JANE AUSTEN

BICENTENARY ESSAYS

Edited by

JOHN HALPERIN

Associate Professor of English
University of Southern California

CAMBRIDGE UNIVERSITY PRESS

CAMBRIDGE

LONDON · NEW YORK · MELBOURNE

Published by the Syndics of the Cambridge University Press
Bentley House, 200 Euston Road, London NW1 2DB
American Branch: 32 East 57th Street, New York, N.Y. 10022

© Cambridge University Press 1975

Library of Congress Catalogue Card Number: 74–25640

ISBNs 0 521 20709 6 hardcovers
0 521 09929 3 paperback

First published 1975

Printed and bound in the United States of America
by R.R. Donnelley & Sons Company

JANE AUSTEN
BICENTENARY ESSAYS

CONTENTS

ACKNOWLEDGMENTS

My chief debts are to Professors A. Walton Litz of Princeton University and Donald Greene of the University of Southern California, both of whom encouraged me to do this book, graciously read my introductory essay in manuscript, and made many useful suggestions for its improvement. Professors Andrew Wright of the University of California, San Diego, and Alistair M. Duckworth of the University of Florida also read my introductory essay in manuscript, and I am grateful to them as well for their kindness in doing so and for their sound critical advice.

I should like to express my appreciation to Mr Jonathan H. Price and the Clarendon Press, Oxford, for allowing me to see uncorrected proof sheets of B. C. Southam's essay on Jane Austen published in the volume edited by A.E. Dyson, *The English Novel: Select Bibliographical Guides*, which was going through the press as I was compiling the select bibliography which appears at the back of this book.

I am also indebted to the College of Letters, Arts and Sciences of the University of Southern California for a grant from its research and publication fund in support of the preparation of this book for the press.

Manhattan Beach, California   J. H.
February 1975

To Max Schulz and Donald Greene
colleagues and friends

I
Some backgrounds

JOHN HALPERIN

Introduction
Jane Austen's nineteenth-century critics:
Walter Scott to Henry James

This book celebrates the 200th anniversary of Jane Austen's birth in 1775 by bringing together in one volume new essays written especially for the occasion by some of the most distinguished scholars and critics of our time – many of whom have already contributed significantly to Jane Austen studies during the past several decades.

What follows in this book represents much of what is going on in Jane Austen studies now, in 1975. Many twentieth-century approaches to Jane Austen and characteristic areas of critical concern are reflected in the ensuing essays.

It is my purpose here to introduce the reader, or perhaps simply to re-acquaint him, with the first 'centenary,' as it were, of Jane Austen criticism, and to sketch the nineteenth-century context out of which modern and contemporary criticism have grown. There are a number of specifically bibliographical studies of Jane Austen criticism.[1] I shall not simply repeat here item by item, in a finer tone or no, what can be found in several standard reference works (for a fuller listing of critical and scholarly books and articles on or about Jane Austen, see the Select bibliography at the end of this volume). Few of the general bibliographical pieces on Jane Austen, however, deal in any great detail with nineteenth-century critical views of the novelist or approach her work from any pronounced historical perspective. Much of what has recently been published of a bibliographical nature understandably emphasizes trends and patterns of the last quarter-century or so, a period that has witnessed such a considerable expansion of interest in Jane Austen and such a remarkable virtuosity in critical approach.[2] What I will attempt to give here, then, is a flavoring of nineteenth-century perspectives upon Jane Austen by examining in some detail the attitudes entertained between 1815 and 1905 by her most important and influential critics.

I

At the time Jane Austen published her novels – that is, during the second decade of the nineteenth century – women did not attend the universities. Men did not study English literature as part of any academic curriculum. Fiction was not deemed an important branch of the literary arts, and readers and critics did not look upon novelists as a literary species likely to add to the world's storehouse of significant art. Fiction was considered a leisurely amusement ('Castle-building,' as Charles Jenner put it in 1770 in *The Placid Man*) and worse, and novelists were rarely esteemed. The novel as serious literature, the novel as written by Aphra Behn, Richardson, Fielding, Smollett, Sterne and others, had been replaced by the novel of their imitators, the novel of sentimentality and sensibility, the circulating library novel. (In 1775, the year of Jane Austen's birth, Sheridan in *The Rivals* has Sir Anthony Absolute tell Mrs Malaprop: 'A circulating library in a town is an ever-green tree of diabolical knowledge!') The rush to the libraries in the latter half of the eighteenth century provoked anti-fiction diatribes, based to some extent on fears of the effects of democratized reading habits on 'people who had no business reading,' from a number of different sources; and, as Richard D. Altick points out, the appearance of hundreds of 'trashy' novels in the later years of the eighteenth century encouraged this reaction against fiction.

Among the pessimists and optimists alike sprang up a rigid
. . . association of the mass reading public with low-grade fiction.
This was to have far-reaching consequences during the nineteenth century, for out of it grew the whole vexatious 'fiction question'
. . . [O]pposition to fiction on religious and moral principles became a convenient stalking-horse for the other motives which it [became] less politic to avow. This tendency was already marked in the eighteenth century; people who, for social or economic reasons, opposed the expansion of the reading public found it handy to conceal their true purposes by harping on the common reader's notorious preference for the novel.[3]

The campaign against fiction was one of the most strenuous activities of both the Evangelical and the Utilitarian movements in the first third of the nineteenth century. Both groups regarded all forms of imaginative literature, and especially the novel, with suspicion. Novels were held to be dangerous because they over-excited the imagination of young people; they were linked to corruption, dissipation and all sorts of immorality, including adultery and divorce. Imaginative literature was considered frivolous; Bentham, of course, excluded it from his ideal republic because it had no practical utility. Random reading was regarded as a waste of time; literature, after all, did not teach skills. Various Methodist tracts even argued that it could be proven from Scripture that God specifically forbade the reading of novels; one of the Utilitarian organs announced to its readers that 'Literature is a seducer; we had almost said a harlot.'[4] No wonder lighter literature was often kept out of the libraries; indeed, many of the early mechanics' institute libraries allowed only books on or about the various branches of science within their walls. By 1800 novels were so numerous and in such bad repute that respectable journals such as the *Scots* and *Gentlemen's* magazines ceased to notice them at all.[5] The reading public had convincingly demonstrated its size and enthusiasm in the 1790s, when Burke's *Reflections on the Revolution in France* sold in the thousands, Tom Paine's rejoinder in *The Rights of Man* sold in the hundreds of thousands, and the Cheap Repository Tracts of Hannah More and others sold, unbelievably enough, in the millions. Political and religious controversy provided stimuli for reading in the nineties and on into the 'teens when thousands of workingmen subscribed to Cobbett's radical journal, the *Political Register*; and some began to fear that it had been a mistake to teach reading to working-class children in Robert Raikes's Sunday schools. The reading of novels, however, was always considered, by the various Establishments, the most frivolous and dangerous form of reading for the half-educated. Coleridge, certainly no literary Establishmentarian, nevertheless spoke for many when he asserted in 1808 that 'where the reading of novels prevails as a habit, it occasions in time the entire destruction of the powers of the mind.'[6] As late as 1826 the publisher Constable launched a series of cheap and popular publications that did not include fiction, and two years later the competing Murray's Family Library did the same. (Things had changed by 1865, however, when the founders of the *Fortnightly Review*, described by Anthony Trollope as 'the most serious, the most earnest, the least devoted to amusement, the least flippant, the least jocose' of literary periodicals, decided that their new journal must always contain a novel.[7])

These things help explain, I think, why there is little serious criticism of Jane Austen during the first half of the nineteenth century.

Attention to her work grows somewhat in the second half, particularly during the period 1859–1870. But between Jane Austen's death in 1817 and G. H. Lewes's 'The Novels of Jane Austen' in 1859, her work attracts little criticism of enduring interest, and only two essays of any distinction whatever (those by Scott and Archbishop Whately). Even from 1870 until the first decades of the twentieth century, Jane Austen criticism – with a few notable exceptions – is scanty and undistinguished. Edmund Wilson is surely wrong when he observes that 'only two reputations have never been affected by the shifts of fashion' in literary taste during the period 1820–1945: Shakespeare's and Jane Austen's.[8] We may agree with him when he goes on to say that Jane Austen's pre-eminent place has remained unchallenged for some years now and that it is likely to remain substantially untouched by future revolutions of taste. But Jane Austen has been a long time getting to the top of the greasy pole; as late as 1900 she was nowhere near it. It is the case, however, that when attention to her novels finally did revive in the twentieth century, its directions and interests were often those of the nineteenth century. Thus, although the nineteenth century contributed only a little to Jane Austen's subsequent literary reputation, what little it did contribute often anticipated and helped to shape the thrust of the later criticism with which most of us are more familiar.

An additional reason for this dearth of early criticism is that the anonymous mode of publication obscured the authorship of Jane Austen's novels for some years (her name never appeared on a title-page during her lifetime; indeed, even her nosy putative cousin Egerton Brydges did not know, as late as 1803, that Jane Austen was 'addicted to literary composition,' as he puts it).[9] The novelist nephew, J. E. Austen-Leigh, tells us that few of her readers

> knew even her name, and none knew more of her than her name. I doubt whether it would be possible to mention any other author of note, whose personal obscurity was so complete . . . Seldom has any literary reputation been of such slow growth . . . her works were at first received [coldly], and . . . few readers had any appreciation of their peculiar merits . . . To the multitude her works appeared tame and commonplace, poor in colouring, and sadly deficient in incident and interest . . . Her reward was not to be the quick return of the cornfield, but the slow growth of the tree which is to endure to another generation.[10]

And clearly Jane Austen had neither the inclination nor the means to 'puff' her work herself, in the manner of Trollope's Lady Carbury. She lived 'in entire seclusion from the literary world: neither by corre-

novelist's characteristic uniformity of tone are particularly incisive – especially, it seems to me, in light of the famous ending of *Mansfield Park*.[45]

The last published item of note before the Austen-Leigh *Memoir* and the reviews which followed it into print is an 1866 unsigned review of George Eliot's *Felix Holt, the Radical* by the well-known literary critic and theorist, Eneas Sweetland Dallas.[46] Dallas opens his review with a comparison of Jane Austen and George Eliot (his opening paragraph is all that need concern us here). Before George Eliot came along, Dallas says, Jane Austen had been at the top of his list of lady novelists. In technical matters, he says, Jane Austen remains pre-eminent; but since she 'scarcely ever gets out of the humdrum of easy-going respectable life . . . she can . . . afford to be calm and neat in arranging every thread . . . she has to weave.' George Eliot may be rougher in this respect, but her subjects, Dallas argues, are more difficult. She deals with the passions, with 'higher thoughts' and 'deeper problems.' The student of a more 'tumultuous life,' George Eliot plays 'with torrents where Miss Austen played with rills.'

In the fall of 1869 J. E. Austen-Leigh, a Berkshire vicar and the son of Jane Austen's eldest brother James, finished writing the *Memoir* of his aunt, whom he knew as a young man and whose funeral he had attended. The volume was published by Bentley in 1870.[47] The *Memoir* is not, strictly speaking, criticism, but its importance in the nineteenth-century history of Jane Austen criticism is threefold. It was the first full-length 'biography' of Jane Austen to appear; because it contained letters and extracts from letters written by the novelist, it marked the first extensive appearance in print of any of Jane Austen's private papers; and it stimulated in response a number of new assessments of Jane Austen, chief among them those by Mrs Oliphant and Richard Simpson. I should say here a few words more about the *Memoir* itself. While it is often informative and interesting, and while it gives us an intermittent but nonetheless fascinating glimpse of Regency life, it extends still farther the Austen family's tradition of protective sanctimoniousness with regard to its authoress, its 'dear aunt Jane.' The family always spoke of her in glowing generalities – whether out of a conscious desire to obfuscate, out of naivety, or out of genuine conviction we may never know, since Cassandra Austen and others systematically destroyed much of the novelist's correspondence after her death. The *Memoir* contains among other things such statements as these:

> Of events her life was singularly barren: few changes and no great crisis ever broke the smooth current of its course . . . Many may care to know whether the moral rectitude, the correct taste, and the

warm affections with which she invested her ideal characters, were really existing in the native source whence those ideas flowed, and were actually exhibited by her in the various relations of life. I can indeed bear witness that there was scarcely a charm in her most delightful characters that was not a true reflection of her own sweet temper and loving heart . . . Of Jane herself I know of no tale of love to relate . . . She did not . . . pass through life without being the object of a strong affection, and it is probable that she met with some whom she found attractive; but her taste was not easily satisfied, nor her heart to be lightly won. I have no reason to think that she ever felt any attachment by which the happiness of her life was at all affected . . . she and her sister were generally thought to have taken to the garb of middle age earlier than their years or their looks required . . . She was as far as possible from being either censorious or satirical. The laugh which she occasionally raised was by imagining for her neighbours . . . her friends or herself, impossible contingencies, by relating . . . some trifling anecdote coloured to her own fancy, or in writing a fictitious history of what they were supposed to have said or done, which could deceive nobody . . . [She had] sound sense and judgment, rectitude of principle, and delicacy of feeling, qualifying her equally to advise, assist, or amuse. She was . . . as ready to comfort the unhappy, or to nurse the sick, as she was to laugh and jest with the light-hearted . . . Above all, she was blessed with a cheerful contented disposition, and an humble mind; and so lowly did she estimate her own claims, that when she received £150 from the sale of 'Sense and Sensibility,' that [*sic*] she considered it a prodigious recompense for that which had cost her nothing . . . She was a humble, believing Christian. Her life had been passed in the performance of home duties, and the cultivation of domestic affections, without any self-seeking or craving after applause. She had always sought, as it were by instinct, to promote the happiness of all who came within her influence, and doubtless she had her reward in the peace of mind which was granted her in her last days. Her sweetness of temper never failed. She was ever considerate and grateful to those who attended on her . . . [Each of her brothers] loved afterwards to fancy a resemblance in some niece or daughter of his own to the dear sister Jane, whose perfect equal they yet never expected to see . . . [Her] course of life was unvaried . . . her own disposition . . . remarkably calm and even. There was in her nothing eccentric or angular; no ruggedness of temper; no singularity of manner; none of the morbid sensibility or exaggeration of feeling, which not unfrequently accompanies great talents, to be worked up into a picture. Hers was a mind well balanced on a basis of good sense, sweetened by an affectionate heart, and regulated by fixed principle.[48]

It should not be difficult to see why subsequent critics so often react with annoyance to the stilted banality of this picture of angelic perfection. Clearly what Austen-Leigh is most zealously bolstering and defending here is Jane Austen's disposition, which, the family apparently always felt – because of the novels' sometimes astringent satire – represented that facet of the novelist's posthumous 'image' most vulnerable to subsequent speculation. Such, of course, has been the case in the twentieth century – as inevitably there would be speculation about any celebrated woman who reportedly welcomed a premature middle age and of whom it is said by an official biographer that she never felt any attachment which affected her happiness.

Austen-Leigh offers as an explanation for the family's prodigious destruction of Jane Austen's private papers its 'extreme dislike to publishing private details' and its disinclination to believe 'that the world would take so strong and abiding an interest in her works as to claim her name as public property.'[49] The second reason is particularly questionable when it is recalled that for some years after Jane Austen's death the family hoped that Macaulay would write her biography and underwrite a monument to her memory in Winchester Cathedral (he did neither).

Here, then, is a prime source of the picture – sometimes defended, sometimes attacked, but almost always considered in some way by modern critics – of Jane Austen as a saintly, gentle, uncomplicated spinster who constructed harmless literary amusements for her friends and relatives. The twentieth century inherited the picture from the nineteenth, and it has seemed at times uncertain whether to put it over the fireplace or into it.

Near the end of his narrative, Austen-Leigh indulges himself long enough to give us his own assessment of his aunt's novels, an assessment very much in accordance with the tenor of much that had previously appeared. He emphasizes 'the fidelity with which [the novels] represent the opinions and manners of the class of society in which the author lived . . . they make no attempt to raise the standard of human life, but merely represent it as it was.'[50] The novels, he adds, 'were not written to support any theory or inculcate any particular moral, except . . . the superiority of high over low principles, and of greatness over littleness of mind.'[51] He compares the novels to 'photographs, in which no feature is softened; no ideal expression is introduced, all is the unadorned reflection of the natural object.'[52] He concludes by expressing his preference for the last three novels (*Mansfield Park, Emma* and *Persuasion*); here, he says, 'are to be found a greater refinement of taste, a more nice sense of propriety, and a deeper insight into the delicate anatomy of the human heart, marking the difference between the brilliant girl and the mature woman.'[53] One always senses, in reading what the Austens have had to say about 'dear aunt Jane,' that they quietly fear future generations may take Elizabeth Bennet as the author's self-portrait, and thus that they do all they can to play down the frivolous and satirical side of their aunt, the novelist. This certainly helps to explain their usual preference for the later novels, which may perhaps be said to be less witty and more 'sensible' than the earlier ones.

The two most important published reactions to the *Memoir* are Margaret Oliphant's and Richard Simpson's; both used their reviews as occasions to write critical essays of substantive importance on Jane Austen's work. Mrs Oliphant, a novelist herself and a regular reviewer (with notoriously undependable opinions) for *Blackwood's,* begins her 1870 unsigned article,[54] a comparative study of 'Miss Austen and Miss Mitford,' with a generalization. Because Jane Austen wrote only about what she knew at firsthand, her characters are not very different from one another. Mrs Oliphant then goes on to tell us what kind of people these are, and what their existence tells us about their creator; and in the process she draws some interesting conclusions about the novelist herself, conclusions which often sound more like those of the twentieth century than the nineteenth.

Mrs Oliphant deals primarily with the question of Jane Austen's disposition, a subject the *Memoir* has unwittingly led her to conjecture upon. Even Mrs Oliphant, so often emphatically wrong in the review section of *Blackwood's,* finds Austen-Leigh's sugary generalizations suspect. Jane Austen's character, says Mrs Oliphant, 'is not the simple character it appears at first glance.' Her 'fine vein of feminine cynicism' is often repressed ('disbelief . . . without showing any outward discomposure'), but her 'stinging yet soft-voiced contempt' is readily apparent. Jane Austen is not, Mrs Oliphant says, simply a good-humored delineator of humanity's mild aberrations.

A . . . despair of any one human creature ever doing good to another – of any influence overcoming those habits and moods and peculiarities of mind which [are] more obstinate than life itself – a sense that nothing is to be done but to look on . . . to make the best of it . . . and wonder why human creatures should be such fools – , such are the foundations upon which [this] feminine cynicism . . . is built. It includes a great deal that is amiable, and is full of toleration and patience, and that habit of making allowance for others which lies at the bottom of all human charity. But yet it is not charity, and its toleration has none of the sweetness which proceeds from that highest of Christian graces. It is not absolute contempt either, but only a softened tone of general disbelief – amusement, nay enjoyment, of all those humours of humanity which are so quaint to look at . . . She has . . . the faculty of seeing her brother clearly all round, as if he were a statue, identifying all his absurdities, quietly jeering at him . . . [She] was capable of a tenderness for the object of her soft laughter – a capability which converts that laughter into something totally different from the gentle derision with which she regards the world in general. Humankind stands low in her estimation, in short, as a mass . . . there is a great deal [of] amusement to be got out of . . . mean people, and to them accordingly she inclines.

It is precisely this reading of Jane Austen's nature that Austen-Leigh and his familial predecessors had hoped to discourage. Like Miss Kavanagh, Mrs Oliphant has discovered the cool detachment with which Jane Austen views her characters. She has also discovered the novelist's capacity to jeer, to deride, to be cynical; her low opinion of humanity; and her interest in the 'mean.' The heroes and heroines of the novels are often too pat, Mrs Oliphant argues, because Jane Austen has less interest in them than in her fools, who therefore have more legitimacy for the reader. Accordingly, she finds Mr Collins Jane Austen's most skillful creation in *Pride and Prejudice;* 'his author, with no pity in her heart, walks round and round him, giving here and there a skilful touch to bring out . . . a picture . . . cruel in its perfection.' (The cruelty is extended, Mrs Oliphant argues, through Charlotte Collins's acquiescence in the novelist's assessment of her husband.) Jane Austen's 'perception of the ridiculous' is less likely to make us admire our fellow beings than to make us know them for what they are. In the 'pitiless perfection of art' as practiced by Jane Austen, heroes and heroines are pert and priggish, irritatingly superior to the various vulgarities of their families and friends, and we cannot like them for this. The lovers are commonplace, the fools inimitable.

Mrs Oliphant goes on to attack both *Sense and Sensibility* and *Mansfield Park* for being dull, disagreeable and unbelievable. She likes *Pride and Prejudice* and *Emma* better, and finds in *Emma* a 'sweetness' and a kindness missing in the other novels, which have few characters worthy of our sympathy. We do not hate anyone in *Emma;* the novel is more affectionate, more tender, less maliciously witty than the others: 'human sympathy has come in to sweeten the tale . . . In *Emma* everything has a softer touch.' Highbury is 'absolutely real.' *Northanger Abbey* is 'her prettiest story'; *Persuasion* returns to the old mould, in which 'every character [is] a fool except the heroic pair . . . in the foreground.' Mrs Oliphant concludes on a note of surprise that Jane Austen's novels should be read by anyone at so late a date: 'it is scarcely to be expected that books so calm and cold and keen . . . would ever be popular.' And yet she also grudgingly admits that the literary authorities, in turning these novels into required reading for 'every student of recent English literature,' were 'never better employed . . . [having] laureated a writer whom the populace would not have been likely to laureate, but whom it has learned to recognise.'

Once again, in this reviewer's tone and chief areas of interest, we see some nineteenth-century threads destined to make their reappearance in the fabric of modern criticism.

The last great nineteenth-century appraisal of Jane Austen is by Richard Simpson, a Roman Catholic friend of Newman's and in his own right a distinguished Shakespearian scholar. We may recall here that Whately, Macaulay and Lewes, among others, were inclined to compare Jane Austen with Shakespeare; in the last hundred years Jane Austen studies have had a certain attraction for Shakespearians, including Simpson, and, some forty years after him, A. C. Bradley. Simpson's unsigned review of the *Memoir* in the *North British Review* also appeared in 1870.[55] He begins by echoing Austen-Leigh's statement that Jane Austen never had the advantage of personal acquaintance with professional literary men or women; he suggests, too, that she derived very little from books. He is one of the first to point out the apparent insulation of her novels from the large events of her contemporary world: 'she lived and wrote through the period of the French Revolution and the European war without referring to them once, except as making the fortunes of some of her naval characters.' And then he goes on to define the 'theory of art' Jane Austen seems to him to be working within: 'she began, as Shakespeare began, with being an ironical [critic] of her contemporaries . . . This critical spirit lies at the foundation of her artistic faculty . . . Criticism, humour, irony, the judgment not of one that gives sentence but of the mimic who quizzes while he mocks, are her characteristics.' The critic is by nature detached, judging; Simpson's classification of Jane Austen may help to explain the coldness many readers find in her. She schooled herself, Simpson says, through observation of aberration and pretense, into a sort of mimetic genius; 'she was a critic who developed herself into an artist.' That Jane Austen's artistry grew out of her critical capacities rather than out of a fertile and wholly autonomous imagination is demonstrated first, Simpson argues, by her 'notable deficiency in the poetical faculty. Perhaps there is no author in existence in whom so marvellous a power of exhibiting characters . . . is combined with so total a want of the poetical imagination . . . she has scarcely a spark of poetry . . . She even seems to have had an ethical dread of the poetic rapture.' Secondly, the superiority of the critical faculty to every other in Jane Austen may be seen in her didacticism, which pervades even the titles of some of her novels. Her love stories tell us very little about love itself, in which the novelist is not really interested; instead, each of her novels expresses 'the Platonic idea that the giving and receiving of knowledge, the active formulation of another's character, or the more passive growth under another's guidance, is the truest and strongest foundation of love.' True love for Jane Austen is less a great passion (always untrustworthy) than an adjunct of sober sense. Impetuosity is always damned: 'Her favourite ideal was to exhibit . . . intelligent love in its germ, to eclipse it for a season by the blaze of a great passion, to quench this glare, and to exhibit the gentle light of the first love reviving and waxing greater till it perfects itself in marriage.' People only discover their mutual attraction by their failures to love elsewhere; the proof is at best a negative one. The character begins in ignorance of the real object of his or her love; then 'the mists are dispersed . . . by the heat of a meteoric love which crosses its path, and bursts, and clears the air. The false glare is extinguished, and the . . . light which had long been shining in secret is revealed to consciousness.' Rational love is eclipsed by sudden or irrational love; the passionate blaze burns itself out; the old reliable flame remains. Love is education through contradiction and sorrow, through the agony and wounding of it by a misguided application of principles; 'wisdom is nothing unless it is directed by love,' says Simpson, citing the examples of Emma and Darcy. Love at first sight is always condemned as delusion. Jane Austen's didacticism manifests itself in her plots, then, whenever 'we see . . . her habitual exaltation of judgment over passion, of the critical over the poetical and imaginative faculties.' This in turn also helps to define her place as that of a great critic rather than a great creative genius.

He moves on in the next part of his essay to some hypotheses about the novelist herself. From the novels, he says, one must assume that Jane Austen's personal view of love is as at best 'only an accident of friendship, friendship being the true light of life, while love [is] often only . . . troublesome . . . Friendship . . . was enough for her.' Hers must have been a detached and critical personality: 'She sat apart on her rocky tower, and watched the poor souls struggling in the waves beneath . . . she could consider the struggles of the mariners with an amused and ironical complacency.' She is kindly by nature yet always superior to her subject – a humorist and a sceptic: 'her pervading critical judgment . . . qualifies her humour' throughout; she is always 'self-collected,' and has her imagination under strict control.

Simpson next considers Jane Austen's capacity to create fictional characters. He finds them natural, 'commonplace, but all discriminated from one another far beyond the possibility of confusion, by touches so delicate that they defy analysis, and so true that they elude observation . . . She exhibits no ideal characters, no perfect virtue, no perfect vice.' Her characters gain their strength and believability from being neither wholly good nor wholly bad. Her wicked characters have some good things in them. Never diabolical, they suffer chiefly from 'a weakness of intelligence, an inability of the common-sense to rule the passions.' Her good characters also have weaknesses, caducity being the chief among these. According to Simpson, this rather unmetaphysical view of humanity arises primarily out of Jane Austen's consciousness that man exists only as a social being, that he has no existence apart from society and that he is formed only by social influences. Man, for her (as for George Eliot and Henry James), is completed only in society. Human virtue results from 'continual struggles and conquests . . . [and out of] progressive states of mind, advancing by repulsing their contraries, or losing ground by being overcome.' The individual mind, then, is often depicted by the novelist 'as a battlefield, where contending hosts are marshalled.' A Jane Austen character unfolds itself 'not in statuesque repose, not as a model without motion, but as a dramatic sketch, a living history.' It would be difficult, I think, to find anywhere a more illuminating or cogent analysis of the moral process to which Jane Austen's sentient characters are usually subjected.

She has no interest in the 'heroic passions,' Simpson argues, nor in the larger social and political issues of her day. Nor is there evidence in her novels to suggest that she conceived of society itself as anything other than a coterie of several families 'without any grave social inequalities' among them mixing together.[56] 'She was perfect in dramatizing the combination of a few simple forces; but it never struck her to try to dramatize the action and reaction of all. Platonist as she was in her feelings, she could rise to contemplate the soul as a family, but not as a republic.' These are high standards. She at times seems to prefer good breeding to good nature, says Simpson, who finds this unsurprising in an author who possessed such self-control: 'She is always perfectly calm, perfectly self-conscious.' And so she has the patience to give 'all the minute attention to detail of the most accomplished miniature-painter.'

Simpson now moves to a closer consideration of the novels themselves. He finds the six novels divisible into an early and a late trilogy, with *Mansfield Park, Emma,* and *Persuasion* reproducing, with more art, subtlety, passion, and humor, the themes and lessons of the earlier three novels (like Austen-Leigh, he prefers the last three). The themes and lessons themselves, however, are unvarying in their presentation.

Never sensational or even improbable, 'the events grow out of one another; and the characters of the actors are the sufficient reasons of the acts which are related. The action is such as is necessary to display the characters.' This does not mean, however, that Jane Austen writes with no particular polemical bias; on the contrary, each of her novels has a particular didactic intention. Thus *Pride and Prejudice* is written to expose as nonsense the phenomenon of 'the sudden flash of love which poets and novelists had agreed to make the great characteristic of the passion'; *Sense and Sensibility* is written 'to prove how entirely the sentimental preoccupations which the study of poetry might produce in the young mind are refuted by the logic of facts, and are found inapplicable to real life'; and *Northanger Abbey* is written to combat the confusion of romance and reality, to refute the idea 'that Mrs Radcliffe's novels give a real picture of life.' The first two volumes of the 'second trilogy,' argues Simpson, are also attacks upon the 'mental narrowness' Jane Austen always abhorred. *Mansfield Park* suggests that true love may be founded upon esteem but not upon passion ('Miss Austen would have made Romeo find out that Juliet was not worth having'); while 'the domestic and ironic way of treating love' is continued in *Emma*, in which the logic of events cures the heroine of her misconceptions and ultimately brings her together in marriage with the only man she has rightly esteemed all along. Like some of Jane Austen's earliest commentators, Simpson finds a certain coldness in the novelist's handling of the love theme – at least until *Persuasion*. There follows a long discussion of Jane Austen's last novel, which is clearly Simpson's favorite. Here, he says, Jane Austen indulges in a partial retraction of her former theories; *Persuasion* tells us that 'she never intended really to separate the heart and the head, intellect and passion.' Like Miss Kavanagh, Simpson sees a mighty change of tone in *Persuasion*, but unlike her he does not find it her saddest novel. In it, he says, Jane Austen 'traces the course of a love founded equally upon esteem and passion . . . Anne Elliot is Shakespeare's Viola translated into an English girl of the nineteenth century.' He argues that the novelist must have had *Twelfth Night* in mind while writing *Persuasion:* 'not only is the general conception of the situation the same, but also the chapters which she wrote during the last months of her life are directly founded upon Shakespeare.' Simpson supports his argument with several references to Shakespeare's play, and then concludes his discussion of *Persuasion* with the assertion that the novel is her 'recantation for all her heresies . . . against the Majesty of Love; in it she displays a poetical vein which her previous writings hardly justified one in suspecting.'

Like Mrs Oliphant, Simpson finds Jane Austen's fascination with fools illuminating and indicative. In the next section of this long essay, he examines her fools and her idea of 'folly.' For Jane Austen, he argues, folly consists in 'a thorough weakness either of will or intellect, an emptiness or irrelevancy of thought'; and, often, 'fixed ideas on a few subjects, giving the whole tone to the person's thoughts so far as he thinks at all.' The 'negative fool,' the fool without ideas, is represented in Jane Austen's work by Mrs Palmer and Miss Bates; the 'fixed ideas' fool, the monomaniac, is represented by Mrs Bennet, Mr Collins, and Sir Walter Elliot. Still another class of fools consists of those who are deficient on their moral rather than (or as well as) their intellectual side; this class includes such personages as the John Dashwoods, Miss Thorpe, Wickham, Willoughby, the Crawfords and Mrs Norris. The later novels, however, present this latter class of fools more convincingly, Simpson says. The Crawfords are interesting moral failures where Wickham and Willoughby are not because, in the later novels, 'there is a want of moral understanding, analogous to the want of intelligence in the [negative] fool . . . In the earlier novels wickedness is wickedness; in the later it is ignorance also.' This is another reason why Simpson prefers the later 'trilogy.' In the earlier novels – and indeed, to some extent in all of the novels before *Persuasion* – Jane Austen inclines too pointedly toward didacticism, the heroes and heroines toward priggishness. 'It is only in . . . *Persuasion* [that] these faults are avoided.'

Simpson concludes with a brief consideration of Miss Mitford's characterization (in a letter) of the young Jane Austen as a flirt and Austen-Leigh's vigorous denial at the end of the *Memoir*. If the charge is true, Simpson says, 'it was most likely in Emma's style . . . with a view to show her disengaged manners, and the superiority of which she was conscious.' He also suggests that the charge, again if true, may help explain the tinge of priggishness in the earlier novels. 'If her sympathies were somewhat limited, this was only because her society was limited,' Simpson says in her defense. While Jane Austen may not have understood society in its conglomerate form, she surely understood certain types of people (such as the naval officer). Though she may have felt that there is a little of the fool in every man, 'there is no brandy and cayenne in her farrago'; she is neat, epigrammatic, and incisive, and always a lady. In understanding her own limitations, she is 'altogether an example for the aspiring artist'; for 'Art will make up for want of force.' Simpson's eulogy of the novelist's charm and intelligence, however, unfortunately leads him, in the final sentence of his essay, into bathos, providing a convenient launching site for the less friendly salvos fired off by some of Jane Austen's later critics (notably Henry James): 'Might we not . . . borrow from Miss Austen's biographer the title which the affection of a nephew bestows upon her, and recognise her officially as "dear aunt Jane"?'

Oddly enough, nothing about Jane Austen of substantive critical importance appeared for the next thirty-five years. But in 1905 Henry James delivered himself of a lecture entitled 'The Lesson of Balzac' before the Contemporary Club of Philadelphia.[57] The lecture has only a little in it about Jane Austen, and indeed it is not about her at all; but as the last assessment of her uttered by a major nineteenth-century critical voice, it represents a convenient stopping place for this survey of the last century's critical attitudes toward Jane Austen.

James's attitude toward her is puzzling. It is clear from his own work that he learned a great deal from her. What he actually learned I cannot touch upon here; the subject has been discussed before, and indeed I have dealt with it myself elsewhere.[58] One explanation for James's apparently unfriendly view of her is that he is often reticent and at times even misleading on the subject of the real formative influences upon his own art.[59] In any case, James's comments in 'The Lesson of Balzac' are by no means flattering to Jane Austen. With all her light felicity, James says, she leaves us 'hardly more curious of her process, or of the experience in her that fed it, than the brown thrush who tells his story from the garden bough.' He goes on to remind us how neglected her work was for the first thirty or forty years after her death, and praises the mid-century critics who rediscovered her. Yet he feels that the tide of admiration for her work has now risen higher than the work itself justifies, and blames 'the body of publishers, editors, illustrators, producers of the pleasant twaddle of magazines; who have found their "dear," our dear, everybody's dear, Jane so infinitely to their material purpose, so amenable to pretty reproduction in every variety of what is called tasteful, and in what seemingly proves to be saleable, form.' James goes on to blame Macaulay and his successors for imposing on subsequent readers the effusions of a 'sentimental judgment' – a critical perspective, like that usually encountered in criticism of the Brontës, James says, which assesses her work romantically, in terms of an image of Jane Austen the person ('dear aunt Jane') rather than objectively, in terms of the novels themselves. Thus, although Jane Austen had 'extraordinary grace of . . . facility' as a novelist, actually she was an unconscious, an amateur, genius: 'sometimes, over her work basket, her tapestry flowers . . . [she] fell a-musing [and] lapsed . . . into wool gathering . . . her dropped stitches . . . these precious moments, were afterwards picked up as little touches of human truth, little glimpses of steady vision, little master-strokes of imagination.' Detachment, anything less than a full commitment to the art of fiction, James always condemns. There can be no such thing as a part-time artist. He detested the untutored dilettante, the novelist who shrank from any form of human experience; and while he does not accuse Jane Austen outright of these crimes, he finds nonetheless that in her novels 'we sit quite resigned in an arrested spring.' Balzac is great because he 'penetrates' into his subjects; those who partake of life 'passively, narrowly, in mere sensibility and sufferance' cannot be great artists because they cannot lose themselves in the expanded energy of complete representation, in the direct exposure of the sensibility and the charged consciousness: 'there is no convincing art that is not ruinously expensive' for the artist, emotionally speaking. It is in terms of this 'intellectual spending' that James, by implication primarily, finds Jane Austen deficient. She does not know enough about her characters, about their 'conditions.' She has not thought enough. She has not indulged in that arduous, unceasing work Klesmer talks about in *Daniel Deronda* (a James favorite) as being a prerequisite of artistic achievement.

The truth of these charges is another matter; but there is little doubt that the nineteenth-century view of Jane Austen ends on a note of increasing interest in the novelist's personality – on a note, that is, slightly sour, or at best equivocal. And of course in the twentieth century, as appreciations of Jane Austen have become both more enthusiastic and more fashionable, so too have depreciations of her. Having passed through stages of neglect, belated lionization, and revisionist questioning, she has ultimately reached, long before this bicentenary year, the enviable pinnacle of controversiality.

NOTES

1 The major bibliographical studies are as follows. First, shorter pieces. One of the earliest is that by C.B. Hogan, 'Jane Austen and Her Early Public' (*Review of English Studies*, 1950), which deals mostly with contemporary reactions. Ian Watt in his 'Introduction' to *Jane Austen: A Collection of Critical Essays* (Englewood Cliffs, N.J., 1963), briefly surveys the corpus of criticism up to that time. The volume itself reprints a number of seminal essays on the novelist (see Section v of the Select bibliography at the end of this volume for a full listing). Watt and Joseph Cady, in 'Jane Austen's Critics' (*Critical Quarterly*, 1963), republish much of what is said in the 'Introduction' to the *Collection of Critical Essays* volume. In introducing his *Jane Austen: The Critical Heritage* (London and New York, 1968), B. C. Southam provides an overview of early Jane Austen criticism (the volume reprints much of the material of early Jane Austen criticism discussed in the text of the present essay). Southam gives us another overview, this time with more emphasis on later critical trends, in his essay on Jane Austen in *The English Novel: Select Bibliographical Guides,* ed. A. E. Dyson (Oxford, 1974). In 'A Short Guide to Jane Austen Studies' (*Critical Survey*, 1968), Norman Page rehearses very briefly indeed Jane Austen criticism from Scott to Southam's *Critical Heritage* volume. Now, full-length bibliographical studies. An indispensable early volume is that by Geoffrey Keynes, *Jane*

Austen: A Bibliography (London, 1929), which focuses mainly on nineteenth-century periodical criticism of the novels. A most important volume is R. W. Chapman's *Jane Austen: A Critical Bibliography* (Oxford, 1953; reprinted with corrections, 1955), a survey of the period 1813–1952 in the form of an annotated bibliography (Chapman does not list early reviews, however). In the same year (1953) there is a dissertation by Frederick M. Link, 'The Reputation of Jane Austen in the Twentieth Century' (Boston University, unpublished), which includes an annotated bibliography of criticism from the earliest period to that in which the author is writing. Another unpublished dissertation, Joseph M. Duffy, Jr's 'Jane Austen and the Nineteenth-Century Critics of Fiction 1812–1913' (University of Chicago, 1954), emphasizes the connections between Jane Austen's nineteenth-century reputation and the contemporary state of novel-criticism in general. F. B. Pinion attempts to provide some bibliographical context in *A Jane Austen Companion: A Critical Survey and Reference Book* (London, 1973). And Barry Roth and Joel Weinsheimer, in *An Annotated Bibliography of Jane Austen Studies, 1952–1972* (Charlottesville, Va., 1973), include in their indispensable volume a usefully cross-indexed guide to studies of Jane Austen during the last twenty years and to books and articles as well in which there is discussion of her of substantive importance.

2 Watt, in his introductory essay, and Southam, in his discussion in the Dyson volume, deal briefly and summarily with nineteenth-century critical attitudes towards Jane Austen – nor do they aim beyond this. Southam, in his introduction to the *Critical Heritage* volume, examines the nineteenth-century context in somewhat more detail, but he also expends a goodish amount of energy commenting on anonymous reviews, extracts from letters and diaries, and conversational hearsay. Hogan's article deals mostly with contemporary attitudes. Chapman's book is fairly exhaustive but, in covering so much territory, can say little in depth about any particular trend. And he does not discuss early reviews of Jane Austen's novels. (Full references to all of these items are given in n. 1, above.) I hope here to bring everything together in one place, giving detailed consideration to what the major nineteenth-century critics of Jane Austen actually *say*. I should add that I will pass over anonymous or otherwise unattributable essays on Jane Austen published during the nineteenth century; it is enough for my purposes here to point out to the reader who the major critics are and what they say. The major unsigned or unattributable published pieces on or partially about Jane Austen (*excluding* contemporary reviews of specific novels) in the nineteenth century *not* dealt with in the text of this essay are four in number and as follows: review of *Life and Adventures of Peter Wilkins* in the *Retrospective Review*, 7 (n.m., 1823), 131-5; article on 'Female Novelists,' *New Monthly Magazine*, 95 (May 1852), 17–23; two-part article on 'Miss Austen,' *Englishwoman's Domestic Magazine*, 3rd series, 2 (July 1866), 238–9, and 2 (August 1866), 278–82; article on 'Jane Austen,' *St Paul's Magazine*, 5 (March 1870), 631–43.

3 Richard D. Altick, *The English Common Reader* (Chicago, 1957), pp. 63–5, *passim*.

4 See the *Methodist Magazine*, 42 (1819), 606–9, and the *Westminster Review*, 2 (1824), 346.

5 See Q. D. Leavis, *Fiction and the Reading Public* (London, 1932), p. 145. Other good accounts of popular attitudes toward fiction in the later eighteenth and early nineteenth centuries are provided by J. T. Taylor, *Early Opposition to the English Novel: The Popular Reaction from 1760 to 1830* (New York, 1943); W.F. Gallaway, Jr, 'The Conservative Attitude toward Fiction, 1770–1830,' *PMLA*, 55 (1940), 1041–59; Winfield H. Rogers, 'The Reaction against Melodramatic Sentimentality in the English Novel, 1796–1830,' *PMLA*, 49 (1934), 98–122; and J. M. S. Tompkins, *The Popular Novel in England, 1770–1800* (London, 1932).

6 *Lectures on Shakespeare and Milton*, The First Lecture.

7 See *Fiction and the Reading Public*, pp. 161–3.

8 See 'A Long Talk about Jane Austen,' in *Classics and Commercials: A Literary Chronicle of the Forties* (New York, 1950). The essay was written and first appeared in 1945 in *The New Yorker*.

9 See Brydges' *Autobiography*, Vol. ii (London, 1834), p. 41.

10 J. E. Austen-Leigh, *A Memoir of Jane Austen* (London, 1870), pp. 143 and 166–9, *passim*.

11 *Ibid.*, pp. 142–3.

12 *The Critical Heritage* (see n. 1, above), p. 1. Southam's calculation was made before the discovery of three additional contemporary reviews of *Emma*, all unsigned, which appeared in the *Champion*, the *Augustan Review*, and the *British Lady's Magazine and Monthly Miscellany*. For further details, see William S. Ward, 'Three Hitherto Unnoted Contemporary Reviews of Jane Austen,' *Nineteenth-Century Fiction*, 26 (1972).

13 *Memoirs and Letters of Sara Coleridge*, ed. E. Coleridge, Vol. i (London, 1873), p. 75.

14 See *The Critical Heritage*, pp. 54 and 116–18.

15 Quoted without attribution by Watt in his 'Introduction' to the *Collection of Critical Essays* volume (see n. 1, above), p. 4. This may simply be another version of a comment made by Mrs Carlyle, who says in an 1843 letter that Jane Austen is 'Too washy; watergruel for mind and body.' See Jane Welsh Carlyle, *Letters and Memorials*, Vol. i (London, 1883), p. 186.

16 *The Brontës: Their Friendships, Lives, and Correspondence*, ed. T. J. Wise and J. A. Symington, Vol. ii (London, 1932), pp. 178–81, *passim*.

17 *Ibid.*, Vol. iii, p. 99.

18 *Jane Austen's Letters*, ed. R. W. Chapman (2nd edition; London, 1952), p. 469.

19 Quoted in Watt's 'Introduction' (p. 7) and cited by him as MS. DV 201 (De Voto numbering) among the Mark Twain Papers then unpublished in the University of California Library at Berkeley. The piece was apparently written sometime between 1900 and 1905. I am indebted here to Watt's summary of these manuscript papers.

    Richard Poirier, in an essay entitled 'Mark Twain, Jane Austen, and the Imagination of Society,' discusses at some length the usual antagonism of American writers, and of Twain in particular, to Jane Austen. See *In Defense of Reading: A Reader's Approach to Literary Criticism*, ed.

Reuben A. Brower and Richard Poirer (New York, 1962). A revised and enlarged version of this essay, published as 'Transatlantic Configurations: Mark Twain and Jane Austen,' is also included in Poirer's *A World Elsewhere: The Place of Style in American Literature* (New York, 1966).

20 In *The English Novel* (see n. 1, above), p. 146. I am grateful to Mr Jonathan H. Price and the Clarendon Press for allowing me to see uncorrected proof sheets of the Jane Austen chapter while I was writing the present essay.

21 14 (March 1816), 188–201. I am quoting here, and on subsequent occasions throughout this essay when nineteenth-century periodical views of Jane Austen are cited, sometimes from the primary source itself, whenever available to me, and sometimes from Southam's excellent collection of early perspectives on Jane Austen in the *Critical Heritage* volume. In either case, only the original appearance of the item will be given, even though some of the early essays on Jane Austen have been reprinted a number of times. This for the sake of uniformity and simplicity. However, I should like to express here my indebtedness to Southam's book for its abstracting and reprinting of the important nineteenth-century statements on Jane Austen and for its excellent and illuminating summaries in headnotes and elsewhere of the significance of the material itself.

22 The 'Biographical Notice' has been widely reprinted. I am quoting here from *The Critical Heritage*, pp. 73–8, *passim*.

23 See, for example, D. W. Harding, 'Regulated Hatred: An Aspect of the Work of Jane Austen,' published originally in *Scrutiny*, 8 (March 1940) and widely reprinted since, and Marvin Mudrick, *Jane Austen: Irony as Defense and Discovery* (Princeton, 1952). Mudrick's book in particular has been a seminal influence on some modern attitudes toward Jane Austen, which have undergone a number of substantial revisions in emphasis in recent years.

24 24 (January 1821), 352–76.

25 Cf. the seventeenth chapter of *Adam Bede,* where George Eliot says in part the following: 'let us always have men ready to give the loving pains of life to the faithful representing of commonplace things . . . It is for this rare, precious quality of truthfulness that I delight in many Dutch paintings . . . I find a source of delicious sympathy in these faithful pictures of a monotonous homely existence, which has been the fate of so many among my fellow-mortals'; and, to mention just one other later statement, the thirty-fifth chapter of *The Eustace Diamonds* (1873), in which Trollope expresses his feeling that leading characters in novels should be no less ordinary than those we are likely to find ourselves sitting next to at dinner, and that novelists should confine themselves to painting a 'true picture of life as it is.'

26 I am excepting Lewes's early shorter comments on Jane Austen, which will be considered along with his great appraisal of 1859. There are other published items of some limited interest, but most of them are unattributable (see n. 2, above) or pedestrian or both. An excellent example of the 'both' category is one of the first so-called 'middle-brow' pieces on Jane Austen of substantive length which appeared as part of a

series of articles on 'Female Novelists' in the *New Monthly Magazine* in 1852 (see n. 2, above). The chief aim of this anonymous essay, and of several others like it during this period, was simply to 'introduce' Jane Austen to the reading public. I omit these items here as likely to be of little interest to twentieth-century students of Jane Austen.

27 Unsigned review of *Women as they are*, 53 (July 1830), 448–51.

28 76 (January 1843), 561–2. Madame D'Arblay, of course, is Fanny Burney, and Macaulay goes on in this article to review her *Memoirs of Dr Burney.*

29 76 (July 1853), 200–3.

30 Perhaps the clearest evidence of direct influence is the Austen-like opening of *Middlemarch* (1871–2), a phenomenon noticed by several critics. Certainly another indication, as David Carroll has noted, is the number of similarities between *Daniel Deronda* (1876) and *Mansfield Park,* which George Eliot was reading as she wrote *Deronda.* What is common to both novels is the hero's conflict between his public and private roles – specifically between the roles of clergyman and lover. See Carroll's essay, '*Mansfield Park, Daniel Deronda,* and Ordination,' in *Modern Philology,* 62 (1965), 217–26.

There are other and more ubiquitous similarities between Jane Austen's novels and George Eliot's. What is most striking is the repetition of protagonists (usually women) in the novels of each who begin in moral blindness and narrow selfishness, undergo through social intercourse a series of personal reversals, and achieve finally a more sharply focused moral vision and a more fully developed sympathy for others. This community of theme has only occasionally been specifically noted. See, for example, F. R. Leavis, *The Great Tradition* (London, 1948); John Halperin, *The Language of Meditation: Four Studies in Nineteenth-Century Fiction* (Devon, 1973); and John Halperin, *Egoism and Self-Discovery in the Victorian Novel* (New York, 1974).

A final note. In 1853, before George Eliot and Lewes were living together (though their acquaintance dated from 1851), an unsigned essay appeared in the *Westminster Review,* 60 (October 1853), 358–9, for which George Eliot then regularly wrote, praising Jane Austen in passing for her photographic naturalness, but placing her firmly in the second rank of novelists because of the triviality of her subjects. Gordon S. Haight has suggested, based on internal evidence, that the author of this essay may possibly be George Eliot, but this is difficult to confirm. An incisive discussion of the literary relationship between George Eliot and Lewes, particularly as it affected her view of the novel, may be found in Alice R. Kaminsky's excellent essay, 'George Eliot, George Henry Lewes, and the Novel,' *PMLA,* 70 (1955), 997–1013.

31 An unsigned review, 'Recent Novels: French and English,' 36 (December 1847), 687. This is the review in which Lewes says, erroneously, that Macaulay called Jane Austen a 'prose Shakespeare,' and it is an attribution Lewes continues to make in several subsequent essays on Jane Austen. He himself has no qualms about comparing Jane Austen to Shakespeare; but the phrase, picked up and widely quoted since, is not really his own either, since he seems to think it is Macaulay's. In any case, this is Lewes's first extended comment on Jane Austen, though in a piece published in

the *New Quarterly Review* for October 1845 he mentions her briefly along with Cervantes, Fielding, and Goethe – authors, he says, who have drawn characters with skill reminiscent of Shakespeare and Molière.

32 November 22, 1851, p. 115, where he is discussing an anonymous work, *The Fair Carew.*

33 'The Lady Novelists,' 58 (July 1852), 134–5.

34 He also suggests at the end of this essay that one source of her realism is her disinclination to be 'doctrinaire,' to write 'thesis' novels – a *genre* modern critics from James to Ortega have felt to be inimical to the maintenance of any autonomous 'illusion of reality' in fiction.

35 In an unsigned article, 'A Word about *Tom Jones*,' in *Blackwood's Edinburgh Magazine*, 87 (March 1860), 335.

36 86 (July 1859), 99–113, unsigned.

37 Lewes here sounds somewhat like Henry James discussing his sacred concept of 'foreshortening.'

38 George Eliot's *Adam Bede* appeared in the same year as Lewes's essay. *Scenes of Clerical Life* had come out in *Blackwood's Edinburgh Magazine* two years earlier. The secret of George Eliot's authorship – that is to say, her pseudonym – was still being taken very seriously by Lewes, a married man living with a woman (George Eliot) to whom he was not married. Later, of course, the real identity of George Eliot – and her domestic circumstances – were known to all.

39 He had used the phrase earlier in an article in the *Westminster Review,* 70 (1858), 493–4.

40 'British Novelists – Richardson, Miss Austen, Scott,' 61 (January 1860), 30–5.

41 Pollock's view is perhaps an early version of one later codified by Ortega (among others), who says in *The Dehumanization of Art and Notes on the Novel* (1925) that the 'autonomous' novel by nature abolishes outer reality by entrapping the reader in its own world and keeping him there, and is therefore the most 'realistic' of *genres*. This, of course, is a bald simplification of what he says.

42 *Letters of Edward Fitzgerald,* Vol. II (London, 1894), p. 131.

43 See pp. 251–74.

44 See D. W. Harding, 'Regulated Hatred,' and Marvin Mudrick, *Jane Austen* (both n. 23, above); and Kingsley Amis, 'What Became of Jane Austen?' in the *Spectator* (4 October 1957), widely reprinted since.

45 For a discussion of this and related matters, see John Halperin, 'The Trouble with *Mansfield Park*,' in *Studies in the Novel,* 7(Spring 1975).

46 In *The Times* for 26 June 1866, p. 6.

47 See n. 10, above.

48 *Memoir,* pp. 2–3, 45–7, 107, 115, 125, 172, 226, 228, 230–1, *passim.*

49 *Ibid.,* p. 230.

50 *Ibid.,* pp. 196–7.

51 *Ibid.,* p. 197.

52 *Ibid.*

53 *Ibid.,* p. 199.

54 *Blackwood's Edinburgh Magazine,* 107 (March 1870), 294–305.

55 52 (April 1870), 129–52.

56 This view of Jane Austen is aptly and effectively refuted by Donald Greene, who argues that the novelist was very much a 'Tory democrat' who championed the rising middle classes against the pretensions of Whiggish aristocracy. See 'Jane Austen and the Peerage,' *PMLA*, 68 (December 1953), 1017–31.

57 On 12 January 1905. James apparently gave this lecture several times elsewhere before it was published – originally in the *Atlantic Monthly* in August 1905, then reprinted in *The Question of Our Speech*, also 1905. I shall be quoting throughout from the version, in which several passages omitted in delivery have been restored, provided by Leon Edel in a selective collection of James's literary essays entitled *The Future of the Novel* (New York, 1956), pp. 97–124.

58 In some detail in *The Language of Meditation*, and again, in less detail, in *Egoism and Self-Discovery in the Victorian Novel* (both n. 30, above). Others who hint at what James may have learned from Jane Austen (the subject is by no means exhausted) include F. R. Leavis in *The Great Tradition* (n. 30, above); A. Walton Litz in *Jane Austen: A Study of Her Artistic Development* (New York, 1965); Irène Simon in 'Jane Austen and *The Art of the Novel*' (*Essays and Studies*, 1962); and Virginia Woolf in 'Jane Austen at Sixty' (*Nation*, 15 December 1923). Writers on Jane Austen frequently look forward to her subsequent influence; writers on James do not often enough look back. If he was in any sense the father of the modern novel, he was also very much the stepson of an older tradition.

59 In addition to his professed dislike of Jane Austen, James also suggests at times a lukewarmness toward Dickens which is very much belied by such novels as *The Bostonians* and *The Princess Casamassima* (both 1886) and a more pronounced dislike for Meredith, some of whose later novels are remarkably similar in technique to his own. His debts to Hawthorne, George Eliot, and Balzac are more freely acknowledged, though he undoubtedly took much more from George Eliot, for one, than he himself knew.

REUBEN A. BROWER

From the *Iliad* to Jane Austen, via *The Rape of the Lock*[1]

Let me start this fabulous voyage with a scene from Pope's *Iliad* (XIV, 179–218), a part of the so-called 'Deception of Zeus,' that may remind the reader of a scene in *The Rape of the Lock*. A brief recall of the context in the Homeric original may be helpful. Hera, seeing that Poseidon is now fighting for the Greeks, is delighted, and plans to deceive Zeus; she seduces him and puts him to sleep, while the Grecians win a great victory over the Trojans. When Zeus awakes and discovers what is going on, he sets in motion new and successful attacks on the Trojan side, in which Patroclus will die, and after which Achilles in revenge returns to battle. So 'the will of Zeus is fulfilled.'

In Homer, the episode of Zeus's seduction is a piece of high comedy – the contrast between great, powerful divinities and their susceptibility to being deceived and seduced by sleep and love. The implied ironies go deep in the texture of the episode and the whole poem: the weakness of the gods, Homer is saying, is a part of the nature of the gods, and through the frivolous comedy of deception the poet is making one more criticism of his divine society. 'The gods,' Cedric Whitman says, 'are barred by their deathlessness from the dignity of tragedy, or the greatness of self-mastery.' But the greatness of the gods is never entirely lost even in moments of ironic inconsistency. When in this scene Zeus tells Hera of all his loves, we feel that

43

he must be a very great god indeed to have begotten so many gods and heroes: Perseus, Minos, Rhadamanthos, Dionysos, Heracles . . .

Here is Pope's version[2] of the scene:

Meantime *Saturnia* from *Olympus'* Brow.
High-thron'd in Gold, beheld the Field below,   180
With Joy the glorious Conflict she survey'd,
Where her great Brother gave the *Grecians* Aid.
But plac'd aloft, on *Ida's* shady Height
She sees her *Jove,* and trembles at the Sight.
Jove to deceive, what Methods shall she try,   185
What Arts, to blind his all-beholding Eye?
At length she trusts her Pow'r; resolv'd to prove
'The old, yet still successful Cheat of Love';
Against his Wisdom to oppose her Charms,
And lull the Lord of Thunders in her Arms.   190
    Swift to her bright Apartment she repairs,
Sacred to Dress, and Beauty's pleasing Cares:
With Skill divine had Vulcan form'd the Bow'r,
Safe from Access of each intruding Pow'r.
Touch'd with her secret Key, the Doors unfold;   195
Self-clos'd behind her shut the Valves of Gold.
Here first she bathes; and round her Body pours
Soft oils of Fragrance, and ambrosial Show'rs:
The Winds perfum'd, the balmy Gale convey
Thro' Heav'n, thro' Earth, and all th' aerial Way;   200
Spirit divine! whose Exhalation greets
The Sense of Gods with more than mortal Sweets.
Thus while she breath'd of Heav'n, with decent Pride
Her artful Hands the radiant Tresses ty'd;
Part on her Head in shining Ringlets roll'd,   205
Part o'er her Shoulders wav'd like melted gold.
Around her next a heav'nly Mantle flow'd,
That rich with *Pallas'* labour'd Colours glow'd;
Large Clasps of Gold the Foldings gather'd round,
A golden Zone her swelling Bosom bound.   210
Far-beaming Pendants tremble in her Ear,
Each Gemm illumin'd with a triple Star.
Then o'er her Head she casts a Veil more white
Than new fal'n Snow, and dazling as the Light.
Last her fair Feet celestial Sandals grace.   215
Thus issuing radiant, with majestic Pace,
Forth from the Dome th' Imperial Goddess moves,
And calls the Mother of the *Smiles* and *Loves.*

(Pope: *The Iliad of Homer,* xiv, 179–218)

Pope's gods are great too, though not in quite the same way as
Homer's were. Homer's deities were more elementary powers – Zeus
is still 'the cloud-gatherer' even in this charming narrative – and their
desires were more elementary too. In the Greek Zeus quite simply,
directly *wants* Hera:

> when he saw her, desire was a mist about his close heart as much as
> on that time they first went to bed together and lay in love, and their
> dear parents knew nothing of it.
>
> (*Iliad*, XIV, 294–6 [Lattimore])

Like two great children at play the son and daughter cheated their
parents, Kronos and Rheia. (We get a glimpse in passing of the coarse
and happy gods of pre-Olympian times.) By comparison, Pope's gods
are Romanized, Hebraicized, and much more solemn. Juno is
'Saturnia'; Neptune is her 'great Brother'; Jove, 'the Lord of Thunders,' is like the Old Testament deity manifest in 'thunders and lightnings'; and Juno is 'th' Imperial Goddess,' who moves 'with majestic
Pace.' This last reminds us of Virgil's *vera incessu,* 'the genuine pace
of a goddess.'

In Pope's version greatness and glamor are often expressed in
language reminiscent of *Paradise Lost.* In Juno's chamber

> the Doors unfold;
> Self-clos'd behind her shut the Valves of Gold.
>
> (195–6)

In the palace of the fallen angels,

> straight the doors
> Opening their brazen folds

and the walls of Pandemonium 'rose like an exhalation.' In Pope an
'exhalation greets/The Sense of Gods' from Juno's perfumes. The
goddess's beauty is described in language that recalls another woman
who was like a goddess,

> Shee as a vail down to the slender waste,
> Her unadorned gold'n tresses wore
> Dissheveled, but in wanton ringlets wav'd.
>
> (*Paradise Lost,* IV, 304–6)

And we hear a little later in Milton of Eve's 'modest pride.' Compare:

> Thus while she breath'd of Heav'n, with decent Pride
> Her artful Hands the radiant Tresses ty'd:
> Part on her Head in shining Ringlets roll'd,
> Part o'er her Shoulders wav'd like melted Gold.
>
> (203–6)

But it is one thing to compare a woman to a goddess, another to compare a goddess to a woman. Pope's Juno, with her 'Charms,' 'her swelling Bosom,' seems more and more a woman of the world,

> resolv'd to prove
> 'The old, yet still successful, Cheat of Love.'

(187–8)

This line, as William Frost points out,[3] was taken from Tooke (not a play on words, but a reference to the poet Charles Tooke, whose translation of the scene came out in a 1701 *Miscellany* including many of the best known writers of the Restoration). The line fairly reeks of that society and its jaded loves: we can hear in anticipation the tone of Lady Bellaston setting out to seduce Tom Jones. Sexual desires and motives so expressed have been through a considerable social education, and though Homer's Hera has her social quality, her mores belong to a high heroic world, more vigorous, less polite. There are in Pope's translation of the whole episode many traces of the idiom, partly Ovidian in origin, of 'am'rous' escapades in eighteenth-century verse: 'pleasing [and 'softer'] Cares,' 'the Pleasing Fire,' 'melts . . . in fierce Desires,' 'Fond Love,' 'gay [and 'soft'] Desire,' 'Love's entrancing Joys,' 'Mix'd with her Soul' [not body], 'Transport,' 'the pleasing Fire.'

There is visual splendor in Homer's dressing scene, but much more in Pope's, where the glamor is equally convincing but far more worldly:

> Large Clasps of Gold the Foldings gather'd round,
> A golden Zone her swelling Bosom bound.
> Far-beaming Pendants tremble in her Ear,
> Each Gemm illumin'd with a triple Star.

(209–12)

Pope's comedy, then, arises from a contrast 'parallel to Homer's, but not the same,' the contrast between solemn Roman deities and all this social gallantry and *luxe*. There is greatness and beauty and comedy, as in Homer, but the definition of the elements that compose these qualities has been altered considerably. This blend, and the character of the translation, can be better understood after a look at the corresponding scene in *The Rape of the Lock*:

> And now, unveil'd, the *Toilet* stands display'd,
> Each Silver Vase in mystic Order laid.
> First, rob'd in White, the Nymph intent adores
> With Head uncover'd, the *Cosmetic* Pow'rs.
> A heav'nly Image in the Glass appears,

125

To that she bends, to that her Eyes she rears;
Th' inferior Priestess, at her Altar's side,
Trembling, begins the sacred Rites of Pride.
Unnumber'd Treasures ope at once, and here
The various Off'rings of the World appear;   130
From each she nicely culls with curious Toil,
And decks the Goddess with the glitt'ring Spoil.
This Casket *India's* glowing Gems unlocks,
And all *Arabia* breathes from yonder Box.
The Tortoise here and Elephant unite,   135
Transform'd to *Combs,* the speckled and the white.
Here Files of Pins extend their shining Rows,
Puffs, Powders, Patches, Bibles, Billet-doux.
Now awful Beauty puts on all its Arms;
The Fair each moment rises in her Charms,   140
Repairs her Smiles, awakens ev'ry Grace,
And calls forth all the Wonders of her Face;
Sees by Degrees a purer Blush arise,
And keener Lightnings quicken in her Eyes.
The busy *Sylphs* surround their darling Care;   145
These set the Head, and those divide the Hair,
Some fold the Sleeve, whilst others plait the Gown;
And *Betty's* prais'd for Labours not her own.

                                          (I, 121–48)

Not with more Glories, in th' Etherial Plain,
The Sun first rises o'er the purpled Main,
Than issuing forth, the Rival of his Beams
Lanch'd on the Bosom of the Silver *Thames.*

                                          (II, 1–4)

As more than one critic has pointed out, it is almost impossible to
tell whether Pope in *The Rape of the Lock* is parodying his *Iliad,* or
whether in his *Iliad* he is imitating *The Rape of the Lock*! (Uncertain-
ty as to dates of composition make this in fact difficult to determine.)
Whatever the explanation, parallels to our passage and to many others
in Pope's *Iliad* are not hard to find: 'Cosmetic Pow'rs' and the 'Pow'rs'
of Olympus; the 'heav'nly Image' in *The Rape* and the 'celestial
Sandals' in the translation; the 'Pride' of the woman and the 'decent
Pride' of the goddess; the 'Charms' of both, and the marvellous
fragrance – 'all *Arabia* breathes' and 'she [Juno] breath'd of Heav'n';
in *The Rape* the 'glowing Gems' and in the *Iliad* the 'Colours' that
'glow'd' and

Each Gemm illumin'd with a triple Star.

In the first line of Canto II, 'th' Etherial Plain' (a favorite adjective of Pope's *Iliad*) parallels 'th' aerial Way' of the translation.

Finally, the woman, Belinda, emerges as a 'goddess' indeed, like 'The Sun,'

> issuing forth, the Rival of his Beams

recalling Juno:

> Thus issuing radiant, with majestic Pace,
> Forth from the Dome th' Imperial Goddess moves.

We can see that up to a point what Pope was doing in the translation and in *The Rape of the Lock* are very nearly the same – the creation of divine glamor and beauty; and the impression is achieved in part in the same way by the use of Miltonic and Virgilian echoes.

But the effects in the context of *The Rape of the Lock* are hardly identical. There is an impression, as in the *Iliad,* of a mysterious and beautiful rite, and of an epiphany, the metamorphosis of a woman and the birth of a goddess; but all that is infused with the fine absurdity of the cult of beauty, 'beauty' in the 'cosmetic' or 'beautician's' sense, and in the sense of sexual attraction. The scene as a whole is highly aphrodisiac. The main difference lies in the wit, the kind that focusses in a phrase like 'the sacred Rites of Pride,' which is both climactic and anticlimactic. But this is an easier sort of wit compared with the quiet irony that runs through the whole scene – all this preparation for the social game of love, for an afternoon cards-and-coffee party, all this to flatter a woman's ego.

But Pope, like many ironists, loves the folly he mocks. Inseparable from his wit, often the condition of its surprise, is the wonderful richness of sensuous and literary texture. Let us consider in order a few characteristic expressions, remembering Homer, Milton, and Pope's translation. (For the reader's convenience, line numbers are given at the left.)

122 'Mystic Order' suggests a secret cult known only to the initiate, and the formulae of cosmetics; 'Order' also suggests the harmony of the process. This is a 'ceremony of innocence,' of the 'Fair and Innocent' who should be protected by the Sylphs.

124 In 'the *Cosmetic* Pow'rs' and 'the glitt'ring Spoil' (132), note the generalizing, eternalizing effect of the article and epithet, as in many epic formulae of Pope's translation. 'Glitt'ring,' (almost standard in Pope's *Iliad* for heroic splendor) here evokes the beauty to the eye of gems and gold, while suggesting that the glitter is transitory – perhaps fake.

135 The union of the Tortoise and the Elephant is grotesque and prodigious (the elephant, we know, is slow to mate)–perhaps a disturb-

ance of the Law of Nature, perhaps an echo of a far-off primitive
world of myth where such things 'really' happen.

136 With 'Transform'd' we feel the presence of the *Metamorphoses:*
the word sets the note for the whole description. A court belle
becomes Juno or Venus or an Augustan Queen, 'Great *Anna!* whom
three Realms obey,' the presiding divinity of this not-so-heroic society.

139 'Now awful Beauty puts on all its Arms . . .' is absurdly beautiful, but taken with 'Wonders' and 'Lightnings' (like the 'lightnings
and thunders' on Sinai); the line puts us in mind of the other 'awful'
deity, the 'majestic' goddess of Pope's *Iliad.*

148 The end of the scene is not mere anticlimax, and more than an
Ovidian dig at make-up. Betty's 'Labours' are '*not* her own.' We are
witnessing the comically marvellous miracle of a woman's getting
herself up for an occasion – the perfect prelude for the beginning of
Canto II, where Belinda appears as a sun-goddess.

By echoes of heroic-mythical and religious worlds, by immediate
appeals of sight, scent, and touch, and by the ordered progress of his
verse, Pope has invested the scene and woman's role in social,
'am'rous' relations, with wonder, while evaluating the role by the
anticipated contrast with the trifling game of love to be played at
Hampton Court. And where are we in relation to the translation? Pope
has created another parallel to the comedy of contrast in the passage
from his *Iliad* and in Homer's original. But with a difference: in
Pope's *Iliad* great Roman deities are seen as glamorous belles; here,
belles are seen as Roman deities, as heroines in an epic scene. The
direction of our amusement has changed, but the techniques of the
poetry – the allusions to Milton, Virgil, and other poets – are surprisingly alike.

The direction of our amusement in *The Rape of the Lock* toward
laughter at contemporary foibles and love-making was not altogether
absent from the expected reading of the scene in Pope's *Iliad.* Parody
of the heroic was in the air, if not explicit, as in *The Rape of the Lock.*
Though Pope's prefatory remarks and most of his performance show
him translating resolutely in the high Roman fashion of Dryden and
other seventeenth-century predecessors, mocking intonations break in
– and where more appropriately than in Book XIV, a scene of Homeric
comedy? Though Pope rejected the hearty burlesque of Dryden's
version of the quarreling Juno and Jove in Book I, there is at least one
couplet to prove that he nearly succumbed to burlesque in rendering
Book XIV:

> At length with Love and Sleep's soft Pow'r opprest,
> The panting Thund'rer nods, and sinks to Rest.

> (405–6)

49

If we recall the lines on Jove's awful nod in Homer, Virgil, or Dryden, the parodic, if not burlesque, overtone is inescapable. (There is – by the way – nothing in the original like the second line.)

That Pope – and his audience – had other than properly heroic feelings about the episode in Homer, and about the style it suggested, is clear from his Observations, which offer plenty of evidence that Pope kept up the heroic decorum of his version uneasily,[4] and that the direction of his personal response to the 'Deceit of Jove' was more like that of the poet who had recently been revising *The Rape of the Lock.* His first note on the scene opens like this: 'I don't know a bolder Fiction in all Antiquity, than this of *Jupiter's* being deceiv'd and laid asleep, or that has a greater Air of Impiety and Absurdity' (l. 179). Though an Homeric singer might have cheerfully assented to the last phrase, it is unlikely that he would have been troubled, as Pope was, by the lack of truth and morality in the 'Fiction.' 'I must needs, upon the whole, as far as I can judge, give up the Morality of this Fable . . . The present Passage will appear with more Dignity,' if the observation of Diodorus is accepted – that the narrative is a symbolic 'Representation of a religious Solemnity.'

The tone in which Pope introduces his next learned comment is worth hearing: 'In the next Place, if we have recourse to Allegory, (which softens and reconciles every thing) it may be imagin'd that by the Congress of *Jupiter* and *Juno,* is meant the mingling of the *Æther* and the *Air.*' Citing as an example the lines on Spring from the *Georgics,* he continues, '[Virgil] calls *Jupiter* expresly *Æther,* and represents him operating upon his Spouse for the Production of all things.' This pedantic if not salacious fantasy is airily dismissed with

> But, be all this as it will, it is certain, that whatever may be thought of this Fable in a theological or philosophical View, it is one of the most beautiful Pieces that ever was produc'd by Poetry. Neither does it want its Moral; an ingenious modern Writer [*Tatler,* 147] . . . has given it us in these Words: 'This Passage of *Homer* may suggest abundance of Instruction to a Woman who has a mind to preserve or recall the Affection of her Husband.'

More 'instruction' in the same vein follows from Pope himself, in 'the Spectator tone' that Sherburn detected in *The Rape of the Lock.* The next note (l. 191) descends to the tone of Rymer on *Othello:* 'some nice Criticks are shock'd in this Place of *Homer* to find that the Goddess washes herself, which presents some Idea as if she were dirty. Those who have Delicacy will profit by this Remark.' The scene of Juno's perfuming herself (ll. 198, 203) is commented on in chatty tones combining praise for Greek 'Simplicity' in dress, Scriblerian pedantry, and kittenish advice to 'the Ladies':

The good *Eustathius* is ravish'd to find, that here are no Washes for the Face . . . the Dress of *Juno* (which is the same they see in *Statues*) has manifestly the Advantage of the present, in displaying whatever is beautiful: That the Charms of the *Neck* and *Breast* are not less laid open, than by the modern Stays.

Of Venus's 'wonder-working Girdle,' Pope notes (l. 218) that 'The Allegory of the *Cestus* lies very open, tho' the Impertinences of *Eustathius* on this Head are unspeakable.' The twentieth-century reader (and Pope, we may assume) may view with scepticism William Frost's comment on the 'panting Thund'rer' couplet – that it is 'consistent both with his [Pope's] version of the episode as a whole and with his conception of the Juno and Jupiter story in Book XIV as perhaps deriving ultimately from the fertility observances of the eastern Mediterranean.'[5] The protective 'perhaps' must cover the ironic and sexy tones of Pope's commentary, which are hardly represented by 'deriving ultimately from the fertility observances of the eastern Mediterranean.' (Oh Fertility – what crimes are committed in thy name by 'anthropological' literary critics!) The 'conception' of the gods implied in the language of the translation is nearer to that of Homer's divine comedy and the worldly comedy of *The Rape of the Lock*. Douglas Knight notes the mixed effect that sometimes results from using the Augustan 'high style' in certain contexts,[6] as for example in Paris's appeal to Helen to 'snatch the hasty Joy':

> Thus having spoke, th'enamour'd *Phrygian* Boy
> Rush'd to the Bed, Impatient for the Joy.
>
> (III, 557–8)

The last line anticipates Byron and in fact echoes Dryden on the illicit love of noble Sigismonda and clownish Guiscard.

We may return to *The Rape of the Lock* for an example of this 'effect' in the blended wonder and ridicule of Pope's treatment of the 'busy Sylphs.' The mixed style in which Pope presents these creatures makes them seem most ambiguous spiritual powers:

> What tho' no Credit doubting Wits may give!
> The Fair and Innocent shall still believe.
> Know then, unnumber'd Spirits round thee fly,
> The light *Militia* of the lower Sky.
>
> (I, 39–42)

But the Sylphs *are* the defenders of beauty and innocence – '*Militia* of the Sky.' At first sight this sounds like Milton's guardian corps of angels, but *'light'* gives them an elfin charm, making them seem diminished compared with angels. 'Light' also implies that they may

51

be unsubstantial and unreliable: Pope's style gives an impression of grandeur and of a nobler spiritual world, while imparting charm and ridiculous ineffectiveness to his deities. We are given the lightest assurance that innocence has strength and resources in an evil society.

But however frail charming Innocence seems, it is preferable to Prudery:

> Soft yielding Minds to Water glide away,
> And sip with *Nymphs,* their Elemental Tea.
> The graver Prude sinks downward to a *Gnome,*
> In search of Mischief still on Earth to roam.
> The light Coquettes in *Sylphs* aloft repair,
> And sport and flutter in the Fields of Air.

(I, 61–6)

Pope comes out strongly, here and elsewhere, on the side of generosity and love:

> Some Nymphs there are, too conscious of their Face,
> For Life predestin'd to the *Gnomes'* Embrace.

'Coquettes' may be 'light,' their realm the less serious one of 'air' – of feminine wiles – *but* they sport in '*the Fields* of Air.' Again there is a touch of heroic quality, of epic generality, as in 'the fields of battle,' or in Chapman's 'the fields of fight.' Just enough weight is given these defenders of innocence to make us regard them with some respect.

Their special skill lies in 'guiding' women in 'mystick Mazes' of gallantry:

> Oft when the World imagines Women stray,
> The *Sylphs* thro' mystick Mazes guide their Way.

(I, 91–2)

They are skillful navigators in the 'Elemental Tea' of social life. But the power of Ariel is not all-sufficient. At the moment the lock is cut, 'resign'd to Fate,' he retires. If a woman is to escape Prudery, Innocence must fall, if only in a symbolic game.

The Baron is helped by Clarissa, who

> drew with tempting Grace
> A two-edg'd Weapon from her shining Case.

(III, 127–8)

This is the same Clarissa who later appears as the voice of Good Sense. Throughout the fuss that follows the rape of the lock, we see the triumph of the Gnomes and Spleen, of prudishness and ill-nature. The speech of Clarissa in Canto V which makes its moral point

52

through parody, not in spite of it, also makes clear that the only way to rise above prudery and attain inner beauty of soul is to

> keep good Humour still whate'er we lose.
>
> (v, 30)

Both Belinda's ravings and the crude boasting of the Baron – the excess of virginity and the excess of triumphant sex – are put in their place. As in a more serious epic, there can be a loss that is not a loss, but glory. Belinda's too is a 'fortunate fall.'

> Then cease, bright Nymph! to mourn thy ravish'd Hair
> Which adds new Glory to the shining Sphere!
>
> (v, 141–2)

Beauty and innocence, guided by Good Sense, may find a way. The woman who achieves this balance comes close to being a goddess of love:

> This, the blest Lover shall for *Venus* take.
>
> (v, 135)

And what – the reader may well ask – does all this have to do with Jane Austen? Let me suggest a few ways. First, we can say that the situation with which Pope deals is very novelistic – a woman and man sparring in a game of love. Second, the situation is novelistic in another sense: the game is in part a social game, and it is played within all the complexities of modern social life. Finally, Pope is picturing a particular, historic society, not only an ideal world of heroism (and comic fantasy), but the actuality of Queen Anne's London. The setting is local, and the action can be dated, as in most novels. Part of the fun comes from seeing this society in the light of an unchanging heroic one, the 'elite' of Homer's imagination.

Two main strands in the developing English novel of the eighteenth century might be noted here: the journalistic, in Defoe, and the parodic, in Fielding.[7] Pope's heroi-comical poem embraces both modes, and anticipates their union in the full blown prose epic of *Tom Jones.* Let us look now at a scene from a novelist who began with parody, who left parody in the strict sense behind but who owed much to the traditions of satire in which *The Rape of the Lock* was written. It is worth noting that in the latter part of *The Rape,* the to-do over Belinda's loss, dialogue becomes more frequent, and, though the heroic style is not sacrificed entirely, the effect comes closer to drama, to comedy of manners.

Fielding – to recall something everyone knows or ought to know – began as a writer of plays, and many of his scenes could be easily transferred to the stage. Jane Austen had the advantage of his example before her. (A word of protest should be entered in passing against the current critical fashion of setting up Jane Austen against Fielding.[8]) Jane Austen is also in her way a poet: her control of sentence rhythm, of ironic play on words, is often almost as precise as Pope's. Consider for example the brief dialogue early in *Pride and Prejudice* in which the seemingly proud and conceited Mr Darcy surprises the very penetrating, very self-assured Elizabeth Bennet by asking her to dance with him:

> After playing some Italian songs, Miss Bingley varied the charm by a lively Scotch air; and soon afterwards Mr. Darcy, drawing near Elizabeth, said to her –
>
> 'Do you not feel a great inclination, Miss Bennet, to seize such an opportunity of dancing a reel?'
>
> She smiled, but made no answer. He repeated the question, with some surprise at her silence.
>
> 'Oh!' said she, 'I heard you before; but I could not immediately determine what to say in reply. You wanted me, I know, to say "Yes," that you might have the pleasure of despising my taste; but I always delight in overthrowing those kind of schemes, and cheating a person of their premeditated contempt. I have therefore made up my mind to tell you, that I do not want to dance a reel at all – and now despise me if you dare.'
>
> 'Indeed I do not dare.'
>
> Elizabeth, having rather expected to affront him, was amazed at his gallantry; but there was a mixture of sweetness and archness in her manner which made it difficult for her to affront anybody; and Darcy had never been so bewitched by any woman as he was by her. He really believed that were it not for the inferiority of her connections, he should be in some danger.
>
> (Vol. I, ch. x)

This dialogue is almost as full of ironic ambiguities as any of the wittiest passages in *The Rape of the Lock*.[9] Consider a few instances. Darcy's question about 'dancing a reel' can be taken as Elizabeth takes it, as expressing 'premeditated contempt' of herself, or of the vulgar heartiness of country dancing. When Darcy repeats the question 'with some surprise' it may be interpreted, quite differently, as another sign of his egotism – that any girl should not jump at the chance – or as a sign of some interest in Elizabeth: a decided warming-up of this formidable man who dances with no one. After his 'Indeed I do *not* dare,' his repeated question can be interpreted as a timid gesture of love: he was, we discover, 'bewitched.' If we look at Elizabeth's remarks, we find that they are equally alive with double possibilities. Her very knowing rejection – 'despise me if you dare' – is based on *her* supposition that she has interpreted Darcy's motives correctly. 'She was amazed at his gallantry' implies (though she does not know it yet) the first sign of an attraction on her part to Mr Darcy. Her 'mixture of sweetness and archness' bewitches, when she intended the opposite effect, to cut Darcy down to size. Note also that her 'archness' defends her 'sweetness' from any over-easy giving in. (We may recall Belinda and her defenders.)

But there are no sylphs here – or rather, they have undergone a new transformation, having become a part of the inner consciousness and life of the heroine. Their skillful navigation now takes the form of Elizabeth's artful way of turning off Darcy's attempts to win her interest. A new diplomacy of the heart has taken the place of Pope's epic machinery. As in *The Rape of the Lock,* the strategy that attempts to defend innocence also attracts the attacker. The sylphs were not altogether reliable defenders: they made Belinda more 'bewitching' than ever.

There is a deeper likeness to Pope that can be seen only by relating this and similar dialogues to the whole of *Pride and Prejudice.* Elizabeth, like Pope's heroine, is being educated (though she doesn't suspect it) in Good Sense; just as Darcy is being educated in love and openness of mind. Through the irony of the dialogue we are being gently reminded that the egotistical pride of Darcy and the self-assurance of Elizabeth are not adequate attitudes for a mature man and woman. Both – without knowing it – are very 'gnomish.' The small hints of possible illumination, of generous response, point to another way, a way between frigidity or pride and mere helpless subjection to another personality. Jane Austen would call it the way of 'rational happiness' – the reward of Pope's 'Good Sense.'

There is no case, or at best a slight one, for proving direct influence of Pope or of *The Rape of the Lock* on Jane Austen. It can be said, however, that her literary temper, the temper expressed through the ironic dialogue and comment of her drawing- and morning-room comedies, had its natural alliances with that of the earlier eighteenth century and with the Augustans, rather than with her immediate ancestors, the sentimental, domestic, and Gothic novelists. Certain traits of mind, views of character and social life, with their accompanying modes of irony and moral evaluation, which become salient in Jane Austen, had been anticipated in eighteenth-century satire. The line of connection and development is suggested by Rachel Trickett in her admirable study of eighteenth-century poetry, *The Honest Muse:*

The movement from fable to fact in subject-matter, and from myth to history as a mode of understanding and reflecting experience, is as vividly reflected in the poetry of the Honest Muse as in the development of the new literary form of the novel to which these changes gave rise.

The Augustan poets, particularly the satirists, 'shared the common assumption of the time that men and manners, matters of fact rather than fiction, were the true substance of an art which, at its highest, must come home to the business and the bosom of every man.'[10]

By family relationship, Jane Austen had at least one link with the great world of Pope and his contemporaries: she was 'great-grand-niece of the magnificent first Duke of Chandos,' and it is likely that both her sister's and her mother's first name came from the Duke's second wife, the Duchess Cassandra.[11] Though Chandos was almost certainly not Pope's Timon, his house, Canons, was grand enough to make the identification a natural one.

Jane Austen's easy familiarity with eighteenth-century writers is also known, especially with 'dear Dr Johnson.' She did not often model her style closely on her hero's, though she made one unfortunate attempt to imitate him in verse. She loved Cowper and Crabbe, and quoted one of Cowper's most Augustan poems. She had a re-play of Pope's *On the Art of Sinking* in her brother James's periodical, *The Loiterer:* the ironic 'Rules for *Prose Composition*' (in No. 5)[12] 'is a compendium of those affectations in style and manner which were ridiculed in the Austen household' and which Jane often made fun of in her *Juvenilia.* Even Johnson and Pope are parodied, Pope in a letter from a young lady crossed – many times! – in love. A friend now widowed tries to brighten her up by introducing the subject of riding.

> Then repeating the following line which was an extempore and equally adapted to recommend both Riding and Candour – 'Ride where you may, Be Candid where you can,' she added, '*I* rode once, but it is many years ago' – She spoke this in so low and tremulous a Voice, that I was silent.
>
> (*A Collection of Letters,* Letter the Second)

The context in the original must have been congenial to the novelist:

> Eye Nature's walks, shoot folly as it flies,
> And catch the Manners living as they rise;
> Laugh where we must, be candid where we can.

(These lines are a better introduction to Jane Austen's novels than to the 'specious' and 'solemn' argument of the *Essay on Man.*) A. Walton Litz says that Jane Austen's 'works must be seen against the background of an eighteenth-century dialectic involving Reason and Feeling, Judgement and Fancy . . . By education and temperament, Jane

Austen was uniquely suited to dramatize in her art the classic debates of the century that lay behind her.'[13] 'Sense and Sensibility' might serve as a sub-title for *The Rape of the Lock*, as 'Benevolence and Prudence' might, for *Tom Jones*. Both novelists – Fielding quite consciously – belong to the 'line of Pope.'

Richard Simpson, one of the earlier critics to point out Jane Austen's links with the Augustans, echoes Lewes's and Macaulay's view of her as close to Shakespeare in 'her power of composing characters. She does not give any of them a hobby-horse, like Sterne, nor a ruling passion, like Pope, nor a humour, like Ben Jonson, nor a trick, like Mr Dickens.'[14] We may want to qualify this if we think of the fixed characters or 'fools' in Jane Austen, and we can accept the remark about the 'ruling passion' only if we add – not 'like Pope' at his best. The lines I just quoted from the *Essay on Man* suggest that the doctrine of the 'Ruling Passion' was not likely to offer an adequate rationale for Pope's mature satirical portraits. The great passage on Man –

> Chaos of Thought and Passion, all confused

– expresses better than his theory Pope's sense of the paradoxical complexity of human nature. In the *Epistle to Cobham*, the satire in which he tried hardest to impose the doctrine on particular cases, the portraits keep exceeding their assigned Passion. In the first half of the poem Pope sets forth a quite different account of 'human kind,' expressing over and over his scepticism about easy explanations.

> Our depths who fathoms, or our shallows finds,
> Quick whirls, and shifting eddies, of our minds? . . .
>
> On human actions reason tho' you can,
> It may be Reason, but it is not Man:
> His Principle of action once explore,
> That instant 'tis his Principle no more.
> Like following life thro' creatures you dissect,
> You lose it in the moment you detect.
>
> (29–30; 35–40)

The dazzling contradictions of Wharton's character hardly illustrate his Ruling Passion, 'the lust of Praise.'

> A constant Bounty, which no friend has made;
> An angel Tongue, which no man can persuade;
> A Fool, with more of Wit than half mankind,
> Too rash for Thought, for Action too refined.
>
> (198–201)

Though we may trace the lines of a moral dialectic in many of Pope's satirical portraits, the greatest ones – like the central characters of Jane Austen's novels – cannot be reduced to a single pair of warring vices and virtues. Though both Jane Austen and Pope were equally clear about the meaning of the large moral abstractions on which their judgments rested, in their great cases they expressed a common love of 'intricacy' in character. Belinda surprises us by being more than a featherhead, and Darcy, by being more than an allegorical embodiment of Prejudice. Elizabeth Bennet may speak for both the novelist and the satirist: 'intricate characters are the *most* amusing.' When Pope tells Swift that 'Your lady friend Martha Blount – is *Semper Eadem*, and I have written an Epistle to her on that qualification in a female character' he is not giving an adequate account of the tenderly mocking picture with which he concludes the *Epistle to a Lady:*

> And yet, believe me, good as well as ill,
> Woman's at best a Contradiction still.
>
> (269–70)

'Heav'n . . . Blends,' he continues,

> Reserve with Frankness, Art with Truth allied,
> Courage with Softness, Modesty with Pride;
> Fixed Principles, with Fancy ever new;
> Shakes all together, and produces – You.
>
> (277–80)

Pope did not always write like this, but he did more than once – in poems to Martha Blount, and in *The Rape of the Lock:*

> Her lively Looks a sprightly Mind disclose,
> Quick as her Eyes, and as unfix'd as those;
> Favours to none, to all she Smiles extends:
> Oft she rejects, but never once offends.
> Bright as the sun, her Eyes the Gazers strike,
> And, like the Sun, they shine on all alike.
> Yet graceful Ease, and Sweetness void of Pride,
> Might hide her Faults, if *Belles* had Faults to hide:
> If to her share some Female Errors fall,
> Look on her Face, and you'll forget 'em all.
>
> (II, 10–18)

'The tone is ironical,' as Cleanth Brooks reminds us, 'but the irony is not that of a narrow and acerb satire; rather it is an irony which accords with a wise recognition of the total situation.'

In this 'Shakespearean' treatment of the heroine and in other features, *The Rape* differs markedly from its more obviously mock-epic predecessors. After reviewing Pope's indebtedness to Tassoni,

Boileau, and Garth, Joseph Warton concludes 'that [*The Rape of the Lock*] contains the truest and liveliest picture of modern life; and that the subject is of a more elegant nature, as well as more artfully conducted than that of any other heroi-comic poem.' 'The important difference lies in the subject,' says Ian Jack: 'while Boileau and Garth describe the quarrels of lazy priests and grubby physicians, Pope is concerned with a quarrel in the *beau monde.*' Pope's world is 'beautiful' in every sense, and his poem presents a credible society of families and lovers in 'a palpably credible plot.'[15] This world of parodied crises and of deeper and more permanent moral and emotional concerns lightly implied in an ironic surface approaches closely to the fictional creations of Jane Austen. Fielding had led the way in his dramatic scenes from the life of a hero who was both warm-hearted and imprudent; and Crabbe, another sturdy Augustan, may have offered models nearer to Jane Austen's chosen milieux in tales like 'The Frank Courtship,' 'Arabella,' and 'The Lover's Journey,' with their scenes of village middle-class wooing and romantic deceptions coolly unmasked. But the outright irony of Crabbe was not adequate to the more complex vision of Jane Austen. To bring the multiple perspectives of irony *and* tenderness to bear simultaneously on the social case, whether Elizabeth Bennet or Marianne Dashwood or Emma Woodhouse, demanded another model for revising the prose sentence to serve its new function. And where could the last of the Augustans and the first of the nineteenth-century novelists find a more apt teacher than in the master of 'intricacy' and politeness, the creator of an idealized yet imperfect Martha Blount and Arabella Fermor? If we shudder at the notion of conscious or unconscious 'influence,' we may change our metaphor and suggest that in Jane Austen the mind and art of Pope found its reincarnation, as the heroi-comical poem found *its* reincarnation in novels of 'Love and Freindship.'

NOTES

1 This essay was previously published, in slightly different form, in *Mirror on Mirror: Translation, Imitation, Parody* (Harvard University Press, 1974), copyright 1974 by the President and Fellows of Harvard College.

2 Text of this and other quotations from Pope's original poems and from his *Homer* is that of the Twickenham Edition of the *Poems of Alexander Pope*, ed. John Butt, vols. I–X (London and New Haven, 1939–67). (Hereafter referred to as 'TE'.)

3 TE, VII, cxlv-viii.

4 'The Notes of others are read to clear difficulties, those of Pope to vary "entertainment." It has, however, been objected with sufficient reason that there is in the commentary too much of unseasonable levity and affected gaiety; that too many appeals are made to the ladies, and the ease

which is so carefully preserved is sometimes the ease of a trifler.' Samuel Johnson, *Lives of the English Poets,* ed. G. Birkbeck Hill (Oxford, 1905), III, p. 240.

5 TE, VII, cliv.

6 TE, VII, clxxxi–iii.

7 See Ian Watt on Defoe's power of 'convincing us completely that his narrative is occurring at a particular place and at a particular time' and on his similarity to Richardson in this respect. *The Rise of the Novel* (Berkeley and Los Angeles, 1957), p. 24.

8 For a more balanced view of Jane Austen's relation to Fielding and to Richardson, and to 'late eighteenth-century fashions in fiction,' see A. Walton Litz, *Jane Austen: A Study of Her Artistic Development* (New York, 1965), pp. 3–18. On Fielding and Jane Austen as writers of 'anti-romance' in the line of Cervantes, see Harry Levin, 'The Example of Cervantes,' *Society and Self in the Novel: English Institute Essays, 1955* (New York, 1956), p. 24. The whole essay is of importance for demonstrating how the novelist passes 'from the imitation of art through parody to the imitation of nature.' (The description also applies to Pope's development as a satirist.)

9 A more detailed analysis of 'Popeian' irony in this and other passages is given in Reuben A. Brower, *The Fields of Light* (New York, 1951), pp. 167–70.

10 *The Honest Muse* (Oxford, 1967), p. 15.

11 Donald Greene, 'Jane Austen and the Peerage,' *PMLA*, 68 (1953), 1019.

12 Litz, p. 46. On *The Loiterer* and its possible effect on Jane Austen's 'comic techniques,' see pp. 15–17.

13 *Ibid.*, p. 8; compare p. 135.

14 'Jane Austen,' *The North British Review,* LII (1870), 136; quoted in *Jane Austen: The Critical Heritage,* ed. B. C. Southam (London, 1968), p. 249. For Lewes's and Macaulay's views, see Southam, items 26, 30, 36. 'It is clear that she began, as Shakespeare began, with being an ironical censurer of her contemporaries. After forming her prentice hand by writing nonsense, she began her artistic self-education by writing burlesques . . . her parodies were designed not so much to flout at the style as at the unnaturalness, unreality, and fictitious morality, of the romances she imitated.' Simpson, *op. cit.,* p. 130.

15 G. S. Rousseau (ed.), *Twentieth Century Interpretations of 'The Rape of the Lock'* (Englewood Cliffs, N.J., 1969), p. 3.

STUART M. TAVE

Jane Austen and one of her contemporaries

A birthday volume seems to say that dates have meaning. If Jane Austen was born in 1775 that means she was born in the middle of the decade which made her an exact contemporary not only of Scott but of Wordsworth, Coleridge and Southey – and they all read her – of Hazlitt too. It means that, like them, the decade in which she comes to maturity and begins serious authorship is the 1790s. If she seems to be removed from the history this implies, from a highly eventful or a palpable gross reality, then it is well to remember that in the novels of Jane Austen as there are pigs and there are dung carts – and with no fuss, casual mention, known parts of the daily scene – so there are passing allusions to a contemporary history that included the flogging of soldiers, the slave trade, the enclosure of commons, new seed drills, émigrés eking out livings in London, bloody political riots, major and minor battles on land and sea, including privateering, even the American War of 1812. What is 'modern' and what is 'old-fashioned' is of frequent concern to her characters, in questions of morals and manners and homes. The modern circular table Emma introduced at Hartfield, and which none but Emma could have had power to place there and persuade her father to use (E 347),[1] was such a thing as still struck heat from Archdeacon Grantly, having associations with the unorthodox, new-fangled, democratic, parvenu (*Barchester Towers*, ch. xxi). These polished surfaces reflect deeply. If Jane Austen were obviously on the side of the modern or of the old-fashioned she would

61

make it easier for us to find her in or out of favor with our tastes, but she never allows us simple-minded pleasures. Darcy's library at Pemberley is a good one, the work of many generations, as he says, and he has added much to it himself: he cannot comprehend the neglect of a family library, he says, 'in such days as these' (*PP* 38). One of the opinions of her novels recorded by Jane Austen was the uneasiness of the lady who thought her wrong to draw such clergymen as Mr Elton and Mr Collins 'in such times as these' (*MW* 439). Both Darcy and the lady, with equal words but unequal minds, speak to the preservation of the life of a valued inheritance. For Jane Austen the library of an old established family, if it were Pemberley, might be a treasure beyond price or imitation, and a clergyman of an old established church, if he were Mr Collins, might be a priceless and inimitable fool – in such times as these, or at any time. Apart from the stirring scene, her clear eye, both witty and loving, is on the unnoted particular which discloses daily meanings.

Such times as these make demands on art, but varied demands, and Jane Austen's response is neither outside her day nor singular in it. Captain Benwick of *Persuasion* seems to be a man very much at the center of his times. He has been at sea fighting the French and while he has been bravely earning his fortune the superior woman he loves has died; he suffers heavily, as his friends are made aware. He is a reader of poetry too, who talks of 'the richness of the present age,' Scott and Byron, has read those tremendous tales of the *Giaour* and the *Bride of Abydos*, wants to ascertain their ranking, and how to pronounce the *Giaour*; he is so intimately acquainted with 'all the impassioned descriptions of hopeless agony,' repeats with tremulous feeling various lines which imaged a broken heart, or a mind destroyed by wretchedness, and looks so entirely as if he meant to be understood, that Anne Elliot ventures to recommend a larger allowance of prose in his daily study (*P* 100–1). Jane Austen has read Byron too, drops him into a letter she writes to her sister on a day when the weather makes it impossible to get out: 'I have read the Corsair, mended my petticoat, & have nothing else to do' (*L* 379). That's informative literary criticism; it tells us something about Byron; there were readers who did not need him because most times there was something else to do. There was another function for art in such times as these and at least one of her contemporaries insisted that what the age needed most was not the art which chooses the great and unusual subject and aims at the most striking effect. He admired those minds which build up greatest things from least suggestions. They need not extraordinary calls to rouse them (*Prelude*, xiv, 101 ff.).

When Hazlitt made his first acquaintance with Wordsworth the poet had just seen the *Castle Spectre* by Monk Lewis, the latest exciting play, and described it very well. He said 'it fitted the taste of the audience like a glove.' This *ad captandum* merit, however, Hazlitt says, was by no means a recommendation, according to the severe principles of the new school, which rejected rather than courted popular appeal.[2] Wordsworth, as he talked, was making havoc of the half of a Cheshire cheese on the table; if his taste was not for the popular it was not because he wanted stronger or more uncommon stimulants. 'For the human mind,' he wrote shortly afterwards, 'is capable of being excited without the application of gross and violent stimulants'; the man has a very faint perception of its beauty and dignity who does not know this and who does not know that one being is elevated above another in proportion as he possesses this capability. The question is central to Wordsworth's choice of subjects and to his aim in his poetry; to endeavor to produce or enlarge this capability is one of the best services in which at any period a writer can be engaged, but 'especially so at the present day.' A multitude of causes unknown to former times are blunting the discriminating powers of the mind, unfitting it for all voluntary exertion, reducing it to torpor: the great national events daily taking place, the accumulation of men in cities where the uniformity of their occupations produces 'a craving for extraordinary incident' which is gratified by the rapid communication of hourly news. To this tendency of life and manners the literature and theatrical exhibitions of the country have conformed themselves; the invaluable works of our elder writers are driven into neglect by 'frantic novels, sickly and stupid German Tragedies, and deluges of idle and extravagant stories in verse.' This degrading thirst after outrageous stimulation he will endeavor to counteract.[3]

If there are, certainly, differences between this and Jane Austen's subjects and aims there are, certainly too, points at which they touch. She had an interest, stronger than his, in the thirst after the violence and stimulation of frantic novels. It is the theatrical representation of a sickly and stupid German play[4] which forms a major and extended incident of *Mansfield Park*, testing the discriminating powers of every major character, presenting parallels to the roles many of them are eager to enact in their own lives and thereby make those lives more exciting. The public causes which Wordsworth says are the most effective in producing the craving for extraordinary incident are not immediate in Jane Austen. She is more interested in young girls living in conventionally good provincial homes, and she knows that they too, if they have been brought up in 'an ordinary parsonage-house,' like Catherine Morland, may well be eager for an abbey and the literature of extraordinary incident which gives them a mind 'craving to be frightened' (*NA* 157, 200).

As Catherine is initiated into that new sensation, the luxury of a raised, restless and frightened imagination over the pages of *Myster-*

ies of Udolpho (*NA* 51), another and related artful vision rises. There is a 'want of taste, which is universal among modern novels of the Radcliffe school,' Wordsworth said; 'I allude to the laborious manner in which everything is placed before your eye for the production of picturesque effect.' Unlike good narration where pictures rise up before the sight and pass away from it unostentatiously, here they are fixed upon an easel for the express purpose of being admired.[5] 'I never look at it,' Catherine says of Beechen Cliff at Bath, 'without thinking of the south of France.' 'You have been abroad then?' Henry Tilney asks, a little surprised; nothing in what he knows of her gives sign of much experience. 'Oh! no, I only mean what I have read about'; it puts her in mind of the country in *Udolpho* (*NA* 106). She needs more instruction in how to admire expressly. When the conversation turns from Mrs Radcliffe to the picturesque Catherine is quite lost, because she knows nothing of taste and the phrases she hears convey scarcely any ideas to her. 'It seemed as if a good view were no longer to be taken from the top of an high hill, and that a clear blue sky was no longer a proof of a fine day. She was heartily ashamed of her ignorance.' It is a misplaced shame because it gives Henry his opportunity to deliver his lecture on the picturesque. He talks of foregrounds, distances, and second distances, side-screens and perspectives, lights and shades, and she is so hopeful a scholar that when they gained the top of Beechen Cliff 'she voluntarily rejected the whole city of Bath, as unworthy to make part of a landscape' (110–11). She is disliking here, and there liking, by rules of mimic art, as Wordsworth says of his own past interest in the picturesque, that strong infection of the age (*Prelude,* xii, 109 ff.). Henry Tilney is interested in it, but takes his pleasures pleasantly, as he does the novels of the Radcliffe school. He uses the stimulation of the arts to teach discrimination in observation and feeling. The infection of the picturesque lies deeper in those who long to imitate characters in exciting romances, like Marianne Dashwood and her need for more violent passion, or Henry Crawford and his continual need for stimulation. With them, each in a different way, the superficial novel sight and its excitement of feeling become desires detached from the integrity of the mind. More like the younger Wordsworth they roam 'Still craving combinations of new forms,' laying the inner faculties asleep, and unlike Dorothy Wordsworth: 'She welcomed what was given, and craved no more' (*Prelude,* xii, 144, 158).

If we follow further the sequence of the same conversation between Catherine Morland and the Tilneys there emerges that relationship which so interested Wordsworth between public and aesthetic excitements. Having gone from Mrs Radcliffe to his lecture on the picturesque, Henry is delighted with Catherine's progress as a pupil in that art, and fearful of wearying her with too much wisdom at once he suffers the subject to decline. By an easy transition from a rocky fragment and a withered oak, to oaks in general, forests, enclosure, waste lands, crown lands, and government, he shortly finds himself at politics, and 'from politics, it was an easy step to silence.' The phrase is often cited in evidence of Jane Austen's killing a subject which can have no interesting sequel. But the conversation is about to jump. The pause succeeding Henry's short disquisition on the state of the nation is ended by a solemn utterance from Catherine: 'I have heard that something very shocking indeed, will soon come out in London.' Miss Tilney is startled. Catherine does not know what its nature will be or who is the author, but it is to be more horrible than anything we have met with yet. A particular friend of Catherine's has had an account of it in a letter from London. It is to be uncommonly dreadful, with murder and everything of the kind. Miss Tilney hopes that proper measures will be taken by government to prevent the dreadful riot. Henry, who has been enjoying this confusion of parallel horrors of London authorship, must then make the ladies understand each other. 'My dear Eleanor, the riot is only in your own brain . . . Miss Morland has been talking of nothing more dreadful than a new publication . . . in three duodecimo volumes, two hundred and seventy-six pages in each, with a frontispiece to the first, of two tombstones and a lantern – do you understand?' The horrors in London which Miss Tilney immediately pictured to herself – a mob of thousands assembling in St George's Fields, the Bank attacked, Tower threatened, blood in the streets, the troops called up – were the details contemporaries would recognize as a repetition of the Gordon riots (*NA* 111–13).

London is the readiest prompter of the riot in the street or in the brain. Catherine begins her reading of horrid tales when she is initiated at Bath by a smart-looking female from 'near London' – Putney we later learn parenthetically when it does not surprise us – who knows the fashions and tastes of London (*NA* 33, 122); that is the mock-romance of a girl from a parsonage in Wiltshire. But the multiplied sensations of the city can become, for both poet and novelist, destructive of life, both of community and of individual wholeness. They are perhaps the last generation who can say without nostalgia that the center of life is in the provinces. Henry Crawford should have stayed there, Michael's Luke should have stayed there, rich man and poor man, at home, on the land, where they properly belong, fulfilling their duties to their estates – in whatever sense – and to their families. Both authors are celebrants of place and of the intimate relationship between landed property and domestic affections.

They are both of them authors who set themselves, programmatically, against the mode of violent stimulation as degrading to the mind and destructive of society, to choose their subjects from what they call common life and their language from the real language of men. His impulse is, initially, more political, hers more moral. His low and rustic life where the essential passions of the heart are under less restraint and speak a more emphatic language is not her landed gentry and baronetage where a lady says 'just what she ought, of course.' But the similarity is that both look for significance in the quiet unregarded daily round of life, the places unheard and unseen by a literature of violent stimulation. His poems are distinguished from the popular poetry of the day, Wordsworth says, in that 'the feeling therein developed gives importance to the action and situation, and not the action and situation to the feeling.'[6] That was not how Jane Austen constructed her plots, but when Fanny Price watches Miss Bertram walk around a gate, or Emma Woodhouse says a thoughtless word to Miss Bates, or Captain Wentworth assists Anne Elliot into a carriage, such actions and situations have no importance at all except as the feeling, usually the different feelings of several people, each feeling complex in itself, makes them greatly important, sometimes the turning point of a valued life. What Jane Austen calls 'the little particulars of the circumstance' (*P* 80), like Wordsworth's one particular rock ('The Brothers,' 366), one particular flower ('Artegal and Elidure,' 58), one particular hour (*Prelude,* iv, 308), are the common details of life seen full with meaning. They are unexciting and unfelt except as the poet and novelist make them available to our perception, enlarge the capability of our mind, its beauty and dignity. The diffusive influence upon those about them exerted by Elinor Dashwood, Fanny Price, Mr Knightley, Anne Elliot, reveals that at least some portion of a good man's, or woman's, life lies in 'the little, nameless, unremembered, acts' ('Tintern Abbey,' 34). Hazlitt, writing on the spirit of his age, says Wordsworth is 'the most original poet' of the age. Scott, sketching a history of the novel and its contemporary development, speaks of Jane Austen's 'spirit and originality,' 'originality and precision.' Hazlitt did not love Wordsworth, and Scott could have claimed the originality in the contemporary novel for himself, but they are honest in criticism and knowledgeable and acute, and what they have in mind is something similar. Wordsworth, more than any important poet, Jane Austen, more than any important novelist, have been held deficient in flight, prosy dwellers in the matter-of-fact or on the surface. Interested in representing the dull and the garrulous they have been judged too literal in their success; a credulous old man in a village narrates 'The Thorn,' a tiresome old maid chatters in Highbury. Hazlitt and Scott take note of this but it is not what is most notable for them. For Hazlitt, Wordsworth takes 'the commonest events and objects,' the trivial and familiar, and brings a depth of feeling to the meanest flower, to do what no one else had done before him; for Scott, Jane Austen takes 'common incidents' and ordinary characters and displays such a depth of knowledge, almost alone in her originality, that we never miss the excitation of uncommon events.[7] Both critics see their authors as turning from an old artifice of pretentious significance to a fresh subject matter and a new depth.

In both authors, we can add parenthetically, there is a strong feeling about the kind of language appropriate to an art which refuses artifice. 'His style is vernacular: he delivers household truths,' Hazlitt says of the poet.[8] The two things go together. The reader of Wordsworth will find little of what is usually called 'poetic diction,' the reader of Jane Austen little of 'novel slang'; he wants none of that 'gaudiness and inane phraseology' of modern poets, she none of the 'unmeaning gibberish' of the novelists.[9] They are both disgusted with the style and the morality of a hackneyed language; it is a formula to express high feelings without origin in the present reality of the speaker; it is unfriendly to what Wordsworth calls 'one property of all good poetry, namely, good sense.'[10] Good sense, in Wordsworth or Jane Austen, favors a 'plain' language; it makes them notorious, among their kind, as unfigured and unmetaphorical authors.

But to stay here with the household truths, we can be a little more specific. For both authors the wisdom of daily life is expressed notably in what both call a cheerfulness. There is in some of Jane Austen's characters – Mr Weston, Mrs Jennings, for example – a cheerfulness of mind without strong feelings, a simple good-tempered ease and good will, which is pleasant and useful, and also a little exasperating at times to others in its impermeability; but there is a more valued sort, of the mind fully aware, emotionally capable, knowing pain and loss and the greater for them. Cheerfulness can rest on a serenity of mind: 'that cheerfulness' which characterizes Jane Bennet, 'proceeding from the serenity of a mind at ease with itself, and kindly disposed towards every one . . . scarcely ever clouded' (*PP* 188); in Wordsworth there is the pleasure in the life in common things, every day found all about him in one neighborhood, which becomes a self-congratulation and 'from morn/To night, unbroken cheerfulness serene' (*Prelude,* i, 108–13). This quality seems to be part of a natural idyll, scarcely ever clouded, from morn to night, a heavenly serenity; indeed there is a language of religious tradition behind it, a *risus ex serenitate conscientiae.*[11] But it has an unbroken self-containment which, for all its benignity, is isolating and needs to be shaken to become more humanly interesting. In both these instances we hear of it at a moment when it is being cracked and tested. But in both it will return with a better assurance. Jane Austen has no illusions about the weariness of 'every day remarks, dull repetitions' (*E* 219), 'no poverty . . . except of conversation' (*SS* 233) and the mean wounds inflicted with daily propriety; nor has Wordsworth about 'the sneers of selfish men,' 'greetings where no kindness is,' 'all/The dreary intercourse of daily life.' But that does not prevail against either of them or disturb 'Our cheerful faith, that all which we behold/Is full of blessings' ('Tintern Abbey,' 128–34). The ground of the faith and the kind of blessing is not the same, but both have a quiet certainty that can always look forward to a length of human time which rests within a larger scheme. Wordsworth puts on his priestly robe for the holy services of poetry with 'A cheerful confidence in things to come' (*Prelude,* i, 58). Anne Elliot could have been eloquent on the side of 'a cheerful confidence in futurity' which does not distrust Providence. It is what Jane Austen is not afraid to call, at that point, 'romance' (*P* 30). Anne learned romance as she grew older. It is an earned confidence that must, as with Wordsworth, be earned continually.

There is, further, a sense of duty understood and deeply felt by those who see the integrity and peace of their own lives as essentially bound to the lives of others and see the lives of all in a more than merely social order. Jane Austen and Wordsworth both had younger brothers who were officers in British ships in the heroic years of the early nineteenth century and those happy warriors were impulses to triumphant and serious composition. The Englishness of character of the sort both authors admire is an inner wealth supportive in its strength of a community. Mr Knightley, with his strong sense of duty, with his manner, morals, and estate all in 'the true English style' (*E* 99, 149, 360), enters the novel in chapter 1 to be immediately cheerful where he is needed. Anne Elliot, who has submitted and suffered in acting with a perfect rightness, has not suffered in her conscience and has nothing to reproach herself with: she has no fortune and no family to bestow on her husband, but 'if I mistake not,' she says, 'a strong sense of duty is no bad part of a woman's portion,' and that she brings to her English captain (*P* 246). She can bring only her own dowry because her father, who had not principle or sense enough to maintain himself in the situation in which Providence had placed him (248), has lost his estate; her father has lost, in Wordsworth's language, the fireside and heroic wealth of hall and bower which, in selfishness, forfeited 'the ancient English dower/Of inward happiness.' That last phrase is from the sonnet on the Milton who should be living at this hour; if Milton's great soul was like a star and dwelt apart, in the concluding lines he brings us this compendious example of manners, virtue, freedom and power:

So didst thou travel on life's common way,
In cheerful godliness; and yet thy heart
The lowliest duties on herself did lay.

announce his inconsistent and self-deceiving decision to take his part in the play-acting, leaving Fanny isolated, he thinks Fanny will find comfort and composure in reading her book of travel. '*You* in the meanwhile will be taking a trip into China, I suppose.' But there is no China and no reading for Fanny that day. Edmund's perception is a little better when he notices, 'And here are Crabbe's Tales, and the Idler, at hand to relieve you, if you tire of your great book' (158). Crabbe's *Tales* (1812) was a brand new book, the *Idler* was more than half a century in the past, but there was a continuity in Fanny's taste. Johnson had praised Crabbe's earliest work, corrected it in manuscript, and though we may feel with Hazlitt some surprise that Johnson here admired the simple and the minute, with Hazlitt we can see the connection. Johnson was 'an acute, strong-minded man, and could see truth when it was presented to him, even through the mist of his prejudices and foibles.'[16] It is a question of a mode of vision, of lights and transparencies, of seeing the truth through a mist. When Wordsworth says that Jane Austen does not clarify the truth there is a question of what it is that needs clarification in the medium between the eye and the object – and, therefore, of what it is that is seen when the truth is seen clearly.

Wordsworth climbs to his mountain vision in the mist that girts him round; as at other times it is in his blessing that the misty mountain-winds will be free to blow against his sister; as Michael, who knew the meaning of all winds on his heights, had been alone amid the heart of many thousand mists (*Prelude*, xiv, 15; 'Tintern Abbey,' 136–7; 'Michael,' 58–9). The vision and the blessing and the meaning come by the enveloping union of that mutual intimacy of the self and the surrounding. In life's everyday appearances Wordsworth gains 'clear sight/Of a new world' in which there is an ennobling interchange of action from without and from within, the object seen and the eye that sees (*Prelude*, xiii, 366 ff.). What a Jane Austen heroine learns to see does not come in misty winds. When a sudden 'scud of rain driving full in her face' makes it impossible for her to observe anything further (*NA* 161), we know that a blindness has descended; the eye begins its interchange with the object seen. The truth is clarified by a different and later light. The moment of truth in Jane Austen is usually that traditional moment when, after a slow preparation, the blindness ends, clarity comes with a rush. Catherine Morland, completely awakened, suddenly sees that 'nothing could . . . be clearer' (*NA* 199). Emma 'saw it all with a clearness which had never blessed her before' (*E* 408). The blessed clarification is a humiliating discovery, because what they see is not a new world, but themselves. The blindness has been self-created by a mind too eager and busy in its previous conceptions and views to hear impartially or see with clear vision (*E* 110). In that sense the truth is clarified by a conquest over an imagination which imposes itself upon the world. The end of that delusion of the self comes as an arrow of self-hatred. Catherine Morland 'hated herself more than she could express' (*NA* 199). Marianne Dashwood sees what has 'made me hate myself forever' (*SS* 264). 'How despicably have I acted!' Elizabeth cries (*PP* 208). For Emma, with one exception 'Every other part of her mind was disgusting' (*E* 412). In each instance the extravagance of the language is the guarantee that this touch at the bottom will have its sequel in a better emotion. The one exception for Emma is her affection for Mr Knightley. The moment of shame, which is the clear sight, is the necessary prelude to the next movement, which is the marriage, the fulfillment of the truth of the new self.

They are both of them, Wordsworth and Jane Austen, poets of marriage, singers of prothalamia. Wordsworth is worried about the mind that lives alone, under tyrannies from within and without, and it would seem that for him a single mind in possession of a good man must be in want of a universally acknowledged truth. His subject is the wedding of the discerning intellect and the goodly universe, and long before the blissful hour arrives he chants the spousal verse of this great consummation (Prospectus of *The Recluse*, 52 ff.). Marriage for both is a way of controlling and completing the self. Cheerfulness is finding the place for the self, and duty its comprehending act, in the larger scheme of things. There are two forms of blessing for the self beset by violence, or for the self that will not be the mere thing of stimulus; one is to marry the universe, the other is to marry Mr Knightley. The one is the egotistical sublime. The other is not negative capability but it is what Anne Elliot calls 'the art of knowing our own nothingness' beyond our own circle. It is an art that requires what she too calls 'imagination,' the imagination that can become a not unworthy member of another commonwealth than the self and its circle (*P* 42–3). That is the imagination of limits, of definites, making no transparencies of other objects, seeing through its own mists. It is the kind of imagination that clarifies not like the poet Cowper gazing into the fire, 'Myself creating what I saw,' the example Mr Knightley wants to avoid (*E* 344); and it is not like the poet Wordsworth who both half creates and perceives ('Tintern Abbey,' 106–7). It takes the claims of the self entirely out of the determination of what it sees. But it does not negate the self, like the chameleon, because it requires both an experience of the varieties of human nature and an achieved strength to clarify the self from the selfishness that obscures perception of what others feel outside the circle. Before they marry the heroines must lose the self to gain the self, or, in social and moral terms, achieve their identity; and that identity has great force. In the moments of self-hatred and disgust they struggle to retain or regain what Emma thinks of as 'Some portion of respect for herself' (408). What makes the unseeing, self-assertive Marianne Dashwood terribly attractive to some romantic readers, and shocking in the novel, is that she has so little of that respect. She has no pride, as she insists in misery, and the world may triumph over her (*SS* 189), as it does. But the observant and self-effacing Anne Elliot, surrounded by the proud, all of them solicitous for their places and forcing their identities, says with her smile, 'I suppose . . . I have more pride than any of you' (*P* 151). And Fanny Price, that heroine who is the most shrinking, most self-doubting, who seems so old-fashioned, dependent, spiritless, in tears stands against the authority of all her world, bearing accusations of self-conceit, self-will, selfishness, 'and every tendency to that independence of spirit, which prevails so much in modern days' (*MP* 318 ff.). Her spirit is neither modern nor old. She holds her place because for all her tears she alone has made the observations of what is before her, has seen the facts and seen the principle. She redeems her society. It is their ability to see through the mists, through the confusion and disorder of their own mixed feelings, which makes Fanny Price and Anne Elliot such witnesses of a powerful clarity and makes them actors of power.

It makes them half-creators of their world so far as they bring its necessary moral cohesion and its shaping love. If Captain Wentworth thinks Anne must feel only strong disgust for a place where she has borne pain, Anne has a better understanding: 'One does not love a place the less for having suffered in it' (*P* 184). Fanny in her little fireless room looks at each object there and remembers all the occasions of the suffering she has borne at Mansfield Park, in tyranny, ridicule and neglect, but remembers too each consolation and the proofs of affection she has found, 'and the whole was now blended together, so harmonized by distance, that every former affliction had its charm.' She looks at the faded furniture, at the transparencies of Tintern Abbey and the moon-light lake in Cumberland; she looks at the sketch of his ship sent by her brother, with its name at the bottom in letters as tall as the mainmast (*MP* 152), the imperfect gift of affection, oddly reconciling. Jane Austen's is an imagination which clarifies by seeing each part in its limits, in its painfulness and its comic disproportion, and then brings all parts to a unified vision created by the meaning of one life; it is capable of both wit and love.

NOTES

1 I have used R. W. Chapman's editions of *The Novels of Jane Austen,* 5 vols. (London: Oxford University Press, 3rd ed., 1932–4); *Minor Works*

(1954); *Letters*, 2nd ed., corrected reprint (1959). The usual abbreviations have been used:

    NA   *Northanger Abbey*
    SS   *Sense and Sensibility*
    PP   *Pride and Prejudice*
    MP *Mansfield Park*
    E   *Emma*
    P   *Persuasion*
    MW *Minor Works*
    L   *Letters*

2 Hazlitt's *Works*, ed. P. P. Howe (1930–4), xvii, 3368.

3 'Preface' (1800), in *Poetical Works*, ed. de Selincourt, 2nd ed. (Oxford, 1952), ii, 389.

4 By Kotzebue, whom Wordsworth probably had in mind as an example; see Coleridge's letter to Wordsworth, 23 January 1798, where Kotzebue appears with *Castle Spectre* as instances of contemporary theater; the reference to what Wordsworth has said of theatrical 'situation' is another link with the 1800 'Preface.' Coleridge's *Letters*, ed. E. L. Griggs (Oxford, 1956–71), i, 378–9.

5 Wordsworth to R. P. Gillies, 25 April 1815, in *Letters*, ed. de Selincourt, iii, 2nd ed., rev. Moorman and Hill (Oxford, 1970), 252.

6 'Preface,' *Poetical Works*, ii, 388–9.

7 Hazlitt, *Works*, xi, 87–9; Scott, *Quarterly Review*, xiv (1815), 193.

8 *Works*, xi, 86.

9 Wordsworth, 1800 'Preface,' *Poetical Works*, ii, 390 (and 398), and 1798 'Advertisement,' *Poetical Works*, ii, 383; Jane Austen, *Letters*, 404, and *Minor Works*, 81.

10 'Preface,' *Poetical Works*, ii, 390.

11 See Tave, *The Amiable Humorist* (Chicago, 1960), p. 7.

12 Tave, *Some Words of Jane Austen* (Chicago, 1973), pp. 112–15.

13 'Essay, Supplementary . . . ' (1815), *Poetical Works*, ii, 420, 423.

14 From a letter by Sara Coleridge, 1834, in *Memoir and Letters of Sara Coleridge* (1873), i, 75.

15 E.g., the Fenwick note to 'Lucy Gray,' *Poetical Works*, i, 360. See also the excerpt from Scott's *Diary* in Wordsworth's *Prose Works*, ed. Grosart (1876), iii, 503.

16 *Spirit of the Age, Works*, xi, 165.

JANE AIKEN HODGE

Jane Austen and her publishers

Born in the year of Bunker Hill, Jane Austen died two years after Waterloo. During two thirds of her short life, England was at war. I have no intention here of discussing the well-tried question of the effect on her books. Of the effect on their publication and sales there can be little doubt. Prices of new books were high when she was born. By 1800, they were almost prohibitive. Quartos had jumped from ten or twelve shillings to eighteen, or even a guinea. The general cost of living had also risen sharply; books were, as always, an obvious economy. And publishers preferred to play safe with small, expensive editions aimed at the circulating libraries that then played a major part in the book trade. Novels, the mainstay of the libraries, were published in several volumes for the convenience of librarian and reader alike. Mrs A. could be reading Volume I of the latest Gothic romance, while Miss B. got on with Volumes II and III. But as the long war with France continued, even the smaller libraries were at risk. Jane Austen, in her letters, describes the fate of Mrs Martin's library. Set up in 1798, and subscribed to by the Austens – 'great novel-readers and not ashamed of being so' – it had failed by 1800. The great days of Mudie's Circulating Library and the three-decker novel were well in the future.

Altogether the climate for authors was about as unpropitious as it is today. While a few lucky ones like Byron or Scott might make enormous sums, the majority, then as now, could not hope to earn a living from their work. There was one significant difference, which was to

75

affect Jane Austen throughout her career. While the author – publisher relationship was still extremely fluid, there were neither authors' associations nor literary agents to see fair play. To make matters worse, the novel had fallen into disrepute. The enormous eighteenth-century success of *Clarissa Harlowe, Evelina* and, later, Gothics like *The Mysteries of Udolpho* had brought the inevitable swarm of imitators. Publishing houses such as the Minerva Press were busy turning out romantic trash to satisfy the library demands of a rapidly growing, semi-educated lower middle class. Once again, the modern parallel is obvious.

Jane Austen began her own writing career, as a young girl, by parodying the absurdities of the Gothic and sentimental schools, but it is significant of the depressed condition of the novel in her day that she – an intensely private person – should have allowed herself the indulgence of defending it in *Northanger Abbey*: 'Only a novel . . . Only *Cecilia*, or *Camilla*, or *Belinda* . . . Only some work in which the greatest powers of the mind are displayed, in which the most thorough knowledge of human nature, the happiest delineations of its varieties; the liveliest effusions of wit and humour are conveyed to the world in the best chosen language.'

These are strong words, and it does not matter, for our purposes, when they were written. When she revised *Northanger Abbey* (or *Susan*, or *Miss Catherine*) for publication at the end of her life, Jane Austen does not seem to have revised them much. If she had, would she not have added *Waverley* to her list of novels? *Cecilia* and *Camilla*, both by Fanny Burney, had been published in 1782 and 1796 respectively, *Belinda*, by Maria Edgeworth, in 1801. Scott published *Waverley* anonymously in 1814, but Jane Austen was in no doubt as to his authorship. 'Walter Scott has no business to write novels, especially good ones – It is not fair. – He has fame and profit enough as a poet, and should not be taking the bread out of other people's mouths. – I do not like him, and do not mean to like *Waverley* if I can help it – but fear I must.'

As so often with Jane Austen, there is the hard grit of truth under the humour. She suffered, throughout her life, from the unpopularity of the novel, and here was the Wizard of the North making an instant success with his first one. In fact, where *Mansfield Park,* published in the same year as *Waverley,* sold out its small edition (probably about 1,000 copies) in six months, *Waverley* sold 1,000 in five weeks, and, by 1817, the year of Jane Austen's death, its sales had exceeded the total sales of the first editions of all her novels.

Dr Johnson told Boswell that no one but a blockhead ever wrote except for money. It was, of course, one of the magnificent over-simplifications with which he enjoyed teasing Boswell, but it had its grain of truth, and Jane Austen would have recognized it. She needed the money. Even then, when a young couple might set up house on £500 a year, her annual allowance of £20 was small. The less perceptive critics of her letters have mocked her for her preoccupation with small economies, the dyeing of hats and the refurbishing of gowns. She did not like having to arrange her journeys to suit the convenience of her carriage-owning brothers, but, 'Till I have a travelling purse of my own I must submit to such things.' She was frank in her enjoyment of the money her books brought her. 'I have now therefore written myself into £250 – which only makes me long for more.' It is sad to think that in her lifetime her novels earned less than £700.

Why was this? After all, the novel may have been in disrepute, but Maria Edgeworth was making a comfortable living from hers, and Fanny Burney helping to support Monsieur d'Arblay. Of course Jane Austen, like all innovators, had to create the taste she would satisfy. What did she really think, I wonder, when a niece scornfully passed over the anonymous *Sense and Sensibility* in their local library? Whatever she thought, she did not change her style in titles. *Elinor and Marianne* had become *Sense and Sensibility*. *First Impressions* would be *Pride and Prejudice:*

> I do not write for such dull elves
> As have not a great deal of ingenuity themselves.

They were brave words, and it must sometimes have been hard to live up to them. Because, there is no doubt about it, Jane Austen was not lucky with her publishers. Since there were no literary agents, an author had to find his or her own way through the publishing jungle. Worse still, in those days women did not do business. The Brontë sisters, when they started to write in the mid-nineteenth century, simply took male pseudonyms and acted for themselves. They had little option. Neither their father nor their brother Branwell would have been much use as an agent. Jane Austen, on the other hand, had plenty of male relatives. Of her six brothers, one was mentally deficient, and two in the navy and away most of the time; but that still left the clergyman James, rich Edward, and the man of the world, Henry.

The first, and least successful, attempt at negotiation was made by their father, the Reverend George Austen. He wrote, on 1 November 1797, to Thomas Cadell, a well-established London publisher, offering him:

> A manuscript novel, comprising 3 vols., about the length of Miss Burney's *Evelina*. As I am well aware of what consequence it is that a work of this sort should make its first appearance under a respectable name, I apply to you. I shall be much obliged therefore

if you will inform me whether you choose to be concerned in it, and what you will venture to advance for the property of it, if on perusal it is approved of. Should you give any encouragement, I will send you the work.

It is hardly surprising that this lukewarm letter failed to catch the imagination of a publisher who had doubtless been rejecting hopeful imitations of Miss Burney's *Evelina* for years. Cadell is reported to have rejected the offer by return of post, thus leaving it open for *First Impressions* to be developed into *Pride and Prejudice*.

So much for the first try. Jane Austen must have been disappointed, but it did not stop her writing. Why should it? Cadell had not even seen her book. According to Cassandra's dating, *First Impressions* was finished in August 1797, and *Sense and Sensibility* (a redraft of an earlier novel in letters, *Elinor and Marianne*) was begun in November, the very month in which Cadell rejected *First Impressions*. Jane Austen still had the audience she was used to, the all-important immediate one supplied by her family. The light-hearted early works bear all the marks of composition for a reliable and intimate audience.

No other attempt at publication was made until 1803, and by then the Austens' circumstances had changed enormously. The boys had long since grown up and left home, and in the autumn of 1800 Mr. Austen had made his surprise decision to retire, at the announcement of which, according to family tradition, Jane fainted. Books, furniture and piano were sold; the diminished family of father, mother and two devoted sisters moved to Bath, a place Jane Austen was known to dislike, to be near a rich aunt whom it was impossible to love. And, somewhere about this time, very likely during one of the summer holidays that were supposed to make the town life of Bath tolerable, Jane Austen's one real romance seems to have taken place. According to the family, there was a young man, perhaps a Dr Blackall. He went away. Perhaps he died. It is all conjecture based on conflicting family traditions. But if it happened, for instance, in the summer of 1802, it would have provided a good reason for another attempt at publication. Jane Austen said later of her brother Henry that he did not have 'A mind for affliction. He is too busy, too active, too sanguine.' She resembled him in this. For her, women who gave way under adversity were 'poor honeys.' It would have been like her to try to cure a heart, however damaged, by publishing a book.

According to Cassandra's dating, the three early books, *First Impressions, Sense and Sensibility* and *Northanger Abbey* (then called *Susan*) had all been finished by 1798. Presumably the three precious manuscripts had travelled to Bath in the writing box that once nearly went to sea by mistake. No one outside the immediate family and its closest friends had seen them. That earlier refusal of *First*

Impressions must still have rankled, because otherwise it was the obvious choice. There is a special note in Jane Austen's letters when she refers to it. 'I do not wonder at your wanting to read *First Impressions* again, so seldom as you have gone through it, and that so long ago.' And, again: 'I would not let Martha read *First Impressions* again upon any account . . . She is very cunning, but I saw through her design; she means to publish it from memory, and one more perusal must enable her to do it.'

With such backing for *First Impressions,* why did she choose *Susan* for her second try? True, according to Cassandra it was the most recently finished of the three books, and, in fact, in the *Advertisement* that Jane Austen later wrote for the book she refers to it as 'finished in the year 1803' – so she must have been revising it, putting in, among other things, that reference to *Belinda.* Unfortunately, we are in no position now to discuss the comparative merits of the three books. No early drafts survive, so it is impossible to tell what *First Impressions* and *Sense and Sensibility* were like before the final revision, that ruthless lopping and cropping they underwent later on. Perhaps Jane Austen chose *Susan* for its topicality. The Gothic romances that it parodies were then at the height of their vogue, and of this she was well aware. In the later *Advertisement* she says: 'The public are entreated to bear in mind that thirteen years have passed since it was finished, many more since it was begun, and that during that period, places, manners, books, and opinions have undergone considerable changes.'

In 1803 she did not ask her father to act for her. 'The handsome proctor' of St John's was an old man now, and, one suspects, a bit of a bore. Instead, she turned to Henry, four years her senior, her favourite brother as Edward was Cassandra's. Did Henry, perhaps, see himself in the charming Henry Tilney and help to influence her choice? Henry was brilliant but erratic. He had had thoughts of the church, fallen in love, and married a sophisticated older cousin, joined the army for her sake (she shared Mary Crawford's view of the church), and sent in his papers after the peace of Amiens. Now a banker, he was living 'quite in style in Upper Berkeley Street.' James and Edward spent most of their time in the country. Jane Austen was probably right in thinking that Henry was the most likely member of her family to have the kind of connection that is so useful in getting a first book published. 'Henry at White's!' she would write, later. 'Oh, what a Henry!'

At first, things did indeed go better. Henry's man of business, Mr Seymour, approached Richard Crosby & Co., who agreed to pay ten pounds for the copyright of *Susan.* This was not quite the pitifully small sum that it seems today. Fanny Burney had accepted twenty pounds for *Evelina* in 1778, and her publisher, Lowndes, had merely added a further ten pounds when the book achieved its surprise success. At the turn of the century novelists were receiving as little as five or six pounds a volume. The outright sale of the copyright was not unusual either. Indeed, James Lackington, the bookseller who first traded in remainders, and should have known, urged authors in his *Memoirs* to sell their copyright as this gave the publisher a maximum stake in the book. Where Jane Austen (or Henry's Mr Seymour on her behalf) probably erred was in accepting so little. Her position was like that of an author taking a very small advance today. The larger the advance the greater the publisher's risk, and, obviously, the greater his effort. Advance (or, for Jane Austen, payment) and advertising go hand in hand. In the case of *Susan,* Crosby, with only ten pounds to lose, decided to lose it. The book was advertised once and then let sink without a trace. It is possible that as a publisher of the Gothic romances it satirized, he may have had second thoughts.

For Jane Austen it must have been a time of slow, agonizing disappointment, about which not a word remains. Getting a rejected manuscript back is bad enough. To have it taken and then simply let drop must be a still worse blow to an author's self-confidence. It is interesting that, according to family tradition, *The Watsons* was begun in 1804. Its paper, in fact, is watermarked 1803. At all events, it was never finished. The pompous author of the *Memoir* of Jane Austen thought that this was because his aunt decided she had set her scene in too low a class of society. Doubtless he was as shocked as Jane Austen intended her less intelligent readers to be by the introduction of that plebeian knife-case. But in fact she had all too good grounds for a period of spiritual dryness. Bath life did not suit her; there was probably even less privacy in the houses they rented there than in that shared bedroom at Steventon. The long disappointment over *Susan* may well have been a last straw.

By 1809 the picture had changed. Mr Austen was dead, and Edward had (somewhat belatedly) offered his impoverished mother and sisters the use of a house of his at Chawton. Jane's spirits rose. 'Yes, yes, we *will* have a pianoforte, as good a one as can be got for thirty guineas.' And she made one more effort on *Susan*'s behalf. She wrote to Crosby (she spelt it Crosbie) offering to supply another copy if the original manuscript had 'by some carelessness' been lost, and threatening to make other arrangements for publication should she receive no answer. She signed herself Mrs Ashton Dennis and got a prompt reply to the Post Office, Southampton. Richard Crosby admitted purchasing the book, pointed out that no time had been stipulated for its publication, threatened proceedings if she published elsewhere, and offered her the manuscript back for the ten pounds he had paid for it. If Mr Austen's letter to Cadell was a classic of the bungling agent, Crosby's was equally the prototype of all those publishers' snubs that have driven authors to drink and protective associations. But this story had a happy ending – in the end. In 1816 one of Jane Austen's brothers did buy *Susan* back and then told Crosby who had written it.

And in 1809 Jane Austen cannot have let the refusal discourage her unduly. Unluckily, a two-year gap in her letters between 1809 and 1811 leaves no evidence of her next move, but by the spring of 1811 she was staying with Henry and his wife in Sloane Street, seeing *Sense and Sensibility* through the press. 'No indeed, I am never too busy to think of *S & S*. I can no more forget it than a mother can forget her sucking child.' Once again, Henry had acted for her. *Sense and Sensibility* was published by Thomas Egerton of the Military Library, Whitehall, which inevitably suggests the connection with Henry, the ex-officer. Egerton was not a major publisher, and he took no great risk over *Sense and Sensibility*. Jane Austen had ended by publishing on commission. This meant that she paid the expenses of printing the book and took the receipts, subject to a commission paid to the publisher for his handling of it. This was not the most hopeful method of publication. A publisher who was confident of a book preferred to buy the copyright outright, or, perhaps, to pay all expenses and then share the final profit with the author (the basis of the modern royalty system). Family tradition tells us that Jane Austen was so uncertain of success that she set aside a contingency fund in case of failure, but as it then cost between one and two hundred pounds to produce an average edition of a two- or three-volume book, Henry must have helped her over the initial expense. She wrote, later, of the second edition: 'I shall owe dear Henry a great deal of money for printing etc.' It is good to know that she covered her costs and netted £140 with the first edition of about 1,000 copies at 15 shillings, which Egerton advertised at least three times in the autumn of 1811 and which received good but short notices in the *Critical Review* and the *British Critic* in the spring of 1812.

Egerton was encouraged. He offered to buy the copyright of *Pride and Prejudice*. Jane Austen asked for £150 – too modest a sum considering the £140 she had made from *Sense and Sensibility*. She then made the further mistake of letting Egerton beat her down to £110. Egerton got a good bargain. The first edition, probably of about 1,500 copies at 18 shillings, came out in January 1813 and was sold out by July. Once again there were good notices in the *British Critic* and the *Critical Review,* and Egerton printed a second edition in November, presumably without telling Jane Austen, who might have asked for more money and would certainly have corrected the errors she had pointed out in the text. The second edition of *Sense and Sensibility* came out in the same month, and it is undoubtedly to it that Jane

Austen refers when she writes to Cassandra: 'Since I wrote last, my second edition has stared me in the face . . . I cannot help hoping that *many* will feel themselves obliged to buy it.'

This mild success must have been stimulating. In 1813 Jane Austen was busy with her first new book since the fiasco of *The Watsons*. 'Now I will try to write of something else, and it shall be a complete change of subject – ordination.' *Mansfield Park* is not many people's favourite among Jane Austen's novels, though it is, in some ways, her richest, and perhaps the one that will stand the most rereading. Egerton, however, cannot have been enthusiastic. Once again Jane Austen published on commission, but this time she had her £250 behind her as a contingency fund. Perhaps she had realized that she had made a mistake over that outright sale of *Pride and Prejudice,* which went into a third edition in 1817 – the only one of her books to do so.

Mansfield Park was published, at 18 shillings, in the spring of 1814. Egerton does not seem to have tried very hard. Henry Austen refers to it as a surprisingly small edition, which suggests that it may have been less than 1,000 copies. It was also very badly printed, advertised twice, and not reviewed at all. We do not know precisely what Jane Austen earned from it, but by the autumn she was considering a second edition, presumably because the first one was nearly sold out. 'It is not settled yet whether I *do* hazard a second edition. We are to see Egerton today. People are more ready to borrow and praise than to buy . . . Though I like praise as well as anybody, I like what Edward calls pewter too.' She had become a professional. In the end, Egerton did not choose to publish a second edition. Jane Austen did what any sensible author would have done. She changed her publisher. But she kept her agent. By October 1815, *Emma* was finished and Jane Austen was staying with Henry, who was negotiating with John Murray, Byron's 'gentleman publisher,' on her behalf.

The choice of publisher was good: the terms offered for *Emma* lamentable. 'Mr Murray's letter is come. He is a rogue, of course, but a civil one. He offers £450 but wants to have the copyright of *Mansfield Park* and *Sense and Sensibility* included. It will end in my publishing for myself I daresay. He sends more praise however than I expected.' Murray, like Egerton, had an eye for a bargain. And, most unluckily, Henry took ill at this point. He dictated his answer to Murray:

> The choice of publisher was good, the terms offered for *Emma,* la-
> of the author's expectation and my own. The terms you offer are so
> very inferior to what we had expected that I am apprehensive of
> having made some great error in my arithmetical calculation. The
> sum offered by you for the copyright of *Sense and Sensibility,*
> *Mansfield Park,* and *Emma* is not equal to the money which my
> sister has actually cleared by one very moderate edition of

Mansfield Park – you yourself expressed astonishment that so small an edition of such a work should have been sent into the world – and a still smaller one of *Sense and Sensibility*.

Like everyone else, Murray was more ready to praise than to buy. Busy nursing Henry, who was really ill, Jane Austen settled, as she had with Egerton, for publication on commission, thus leaving Murray with too small a stake in *Emma*. The ledgers of the firm are still extant and show that Murray published Jane Austen's books for a straight 10% commission. He printed 2,000 copies of *Emma*, at 21 shillings a copy, so that he stood to gain, at the outside, £210. It is no wonder if he did not over-exert himself in promoting the book. Gifford, editor of the *Quarterly Review*, which Murray had founded, read *Emma* for him, and had 'nothing but good to say' of it. The Prince Regent, an admirer of Miss Austen's, indicated, through his librarian, that he would accept the dedication, but even this seems not to have stimulated John Murray. Roworth, who had printed *Sense and Sensibility*, was also printing *Emma* – slowly. Jane Austen, still nursing Henry, was correcting proofs a few sheets at a time, and writing with increasing indignation to Murray, who 'soothed and complimented' her into 'tolerable comfort,' blaming the delay on the stationer who had failed to produce the paper.

The publisher who had infuriated Byron by his assiduous advance puffing of *Childe Harold* in 1809 did make one effort on behalf of his new author. 'Have you any fancy to dash off an article on *Emma?*' Murray wrote to Sir Walter Scott. 'It wants incident and romance does it not?' As between publisher and reviewer, this can hardly be looked on as high praise. Scott, of course, was more enthusiastic about *Emma* than Murray deserved. Writing in the *Quarterly Review*, he used the book as a basis for a defence of the novel almost comically similar to Jane Austen's own as yet unpublished passage in *Northanger Abbey*. This was not, he said, the kind of novel where the heroine suffers from 'an insidious ravisher, a cloak wrapped forcibly around her head, and a coach, with the blinds up, driving she knew not whither.' *Emma*, on the contrary, was 'a story which we peruse with pleasure. The subjects are not often elegant, and certainly never grand, but they are finished up to nature, and with a precision which delights the reader.'

Emma was also reviewed in the *Literary Panorama*, the *Monthly Review*, the *British Critic* and the *Gentleman's Magazine*, but the general tone is summed up in a sentence from the *British Critic*: 'It rarely happens that in a production of this nature we have so little to find fault with.' It is not the kind of praise that is likely to double the sales of a book, and no doubt Murray decided that he had been right in his estimate of Miss Austen.

In fact *Emma*, published in December 1815, sold somewhere over

1,200 copies in 1816, yielding an author's profit of £221 6s 4d for that year. Unfortunately, the second edition of *Mansfield Park*, 1,750 copies at 18 shillings, published in February 1816, made a loss of £182 8s 3d that year. Perhaps Egerton had been right in his decision not to reprint. And, of course, a reprint should have been cheaper for him. Presumably Murray had to start from scratch. Egerton's edition was printed by G. Sidney and Murray's by J. Moyes. At all events John Murray, a practical man, set the initial loss on the second edition of *Mansfield Park* against the author's profits from *Emma*. On 21 February 1817, Jane Austen received a cheque for 38 18s, 'first profits from *Emma*.' For an author who had made £140 with her first book, it must have been a daunting experience, and it came at a bad time.

At the very end of her life, Jane Austen listed her total earnings from her books. She had £600 in the Navy Five Percents, which represented 140 for the first edition of *Sense and Sensibility*, £110 for the copyright of *Pride and Prejudice*, and, presumably, a total of £350 for the first edition of *Mansfield Park* and the second one of *Sense and Sensibility*. Over and above this, she had received £13 7s representing 'Residue from the first edition of *Mansfield Park* remaining in Henrietta Street, March 1816'; a further £12 15s from Egerton for the second edition of *Sense and Sensibility*, March 1816; 38 18s first profits on *Emma*, February 1817; and another £19 13s from Egerton for the second edition of *Sense and Sensibility*, March 1817. The figures may well have made her wonder about her change of publisher.

The 13 7s for *Mansfield Park* must represent a few copies still in Egerton's hands when Jane Austen announced that she was leaving him. In fact, she was lucky to get the money, since Henry, who was then living in Henrietta Street, went bankrupt in 1816. It was one of a series of moral and financial blows that must have exacerbated the Addison's Disease from which Jane Austen had been suffering since 1816 or even earlier. The knowledge that her four books had netted her a total of £684 13s can hardly have been a tonic. Maria Edgeworth, writing at the same time, got more for a single book. It was lucky for Jane Austen, and for us, that she shared something of Henry's sanguine temperament. He rebounded from bankruptcy and entered the church. She collected the opinions (not all of them favorable) of family and friends. She knew, and cared, that Lady Robert Kerr had praised *Mansfield Park* and that Mr Jeffery (of the *Edinburgh Review*) had been kept up three nights by *Emma*. Money is not just money to an author: it is also tangible evidence of a receptive public, and Jane Austen was no Proust. She had always written for an audience.

She began her last completed book, *Persuasion*, in August 1815 and finished it a year later, before she had had the bad news about the second edition of *Mansfield Park*. She was also working on the revision of *Susan*, now renamed *Catherine* (an anonymous *Susan* had been published in 1809). It may be coincidence that she received that miserable £38 18s from Murray in February 1817 and wrote to her niece Fanny in March that 'Miss Catherine is put upon the shelf for the present . . . but I have a something ready for publication, which may perhaps appear about a twelvemonth hence.' Jane Austen always liked to take time to polish and repolish her books, revising one while she started work on the next, but at this point she may well have felt that the publishing omens were not propitious. Nor does it seem likely that Murray was pressing her for her next book.

In January 1817 she started a book that was to be an entirely new departure. She went on working at what she called *The Brothers* and we call *Sanditon* until 17 March, defying her illness, reclining on a makeshift sofa and writing in pencil when she was too weak for pen and ink. Then, three months to the day from the brave start, she gave up. In April she made her will, leaving everything, after a few minor legacies, to Cassandra. It would have pleased her to know that Murray's figures show further payments of £151 6s 7d for *Emma*, £118 18s 4d for the second edition of *Mansfield Park*, and £595 17s 7d for *Northanger Abbey* and *Persuasion* – 1,750 copies published, with a biographical note by Henry, at 24 shillings in December 1817. It would probably not have surprised her that in 1821 Murray remaindered her books. The last ledger entries for *Emma* and *Mansfield Park* represent 'Balance of copies sold at sale.' Twelve years later Henry and Cassandra sold the copyright of the five books they still owned to Richard Bentley for £250. By then Jane Austen and her heirs had made a grand total of £1,800 15s 6d from her books. But Jane Austen had died – quietly, as she lived – in July 1817. Her death is not mentioned in the Annual Register for the year, and the family who mourned and missed her did not think to mention on her tombstone that she had, among other things, written six novels.

It is hardly a success story, either for Jane Austen or for her publishers. Of course it was partly her fault. She did not want to be a lion. She published anonymously and was appalled when Henry revealed the secret of her authorship of *Pride and Prejudice*. When publicity offered itself in the shape of the Prince Regent and his egregious librarian, she backed away as best she could. It is no wonder that Murray seems never to have invited her to the literary parties where he introduced one lion to another. Miss Mitford's 'poker of whom everyone is afraid' would probably have been no addition to a literary soirée.

II
The novels

KATRIN RISTKOK BURLIN

The pen of the contriver':
the four fictions of
Northanger Abbey

In *Northanger Abbey*,[1] Jane Austen came to terms with her art in a
single, complex treatment of the theme of fiction.[2] Every character in
this novel is implicated in the fictive process. Its heroine is a novel-
reader, its hero an inveterate inventor of fictions, its villains liars,
contrivers of fictions. The complicated plot is based totally on fictions,
each of its major crises being precipitated by a fiction. The first crisis
is obviously Catherine's discovery of the delusive nature of Gothic
romances, the second crisis, her discovery of the delusive fictions of
Bath. The third, and most important crisis, Catherine's sudden and
violent expulsion from the Abbey, is curiously precipitated by a
mysterious, self-contradictory double-fiction, told at Bath but
revealed only retrospectively. The secret working out of this double-
fiction is the real plot of *Northanger Abbey,* responsible for its principal action, but kept deliberately a secret from heroine, hero, and reader alike. From the distressing perplexities of this mystery her favorite
characters can be extricated only by the timely 'intrusion' of the
author, who, with her superior knowledge as the supreme fiction-maker, demonstrates the necessity for the professional novelist in a world
thoroughly permeated by delusive fictions. From her astonishingly
aggressive authorial 'intrusion' near the opening pages of *Northanger
Abbey* to defend the novel, to her noisy re-entrance at its end, Jane
Austen's motive is to fight for her craft, to prove that it is the responsi-

ble novelist who protects us by teaching us through his art to recognize and discriminate among the fictions of life and art alike.

The traditional reading of *Northanger Abbey* sees it as falling unhappily into two disparate halves: a satisfying 'Bath' volume of realistic fiction, exploring social and moral values, and a disappointing 'Northanger' volume of rather flat burlesque of the Gothic, sentimental novel. But A. Walton Litz offers the key to unlock the door between these volumes by suggesting that 'in learning to handle the fictions of the Gothic world Catherine comes to recognize the other fictions which haunt her life.'[3] Those 'other fictions' are, in fact, the principal concern of *Northanger Abbey*. Jane Austen's method is to expose the reader to four kinds of fiction: (1) the absurd extravagance of sentimental Gothic fictions; (2) the satiric, educative fictions of Henry Tilney; (3) the manipulative, egotistical fictions of the Thorpes; and (4) the satiric and realistic fiction of *Northanger Abbey* itself. Volume I (Bath) is dedicated to the creation of fictions; Volume II (Northanger Abbey), to their realization. The elegant thematic and structural transition between the volumes is effected by Henry Tilney's creation of a burlesque fiction, as he drives Catherine in his curricle from the one locale to the other.

Since the basic structural unit of all these fictions is language, the relationship between fiction and the chosen word is a major theme in *Northanger Abbey*.[4] How Jane Austen's characters use language serves as an index to the kinds of fiction they create, as Joseph Wiesenfarth has elegantly demonstrated in *The Errand of Form*. There are four different kinds of language: (1) the 'best-chosen language,'[5] the tool of the responsible novelist; (2) 'novel slang,'[6] the vocabulary of the sentimental, Gothic novelist; (3) 'common cant,' the basis for social fictions; and (4) 'nice' diction, the instrument of corrective fiction. The battle for the heroine's understanding[7] as well as her person, waged among these fictions with their distinctive linguistic weapons, creates the strategy of *Northanger Abbey*'s action and structure.

Because it begins as a burlesque, the novel initially invites laughter at its heroine's expense. But some important suggestions lurk beneath that burlesque. In the exploration of Catherine's early response to fiction the emphasis, however comic, falls on the unthinking nature of her enjoyment, 'for provided that nothing like useful knowledge could be gained from them, provided they were all story and no reflection,' she liked fictional narratives very much. Unheroically normal, Catherine's 'mental development' fits neatly into Dr Johnson's outline of 'The Climacterics of the Mind':

If we consider the exercises of the mind, it will be found that in each part of life some particular faculty is more eminently employed. When the treasures of knowledge are first opened before us, while novelty blooms alike on either hand, and every thing equally unknown and unexamined seems of equal value, the power of the soul is principally exerted in a vivacious and desultory curiosity. She applies by turns to every object, enjoys it for a short time, and flies with equal ardour to another. She delights to catch up loose and unconnected ideas, but starts away from systems and complications which would obstruct the rapidity of her transitions, and detain her long in the same pursuit. (*Rambler* No. 151)[8]

Catherine's 'slovenly'[9] attitude to 'complications' leads characteristically to the adolescent's problem of discriminating among fictions.

If *Northanger Abbey* is Catherine's 'introduction into life' through fiction, Henry Tilney is the master of ceremonies. He is to enrich her understanding by making her acquainted with a complex world of fictions, to guide her to the point of his own cool judgment of literary fictions and keen sense of social fictions. But why should this experienced critic of both society and fiction, this wit and champion of the integrity of language, take interest in an inexperienced, literal-minded, uncritical young girl with a small stock of ideas and utter ignorance of the implications of language? If *Northanger Abbey* is to be more than a burlesque, if it is to meet the standards set by the new realistic novel, we must be made to believe in Henry Tilney's attraction to Catherine. One realizes through Jane Austen's success in achieving this in *Northanger Abbey* how much less schematic and more subtle it is as a novel than *Sense and Sensibility*, where Jane Austen 'flattened' her characters for the sake of its argument. Surely *Northanger Abbey* bears the marks of a mature re-working. Catherine never loses her youthful 'roundness.'

The relationship between Henry and Catherine is believable for many reasons: he is an eager teacher, she, an ardent pupil; she is fond of him, he is fond of admiration. But what makes the relationship most persuasive is that Catherine is unaffectedly good, and Henry, like Jane Austen herself, admires goodness more than cleverness. Jane Austen thinks this an important point, and indicates so by qualifying the disparaging remarks on Catherine's 'mental endowments' with which she had opened the novel with the more flattering remarks on the excellence of Catherine's disposition, with which she opens the chapter immediately following. It is *she* who tips the scale from 'mind' (ignorant) to heart ('affectionate').

Catherine's simplicity, her tendency to express honestly what she thinks and feels, and her puzzlement when confronted with deliberate ambiguity are exploited by Jane Austen to expose the fictions of the society to which she is now introduced. As Hugh Blair indicated, however, 'The great advantage of simplicity of style, like simplicity of manners, [is] that it shows us a man's sentiments and turn of mind, laid open without disguise.' To effect her exposure of social fictions, the novelist endows her heroine with what Blair terms, for want of a better English adjective, 'the naive style':

> It always expresses a discovery of character . . . that sort of amiable ingenuity or undisguised openness which seems to give us some degree of superiority over the person who shows it; a certain infantine simplicity, which we love in our hearts, but which displays some features of the character that we think we could have art enough to hide; and which, therefore, always leads us to smile at the person who discovers this character.[10]

For those who want to hide sordid motives behind the cloak of ambiguity, Catherine's simple requests for clarification and explanation prove a source of perpetual embarrassment. This aspect of her naïveté delights Henry. He uses it both to teach her to understand the meanings to which she may give unconscious expression and to give her innocent satires a sophisticated thrust. In a typical scene (pp. 132–3), the interplay of dialogue between Catherine's naïve and Henry's sophisticated styles satirizes common social fictions and abuses of language, while suggesting the novel's fundamental theme.[11]

The task, then, of teaching Catherine falls to Henry, whom most critics have perceived as her mentor, or guide, or even as Jane Austen's surrogate. She is rescued from the tedium of a conventional Bath ballroom by the witty fictions of Henry Tilney precisely at the moment she is most conscious of 'intellectual poverty' (ch. III, pp. 25–9). It is Henry's ability to bewilder her through those fictions that charms Catherine immediately; there is a mystery in his manner, and she finds mystery intriguing. As Stuart M. Tave points out, 'Henry knows how to use art' (p.36). Like his author, he has a multiplicity of poses,[12] and in this scene he adopts that of a conventional Bath beau, satirizing ballroom dialogue while testing the quality of Catherine's responses. He is able to create such a fictional character of himself because Bath beaux have, in fact, begun to model themselves after the pattern established by heroes of sentimental novels. As Howard S. Babb points out, Henry's satire is designed to prick the bubble of false emotionality, and his artificial manner ought to warn Catherine that she is entering a world of 'assumed' poses and affected responses.[13]

When he perceives that his first fiction has puzzled Catherine, for she has 'turned away her head,' Henry reshapes the situation with yet another fiction: Catherine must keep a journal (pp. 26–7). Each entry in this fictive journal is cleverly 'contrived' as an explicit expression of Catherine's interest in Henry; implicit in each is Henry's interest in

Catherine. The verbal artifact of the fictive journal permits him to indulge himself in the novelist's delight in exploring points of view. He shows Catherine how different he might appear from two possible views: he is the subject of both fictive entries, but each presents him as an utterly different character. And through the medium of this fiction he also immediately shapes her point of view: the 'heroine' in the 'sprigged muslin robe with blue trimmings – plain black shoes' is delighted with her author and eager to review his future 'novels.' And indeed, Henry has invented this fictive journal precisely to win her critical esteem.

But if the fiction of Catherine's journal was invented largely to foster intimacy between author and reader, Henry must abandon it if he is to generalize about 'journalizing'; her journal had to be flattering, and Henry's real opinion of the habit directly contrasts with his ironically expressed praise.[14] When he enlarges his attack to incorporate journal-keeping in general, it becomes difficult, if not impossible, to separate as objects of Jane Austen's irony the language and conventions of the popular novel from those of Bath society. The shift from creator of verbal artifacts to critic, however, clearly points to the novel's theme; while Norman Page has said that all of Jane Austen's early novels are '*about* language' (pp. 12–13), I would prefer to say of *Northanger Abbey* that it is about language as it is shaped into pseudo-fictions, imitations of novels.

Henry's satire of the trivial and narcissistic journals kept by young ladies at Bath alludes also to the tiresome convention by which popular novelists expediently advance a narrative: the journal kept for 'absent cousins' that enables a heroine to detail her adventures at length. Henry's distaste is provoked by the carelessness of style all journal-keeping fosters. Preserved as a journal must be from rigorous critical scrutiny, it makes no demands on its author, and only reinforces bad habits of language and insipidity of thought. Dr Johnson's contemptuous description of the familiar letter as 'pages of inanity' (*Rambler* No. 152, v, p. 44) would perhaps best express Henry's real opinion of ladies' journals. His extravagant praise of 'journalizing' as leading 'to the easy style of writing for which ladies are so generally celebrated' is Catherine's introduction to irony. For the first time she perceives that words may be used to convey the opposite of their literal meaning. Henry does *not* admire an 'easy style of writing,' which he sees as compounded of 'a general deficiency of subject, a total inattention to stops, and a very frequent ignorance of grammar.' To call such a style 'easy' is to cover careless and hasty execution with a flattering cliché. It is a misplacement of value on 'quickness' or on 'ease' above precision and care that Henry isolates as pernicious to good writing and rational communication.

Henry's notorious concern for precision in language, first commented upon by his sister, has been too frequently rehearsed to require elaboration here. His lectures on correct usage are scattered throughout the novel, his own tutors having been, as Eleanor points out, Johnson and Blair. The words whose misuse offends Henry, such as 'nice' and 'amazingly,' had in some part been collected by Blair in a list of synonyms 'to show the necessity of attending to the exact import of words' (I, pp. 196–7). His definition of 'amazement' ('I am amazed, with what is incomprehensible') indicates the direction in which Henry works to disabuse Catherine. Henry, the inveterate fiction-maker, possesses in his artful language those qualifications Dr Johnson set for modern fiction: 'It requires, together with that learning which is to be gained from books, that experience which can never be gained by solitary diligence, but must arise from general converse, and accurate observation of the living world.' Learned, sociable, articulate and critical, Henry creates fictions 'to initiate youth by mock encounters in the art of necessary defense, and to increase prudence without impairing virtue' (*Rambler* No. 4, III, pp. 20–3).

His fictions are thus very much like Jane Austen's: delicious inventions with a moral core. Satiric by nature, he too believes that fiction ought 'to give the power of counteracting fraud' (*Rambler* No. 4, III, p. 23). His expressed opinions are nearly always consistent with his author's; he teaches in the same way and with nearly equal success. But his own fictions, those made up quite independently of his author, ought not to be accepted uncritically, as if they were hers. Henry is but the creature of Jane Austen's imagination, with a properly subordinate place in her work.

Ardent, eager, and empty, Catherine's mind is stimulated by Henry's fictions and prepared to encounter the world of the novel itself, experience heightened by fiction. But when removed from his direct influence, she is shown to have been rendered vulnerable to the world of real fictions, the novels of the circulating library. Again Jane Austen, in drawing a realistic picture of her heroine's intellectual development, seems to follow the guidance of Dr Johnson's analysis of the growing mind in *Rambler* No. 151.

> While the judgment is yet unformed and unable to compare the draughts of fiction with their originals, we are delighted with improbable adventures, impracticable virtues, and inimitable characters. (V, p.39)

With one important qualification, her solid integrity, Catherine's mind is the prototype of the typical novel-reader's, described by Dr Johnson in *Rambler* No. 4. As such, it would seem vulnerable to the dangers Johnson finds in 'The Comedy of Romance' (p.19). This is his term for the new novel, dangerous in providing

the entertainments of minds unfurnished with ideas, and therefore
easily susceptible of impressions; not fixed by principles, and
therefore easily following the current of fancy; not informed by
experience, and consequently open to every false suggestion and
partial account. (III, p. 21)

Perhaps one of the happiest uses of fiction is its capacity to teach
those who, like Catherine, are 'not altogether . . . particularly friendly to very severe, very intense application.' It would be foolish to
patronize Catherine because she prefers fiction to history. Her choice
of fiction and her infatuation with it are silly. But the tendency of her
mind, its bent towards fiction, is not.[15] What it manifests is a craving –
in the midst of a trivial little world – 'for a more splendid order of
things.' Blair discovers a satisfying explanation for man's urge for
fiction in Lord Bacon:

> Lord Bacon takes notice of our taste for fictitious history, as a proof
> of the greatness and dignity of the human mind. He observes very
> ingeniously, that the objects of this world, and the common train of
> affairs which we behold going on in it, do not fill the mind, nor give
> it entire satisfaction. We seek for something that shall expand the
> mind in a greater degree: we seek for more heroic and illustrious
> deeds, for more diversified and surprising events, for a more
> splendid order of things, a more regular and just distribution of
> rewards and punishments than what we find here: *because we meet
> not with these in true history, we have resource to [the] fictitious. We
> create worlds according to our fancy, in order to gratify our
> capacious desires.* (italics mine; II, pp. 304–5)

The Thorpes, too, have a 'taste for fictitious history,' but it is a
corrupt taste, 'satisfying' a corrupt palate. They do not crave 'a more
splendid order of things,' but the 'things' themselves. They do not
have the novelist's passion for an 'ordered' world. The issue they take
with 'the common train of affairs' is not that it does not 'fill the mind'
but that it fails to fill the pocket. They seek, through their fictions, not
to celebrate heroic deeds or the triumph of justice – as do even the
'romancers' *Northanger Abbey* often mocks. Their fictions are a mockery of poetic justice, for the Thorpes want to pervert justice to reward
only themselves. Neither Thorpe as 'novelist' is interested in the
possibilities of the imagination for 'expanding' the mind; imagination
is not something they value except as a means to an end. Their fictions,
therefore, are not a 'proof of the greatness and dignity of the human
mind,' but of its meanness and egotism. They do, indeed, 'create
worlds according to their fancy, in order to gratify their capacious
desires,' but those desires are 'capacious' only in the sense of the
largeness of their greed.

Isabella's quick intimacy with Catherine is itself a borrowing from the novel of sensibility, but Catherine is too naive to perceive that her new friend is herself a fiction, her character, vocabulary, and sentiments all emanating from the circulating library to which she now introduces Catherine. The further introduction to John Thorpe merely precipitates the heroine deeper into the 'land of fiction,'[16] a world of factitious novelists. Under the influence of a self-created delusion that Catherine is rich, Thorpe affects not only admiration for her, but, through the 'cant terms of men of fashion,'[17] a fictional presence that he thinks will win her. His steady stream of aggressively masculine fabrications rather offends than pleases Catherine. Despite his vigorous assertion that he has 'something else to do' than read novels, 'the stupidest things in creation' (p. 48), that 'something else' proves to be the business of creating fictions and plots of his own to entrap the presumed heiress.

To alert the reader to the complexity and subtlety of social fictions, Jane Austen makes the Thorpes not only the fiction-makers we are accustomed to meet in society, but ironically turns them into 'novelists.' They structure their fictions according to the novel's conventional form, incorporating plots (often unfolded by consequent action), detailed description, the creation of character and dialogue, and the establishment of setting. All these novelistic devices are intended to create the illusion of verisimilitude.

Though the reader has been prepared for John's first major 'novel' (ch. XI, pp. 85–8) by his history of petty fictions, its extravagant inventiveness and richness of detail[18] still astonish – extravagance and richness directed, however, to 'exalt' neither the mind nor the morals. He simply wishes to alter circumstances to suit his present ambitions. Starting with a simple though false eye-witness account, claiming four times to have seen the fictive Tilneys abandoning Catherine, he proceeds rapidly from false journalism to the creation of a 'novel' of betrayed friendship, always adapting his technique to the ideals of 'the Familiar Novelists'[19] whose complex constructs attempt to create the illusion of truth.

When one realistic possibility still holds Catherine back from crossing the threshold of Thorpe's fictive world, he brings together all the elements of his fiction to dramatize its fable (p. 86). It is a final extension that comes closest to a piece of literary fiction, incorporating the creation of character and circumstance, illustrated with a piece of action, again characteristic of Thorpe's horseflesh-fancy ('a man who was just passing by on horseback').

Catherine's hesitation ends with the ending of the fiction. For not having recognized Thorpe's story as a fiction, she is forced to pay the consequences, which, ironically, take the form of the romantic heroine's most conventional dilemma – being kidnapped by the villain and misunderstood by the hero. A moment later Thorpe falls through the trap-door of his own staged fiction when he unwittingly tests it by reality (p. 87). Catherine's reflections at the moment of revelation are a mixture of Thorpe's fiction and Mrs Radcliffe's, unconsciously battling with Henry Tilney's truth. Each of her discoveries about fiction is made in a context richly confected with layer upon layer of fictions, each serving as an ironic commentary on the other. Thus Catherine submits to Thorpe's novel because she had already so extravagantly tasted of Mrs Radcliffe's.

The Thorpes' second major fiction lies at the heart of the novel (ch. XII, pp. 97–102) and is co-authored; its intent is to reshape the existing situation. Isabella provides the conventional social fiction of the 'previous engagement'; John invents the detail, embroidering the dull social fiction with a novelist's delight in particularity and fitness. While Catherine energetically strives for the truth, Thorpe has put Isabella's social fiction into action (p.100), playing author to a fictive Catherine, making her his creature, writing her dialogue, endowing her with his own motives and morals, determining her actions, and deciding her fate. Clearly, had Catherine not denied Thorpe the right 'to *invent* any such message,' it would have altered relationships, changed attitudes, and settled an impenetrable mist of indistinctness[20] upon the heroine's language, style, and judgment.

Henry, on the other hand, uses his witty fictions to introduce Catherine to the complexities of the real world and the abuses of the Thorpes. Because Babb has offered so excellent an analysis of the materials of Henry's most elegantly witty fiction, the marriage/country-dance emblem, I will not discuss it here. I will point, however, to its being clearly a fiction, and not the product of a technique Babb terms 'metaphoric indirection.'[21] Henry is not only making a fiction, but acting the part of the novelist. Having no space to prove the point at large, I introduce two excellent witnesses to the character of my argument: Dr Johnson and Jane Austen herself. Henry's invention of the emblem is 'an effusion of wit,' a product of the same qualities we saw mapped out by Dr Johnson as necessary for the novelist in *Rambler* No. 4; in *Rambler* No. 194, he identifies the same qualities as necessary for such an 'effusion':

> Wit, you know, is the unexpected copulation of ideas, the discovery of some occult relation between images in appearance remote from each other; *an effusion of wit* therefore presupposes an accumulation of knowledge: a memory stored with notions, which the imagination may cull out to compose new assemblages. (v, p. 251)

Jane Austen, in her own 'Defense' of fiction, cites the requisite qualities for the novel, or for the kind of mind necessary to produce it:

'some work, in which the greatest powers of the mind are displayed, in which the most thorough knowledge of human nature, the happiest delineation of its varieties, the liveliest *effusions of wit* and humour are conveyed to the world in the best chosen language' (p. 38; my italics).

Henry's third attempt at fiction-making occurs in the context of one of the most significant chapters in *Northanger Abbey*. Chapter XIV, almost entirely taken up with the walk 'round Beechen Cliff,' forms the nexus of the central themes of this novel:[22] it explores at many levels the consequences of the abuse of language[23] and is rich in implications about the use and abuse of fiction. During the walk, Henry is to discover how lost in fiction Catherine has become, and how her originally simple point of view and small vocabulary have been limited by the narrow scope of her reading and acquaintance – the novels of Mrs Radcliffe and of the Thorpes.

The walk begins with a significant discussion of fiction. Catherine discovers the error of one of her commonplace assumptions, that 'young men despised novels amazingly' (p. 107), for in his witty defense of *Udolpho,* Henry allows that once he had begun that romance, 'I could not lay it down again – my hair standing on end the whole time.' He defends romances, though satirically, and attacks facile generalizations instead. Continuing in the parodic mode, he further encourages Catherine in her naïve acceptance of the Gothic as real, referring to the 'Julias and Louisas' of that world as if he assumed them to be as intimate with her as 'your friend Emily.'

When Eleanor turns the subject to history, we learn something crucial; what Catherine 'cannot be interested in' is 'history, real solemn history'; her preference again is for the ideal over the real. But Jane Austen also uses Catherine's candor to score a few points for her own craft. Catherine finds history to be more sensational than fiction – 'the quarrels of popes and kings, with wars and pestilences, in every page.' It is 'tiresome' in that it has no mixed characters, less relevance to everyday experience than novels, and, though 'a great deal of it must be invention,' that invention is 'dull.' By pointing to the strong element of fiction in any history,[24] Jane Austen indirectly argues for the role fiction plays in revealing truth. As the recorder of more commonplace events, the novel has a respectability of its own and need not descend to that common dodge of beleaguered novelists and masquerade as 'history.'[25]

In the ensuing discussion of picturesque beauty, Jane Austen unites the three themes of point of view,[26] language, and fiction. The Tilneys, in their knowledge of the picturesque, have a better vantage point and richer vocabulary than Catherine's. Henry attempts to teach these to Catherine: 'He talked of fore-grounds, distances, and second

distances –side-screens and perspectives –lights and shades' (p. 111).
Correcting Catherine's conventional and limited point of view, he
again attempts to teach her to see imaginatively, and critically. But
while Jane Austen allows Henry thus to jostle Catherine's mind into
action, she also uses his lessons to satirize a fashionable cult[27] with its
own slang and advances her theme of fiction. For Catherine is 'so
hopeful a scholar' of the picturesque that she dismisses what her
common sense tells her, even of present realities, so 'that when they
gained the top of Beechen Cliff, she voluntarily rejected the whole
city of Bath' (p. 116). Adopting Gilpin's point of view, she populates
the land with romantic figures.

The discussion of the picturesque forms 'an easy transition' from
the regions of rhetoric back to the 'fields of fiction.' Jane Austen is
forcing us to realize that the real world *does* serve as a source of fiction
if looked at from the imaginative point of view, with a mind alive to
the possibilities of the scene presented. In his 'Observations on the
Mountains and Lakes of Cumberland and Westmorland,' Gilpin
himself suggests the relation of the picturesque – as it comprehends
the sublime – to the imagination and its creation of fiction:

> It is impossible to view such scenes as these without feeling the
> imagination take fire . . . Every object here is sublime, and
> wonderful: not only the eye is pleased; but the imagination is filled.
> We are carried at once into the *'fields of fiction,'* and romance.
> Enthusiastic ideas take possession of us; and we suppose ourselves
> among the inhabitants of fabled times. The transition, indeed, is
> easy and natural, from romantic scenes to romantic inhabitants.[28]

The more sensible Henry, viewing the land, ponders instead 'inclo-
sures' and 'the state of the nation.'

In the context of Henry's 'short disquisition' on politics, Catherine's report (pp. 111–12) of having heard 'that something very shocking indeed, will soon come out in London,' is not recognized by
Eleanor as 'novel slang,' but to mean the coming of a dreadful riot.[29]
By repeatedly stressing that the words Catherine uses are a friend's
(probably Isabella's), Jane Austen deliberately transfers the responsibility from Catherine's intimacy with the wrong kind of fiction to one
with the wrong kind of person. Eleanor's fears are a fiction based on a
fiction, which Henry clarifies by turning Catherine's repetition of
novel slang into the thing itself: 'Three duodecimo volumes, two
hundred and seventy-six pages in each, with a frontispiece to the first,
of two tombstones and a lantern' (p. 113). But the danger of a careless
use of violent words is expressed in Henry's fabrication of his own
vivid but realistic horror-story. He is not content to relegate the
'horrors' Catherine had inadvertently raised to the world of the

circulating library; these dangers have to be expressed through a novel different in quality from *Udolpho*. His novel is a vivid but realistic horror-story. He even makes his fiction personal, bringing truth home, by exercising the authorial prerogative to dispense with his characters, and knocking down his brother Frederick with a brickbat for the sake of his theme. His exploitation of extravagant cliché – 'the streets of London flowing with blood' and 'the hopes of the nation' – suggests that such language is not limited to novels where it titillates the private sensibility, but may be exploited by the unscrupulous to work up the emotions of a mob into acts of violence. Henry is remembering the Gordon Riots[30] as he reminds Catherine of the consequences of inflammatory language in the real world. Page comments perceptively on this passage: 'an illustration, very pertinent to the central theme of the novel, of the confusions arising when the make-believe of fiction is mistaken for reality' (pp. 16–17).

The first volume seems to end with a stalemate in the battle of fictions for Catherine's mind. Isabella has successfully carried off her fiction of love and friendship, for she is engaged to James. But, through the power of his story-telling, Henry has strong hold of Catherine's mind. We do not yet know that Catherine is being carried to Northanger Abbey because of a fiction. During the journey, however, when Henry tries through his last fiction to laugh Catherine out of her romantic expectations of the Abbey, he succeeds instead in inadvertently persuading her of their truth. What makes this fiction of Henry's different from his others is that he yields to the temptation to go beyond his parodic intent.[31] Catherine's flattering comparison of his fiction with those she has read, and his own delight in his skill of invention, is so gratifying that he is unable to resist taking advantage of the novelist's power to control – even to infatuate – his audience. For the first time Henry takes conscious advantage of Catherine's naïveté, and does so to her disadvantage. Because he forms his parody from the materials of her reading at Bath, it releases the effects of 'that sort of reading' in which she had there 'indulged' and seizes such power over her imagination as to determine the major portion of her actions at Northanger.

Unthinkingly, or perhaps because he is a 'novelist' of the commonplace by nature after all, Henry furnishes his fictional abbey with the chests and cabinets of the real Abbey. Unfortunately, he has transformed them through the medium of his fancy into enchanted objects. When Catherine finds herself surrounded by the apparatus of Henry's fiction at the Abbey itself, she believes quite naturally that she is indeed in a world ruled by the laws of fiction. Henry's 'novel' eases her over the threshold of the fictional world by making her feel familiar with its interior. But what is most significant about *this* fiction is that at the crisis of his narrative Henry abdicates his authorship, telling his heroine 'to use her own fancy' to complete it. If Catherine is indeed preoccupied with her 'fancy' during the first portion of her stay at Northanger Abbey, she has been given leave to do so. This is the first fiction Henry has not finished, and the first he has not wholly shaped to fit satiric or pedagogic purposes. With the interruption of the story, a temporal dimension is for the first time introduced into Henry's fictions. All his other fictions were carefully separated from reality, established as verbal artifacts, a 'journal,' an 'emblem,' the circulating library 'history' of the 'riot.' When Henry fails to enclose *this* fiction, it breaks loose and invades the rest of the novel.

Her Gothic adventures at Northanger are frequently referred explicitly to the influence of Henry's fiction by Catherine herself. Ultimately she blames him for some of her 'folly.' The 'darkness impenetrable' of Catherine's mind symbolizes the point of greatest submission to fancy; the illusions of fiction do not stand the test of daylight. But each time experience reveals to Catherine the absurdity of a romantic expectation she repents heartily – only to fall again the next moment a victim to further temptation. Her unconscious persistence in imaginings is indicated to us by the way in which she assigns malignant motives to inanimate objects, blaming a chest or cabinet for misleading her instead of herself for being misled.

Jane Austen herself deflects the responsibility for her heroine's delusions from Mrs Radcliffe's professional fiction to Henry's arrogantly amateurish interpretation of it. Whatever the cause, the effect is to call into question Henry's wisdom as satirist and maker of fictions. In this last fiction Henry is 'dangerously' close to usurping the author's place. 'Dangerously,' because without the author's providential powers he involves his heroine in perplexities he has not foreseen, while even the popular novelist is responsibly capable of seeing the heroine through to the resolution of her troubles. And there are perplexities he cannot foresee, such as those brought about by his own father's involving Catherine in fictions. General Tilney is as interested as the Thorpes in seducing Catherine for his own 'interest' through the creation and manipulation of fictions; like the Thorpes, the General maintains a fiction about himself. To realize his ambitions he uses language much as the Thorpes do.[32]

But General Tilney is himself to prove more naïvely and dramatically susceptible to the most extravagant of fictions than Catherine. It is *his* belief in fictions, not hers, that is to change the course of her life. Though we cannot know that the sudden and excessive fiction of his friendship for Catherine has originated in his belief in John Thorpe's tales about her, we ought as alert readers to have suspected it, for even Catherine notes the change in the General's attitude to her after he has

101

been talking to Thorpe. To dramatize the dangerously secret perva-
siveness of fiction, Jane Austen keeps deliberately silent about *this*
fiction while keeping the reader distracted at the forestage of her fable
– trying to keep him, that is, abreast of the fictions in which Catherine
is steadily entangled despite her own efforts to understand her experience.

As Catherine attempts to act out Henry's fiction, experience helps
dissipate its effects. She comes to perceive its absurdity, to discover
that it is impossible to sustain a fiction of this kind in the real world.
But the more powerful and therefore more pernicious influence of
Gothic fiction cannot be cured by experience alone. Jane Austen is
careful to deflect responsibility away from Henry to Mrs Radcliffe for
Catherine's most horrid delusion about the Abbey: her impertinent
suspicions about his father's involvement in his mother's death.
These distasteful speculations are clearly related to her reading of
Udolpho – she thinks General Tilney a Montoni – and free Henry
to scold her for her delusions.

Henry has to summon all his energy to address to Catherine that
passionately forthright lecture. He may never engage in fiction-making again. His appeal to her that she use judgment must bring force-
fully home to her that she has never once judged her reading by any
critical standards. Henry's 'address' and Catherine's response to it
have been so fully discussed by critics that I will only point to what
may need further attention. Henry's catalogue of the rational bases of
judgment 'Consult your own understanding, your own sense of the
probable, your own observation of what is passing around you (pp.
197–8)–is really a thinly disguised statement of the laws of probability
Jane Austen feels ought to govern the world of the novel as they do the
real world. Catherine's 'disenchantment' is used similarly. It states
more or less explicitly some of Jane Austen's own convictions about the
limitations of 'romance' (while acknowledging its charms), and suggests some of the values of the new realistic fiction, such as the admission of 'mixed characters' into the 'literary corporation.' Other than
this, it is important for the thematic cohesiveness of *Northanger Abbey*
that Jane Austen should in both passages nominate language as a means
by which evil is dissipated.

Catherine's new anxieties are realistic, for they originate in her
acquaintance with the illusory realities of the Thorpes, 'mournfully
superior in reality and substance' to those caused by Mrs Radcliffe –
not because their fictions are more real or substantial than hers, but
because their *consequences* are more painful and lasting in reality and
substance. She is the innocent victim of their deceptions; she has
played no conscious part in their illusions.

Isabella's letter is important but again so commonly discussed that I will only note its salient features for this argument. Isabella writes obviously in hopes of salvaging a fiction of feeling for James, and tries to invoke Catherine's help to remake the illusion. Her letter is, therefore, a testament to the Thorpes' faith that false words can 'set all to rights,' that they can talk into and out of existence whatever they wish. This letter is replete with fictions besides those of love and friendship: the language of fiction ('He is the only man I ever did or could love'), the fiction of the 'cold, or something,' the fiction of not understanding the quarrel, perhaps even the fiction of having 'mislaid' James's 'direction.' Isabella's shoddy reconstruction of the fiction of sentiment no longer deludes a Catherine made sensitive to fictions. Catherine acknowledges that she has never known the real Isabella at all: 'So much for Isabella,' she cried, 'and for all our intimacy!' When Catherine wishes she had never known an Isabella, Henry assures her, 'It will soon be as if you never had.'

But the Thorpes' fictions are not as easily dissipated as Henry's assurance to Catherine would suggest. The atmosphere created by delusions is so thick that it confuses even the deceivers. The Thorpes' lies actually change reality. We now see Catherine become the 'involuntary, unconscious object of a deception' over which she has no control. When the General discovers the futility of his fiction of friendship for Catherine, he dismisses her from the Abbey in a rage that postpones explanations. Catherine is violently forced into acting out the violence the Thorpes have done to language. Henry's retrospective narrative at Fullerton of John Thorpe's double-lie (pp. 244–5) reveals that when Thorpe boasted to Henry's father about Catherine to enrich his own image, the wily General had planned to plunder him of his spoils. But to believe either of Thorpe's extravagant fictions (Catherine as the 'heiress of Fullerton,' possessing a 'rich aunt,' and 'sinking' siblings, etc.) the General must indeed have read pamphlets to the exclusion of novels, or he would have recognized in Thorpe's stories the sentimental clichés John has so obviously borrowed from the circulating-library novel.

The General's easy acceptance of Thorpe's double-fiction as real explains that violent act of his in expelling Catherine from the Abbey, an act for which Jane Austen has been so roundly criticized. Maria Edgeworth protested that 'the behaviour of the General in "Northanger Abbey," packing off the young lady without a servant or the common civilities which any bear of a man, not to say gentleman, would have shown, is quite outrageously out of drawing and out of nature.'[33] But the General's act is psychologically consistent and 'artful' as well.

Subject to his fictions about himself and what is truly valuable, the General has ceased to be real and thus become susceptible to behaving like a figure in a novel rather than a real man. He *is* a villain, just as Catherine thought, but in a fiction of John Thorpe's making rather than Ann Radcliffe's – or even Jane Austen's. If the General cannot judge Thorpe's fictions rationally, how can he be expected to behave rationally? If he somehow does believe in romantic nonsense, why should he not follow its codes?

When Thorpe discovers the reality that negates his original fiction, he contradicts it with another of equal but negative extravagance. This double-lie about Catherine to the General is therefore clearly prefigured in the earlier double-lie to Catherine about James's gig (pp.65–6). We are thus shown that the trouble with a personal, impulsive motive behind the creation of fictions is the subjectivity that leads the creator to destroy as impulsively as he creates. Life imitates art, and by exposing Thorpe's double-lie Jane Austen reverses the formula by demonstrating how easily she can manipulate such conventional plots as Thorpe's, how casually create and destroy at will. The damage done by Thorpe's lies is too extensive for her own characters to cope with successfully. Jane Austen must step in to reorder the world of *Northanger Abbey* – not, indeed, to its original order, for that is permanently changed, but into happier terms than the manipulations of the Thorpes have effected.

For Jane Austen, language is not the appropriate medium for the expression of strong emotion. She *distrusts* the language of emotion: in making the expression of feeling too facile, it dissipates its strength and encourages insincerity and hypocrisy. Language is a corrupt mirror for feeling: it distorts emotion by reflecting it as either grotesquely overblown or excessively shallow. Because Catherine's feelings are fresh and strong, she has neither the need nor the vocabulary to parade them; her emotion is expressed in the 'language of nature,' though she 'knew not what to say':

> her eloquence was only in her eyes. From them, however, the eight parts of speech shone out most expressively, and James could combine them with ease. (p. 120)

The superiority of this silent grammar of emotion is confirmed in Blair's *Lectures:*

> Now the tone of our voice, our looks, and gestures, interpret our ideas and emotions no less than words do; nay, the impression they make on others, is frequently much stronger than any that words can make. . . . The signification of our sentiments, made by tones and gestures, has this advantage above that made by words, that it is the language of nature. It is that method of interpreting our mind, which nature has dictated to all, and which is understood by all;

whereas, words are only arbitrary conventional symbols of our
ideas; and, by consequence, must make a more feeble impression.
(II, p. 204)

Jane Austen exploits the irony that mute gesture is actually more
eloquent than the most extravagant and elevated language of emotion
to point up the absurdity of the Thorpes' parade of sentiment: all their
excesses of sentimental language communicate less feeling than one
look or gesture or movement or silence of Catherine's. In one sense,
the 'silence' into which the 'good' characters fall as the novel reaches
its conclusion is a mute protest against the corruptions of language
that have brought their affairs to a crisis.

Even eloquent, witty, language-conscious Henry, the eager follow-
er of Blair and Johnson, is reduced to silence under the influence of
strong emotion. When, anxious and embarrassed, he arrives at Fullerton, his powers of speech desert him. At the Allens, Henry 'talked at
random, without sense or connection'; to Mrs Morland, who has difficulty 'finding conversation for her guest,' he can say 'nothing to the
purpose.' Henry has come close to usurping his author's role of teaching the importance of precise language. Now he becomes the victim of
her benign irony. For just before the chapter that introduces Henry to
the Morlands, Jane Austen has noisily re-entered her novel to claim
authorship, and to take possession of its characters and materials. The
assertion of herself as the 'contriver' of this fiction is dramatized by
reducing her creations to silence as she raises *her* voice.

Her tone toward her own fiction at the beginning of the novel
(always excepting the 'Defense') is quite different from that of the
voice in the 'intrusions.' Unassuming, unassertive, she affects to be
bemused by the strangeness of the fiction it has devolved upon her to
relate: it is so strangely like life and so unlike romance that she does
not know quite what to make of it. Most of the burlesque of the
Gothic/sentimental fiction in the Bath episodes is characterized by
this ironic tone. In reserving till later most of her intrusions as
acknowledged author, while drawing her reader's attention to the
faults and follies of another fiction, she quietly allows her own fiction-
makers to set their contrivances in motion; as Darrel Mansell says in
another context, 'this puckish withholding on the narrator's
part . . . creates a faint comedy between Jane Austen and her own
characters that runs through the novels' (p. 27).

In fact she does not raise her voice until her heroine finds herself in
perplexities based on fictions from which she is unable to extricate
herself without her author's help. It is Catherine's violent and unex-
plained dismissal from the Abbey and ignominious return to Fullerton which prompt Jane Austen to make her second major 'intrusion'
into *Northanger Abbey*:

A heroine returning at the close of her career, to her native village, in all the triumph of recovered reputation . . . is an event on which the pen of the contriver may well delight to dwell; it gives credit to every conclusion, and the author must share in the glory she so liberally bestows. But my affair is widely different. (p. 232)

Assuming an ironic sympathy with the shallow artistic fulfillment, the 'sweet elation of spirits' for what are essentially fairy-tale devices, Jane Austen implies that not only do such contrived and fantastic 'happy endings' suspend the judgment of the reader by making him too happy to be critical, but they seem to have the same effect on the author.[34]

From such fictions Jane Austen carefully distinguishes her 'affair.' The thrust of *Northanger Abbey,* whose hero falls in love with the heroine from gratitude for her esteem, is a 'blow upon sentiment.' Its attempt is at neither 'grandeur' nor 'pathos' but at the 'midland counties' and 'central parts' of emotion. Appropriately, Jane Austen concludes the passage with a realistic touch, apt to the quality of her fiction different from popular novels – the brief reference to the Sunday loiterers of this small town for whom a passing hack post-chaise is an occasion for the exercise of 'fancy.'

By reminding the reader at the crisis of the novel's affairs that it *is* a novel, the artist's delighted assertion of controlling power points explicitly to fiction as the central theme of *Northanger Abbey.* Jane Austen's rescue of her favorite characters from the consequences of irresponsible fiction-making calls attention to her own supremacy as fiction-maker. In each 'intrusion' she strengthens the novelist's position by speaking out boldly as the contriver of fictions of which she is not ashamed, but proud to shape and control. Making overt her own novel's parody of bad fiction,[35] she explicitly distinguishes what she is doing from the efforts of others. Donald D. Stone cites Frank Kermode's idea that the novel is 'a history of anti-novels,' adding his own observation that 'it is by attacking the conventions of "fiction" that the novel maintains its position as a transcriber of reality' (p. 35).

Frankly acknowledging her craft, Jane Austen draws the reader into the process of fiction-making – even, in one 'intrusion' (p. 247), soliciting his help for the best, i.e., the most probable, disposition of her materials. The reader is obliged to read fictions less passively, and, by taking a creative attitude to the novel, to appreciate it as an intellectual exercise, not as a sentimental escape.[36] Encouraging his consciousness of *Northanger Abbey* as fiction, she opens its materials to him and endows him with some of her own awareness of its possibilities.[37] Emulating Henry's advice to Catherine, she can even appeal to her reader's imagination for help in concluding her fiction satisfactorily: 'Consult your own understanding, your own sense of what is probable, your own observation of what is around you.'

In sharing with her reader the true fictional process, after having shown him the nature and consequence of 'false' fiction, lies Jane Austen's strongest, most telling defense of the novel. But perhaps its most charming revelation is Jane Austen's notion that the real motive for authorship should be the creation of joy in the assembling of materials to express truth. That is the explanation for the cheer with which she breaks into the novel to share directly with her readers her confidence in their mutual happiness at her ingenious invention of a reward for all of Eleanor Tilney's sufferings. The sketchy portrait of Eleanor's lover is, of course, exquisitely appropriate to the merry tone of the passage, while the particular detail with which Jane Austen condescends to 'finish' her depiction of Eleanor's lover mocks the superficial neatness of the Gothic novel.[38] She has constructed her own novel, so surely to expose its 'tendency' – the exploration and resolution of fiction – that she impertinently invites us at the end of *Northanger Abbey* to misinterpret its materials.[39]

She can permit herself the fun of making her heroines patronize the source of their being, the circulating library, itself a world of fictions, and form their friendships through the reading and discussion of fictions, without ever compromising their reality. She even interrupts them in their reading by suddenly exhorting other novelists to defend the fiction her own heroines so richly enjoy. This infamous defense of fiction is strategically placed early (chapter v, pp. 37–8) in her novel. What it achieves in this position is to force the reader to scrutinize the fictive process. With its apparent contradiction of the burlesque opening, the 'Defense' makes it plain that the parodic passages of *Northanger Abbey* are not intended to reject fiction, but to refine and redefine it.[40]

Another such strategically placed defense occurs in her two critical 'asides' (pp. 110–11) – to society, and to 'the capital pen of a sister author' – where Jane Austen yokes fiction with society, making clear at an important stage of the novel that the value of fiction (if it is responsibly handled) lies in the power to tell truth about life. For the source of this kind of fiction, unlike that of an *Udolpho,* is society; the novel pays back its debt through offering society a corrective fiction.

As Catherine increasingly submits her understanding to fiction, before we judge her we ought to remember that we have been warned. The world in which Catherine exists is itself an illusion; we can therefore only judge her foolishness as long as we ourselves foolishly believe in the reality of the fiction that gave *her* being, the 'reality' by which we determine what is 'illusion.'[41] That Henry Tilney believes in the superior power of fiction over 'naked instruction' is demonstrated each time he engages to teach Catherine. For Jane Austen believes as firmly as Blair that it is not the novel but 'the faulty manner of its execution, that can expose it to any contempt' (II, p. 304).

It is in her 'dear Dr Johnson' that we find a practical justification for the novel. For if Dr Johnson intended in *Rambler* No. 4 to warn readers and writers of the 'new' novel's dangerous possibilities, he also saw its use as a safeguard for innocence. In depicting society realistically, the 'modern' novel taught innocence what to fear, and ignorance what to detest:

> These familiar histories may perhaps be made of greater use than the solemnities of professed morality, and convey the knowledge of vice and virtue with more efficacy than axioms and definitions. (III, pp. 21-2)

> The purpose of these writings is surely not only to show mankind, but to provide that they may be seen hereafter with less hazard; to teach the means of avoiding the snares which are laid by Treachery for Innocence, without infusing any wish for that superiority with which the betrayer flatters his vanity; to give the power of counter-acting fraud, without the temptation to practice it; to initiate youth by mock encounters in the art of necessary defence, and to increase prudence without impairing virtue. (III, pp. 22-3)

Northanger Abbey is, of course, a novel of this nature. It offers through the depiction of its innocent heroine in the hands of a manipulative, greedy society – her head the more easily turned because of the irresponsible fiction in which she indulges – a moral lesson for young readers. But it offers also a far more sophisticated lesson, for more sophisticated readers, about the nature of fiction and the art of the novel.

NOTES

1 All quotations from *Northanger Abbey* are taken from *The Novels of Jane Austen,* ed. R. W. Chapman, 3rd ed. (London: Oxford Univerity Press, 1933), Vol. v.

2 John K. Mathison, '*Northanger Abbey* and Jane Austen's Conception of the Value of Fiction,' *English Literary History*, 24 (1957), 138–52, is to my knowledge the first to have called attention to this theme.

3 *Jane Austen: A Study of Her Artistic Development* (New York: Oxford University Press, 1965), pp. 59 and 67. See also Joseph Wiesenfarth, *The Errand of Form: An Assay of Jane Austen's Art* (New York: Fordham University Press, 1967), p. 26: 'The Gothic parody in *Northanger Abbey* correlates perfectly with the realism of false friendship and love. In both cases the attempt to substitute a word-construct for real life is exposed.'

4 Since the early suggestive essays by Frank W. Bradbrook, 'Style and Judgment in Jane Austen's Novels,' *Cambridge Journal*, 4 (1951), 519–24,

and *Jane Austen and Her Predecessors* (Cambridge: Cambridge University Press, 1966); and Knud Sørensen, 'Johnsonese in *Northanger Abbey*: A Note on Jane Austen's Style,' *Essays and Studies*, 50 (1969), 390–7, the most detailed analyses of Jane Austen's language are: Howard S. Babb, *Jane Austen's Novels: The Fabric of Dialogue* (Columbus: Ohio State University Press, 1961); Norman Page, *The Language of Jane Austen* (New York: Barnes and Noble, 1972); Lloyd W. Brown, *Bits of Ivory: Narrative Techniques in Jane Austen's Fiction* (Baton Rouge: Louisiana State University Press, 1973); and Donald D. Stone, 'Sense and Semantics in Jane Austen,' *Nineteenth Century Fiction*, 25 (1970), 31–50, who uses Wittgenstein to point to its philosophic implications. See also Wiesenfarth, p. 29: 'Mastery of language becomes the outward aspect of Catherine Morland's radical human effort to mature,' which the author in turn relates to her mastery of fictions. Since most of the books on Jane Austen which have appeared in the past few years postdate the original formulation of this study, I shall merely refer briefly in these notes to points of significant overlap.

5 Defined by Page, p. 78: ' "The best chosen English" implies not only the choice between more and less desirable alternatives, but also some principle of selection, and desirably some authority to settle doubtful cases.'

6 *Jane Austen's Letters to Her Sister Cassandra and Others,* ed. R. W. Chapman, 2nd ed. (London: Oxford University Press, 1932), p. 404 (28 September 1814).

7 The development of Catherine's understanding or judgment has been the focus of most studies of the novel, the most recent of which are Stuart M. Tave, *Some Words of Jane Austen* (Chicago and London: University of Chicago Press, 1973); Darrel Mansell, *The Novels of Jane Austen* (New York: Barnes and Noble, 1973); and Robert Kiely, *The Romantic Novel in England* (Cambridge, Mass.: Harvard University Press, 1972).

8 *The Works of Samuel Johnson,* ed. W. J. Bate and Albrecht B. Strauss (New Haven: Yale University Press, 1969), v, p. 39. All subsequent references in the text will be to the volume and the page of this edition.

9 *Letters,* 17 November 1798: 'an artist cannot do any thing slovenly.'

10 *Lectures on Rhetoric and the Belles Lettres,* ed. Harold F. Harding (Carbondale: Southern Illinois University Press, 1965), I, pp. 390–1. All subsequent references in the text to Blair will be to the volume and page of this edition. Cf. Chapman's *Novels,* Vol. v, p. 296, for Jane Austen's allusion in *Northanger Abbey* (p. 108) to Hugh Blair's *Lectures.*

11 See Stone, pp. 37–8.

12 Brown, pp. 114 and 217, who sees Henry as the author's surrogate.

13 See Babb, pp. 91–2.

14 See Brown, p. 140.

15 See Litz, pp. 65–7, on Catherine's 'sympathetic imagination'; see also p. 57: Jane Austen's 'early works reflect the gradual formation of a rationale for the novel which could withstand all the Johnsonian objections.' See also Mathison, 150–2.

16 Walter Scott's review of *Emma* in the *Quarterly Review,* XIV (October 1815), 190.

17 See Page, p. 153.

18 As distinct from the often-cited absence of 'fact' in Jane Austen's own fiction; see Mansell, ch. 2, and Page, p. 55.

19 Blair's term for what the 'magnificent Heroic Romance dwindled down to,' II, p. 308.

20 The terms are from Blair, I, p. 195.

21 See Babb, pp. 106–11, and Kiely, pp. 126–7.

22 See Babb, pp. 98–105.

23 See Stone, p. 112.

24 In this she would be supported by Dr Johnson, who also felt compelled to point out that 'We must consider how very little history there is; I mean real authentick history . . . All the colouring, all the philosophy of history is conjecture.' See *Boswell's Life of Johnson,* ed. Chauncey B. Tinker (New York, 1948), p. 595.

25 See Mathison, 150–2; Babb, p. 103; and Litz, pp. 53–4.

26 Cynthia Griffin, 'The Development of Realism in Jane Austen's Early Novels,' *ELH,* 30 (1963), 35–52, stresses the problem of point of view in these novels.

27 See Mansell, p. 7.

28 Cited by Bradbrook, *Jane Austen,* pp. 50–68, with some helpful suggestions about her attitude to Gilpin. Cf. Chapman's *Novels,* Vol. V, pp. 299–300, for Jane Austen's knowledge of Gilpin.

29 See Wiesenfarth, p. 14: 'Eleanor's mistake (taking Catherine's "horrid" verbal reality for a "real-life situation") is a foreshadowing of Catherine's at the Abbey when she imposes a fictional construct on a life situation.'

30 In the 'Introductory Note to *Northanger Abbey* and *Persuasion,*' (p. xiii, n. 2), Chapman states that 'Henry's reference to St. George's Fields makes it certain that he is thinking of the Gordon Riots of 1780.' Litz, pp. 63–4, points to the significance of this historical context for Henry's remarks.

31 Brown's references, pp. 114–18, to this parodic fiction as 'not a self-contained literary exercise on Henry's part' characterize its function in the novel, but not its reflection on Jane Austen's attitude to Henry as fiction-maker. See also pp. 116 ff. for his discussion of the relationship of Henry's parodic style to Catherine's development. Various critics such as Stone, Kiely, and especially Mansell – who sees Henry as the tutor of the improbable – have severely qualified Henry's authority as Catherine's mentor; I myself do not find him unreliable as a teacher through fiction until this point.

32 See Brown, pp. 112–13; Babb, p. 94; and Wiesenfarth, pp. 22 ff., for a discussion of the relationship between the techniques and ambitions of the Thorpes and General Tilney.

33 *The Life and Letters of Maria Edgeworth,* ed. Augustus J. C. Hare (Boston, 1895), Vol. I, p. 260.

34 See Lloyd W. Brown, 'The Comic Conclusion in Jane Austen's Novels,' *PMLA,* 84 (1969), 1582–3.

35 See Mathison, 146ff.

36 See Brown, *Bits of Ivory*, p. 213.

37 See Walter Scott's review of *Emma*, (n. 16, above), 188–201, Litz, pp. 3–6, and, among others, Griffin, Mathison and Frank J. Kearful, 'Satire on the Form of the Novel: The Problem of Aesthetic Unity in *Northanger Abbey*,' *ELH*, 32 (1965), 511–27.

38 See Brown, 'Comic Conclusion,' 1583.

39 Alan D. McKillop, 'Critical Realism in *Northanger Abbey*,' reprinted in Ian Watt (ed.), *Jane Austen: A Collection of Critical Essays* (Englewood Cliffs, N. J.: Prentice-Hall, 1963), p. 61; see also Page, p. 51.

40 See McKillop, p. 58, and Mathison, pp. 146–9.

41 See Alistair M. Duckworth, *The Improvement of the Estate: A Study of Jane Austen's Novels* (Baltimore: The Johns Hopkins Press, 1971), p. 102; Litz, p. 63; and Kearful, who uses the word throughout but extends it to the novel as a whole. This excellent but rather enigmatic article raises many of the issues to which I refer at the conclusion of my essay.

EVERETT ZIMMERMAN

Admiring Pope no more than is proper:
Sense and Sensibility

Sense and Sensibility belongs to the pre-Romantic world. It was not published until 1811, but its first draft, *Elinor and Marianne,* was begun in 1797. Many of the issues of the book are ones that became prominent in Romanticism, but the vocabulary and moral norms of the book are part of what Northrop Frye has called the 'age of sensibility' – neither Augustan nor Romantic but related to both.[1] Jane Austen's analyses of man's ways of knowing and of his relationship to the social world are based on assumptions that were familiar in the eighteenth century. They also show the influence of, and provide a critique of, assumptions that were later identified as Romantic.[2]

Readers have sometimes been annoyed by Jane Austen's preference for Elinor, a preference that seems to validate the importance of the social surface and to derogate feelings. Marianne's feelings are apparent because she acts in accord with them. She cares for essentials, not for superficialities. Elinor, in contrast, is intensely interested in social conventions, indulging often in hypocrisies that hide her feelings from others. She wishes to satisfy the demands of society, as well as of the self. The 'understanding' is crucially important to Elinor's complex perspective. She tries to incorporate into her conception of the world all of the trivial, contradictory, anomalous, and unpleasant – as well as the important, harmonious, and pleasant – aspects of her life, giving each its due weight. Her attempt is to understand the world, not to change it.

112

Marianne's qualities are associated with sensibility and Elinor's with sense. However, all worthy characters in Jane Austen have at least some measure of both qualities. (In the *Juvenilia,* the attack is on perverted and hypocritical sensibility.) One of Jane Austen's earliest reviewers notes that both of the central figures of *Sense and Sensibility* have at least the minimum requirement of the titular qualities: 'The characters of Elinor and Marianne are very nicely contrasted; the former possessing great good sense, with a *proper quantity of sensibility,* the latter an equal share of the sense which renders her sister so estimable, but blending it at the same time with an *immoderate* degree of sensibility which renders her unhappy on every trifling occasion, and annoys every one around her.'[3] Marianne's difficulties, however, result not so much from an excess of sensibility as from a misuse of it.

The article on 'Sensibility' in the 1797 edition of *The Encyclopaedia Britannica* (3rd edition) defines a conception of the term held by Jane Austen's contemporaries: it 'is a nice and delicate perception of pleasure or pain, beauty or deformity. It is very nearly allied to taste; and as far as it is natural seems to depend upon the organization of the nervous system.' This definition presents sensibility as a sensitivity both to self – 'pleasure or pain' – and to the external world – 'beauty or deformity.' It is related to perception, and 'It is capable . . . of cultivation and is experienced in a much higher degree in civilized than in savage nations, and among persons liberally educated than among boors and illiterate mechanics.'

The citations in the *OED* of *sense, sensible* and *sensibility* as used during or near Jane Austen's lifetime show that these words were related to each other in a continuum, without precise demarcation. Each has meanings connecting it to sense experience; to intensities of sensation; and to a proper apprehension of the world. A man has sense, presumably, because his estimate of the world is founded on the information from his senses. Sensibility is allied to emotion and is, therefore, at a greater distance from the senses; consequently it leads to a less precise understanding of the world. Nevertheless, sensibility is also a sharp and full response to the senses and is productive of an insight that the man with little sensibility lacks. A sensible man may be emotional or matter-of-fact. He may be sensible of responses from within or sensible of the world without.[4] These shades of meaning are relevant to *Sense and Sensibility* – not to every usage, of course, but to the generalized conception implied by the title. Jane Austen sees sense and sensibility as related instruments of understanding, sharing some functions and being essential for an adequate insight into the deceptive public and private worlds.

Late-eighteenth-century notions of the perceptive powers in sensibility hover somewhere between empiricism and the Romantic conceptions of imagination (probably somewhat closer to empiricism). In discussing Blake's relationship to eighteenth-century thought, Jean Hagstrum cites contrasting passages to define the opposing views.[5] Locke writes: 'All those sublime thoughts which . . . reach as high as heaven itself take their rise and footing here: in all that great extent wherein the mind wanders . . . it stirs not one jot beyond those ideas which sense or reflection have offered for its contemplation.' Blake writes: 'Man's perceptions are not bounded by organs of perception; he perceives more than sense (tho' ever so acute) can discover.' Jane Austen often suggests that her heroines perceive more than one can attribute to simple sense data; nevertheless their perceptions are nearly always rooted in sensations, even if extraordinarily delicate ones: Elinor 'watched his eyes, while Mrs. Jennings thought only of his behaviour' (p. 305).[6]

Writers before Jane Austen had presented varying views of sensibility. Sterne is known for his conception of sensibility as a force for benevolence; he also shows that sensibility is an instrument for understanding the inner world. Yorick of *A Sentimental Journey* (1768) congratulates himself on his sensibility, but when he pursues his sentiments to their sources he often finds a physical motive instead of the assumed spiritual ones. Sterne excels in describing the delicate interactions of the physical and emotional: 'I fear, in this interval, I must have made some slight efforts towards a closer compression of her hand, from a subtle sensation I felt in the palm of my own – not as if she was going to withdraw hers – but, as if she thought about it – and I had infallibly lost it a second time, had not instinct more than reason directed me to the last resource in these dangers – to hold it loosely, and in a manner as if I was every moment going to release it, of myself.'[7] Jane Austen's work is purged of the more obvious eroticism to be found in Sterne; nevertheless, there is much of the same kind of analysis – a tracking down of sentiments to their lairs. Elinor often pursues the sources of feeling; Marianne rarely does. Elinor is suspicious of her self-justifying, self-congratulatory feelings and attempts to find the suppressed discordant elements. Marianne limits her consciousness to her dominant feelings.

In pointing out the hazards of sensibility, Jane Austen is following a tradition of the sentimental novel. Even some of those more assiduous cultivators of sensibility who eschewed Sterne's ironies recognized the potential dangers of being too susceptible. For example, the lurid life and unfortunate end of Laurentini di Udolpho of *The Mysteries of Udolpho* (1794) are intended to illustrate the effects of unrestrained sensibility. The heroine, Emily St Aubert, whose feelings are admirably powerful, is warned to impose some limits on herself.

Henry MacKenzie's *The Man of Feeling* (1771) illustrates an attitude toward sensibility differing from Jane Austen's. The sensibility of Harley, the central figure, leads him to see and relieve the distresses of others; this same sensibility regularly leads him to misjudgments. Because Harley is a man of feeling, he is unfitted to be a man of the world. The book finally supports Harley's view: 'to calculate the chances of deception is too tedious a business for the life of man!'[8] Jane Austen has little patience for this indulgence. For her, dying of a broken heart is not an adequate response to the world. Sensibility is for Jane Austen an agent of understanding as well as of benevolence. She refused to sever it from sense.

A minor but not insignificant theme of the book – man in nature – is an aid in placing *Sense and Sensibility* in its near-Romantic context. Elinor's attitude falls between Cowper's and Wordsworth's, Marianne's close to Wordsworth's. Elinor shares the late-eighteenth-century taste for the unaltered natural, as her response to her conversation with her silly brother about her sillier sister-in-law's improvements at Barton shows:

> 'Where is the green-house to be?'
> 'Upon the knoll behind the house. The old walnut trees are all come down to make room for it. It will be a very fine object from many parts of the park, and the flower-garden will slope down just before it, and be exceedingly pretty. We have cleared away all the old thorns that grew in patches over the brow.'
> Elinor kept her concern and censure to herself; and was very thankful that Marianne was not present to share the provocation (p. 226).

A differing perspective from Cowper (*The Task,* 1785), a favorite poet of Jane Austen and the Dashwood sisters, helps us to locate Elinor's attitude more precisely:

> Who loves a garden, loves a green-house too.
> Unconscious of a less propitious clime
> There blooms exotic beauty, warm and snug,
> While the winds whistle and snows descend.

> (Bk III, ll. 566–9)

Cowper is more determined than Elinor to subjugate the natural to the human. The difference between Elinor and Cowper is even clearer in the following lines:

> Strength may wield the pond'rous spade,
> May turn the clod, and wheel the compost home;
> But elegance, chief grace the garden shows
> And most attractive, is the fair result
> Of thought, the creature of a polish'd mind.

> (ll. 636–40)

115

Elinor sees less need than Cowper to impose an order on nature; but, on the other hand, she does not wish to merge with it. Wordsworth's 'Lines Composed a Few Miles Above Tintern Abbey' (1798) takes a more insistently personal tone than either Cowper or Elinor; nature is not subjugated but incorporated:

> Five years have past; five summers, with the length
> Of five long winters! and again I hear
> These waters, rolling from their mountain-springs
> With a soft inland murmur. – Once again
> Do I behold these steep and lofty cliffs,
> That on a wild secluded scene impress
> Thoughts of a more deep seclusion; and connect
> The landscape with the quiet of the sky.

(ll. 1–8)

Marianne's apostrophe to 'Dear, dear Norland' is an expression of her desire to establish a personal relationship with a house and trees. Marianne's attitude is mocked by Jane Austen: 'Oh! happy house, could you know what I suffer in now viewing you from this spot, from whence perhaps I may view you no more! – And you, ye well-known trees! – but you will continue the same . . . insensible of any change in those who walk under your shade! – But who will remain to enjoy you?' (p. 27) This mockery of Marianne is repeated. Elinor says, 'It is not every one . . . who has your passion for dead leaves.' Marianne replies, 'No; my feelings are not often shared, not often understood. But *sometimes* they are' (p. 88). Marianne longs for a harmony of understanding and for a unity of man and nature. She seeks to achieve an identity of inner and outer worlds, even in her distress: 'Marianne entered the house with an heart swelling with emotion from the consciousness of being only eighty miles from Barton, and not thirty from Combe Magna' (p. 302).

In *Rasselas,* Samuel Johnson analyzes longings like Marianne's. Man engages in continuous activity, mental and physical, to abrogate the inevitable distances of time and space: 'no mind is much employed upon the present: recollection and anticipation fill up almost all our moments' (ch. XXX); pyramids are erected 'only in compliance with that hunger of imagination which preys incessantly upon life, and must always be appeased by some employment' (ch. XXXII). Marianne, in contrast to Johnson, envisions the possibility of satisfying these longings. She refuses to accept detachment as the norm. Sensing separation, she attempts imaginatively to reconstitute her world. To do so, she must place herself at the center of all she perceives. As difficulties arise in ordering her perceptions, she eliminates those things that resist her order. Her world becomes a part of her, but it is small and distorted.

Marianne attempts to find external counters for her thoughts, refusing to acknowledge a separation of thought from reality. She knows 'what a young man ought to be' (p. 45) and says of Edward, 'His eyes want all that spirit, that fire, which at once announce virtue and intelligence . . . He admires as a lover, not as a connoisseur. To satisfy me, those characters must be united' (p. 17). But in conversing with Willoughby, she discovers that 'The same books, the same passages were idolized by each – or if any difference appeared, any objection arose, it lasted no longer than till the force of her arguments and the brightness of her eyes could be displayed' (p. 47). She wants an emblem, not a man; Willoughby is the generalized figure of the 'hero of the a favourite story' (p. 43). He is one of her clichés.

Willoughby remains in Marianne's mind as an evil force long after his betrayal of her; he becomes a part of her mental topography. Having created a mental world, Marianne cannot escape it, even when her external circumstances change. After losing the stability provided by illusion, she attempts to organize a new order around grief: 'Her mind did become settled, but it was settled in a gloomy dejection. She felt the loss of Willoughby's character yet more heavily than she had felt the loss of his heart . . . and the doubt of what his designs might *once* have been on herself, preyed . . . on her spirits' (p. 212).

Willoughby's lurid interview with Elinor during Marianne's sickness reveals the conventionalized pattern that the romance of Marianne and Willoughby has assumed. Of Marianne's letter, Willoughby comments: 'Every line, every word was – in the hackneyed metaphor which their dear writer, were she here, would forbid – a dagger to my heart. To know that Marianne was in town was – in the same language – a thunderbolt. – Thunderbolts and daggers! – what a reproof would she have given me!' (p. 325) Marianne despises the verbal cliché, but she has actualized the patterns of literature and turned her life into a cliché. Nevertheless her passion – and Willoughby's to a great extent – is genuine. In *Madame Bovary* Flaubert remarks on the difficulties of reconciling language to feeling: 'He had no perception – this man of such vast experience – of the dissimilarity of feeling that might underlie similarities of expression . . . the truth is that fullness of soul can sometimes overflow in utter vapidity of language, for none of us can ever express the exact measure of his needs or his thoughts or his sorrows; and human speech is like a cracked kettle on which we tap crude rhythms for bears to dance to, while we long to make music that will melt the stars.'[9]

Marianne refuses to say what she does not feel (p. 122), but she often has little understanding of her feelings. She deals with everything intensely but from very limited intellectual premises: her categories and judgments are finally crude ones. Neither her passion for Willoughby nor her final acceptance of Colonel Brandon is contemptible, but neither choice is nice. Her enthusiasms are often attractive, her discernment, limited.

The imaginative unity of Romanticism is to Jane Austen an egocentric and false one. It must be combatted by a resolute effort to decenter oneself. One can achieve a mental accommodation of discordant elements but not a resolution of them. Elinor's response to the marriage of Lucy and Robert Ferrars is presented in relation to multiple faculties – heart, imagination, and reason – and to each is assigned a different, and discrete, level of comprehension: 'To her heart it was a delightful affair, to her imagination it was even a ridiculous one, but to her reason, her judgment, it was completely a puzzle' (p. 364). Marianne ascertains that Willoughby admires 'Pope no more than is proper' (p. 47), but Jane Austen's view of mankind is not in many respects markedly different from Pope's in *An Essay on Man:*

Chaos of Thought and Passion, all confus'd;
Still by himself abus'd or dis-abus'd;
Created half to rise, and half to fall;
Great Lord of all things, yet a Prey to all;
Sole Judge of Truth, in endless Error hurl'd:
The Glory, Jest, and Riddle, of the World!

(Bk II, ll. 13–18)

In Pope and Jane Austen, man's conception of the ultimate order is always fragmented.

Jane Austen's comment on Romantic harmonies is clear in a scene early in the third book. While Marianne plays the piano and Elinor and Colonel Brandon talk, we are told what the good-hearted observer, Mrs Jennings, is thinking. Colonel Brandon, to the observer's delight, seems to be proposing marriage, as 'Elinor changed colour, attended with agitation' (p. 281). But we later learn that Colonel Brandon is urging Elinor to communicate to Edward his offer of the living at Delaford, thus bringing Edward closer to marriage with Lucy. Jane Austen prolongs the scene, emphasizing the metamorphosis of Romantic interminglings into a comedy of misapprehension. As happens so often, Marianne's piano-playing is only a diversion, not part of a complex scene of unified emotion.

Elinor's characteristic method of thinking is analytical rather than synthetic. Her judgments are rational, but they are also complex and often more than rational. She is convinced of Lucy's engagement to Edward, 'supported as it was too on every side by such probabilities and proofs, and contradicted by nothing but her own wishes' (p. 139). But as she thinks longer, she is also convinced that Edward's 'affection was all her own': 'She could not be deceived in that. Her mother, sisters, Fanny, all had been conscious of his regard for her at Norland;

118

it was not an illusion of her own vanity.' Deeply suspicious of the distorting effects of her own involvement, she relies on the support of others' perceptions. Nevertheless, her final understanding of Edward is emotional, based on reason but extending past it. Her reverie begins in her own feelings of resentment and ends in full comprehension of Edward's painful position: 'she wept for him, more than for herself' (p. 140).

She does not, however, assume that her emotional and rational certainties about Edward solve any of her problems. Marianne says, 'Edward loves you – what, oh! what can do away such happiness as that?' Elinor replies, 'Many, many circumstances' (p. 186). This statement recalls her earlier comment on Marianne and Willoughby: 'I want no proof of their affection . . . but of their engagement I do' (p. 79). The feelings and the social world are different realms. Certainties about feelings cannot be translated into certainties about actions. Willoughby and Edward must be comprehended within multiple contexts.

Elinor's judgment is subjected to the same distorting tendencies as Marianne's. Sense alone is not enough for full comprehension, but sensibility is unstable and resistant to control. And without its connection to sense, sensibility is a perversion. Elinor's difficulties in maintaining an equilibrium are apparent in her final judgments of Willoughby. Although she gains her fullest understanding of him in the interview that takes place during Marianne's illness, she persistently slides toward misevaluation. She understands his attractiveness, his passion, and his selfishness; but it is difficult for her to comprehend these qualities without making some reductive whole of them.

The mental act of understanding the world tends to be confused with ordering it. Elinor attempts to see clearly, but she sometimes imposes a rational scheme on the non-rational. For Marianne's sake, she 'wished Willoughby a widower,' but then decides that 'the reward of her sister was due' to Colonel Brandon (p. 335). She seems not to understand that her disposing is irrelevant, that she may perceive others' hearts but not command them. Her earlier precise analysis of Edward's qualities is more an ordering of her own feelings than an explanation of them: 'I have seen a great deal of him, have studied his sentiments and heard his opinions on subjects of literature and taste; and, upon the whole, I venture to pronounce that his mind is well-informed, his enjoyment of books exceedingly great, his imagination lively, his observation just and correct, and his taste delicate and pure' (p. 20). The Johnsonian style, both in Jane Austen and Johnson, sometimes conveys exactitude of understanding in relation to a perceived external order. Other times, it is whistling in the dark.

Elinor's understanding is not an active force; it is inhibited by her respect for social conventions. She long understood Lucy's calculations and Edward's misery; nevertheless, she 'gloried' in Edward's 'integrity' in maintaining the engagement (p. 270). Even in situations of much less importance, she observes arbitrary conventions. She pays a formally required visit to Mrs John Dashwood, although their dislike is mutual (p. 294). Decorum tends to become an independent force, separated from understanding and harnessed to no conceivable end.

Elinor contributes to the pattern of deceit that she tries to comprehend: 'Elinor wanted very much to know, though she did not choose to ask'; here is one of her characteristic indirections (p. 229). Much of her energy is devoted to solving puzzles that she herself has helped to make. This activity is sterile and ultimately solipsistic. Her superior knowledge does not result in action but in contempt for a world that she supports: 'But while she smiled at a graciousness so misapplied, she could not reflect on the mean-spirited folly from which it sprung . . . without thoroughly despising them all four' (p. 233).

Why then is Elinor's way to be preferred to Marianne's? To accept Marianne is deliberately to accept an egocentrically distorted view of the world, but to accept Elinor is deliberately to accept the imprisonment of the self within the hardened forms of a sometimes irrelevant social structure. Marianne's Blakean dismissal of Elinor's self-control is forceful, even if not entirely just: 'with strong affections it was impossible, with calm ones it could have no merit' (p. 104); 'Those who restrain desire, do so because theirs is weak enough to be restrained; and the restrainer or reason usurps its place, and governs the unwilling' (*Marriage of Heaven and Hell*). Marianne almost destroys herself, but Elinor is ineffectual. Elinor's understanding of the social structure has no direct connection to her marriage to Edward.

Jane Austen makes vivid the horrors of living socially. The many scenes with the Dashwoods and Middletons are filled with grating stupidity and nastiness, shrieking children and unendurable disputes about their height. Elinor's insight shields her from none of this, but both she and Marianne are finally granted peace – one of the profoundest blessings in their world: 'among the merits and the happiness of Elinor and Marianne, let it not be ranked as the least considerable, that though sisters, and living almost within sight of each other, they could live without disagreement between themselves or producing coolness between their husbands' (p. 380).

The upholders of 'sensibility' in the late eighteenth century were indebted to a tradition of moral thought that had Shaftesbury as its most influential spokesman.[10] He emphasized the importance of emotion as a guide to proper action. Some emotions lead to public good and some to private good; self and society are compatible. An 'economy of the passions' is essential; an imbalance leads to evil.[11] Jane Austen conceives of the self as necessarily interacting with society but also as having a core that must be kept inviolate. She is concerned with the public world not only to strengthen it but also to protect herself from it. To her, self and society are to some degree incompatible. Jane Austen supports Elinor's sometimes extreme concern for social conventions, but she also shows the painfully constricted life that results from this concern.

NOTES

1 'Towards Defining an Age of Sensibility,' *English Literary History,* 23 (1956), 144–52.

2 For commentary on Romanticism that is relevant to this essay, see René Wellek's 'Romanticism Re-Examined,' in *Romanticism Reconsidered,* ed. Northrop Frye (New York: Columbia University Press, 1963), pp. 107–33, which identifies the 'synthetic imagination as the common denominator of Romanticism' (p. 113); and Georges Poulet's *Metamorphosis of the Circle,* trans. Carley Dawson and Elliott Coleman (Baltimore: The Johns Hopkins Press, 1967).

3 *Critical Review,* February 1812 (unsigned). Quoted from *Jane Austen: The Critical Heritage,* ed. B.C. Southam (London: Routledge, 1968), pp. 35–6.

4 Those who wish to pursue these meanings and relationships further may consult Susie I. Tucker's *Protean Shape: A Study in Eighteenth-Century Vocabulary and Usage* (London: Athlone Press, 1967), pp. 249–51; and William Empson's *The Structure of Complex Words* (New York: New Directions, 1951).

5 'William Blake Rejects the Enlightenment' in *Blake: A Collection of Critical Essays,* ed. Northrop Frye (Englewood Cliffs, N.J.: Prentice-Hall, 1966), p. 145. The quotation of Locke is from the *Essay Concerning Human Understanding,* II, i, 24; the quotation of Blake is from 'There Is No Natural Religion' (second series).

6 All citations of *Sense and Sensibility are to The Novels of Jane Austen,* 3rd ed., ed. R.W. Chapman (London: Oxford University Press, 1933).

7 *A Sentimental Journey,* ed. Ian Jack (London: Oxford University Press, 1972), p. 19.

8 *The Man of Feeling,* ed. Brian Vickers (London: Oxford University Press, 1970), p. 53.

9 *Madame Bovary,* trans. Francis Steegmuller (New York: Modern Library, 1957), pp. 215–16; see *Oeuvres complètes de Gustave Flaubert* (Paris: Conard, 1910), vol. 8, p. 265.

10 The following are essential discussions of the development and implications of 'moral-sense' thought in the eighteenth century: R. S. Crane, 'Suggestions Toward a Genealogy of the "Man of Feeling,"' *ELH,*

1 (1934), 205–30; Walter Jackson Bate, 'The Sympathetic Imagination in Eighteenth-Century English Criticism,' *ELH*, 12 (1945), 144-64; A.R. Humphreys, 'The Friend of Mankind (1700–60) – An Aspect of Eighteenth-Century Sensibility,' *Review of English Studies*, 24 (1948), 203-18.

11 See Shaftesbury, 'An Inquiry Concerning Virtue or Merit,' *Characteristics of Men, Manners, Opinions, Times, etc.*, ed. John M. Robertson (New York: E.P. Dutton, 19000, I, 286–91.

ROBERT B. HEILMAN

E pluribus unum: parts and whole in Pride and Prejudice

I

Pride and Prejudice and *Sense and Sensibility* (and we might as well include *Love and Freindship*) are, as titles of fiction go, of a rare type (the titles of Jane Austen's other four major works are of types that appear much more frequently – two place names, a baptismal name, an abstraction). Not that pairs as such are exceptional; they always flourish. There are basic formats: he and she *(Troilus and Cressida, Paul and Virginia)*, he and he *(Gargantua and Pantagruel, Sandford and Merton,* and, plurally, *Fathers and Sons,* or mixed, *Joseph and His Brothers)*, two human types *(The Prince and the Pauper, Manservant and Maidservant, Dr Jekyll and Mr Hyde* – two-in-one, of course), man and beast *(Of Mice and Men, Androcles and the Lion)*, two beasts *(The Owl and the Nightingale)*, two scenes *(The Cloister and the Hearth)*, two basic conditions *(War and Peace)*, two things, concrete or abstract, literal or symbolic *(The Sound and the Fury, The Power and the Glory, The Moon and Sixpence, Bread and Wine, World Enough and Time, The Red and the Black, Decline and Fall, The Web and the Rock)*.

What this title search in literary realty does not turn up is a pair of human qualities, attitudes, personality types, responsive patterns. Oddly enough, the nearest analogue to the Austen titles is *Crime and Punishment* – at least in the sense that one might think of crime as a deviation like prejudice, or a way of life like sensibility; the difficulty, of course, is that punishment is a sequel rather than an alternative. For Austen parallels, however, it would seem likelier to turn to the eight-

eenth century. Yet there the pickings are thin. Such a title as Mrs Inchbald's *Nature and Art* sounds apropos (and it does name a subject to
which Austen turns more than once[1]), but the novel itself is a primiti-
vist tract, than which anything more non-Austen could hardly be
imagined.

But stand *Nature and Art* up beside *Sense and Sensibility:* one
might expect some resemblance between the novels, for *nature* and
sensibility are kindred forms of the new radical feeling after about
1760, and to sharers of this feeling a person committed to 'sense'
might seem equally capable of being ensnared by 'art.' I refer, of
course, to the type of expectation that the titles might create. Yet the
difference is that Mrs Inchbald's dualism is terminal and Austen's is
experimental; Inchbald names exclusive modes, Austen, alternatives
to be neither wholly rejected nor wholly glorified. Though sense and
sensibility may look like absolutes, they are only possibilities that
need the test of experience; though the title may suggest an allegorical
design, it simply names options to be explored.

If Elinor's 'sense' is to be admired, and it is, nevertheless the fact is
that it renders her no less vulnerable to the harrowing vicissitudes of
experience (her lover inflicts almost as much pain on her as
Marianne's does on Marianne) and that it burdens her with additional
responsibilities in a family of which the other members are more
given to emotional self-indulgence. While it is good if people have
sense, nevertheless sense is not an omni-efficient value, a warranty
against the dangers of life and the misery that others impose. What is
more, there is such a thing as too much sense, an excess dramatized in
John and Fanny Dashwood, who live by a chill calculation that insu-
lates them not only against emotional disturbance but against legitimate claims on their human responsiveness. Marianne's ex-lover
Willoughby is another man of sense: assailed by financial pressure, he
denies what he takes to be the dictates of his heart and marries money.
When we cross over to sensibility, we see that Marianne's allegiance
to it produces more pain than gratification; it seems almost a way of
life that might be chosen by a masochist or some other neurotic. Yet
Austen does not allegorize this position and make Marianne illustrate
a thesis. For Marianne's sensibility, troublesome as it is, is also partly
justified in that her intuitive perception of Willoughby's response to
her is not a fantasy; she has seen something real, even though
Willoughby chooses not to act in terms of it. But Marianne's sensibility is more emphatically justified when she is seen in contrast with the
Steele sisters, who have no sensibility at all. Their characteristic
insensibility to others makes Marianne's hypersensitivity look good,
for, while their vulgarity of feeling is incurable, her hypersensitivity
is a modifiable excess of a central warmth and spontaneity of feeling
that are humanly indispensable.

Austen, then, has so arranged her characters that they enact a commentary on the values embodied in her title. She 'outflanks' the two key positions and thus modifies them instead of holding to them inflexibly. 'Sense' is a virtue, but is not an absolute; there can be a disastrous excess of it. 'Sensibility' can be mistaken for an unqualified virtue by cultists, and it can be, if not actually a vice, at least a troubling disorder; yet it is not so much an essential error as it is an excess of a virtue. In sum, though her title suggests a pair of allegorical opposites, Austen is sturdily anti-allegorical: she finds a duality not between clear-cut virtues and clear-cut vices, but within apparent virtues and apparent vices. An *a priori* rightness and an *a priori* wrongness undergo the corrective of experience – linear experience in which unfoldings in time add new perspectives, and analogical experience in which concurrent actions supply panoramic illumination. It is the kind of excellence which keeps *Sense and Sensibility,* despite its shortcomings in detail, alive.

II

As a title, *Pride and Prejudice* resembles *Sense and Sensibility* and yet differs from it. The obvious likeness is that two habits of personality are designated by abstract terms that make us expect the allegorical method. In *Pride and Prejudice,* however, we seem to have not an opposition of superior and inferior but a pair of shortcomings. *Prejudice* can be read in only one way. To a reader consciously on guard against boobytraps, 'pride' might immediately mean 'self-respect,' but the chances are against it. The magnetic field of 'prejudice' influences the connotation of 'pride,' but even without this it would be hard to resist the implication of 'vanity,' 'arrogance,' and 'hubris,' of 'Pride goeth before a fall' and 'pride, the never-failing vice of fools.' A title more like *Sense and Sensibility* would be *Pride and Humility,* for, as we shall see, there is a substantial humility theme, and both opposites are dealt with complexly. But the phrase that Fanny Burney used a number of times in *Cecilia* and that presumably caught Austen's eye was 'pride and prejudice,' not 'pride and humility.'

'Prejudice' is less on target than 'humility' would have been, at least in the sense that prejudice is thematically less evident. It is present, of course, both in Bennets and in Darcys and is modified in the individuals capable of self-modification. Yet it remains relatively subsurface and passive, probably because Austen saw that there isn't really very much to be said about it. It hardly goes beyond banality to inveigh against prejudice. The thematic possibility of prejudice becomes larger only if one approaches it with a strained paradoxicality that might take this line: while prejudice is commonly a pre-judgment that

remains indifferent to evidence, it may also be the lightning intuition
of truth that seems to proceed without evidence but will in time be
confirmed by evidence. But lightning intuition of truth is not the form
of pre-judgment that distinguishes the characters in *Pride and
Prejudice*: they become open to truth only after evidence has knocked
heavily on the doors of their minds. Austen would not seek the rare
virtue in prejudice any more than she would inveigh against the vice
of it. Her natural ground is a central one, equidistant from the tortured
and the truistic.

This hypothesizing grows out of the fact that, while one of the title
words keeps cropping up like a leitmotif, the other appears very little.
Though the two family groups are prejudiced, though Elizabeth is
prejudiced against Darcy and in favor of Wickham, though Wickham
alleges that Darcy is prejudiced against him, though the younger
Bennet girls are prejudiced in favor of men in uniform, and though
Collins lives by prejudice alone, the concept does not often surface in
the verbal specification that would reveal Austen's awareness of it as a
principal counter. The concept is charmingly intimated when, in
passages separated by only a few pages, Austen playfully puts
Elizabeth and Collins into the same emotional boat: Elizabeth fears
'To find a man agreeable whom one is determined to hate!' and
Collins presents 'the determined air of following his own inclination'
(ch. 18).[2] It is just on this occasion that Elizabeth – more playfulness
by Austen – suggests to Darcy that he may be 'blinded by prejudice.'
For another hundred pages (and roughly a score of chapters) the word
is missing; then it has a little flowering of more than casual meaning-
fulness. Rejected accusingly by Elizabeth, Darcy writes a long letter
explaining the actions that had annoyed her. Elizabeth approaches the
letter with 'a strong prejudice against everything he might say,' but in
a little while begins to perceive that 'she had been blind, partial,
prejudiced, absurd' (ch. 36). This comic anagnorisis is at the heart of
Elizabeth's personal drama; her self-perceptiveness is a central
strength of the book. Despite the genuineness of the pain in
Elizabeth's self-understanding, it is right for the tone of the book that
a little later she can jest ironically about herself: 'And yet I meant to be
so uncommonly clever in taking so decided a dislike to him without
any reason. It is such a spur to one's genius, such an opening for wit to
have a dislike of that kind' (ch. 40). Yet the laughter at self does not
preclude straightforward self-censure: 'But the misfortune of speaking with bitterness is a most natural consequence of the prejudice I
have been encouraging.' Two paragraphs later Austen makes
Elizabeth refer to the 'general prejudice against Mr Darcy [which] is
so violent that it would be the death of half the good people in Meryton to attempt to place him an amiable light.' Though the point is not

made overtly, the repetition of *prejudice* lets us infer Elizabeth's recognition that she has been behaving not like a discriminating individual, but like a thoughtless public ever quick to leap to conclusions.

This is virtually the end of prejudice as a publicly identified theme. True, Mr Gardiner attributes 'family prejudice' to Mrs Reynolds, the housekeeper, when she praises Darcy (ch. 43), and Elizabeth explains to Darcy how 'all her former prejudices had been removed' (chs. 58, 60). True, Mrs Bennet's shift from con-Darcy to pro-Darcy when she finds that Elizabeth is to benefit from his 'ten thousand a year, and very likely more' (ch. 59) suggests an indecently hasty reorientation of prejudice. Austen does not push this; nor does she make the point that pre-judgments, which are an inevitable tentative way into experience, become prejudices only when clung to, in the face of modifying evidence, as emotional supports; nor does she go into the distinction between prejudices about individuals and prejudices about classes (fortunately she eliminates the class issue by having virtues and vices easily surmount all social barriers). To make these notations, however, is not to disparage; it is only to say that, as a theme, prejudice never quite takes on the vitality that appears in the treatment of pride. Not that Elizabeth's and Darcy's overcoming of it is not significant, but this conquest, as we shall see, is an auxiliary way of articulating the central drama.

III

Though I have talked as if Austen's two-part titles provide essential keys to general structure, it is clear by now that this assumption needs qualifications. For one thing, Austen fundamentally modifies the expectations that the titles may be supposed to arouse. Again, a title-word such a 'prejudice' may not stir her imagination enough to exert a principal influence on the story, but may simply pop into view now and then. Further, a significant theme such as humility may not appear in the title at all, though it may be implied by the presence of 'pride.' Obviously there are various totally untitled themes. Of these, a major one is marriage. It is important in the present context because the treatment of it is closely interwoven with the treatment of pride; at certain crucial points, the two are hardly separable. This interdependence, however, is not immediately apparent. Hence it is better to postpone a direct look at the marriage theme until we have laid some groundwork by seeing what Austen does with pride.[3]

Pride comes into play very early and then is dramatically active, or is the formal object of attention, in about half the sixty-one chapters. Austen sees that the word itself stands for a medley of psychological and moral states, rooted in a common human ground but growing out diversely as they are nurtured by, and nurture, different personalities. But this absence of oneness appears only after some time has passed. Initially Austen treats pride as if it were wholly unproblematic, a failing no less clear-cut than prejudice.

Darcy is 'discovered to be proud,' 'above his company and above being pleased'; he is called the 'proudest, most disagreeable man in the world,' 'so high and conceited' (ch. 3); likewise the Bingley sisters are 'proud and conceited' (ch. 4); and Mrs Bennet records the community opinion: 'everyone says that he is ate up with pride' (ch. 5). The observers believe that they are seeing sense of superiority, snobbishness, excessive self-approval; yet very soon we also see that what is called pride includes reserve, an apparent unresponsiveness to overtures, a holding back from conventional intercourse, pleasantries and small talk. An accusation of pride, then, may be quite justifiable, but it is also a way of disapproving partial non-compliance with neighborhood social ways; in the observer there may be as much strength of feeling as there is sharpness of eye or even more. Both possibilities are present when Austen observes that 'Elizabeth saw superciliousness in their treatment of everybody' (ch. 6). It gradually becomes evident that one can point to pride perceptively, defensively, aggressively, or even (much later) admiringly.

The faint duality that first hangs over the issue of pride is amplified in a Lucas–Bennet round-table discussion (ch. 5). Charlotte Lucas proposes that Darcy 'has a *right* to be proud' – the right of character, status, and fortune. Elizabeth, on the other hand, 'could forgive *his* pride if he had not mortified *mine*': for the first time pride is less an unarguable vice than an *amour propre* which is a fact of every life. Mary picks this up and articulates it formally in a little essay which she contributes, pedantically but by no means stupidly: 'Pride is . . . very common . . . few of us . . . do not cherish a feeling of self-complacency . . . A person may be proud without being vain. Pride relates more to an opinion of ourselves, vanity to what we would have others think of us.' (Austen uses Mary's sage words against her a little later when Mary sings to entertain others: 'Vanity had given her application . . . likewise a pedantic and conceited manner' [ch. 6] – the first judgment in which we see a virtue and a vice plainly brought together under one name.) When pride is said to be universal and is distinguished from vanity, it is something more than a gross attribute of bad men who because of it can be pointed at by good men. Though the symposium ends anticlimactically with the declaration by 'a young Lucas' that if you have enough money pride need not be worried about, the opinions serve a dramatic purpose: all participants view pride not absolutely as a failing but relativistically, felt and understood differently as different perspectives are brought into play. Interestingly enough, it is not long before Austen has Darcy himself echo Mary's distinction. This occurs when Elizabeth, confident of her assessment of him, inferentially accuses him of 'vanity and pride' (ch. 11). Darcy replies that while 'vanity is a weakness,' 'real superiority of mind' will keep pride 'always under good regulation'; i.e., pride is a neutral quality which becomes undesirable only when it gets out of hand. Elizabeth turns away to 'hide a smile,' and we smile at her.

It is not long, then, before we are pushed beyond the allegorical singleness of meaning which the title might lead a reader to expect. The theme of pride is constantly subjected to modification by new developments. Austen sees pride as very much in people's minds, either as an unspoken attitude of their own egos or as an easy name for displeasing manners and traits in others. Elizabeth has to 'tremble lest her mother should be exposing herself again' (ch. 9) and lest all her family 'expose themselves as much as they could during the evening' (ch. 18). Darcy is 'ashamed of his aunt's ill-breeding' (ch. 31) – she is the only embodiment of the heavy-handed snobbery which for many of the characters is the primary meaning of pride. Since Elizabeth is the Bennet most sensitive to others' obnoxious pride, it is a delightful irony that Miss Bingley should attribute to her 'a mixture of pride and impertinence,' a 'conceited independence' (ch. 8), and 'that little something bordering on conceit and impertinence' (ch. 10). So it works in both directions. Miss Bingley is an unreliable witness, but then Elizabeth may be too.

IV

These bright turns are peripheral to the more searching account of pride achieved through the introduction of the humility motif. Once we see the word *humble* we might well expect a familiar moralistic antithesis of the proud who will fall and the humble who shall inherit. But again it does not work out that way. Austen not only rejects a cliché view; she further undercuts expectation by straining the humility theme through two sharply contrasting characters, Bingley and Collins. The Bingley episode is brief but lively and meaningful. Amiable Bingley says that his thoughts flow faster than he can write them down; hence his letters often do not make sense. With a tinge of gentle irony Elizabeth praises his 'humility.' Darcy then leaps in with the sharpest observation that he has yet made: 'Nothing is more deceitful than the appearance of humility. It is often only carelessness of opinion, and sometimes an indirect boast.' To Bingley he attributes 'The indirect boast, for you are really proud of your defects in writing . . . the power of doing anything quickly is often much prized by

129

the possessor' (ch. 10). Humility, then, is not set up as a virtue countering the vice of pride; rather we have the paradox that qualities accepted as opposites may coincide. Complacency may garb itself in the humility of self-denigration; a man may be vain of his lack of pretension. No truisms here.

Only a little later we come upon the same issue in a different guise – different enough, perhaps, to obscure the thematic identity. Though paradoxicality is suggested by the 'mixture of servility and self-importance' which Mr Bennet gleefully points out in Collins' letter (ch. 13), Collins initially seems no more than a minor Uriah Heep almost four decades ahead of his time. His ceaseless refrain of 'humble abode' and 'humble parsonage' and his assurance in his 'proper humility of behaviour' (ch. 18) suggest only an oafish muddy-eyed insensitivity. Here, we do at first appear to have an allegorical character, one who has turned the traditional virtue of humility into a monstrosity and thus must make one long for pride in any form. But what is striking is that Austen is unwilling to let him go as unrelievedly one-dimensional; she tells us directly that he combines 'humility of manner' and 'the self-conceit of a weak head,' that he is a 'mixture of pride and obsequiousness, self-importance and humility' (ch. 15). Though these are assertions rather than drama, they have the dramatic life inhering in the perception that mutually contradictory elements may co-exist – a carrying on of Austen's essential impulse to shun easy moral categories. When both the likable Bingley and the repellent Collins reveal an essential pride beneath a ritual humility, we perceive not only the spread of pride among contrasting human types, but a further complication of meaning in a word that has already been used to denote both a diversity of qualities in men called proud and the animus of those who level the charge. We might well imagine that Austen is going to solve the problem of definition by declaring for a total relativism.

V

To lead us in this direction is an admirable ploy in one who is of course going to do no such thing. It is Wickham, ironically, through whom Austen first pushes us toward the permanent center of meaning. Wickham's entry into the story, as well as his role, is the source of more than one ironic effect. Collins' objectionableness predisposes Elizabeth in favor of the relatively charming and by no means stupid Wickham, as self-conscious as Collins but much more 'aware.' Elizabeth's antagonism to Darcy, and Wickham's defensiveness against Darcy as the man who has the goods on him (we do not yet know this, of course), bring them into a rapport that, though its central ground is anti-Darcy feeling, still has a freedom which opens the way toward a more reliable definition of pride than has so far been present in anyone's use of the word. Granted, both use the word in conventional, undefined ways. Elizabeth reports with assurance that 'Everbody is disgusted with [Darcy's] pride,' and Wickham asserts, 'His pride never deserts him' (ch. 16). Yet in between these standard-line observations both people – as if freed from narrowness by a congeniality which both ironically take to be greater than it is – slip into usages which imply the broadest and most useful definition of pride so far presented to us. They open up the title theme vastly.

Elizabeth 'wonder[s] that the very pride of this Mr Darcy has not made him more just to you,' that 'he should not have been too proud to be dishonest.' Wickham replies that, indeed, 'almost all his actions may be traced to pride; and pride has often been his best friend. It has connected him nearer with virtue than any other feeling.' Here Elizabeth, her emotions rising, slips back into the commonplace: 'Can such abominable pride as his have ever done him good?' But Wickham, who strikingly combines occasional clarity of mind with deviousness and crass opportunism, goes on to speak of Darcy's pride in terms that at last take us into the thematic center of the book:

> 'Yes. It has often led him to be liberal and generous, to give his money freely, to display hospitality, to assist his tenants, to relieve the poor. Family pride, and *filial* pride, for he is very proud of what his father was, have done this. Not to appear to disgrace his family, to degenerate from the popular qualities or lose the influence of the Pemberley house, is a powerful motive. He has also *brotherly* pride, which with *some* brotherly affection makes him a very kind and careful guardian of his sister.'

(Long afterwards, Wickham is again able to register such a view of Darcy's pride [ch. 41].)

At this point we are compelled, whether we think it through or not, to recognize that while 'pride' can become a cliche of multiple uses but limited usefulness, behind the cliché currency there lies a profound human motive that manifests itself in different ways. The neutral center of pride, the single root nurturing several stems, is a universal self-regard or self-esteem, an inevitable fact of life which can take contrary forms. In one direction it can become self-admiration, in another, self-respect; in one direction, complacency and sense of privilege, in the other, sense of obligation; in one, the assertion of assumed quality, in the other, commitment to a quality to be maintained by constant effort; in one, the freedom to look down on the world, in the other, the need to live up to the standards that claim one's loyalty.

Once such a definition has been put into play, the problem is always how pride operates in each individual, and we see a wide range from abrasive superciliousness at one extreme to a lightminded absence of decent pride at the other. The gradual build-up of this structure of attitudes, working in conjunction with the formal definition made possible by Wickham's analysis of Darcy, puts us in a position of increasing detachment with respect to the attributions of pride made in the second half of the story. We relish the jest at the ordinary use of the word when Mrs Gardiner, on being pushed, 'was confident at least that she recollected having heard Mr Fitzwilliam Darcy formerly spoken of as a very proud, ill-natured boy' (ch. 25). It is less amusing when Elizabeth passionately reverts to her original anger at Darcy: 'his pride and caprice were the cause of all that Jane had suffered,' his 'pride . . . would receive a deeper wound from the want of importance in [the Bennets] than from their want of sense'; yet even in this context she can be capable of a mild modification and term his motive 'This worst kind of pride' (ch. 33). Then he does indeed acknowledge just this 'pride' – that is, his judgment of her family – when he proposes. Here he exhibits candor rather than grace, but when Elizabeth retorts angrily he is shrewd enough to charge, in reply, that her 'pride [has] been hurt by my honest confession of [my] scruples.' He is right, but just stuffily defensive enough to render understandable Elizabeth's falling back on an undiscriminating accusation of 'pride . . . abominable pride' (ch. 34). She wants, needs, to find him guilty of the 'worst kind of pride,' and yet by now we realize that what she charges him with is not the whole truth.

After the proposal crisis Austen goes back to an earlier game of seeing how easily people use the word 'pride,' either as an outcropping of their own emotions or as a loose name for characteristics that they are unable or unwilling to define precisely. When Darcy's housekeeper, Mrs Reynolds, speaks well of him, Mr Gardiner attributes this to 'pride or attachment.' Mrs Reynolds thinks that when people call Darcy 'proud' it is 'only because he does not rattle away like other young men' (ch. 43). Elizabeth herself sees that though Miss Darcy is called 'proud,' she is no more than 'exceedingly shy' (ch. 44); this would make 'those who felt themselves inferior' think her 'proud and reserved' (ch. 45). Hence Elizabeth now understands that Wickham lied to her in calling Georgianna 'proud, reserved, disagreeable' (ch. 47).

More important, Elizabeth is able to see Darcy in a different light. In wanting to meet the Gardiners, he seems to forsake the 'pride' once offended by her family (ch. 43). She notes other changes 'in a man of so much pride' (ch. 44): though she clings to her old word, she is beginning to make excuses for him. The Gardiners take a 'so what' attitude to 'the pride he probably had' and think that if he didn't have it, 'it would certainly be imputed by the inhabitants of a small market-town, where the family did not visit' (ch. 44): social non-participation as pride. While such revaluations are going on, it is only the very silly people who persist in the uncritical usage that was general at the beginning of the book. Kitty still thinks of Darcy only as 'That tall, proud man,' and Mrs Bennet hopes to cook adequately for 'the appetite and pride' of such a man (ch. 53). At the end she insists that he is 'a proud, unpleasant sort of man' (ch. 59) – a joke to the reader, of course, yet more than that. For Mrs Bennet is the thoughtless, indefatigable marrying mother who has no pride at all; anything goes. Besides, Austen has said of her that she was in no way 'humbled' by her daughter Lydia's misconduct (ch. 49). Mrs Bennet has achieved something in the world of the novel: she is incapable of both pride and humility.

When Mrs Bennet calls Darcy 'proud, unpleasant,' Elizabeth replies, 'I love him. Indeed he has no improper pride' (ch. 59). This completes the principal thematic development in *Pride and Prejudice.* But Elizabeth has come to this point only through a crucial central experience – a peripeteia – which I have so far passed over silently. This peripeteia takes place at a point where the pride theme and the marriage are both active and are notably interdependent. To get the full impact of the peripeteia we need to have a clear picture of the marriage theme and how it is established in the over-all structure.

VI

In nineteenth-century fiction we take marriage so much for granted as an objective, or way of life, or resolution of uncertainties and tensions, that we may not immediately notice its role in *Pride and Prejudice* as an object of contemplation. Austen presents six marriages – two established ones and four in the process of being put together. Of the two established marriages, that of the Gardiners is too shadowy to have a dramatic role; we are only dimly aware of it as a satisfactory relationship between two apparently likeminded people. The Bennet marriage affords a detached comic view of a working, if un-ideal, relationship between a featherbrained, humorless, very conventional woman, once very pretty we are told, and a witty but lazy man whose only serious activity is making ironic comments on his family and their associates. Austen is neither satiric nor sorrowful nor protesting; in the imperfections of this match she sees, it appears, less a disaster than a model of ordinary marital relationships which survive some incompatibility in the partners. The portrayal results from a comic acceptance of the way things are.

And that, too, is the tone in which Austen reports on the four marriages that are her central narrative material. These have actional interrelationships: Elizabeth can visit the Collinses and thus be within reach of Darcy, Darcy's interference in the Bingley–Jane affair precipitates Elizabeth's wrathful rejection of Darcy, Collins gloomily condoles on the Lydia–Wickham affair, and his endeavor to interfere with the Elizabeth–Darcy rapprochement is ironically unsuccessful. The Lydia–Wickham elopement convinces Elizabeth that Darcy will never have anything more to do with any Bennet, but everything turns out contrary to her predictions.

Such narrative ties prevent an effect of disjunction, create a sense of unity among strands of action that could seem quite separate stories. But the more important relationships among the four new marriages is that of analogy; *Pride and Prejudice* employs a sophisticated analogical structure very early in the history of the novel. We see the marriages in the light of each other; they represent four different kinds of human relationships. Austen is capable of imagining the different styles, but, more important, refrains from an adversary role. She is not the angry scourge of imperfect arrangements, but the comic observer of different modes that reflect the qualities of the participants and that may fall short of, or resemble, or improve upon the relationship of the Bennets senior. Each represents a certain principle or justification. The Charlotte–Collins marriage is pure convenience; for each party, better this than nothing. The Lydia–Wickham marriage is society's conventional rescue operation for the sexy runaways (Wickham is Richardson's Lovelace scaled down from the demonic to the small-time seducer[4]). The Jane–Bingley marriage is the automatic union of two gentle, amiable, modest, similar souls. The Elizabeth–Darcy relationship is a more difficult, complex affair: both parties are sharp, critical, strong-minded, and given to firm stands upon initial grounds that need modification. Hence both parties have to work through a barrier-ground of unfavorable judgments, misunderstandings, and self-justifying postures.

The novel says, in effect, that these different kinds of marriage all occur, all are inevitable, and all are more or less workable: this is the comic acceptance of the world. Yet it does not simply equate them. It says that each embodies a *modus vivendi* adequate for the participants, but also it never assumes the human equivalence of the participants. In fact, one of the great things in the book is its subtle combination of acceptance and judgment. No character, and no narrative thrust, really makes a case against Charlotte's marrying Collins and Lydia's being married to Wickham, but Austen does use Elizabeth to voice the conventional romantic objections to the former and to criticize society's conventional approval of the latter. Yet Austen is so detached that she does not grant Elizabeth equal authority in both cases. On Charlotte and Collins Elizabeth is so incredulous that she hurts Charlotte's feelings (ch. 22) and so insistently condemnatory that we feel the hyperbole in her polemic and are ready for the quiet defense of the arrangement made by Jane (ch. 24). What is pressed upon us is the comic discrepancy between Elizabeth's unyielding idealist position and the realities of life which introduce the non-ideal and render it workable. On the other hand, when no one at all objects to the matrimonial legitimatizing of the Lydia–Wickham sexual adventure, and when some observers, including Mrs Bennet, regard it as an objectively desirable and valuable outcome, Elizabeth is 'sick of this folly'; as she says, 'How strange it is! And for *this* we are to be thankful' (ch. 49). This is in the best comic spirit: one accepts society's arrangements, but one is not taken in by them any more than one revolts against them.

Austen sets up against each other the planned prudential marriage (Charlotte 'set out to meet [Collins] accidentally in the lane' [ch. 22]), the institutionally rectifying (shotgun) marriage, the spontaneous uncomplicated marriage, and finally the slowly developing *earned* relationship of more complex personalities. Though they are all valid for the appropriate personalities, they are not equally significant or interesting. The less interesting they are, the more quickly Austen disposes of them. Charlotte catches Collins in a chapter, and the comment occupies part of several following chapters (chs. 22–24). We hear quickly about the Lydia–Wickham elopement after it has happened (ch. 46); the aftermath winds on through six chapters (chs. 47–52), its interest lying not in the elopers, however, but in the impact of their escapade on others. The mutual attraction between Jane and Bingley begins to creep into visibility very early (ch. 3), but then external obstacles intervene, and the engagement takes place only near the end (ch. 55). In a sense, then, the story is a long one, but its apparent length is much greater than its bulk. The truly long story is that of Elizabeth and Darcy: Darcy first begins to be aware of Elizabeth fairly early (ch. 6), their engagement is the last one to be effected (ch. 58), and the adjustments between them continue through another session of post mortems (ch. 60). But more important than the duration of the Elizabeth–Darcy story is its fictional magnitude; it is worked out in great detail, and it is at the moral center of the comedy. It *has* to be done fully, since the problems created by independent, assertive, and partly mistaken minds must be worked out with care. For Darcy and Elizabeth this means a greater understanding both of the facts outside the self and of the self. The parties have to learn much to *earn* their accommodation.

VII

We have spoken of the title themes – pride and prejudice – and of the marriage theme. They all come together in the crucial stages of the achievement of reciprocal understanding and confidence by Elizabeth and Darcy, and this makes evident the remarkable structural unity of the novel, or, perhaps better, defines a close coherence which we feel despite the almost lavish multiplicity of procedure. Not only do Elizabeth and Darcy, of all the pairs, have the most serious problem of surmounting barriers of misconception and adverse feeling, but they are the most sensitive – both in susceptibility to injured feelings and in capacity for getting to the center of things – to matters of prejudice and pride. The chief line of action begins to straighten itself out when the two principal characters work out a mutual adjustment in terms of the basic conceptual matters of the book.

The cardinal phase of the clarification begins with Elizabeth's spirited and accusatory rejection of Darcy's proposal, a proposal obviously sincere but burdened with overconfidence and a partial, though by no means total, ineptitude of style. Each has made a note of the other's 'pride.' Then Darcy writes to Elizabeth. 'I write,' Austen skillfully makes him say, 'without any intention of . . . humbling myself' (ch. 35). But in truth he does humble himself, and in the very best sense, not only by writing to her when he might understandably take refuge in offended silence, but by writing at great length and in explaining, fully and in carefully neutral tones, his belief that Jane was not seriously attached to Bingley ('If *you* have not been mistaken here, *I* must have been in an error'), his regret that he 'condescended to adopt the measures of art,' and, finally, the whole Wickham–Georgianna story which accounted for his treatment of Wickham denounced by Elizabeth in her ignorance of the facts. Elizabeth approaches this letter with a 'strong prejudice' against it (as we noted earlier), and with conviction that it is 'all pride and insolence' (ch. 36). But if Darcy humbles himself by refusing to take refuge in offended dignity and by coming down from a high place to explain, Elizabeth humbles herself by gradually retreating from her initial hostility to the letter, by considering the evidence and the probabilities, by gradually revising her whole attitude, and in the end by seeing her own errors. Neither of the principals gets locked into a defensive–aggressive stance that forbids growth; both move from a tendency to be stiff–necked to a saving flexibility. Chapter 36 is a remarkable tracing of Elizabeth's coming around to a completely changed point of view. And Austen makes her couch her new vision in the central thematic terms of the book. She felt that she had been 'blind, partial, prejudiced, absurd. "How despicably have I acted!" she cried, "I, who have prided myself on my discernment! I who have . . . gratified my vanity in useless or blamable distrust. How humiliating is this discovery! Yet how just a humiliation! . . . But vanity, not love, has been my folly. . . . Till this moment I never knew myself."' Thus she reaches the high point that is possible in the comic experience, the anagnorisis, and it is at the center of the thematic progression. She attributes her errors to pride and vanity, which so far have been largely the vices of others. Yet anagnorisis of this kind need not, and does not, lead to somber self-accusation. Elizabeth recurs to the subject readily enough to give dramatic evidence of her sharper sense of truth, but, like the well person she is, she does it playfully or wrily. She thinks of Darcy's proposal and subsequent explanations as matters that 'must . . . so highly gratify whatever of her own vanity she had not yet been able to reason away' (ch. 38). To Jane she acknowledges that she has cultivated her 'prejudices' and has been 'weak and vain and nonsensical' (ch. 40). Her most painful recognition is of 'the reproof contained in [Wickham's] believing' that 'her vanity would be gratified' by a renewal of his attentions to her (ch. 41).

Equally important with Elizabeth's mastery of a new insight into pride and prejudice is the dramatic definition of pride as the acceptance of responsibility. This indispensably fills out a story that has devoted a good deal of time to the view of pride as an easy and blind self-esteem. The new definition of pride picks up where Wickham had left off in attributing Darcy's virtues in part to his pride (ch. 16). It is a pleasant irony that Wickham should then contribute to the definition of pride as a virtue by running off with Lydia – a risky fictional stereotype which Austen handles freshly and originally,[5] making the banal vital. One of Elizabeth's own responses makes a fine contribution to the pride theme. Elizabeth guesses diffidently that Darcy's intervention was 'done . . . for her,' but she also 'felt that even her vanity was insufficient' to let her imagine his going beyond that. Darcy allied to someone allied to Wickham – unthinkable! In Elizabeth's inner words, 'Every kind of pride must revolt from the connection' (ch. 52). Here Elizabeth accepts pride as a kind of irrefutable judgment of flawed being, an inevitable placement of self with respect to defective quality. So we have a double irony: Elizabeth has reversed herself on pride, and she is wrong about Darcy. The revelation of her error is a major part of the remaining action.

We are prepared for the revelation, however, by Darcy's entry into the seduction imbroglio and his contribution to getting the elopers married. Here we have another Darcy-Bennet tension; this time, however, there is a direct contrast between Darcy and Mr Bennet. Mr Bennet has not 'done his duty,' he welcomes a solution 'with so little inconvenience to himself' and 'with such trifling exertion,' and quickly returns 'to all his former indolence,' that is to say, to ironic disengagement (ch. 50). Perhaps nowhere else in fiction is there so shrewd a treatment of the ironic commentator: the source of all his delightful wit is a detachment which also means an incapacity for the attachment, that is, the committed action which is plainly called for in the situation of which he is a part. The thematic point of this episode is that Mr Bennet lacks pride; his failure is not put literally in such terms, but the sense of it is unmistakable. While he has not 'done his duty,' Darcy defines it as his own 'duty to step forward and endeavour to remedy an evil which had been brought on by himself' (ch. 52); that is, to him it is 'mistaken pride' not to have exposed Wickham publicly and thus to have saved others from his opportunism. Darcy's pride was that 'his character was to speak for itself,' without annotation by the facts that he could supply. Interestingly enough, it is an understandable pride – a kind of self-confidence based on knowledge of right conduct. It is quite different from the pride which Elizabeth had imputed to him. Yet he is now a sterner critic of himself than she was, for he repudiates a kind of pride for which a case can be made. What comes into play here is a subtler distinction than those utilized by the earlier narrative – the distinction between the pride which rests with assurance upon genuine achievement (the honorable conduct that we know was Darcy's), and the pride that imposes continuing activity lest achievement itself not be effective against the self-seeking ever present in the world. Darcy rejects the former and elects the latter – in his word, 'duty.' Here the novel reaches the apex in the complex structure of definitions of pride that give both form and life to the story. What looked very simple initially has turned out to contain an exciting and enlightening range of possibilities. Art forces us out of the simple omnibus concept of daily life into the conceptual discrimination on which truth depends.

The drama of definition, we have seen, is not a separable element but is an intimate part of the drama of Elizabeth's and Darcy's earning their relationship. The final accommodation is summed up in three separate but related passages. Before she knows of Darcy's role in getting Lydia and Wickham married, Elizabeth is sure that her family's 'alliance' with Wickham will alienate Darcy permanently. 'She was humbled,' Austen tells us (ch. 50). Austen might have said 'embarrassed' or 'distressed'; but to say 'humbled' is not only to tie this event into the thematic structure but to show Elizabeth in that kind of reversal which life imposes upon people in the growing-up process. Austen underscores this in the next paragraph when she makes Elizabeth think, with a new sense of loss, of 'the proposals which she had proudly spurned only four months ago.' We see her and Darcy both rejecting the kind of pride – the mode of self-esteem – that had actuated them before. Elizabeth is still wrong in another way, however: she is sure that her rejected suitor must be relishing this new contretemps which can only seem to him to have justified all his prejudices. He is 'generous,' she knows. 'But while he was mortal, there must be a triumph.'

Then she learns, with a thrill that she firmly holds in check, that he has had a central role in gracing the runaways' weekend amour with marital sanctions. 'For herself she was humbled,' says Austen (ch. 52), using the phrase for a second time, meaningfully: again Elizabeth comes down from a high place, this time through a new perception of stature in the man who she had thought was only walking stiffly on the stilts of status. Austen goes on immediately: 'but she was proud of him. Proud that in a cause of compassion and honour he had been able to get the better of himself.' Here is a new increment to the ever-expanding significance of *pride:* admiration for the moral quality revealed in the mastery of prejudice. For both, pride as a responsibility to truth leads to humility as an acknowledgment of error.

Yet Austen sees instinctively that the story has not gone quite far enough, that it needs an additional rounding out for the final achievement of form, and she comes up with it in the Elizabeth-Darcy post mortem very near the end. Now it is Darcy's turn to register formally a self-understanding such as has been implicit in his actions and explicit in Elizabeth's various reflections on the course of events. It is remarkable that here indeed Darcy acknowledges the kind of pride that Elizabeth had originally imputed to him. Of his rearing: 'I had been given good principles but left to follow them in pride and conceit' (ch. 58). He goes on to speak of his habit of looking down on the rest of the world. But then came Elizabeth: 'You taught me a lesson, hard indeed at first but most advantageous. By you I was properly humbled' – brought down from high complacency and converted to the more substantial pride of which he had always the capability. Both lovers have gone through self-corrective experiences that can be rendered in the same vocabulary; in being 'humbled,' both have learned to see themselves in a less exalted perspective.

The repeated juxtaposition of 'pride' and 'humility' (or 'proud' and 'humbled') would, in its exploitation of a traditional tension, be effective without any support. But surely it gains something from our recollection, subliminal though it may be, of Collins, whose self-conscious professions of humility scarcely concealed a pressing, if unrecognized, self-satisfaction. The split between Collins and Darcy–Elizabeth, then, is not between admirable humility and lamentable pride, but rather between much richer possibilities in human character: on the one hand a union of vulgar humility and vulgar pride, and on the other, of right pride and true humility. In different qualitative ranges, opposites coexist.

In the final chapters there is another charming accent by contrast, this one overt. Elizabeth, as we saw, is 'proud' of Darcy. Compare Mr Bennet's praise of his new son-in-law Wickham: 'He simpers, and smirks, and makes love to us all. I am prodigiously proud of him' (ch. 53). While the daughter pays tribute to quality, the father ironically pays tribute to its absence. It is the ironic man's comeback from a failure rooted in his irony (his irony is not unlike Wickham's charm, a substitute for principle).

VIII

The term 'multiplicity' which I used earlier applies, it is now clear, both to the pride theme and to the marriage theme: people use the word and manage the institution in many different ways. Comedy examines all options and in effect forgives all (when *all* options are untenable or humanly inadequate, comedy becomes 'black'). Here, comedy accepts all versions of semantic and matrimonial practice – in the sense that it knows these diversities to be inevitable and that, unlike satire, it does not inveigh against any of them. Yet 'accept' does not imply either a chaotic medley of undifferentiable alternatives or a chaotic formlessness in a story embracing too many options to achieve coherence through an order of values. The novel does not say, 'People use *pride* in many ways, and it doesn't really matter how you use it.' It says, rather, 'Some people use the word more discriminatingly than others,' and it makes clear that the more discriminating users, far from being academic precisians, are the better human beings. The novel does not say only, though it does say, 'Everybody has some form of pride'; it goes on to say, 'There are better and worse forms of pride, and happily for the world and for human quality some people are drawn to the better forms.' Again the novel says, but it does not only say, 'There are many types of marital relationships, and they all work more or less.' It also says, 'Some marriages exact more maturing effort from the human being, some bring into play a fuller humanity, and some are more interesting because they entertain a wider and deeper vision of human possibility.' Thus the multiple elements do not lie passively side by side, in value equivalent or indistinguishable; rather they shed light or cast shadows on each other, and thus some become brighter and some dimmer; some become larger, and some smaller. The dramatic relationships, entirely unaided by exegetic discourse, gradually erect, if not a hierarchy, at least a scale, of values, and thus the novel, as a narrative embodiment of thought, takes form. To borrow a phrase from a possibly unlikely source, we can indeed say, of *Pride and Prejudice, e pluribus unum.*

The oneness is served not only by the unobtrusive sense of values that orders the main strands with respect to each other but also by an equally unobtrusive sense of proportion. Austen gives primary and amplest attention to the pair who exhibit the values by which, without thinking about it, we judge the stature of all the other men and women. Elizabeth and Darcy are the characters who experience most deeply the problem of pride (and of prejudice, though less extensively than that of pride); they are capable initially of a commonplace pride but eventually of a superior pride and of a proper humility; they come to use these key words with more accuracy and with a keener consciousness of meaning than nearly all of the others do; and they have to reorder their preconceptions of themselves and of each other. We look longest at this pair who exemplify what I have called the 'earned' relationship, the one which calls most extensively upon human powers of understanding, of revaluation, of self-recognition, and of self-correction. To undiminished vigor they add good sense and courtesy. Thus they bring most fully into play the qualities that make civilized life possible. They have to be the most significant, and hence the most interesting, couple.

Elizabeth had used a cliché term that was inadequate because it represented a conventional point of view that oversimplified truth; Darcy initially employed a conventional point of view that did not do justice to all the Bennets. Incongruity and discrepancy are a central Austen subject, and its most characteristic form is a disparity between cliché or convention on the one hand, and, on the other, the reality for which at first they appear to be a reliable shorthand. This disparity appears repeatedly in her fiction, and it is handled with gradually increasing subtlety. The juvenilia parody various motifs of eighteenth-century popular fiction: the humor turns on the ludicrousness of styles and plots that, losing their lifelines to actuality, have stiffened into clichés and conventions. *Northanger Abbey* increases the complexity of the jest: a literary convention that once seemed to introduce a new reality now cuts off its devotée from an adequate sense of reality. In *Sense and Sensibility* a popular convention of feeling, taken to be intrinsically meritorious, is shown to increase the difficulties of actuality, both for the feeling person and for those affected by what she does; yet here the picture takes on additional dimension, for the conventional feeling, though it leads to unhappy distortions, looks much better than no feeling at all. In *Emma* and *Pride and Prejudice* the situation is markedly richer: complacent individuals, proceeding from stereotyped expectations, try to make circumstances conform to their *a priori* notions. By a slow revision of preconceptions, as we have seen, Elizabeth and Darcy 'earn' the better insight and the rapport that insight makes possible. Emma varies from them by being more managerial, but the range of *Emma* is less: while Emma earns a better sense of fact by dismay and even humiliation, still she is less involved in the misconstrued world, and has a great deal of help from the man whose good sense is a given. In working with a somewhat thinner mixture, *Emma* occupies an intermediate ground between *Pride and Prejudice* and both *Mansfield Park,* written earlier, and *Persuasion,* still to be written. In the latter two what is missing is the earning of a better self and life that is at the dramatic center of *Pride and Prejudice;* Fanny Price and Anne Elliot see things pretty accurately from the start and have little learning, at least about themselves, to do.[6] Their *a priori* rightness, instead of undergoing correction by, secures affirmation by, experience. We wait, not for the ironic graduation toward rectitude of perception, but for people and circumstances to catch up with a rectitude which is a given. This simpler movement, largely without the exploration of the discrepancy between prejudgment (by cliché, convention, complacency, or wilfullness) and reality which is the most characteristic ground of the Austen comic mode, doubtless accounts for the less favorable judgments of *Mansfield Park* and *Persuasion* (which lead in turn to clashes over their merits). To look at these two in these terms, though with a haste that is not quite fair, is to gain an additional perspective on the breadth and depth of *Pride and Prejudice.*

NOTES

1 Austen's relationship to eighteenth-century fictional types and motifs is fully canvassed in well-known works by C. Linklater Thompson, Henrietta Ten Harmsel, F. W. Bradbrook and Kenneth L. Moler.

2 Quotations are from the text in the Rinehart Edition (1949).

3 The themes and issues dealt with in this essay have been much discussed in articles and books in the last two decades. It is a rare study of *Pride and Prejudice* that does not allude to the two title themes, to irony as central in Austen's method, to the learning process that Elizabeth and Darcy undergo. The marriage theme has received a good deal of attention. Various passages that I quote have been quoted before, and some have been discussed in ways similar to my own. To record all parts of previous criticism that mention the subjects I deal with, that at some point or other I parallel or diverge from, that quote the same passages with similar or different emphases – this would, I believe, create a wilderness of notes more extensive than useful to readers. When there is such a wealth of commentary, one may indeed have missed something relevant to one's own argument. However, to the best of my knowledge, the familiar aspects of *Pride and Prejudice* which I notice have not previously been combined and interpreted as they are here.

4 See note 1.

5 In some previous criticism there is a tendency to censure Austen for the stereotype and not to notice the major innovation by which she pushes the stereotype into the background.

6 This view is set forth at length in C. S. Lewis's 'A Note on Jane Austen' in *Jane Austen: A Collection of Critical Essays,* ed. Ian Watt (Englewood Cliffs, N.J.: Prentice-Hall, 1963), pp. 25–34. Lewis's essay first appeared in 1954. *Mansfield Park* is of especial interest in that it suggests the

presence in Jane Austen of a kind of split first discussed by Kenneth
Burke in *Attitudes to History* (1937) – the split between formal
commitment and imaginative allegiance. Fanny has all the standard
virtues and has to win, but the Crawfords, who are wrong and have to
lose, have almost a corner on the charm. The theoretical issue is discussed
in my 'Two-Tone Fiction' in *The Theory of the Novel: New Essays,* ed.
John Halperin (New York: Oxford University Press, 1974), pp. 305–22. A
major argument to the effect that Fanny and Anne are treated more
complexly than I suggest here appears in Kenneth L. Moler, *Jane Austen's
Art of Allusion* (Lincoln, Neb.: University of Nebraska Press, 1968), pp.
109–54 and 187–223.

KARL KROEBER

Pride and Prejudice:
fiction's lasting novelty

If criticism, like philosophy, should begin in wonder, where better to start than celebrating Jane Austen's birthyear with scholarly essays? Only she could do justice to the irony of an anthology devoted to 'the most unlearned and uninformed female who ever dared to be an authoress,' as she described herself. But any excuse for the pleasure of talking about Jane Austen's irony is worth seizing, and in 1975 her fiction is peculiarly useful in helping us to understand the paradox of how novels endure.

Although Jane Austen's esteem as a superior artist is secure, the exemplarity of her art is seldom celebrated.[1] One suspects that it never occurred, even in passing, to Erich Auerbach that her fiction might have special value to the history of the 'representation of reality' he traced in *Mimesis*. In fact, her work illustrates a limitation in Auerbach's study, suggested by his failure to comment significantly on any fiction in English between Fielding and Joyce.[2] Her novels reveal how and why fiction works along a borderland, as Roman Jakobson has called it,[3] between referential language and metalanguage, how and why the 'representation of reality' is but half a novel's function.

Long ago Kipling in his story 'The Janeites' made the point that the circle of her admirers has never been a coterie, even though Jane Austen's distinguishing quality is impeccable stylistic tact. She is as incapable of Flaubert's occasional vulgarity as of Joyce's lapses into pedantry. And 'The Master' is a clumsy craftsman compared to her. *Pride and Prejudice*'s first sentence contrasts with the characteristical-

144

ly Jamesian opening of 'The Birthplace': 'It seemed to them at first, the offer, too good to be true, and their friend's letter, addressed to them to feel, as he said, the ground, to sound them as to inclinations and possibilities, had almost the effect of a brave joke at their expense.'

Although conventions of spelling, punctuation, and grammar have altered enough since the early nineteenth century that some of Jane Austen's phrasing surprises us, and even though some words have betrayed her by shifting their meaning, her language remains entirely clear, in part because her commitment to a firm verbal design saves her from misusing words, as James sometimes does: 'Strether seemed to make it out, from their position, between the interstices of arrayed watches, of close-hung dangling gewgaws.'[4]

It is remarkable that quiet exactness of style should be appreciated in the United States. Yet recognition of Jane Austen's skill by American critics triumphing over the illusion of a common language saves her from the category of a merely nationally popular novelist, like Scandinavian Nobel prize winners. But language aside, her social prejudices would seem to make her uncongenial to Americans. And Mark Twain's 'animal repugnance' to her no doubt represents a persisting American attitude. Today, the instinctive, democratic, Twainian distaste for Jane Austen must be discriminated from the complex, elitist, Joycean distaste of young people whose reading has been almost exclusively in twentieth-century literature and who are sophisticated in contemporary theories of fiction and prose style. These students, mostly English majors, we should attend to, for they reflect, as in a multifaceted mirror, images of the aesthetic sensibility we now inculcate.

If today we praise Jane Austen, we ought to recognize how antithetical to prevailing theories of literary, especially fictional, art her practice is. In a 'creative writing' class her fondness for pallid verbs and vague adverbs, as well as her lack of sensory specificness, would be condemned. Worse, perhaps, is her failure to use metaphors – except when they are clichés. One has to strain to discover symbolism in her works, and even imaginative critics have not unearthed convincing archetypes from her novels. How can her fiction continue to be so widely praised?

We might begin an answer by considering the complementarity of the two commonest strictures on her fiction, that her subject-matter – middle-class girls getting married – is narrow and limited, while her language is generalized and abstract. Her language may be illustrated simply by the use of 'trade' in early chapters of *Pride and Prejudice*. Of the Bingleys it is observed: 'They were of a respectable family in the north of England; a circumstance more deeply impressed on their memories than that their brother's fortune and their own had been acquired by trade' (p. 15).[5] Sir William Lucas 'had formerly been in trade in Meryton.' And Mrs Bennet's brother is 'settled in London in a respectable line of trade.' What any of these people traded in we are never told. Referentially, 'trade' is abstract. But how 'trade' functions in the novel, what it stands against – namely, 'landed property' – is specific. Whatever his moral defects and lack of income, Mr Bennet is not in trade; Elizabeth's claim to an equality with Darcy because she is 'the daughter of a gentleman' is allowed by Lady Catherine. Because 'trade' has minimal referential specificity, the word possesses special strength in the verbal organization of the novel. The effectiveness of the verbal order depends on dramatic self-consistency, not upon the accuracy or vividness with which it refers to other, non-linguistic reality. In *Pride and Prejudice*'s verbal structure what counts is the potency with which 'trade' and 'property' (and other such terms) confront one another, not the exactness nor the comprehensiveness with which they refer to physical actualities outside the novel.

If we pay heed to the book's linguistic pattern, we can understand how Jane Austen succeeds in a style so dense – as Mark Schorer observed long ago – with dead metaphors, especially those deriving from the counting-house and the inherited estate.[6] Schorer's 'dead metaphor' is itself a dead metaphor. Jane Austen's metaphors are 'dead' as language referring to non-linguistic concerns. That does not prevent them from constituting the 'living' tissue of a novel as a self-consistent verbal design. One advantage of dead metaphors is that they can no longer die: they retain for us virtually the same effectiveness they possessed for Jane Austen's first readers. More important, dead metaphors function abstractly rather than concretely, strengthening the non-referential organization of the novel. They reinforce Jane Austen's mode of characterizing. In much the same fashion that she maneuvers 'trade' and 'property' she maneuvers the names we call her characters. They exist vitally only in opposition to one another. We know almost nothing of how they appear, or any sensory peculiarities. What we know about a character is how his or her personality contrasts against others.[7] So the more generally similar the characters are, the more effective are differentiations among them. Aesthetically, then, Jane Austen gains power by confining her characters to a single stratum of gentlefolk and by focusing on the sex whose activities were more inhibited by convention – the gain reflected by the minor value of her works as historical documents.

Her 'major' characters are not more historically significant than others but those most carefully distinguished from the greatest number of other characters. We know how Elizabeth is *un*like all the other characters. A minor figure, such as Mary, is differentiated specifically from only a few others. Yet if the 'minor' Mary engages in few differentiating relations, the relatively minor Jane encounters almost as many other people as Elizabeth. But Jane is discriminated in a simpler and more consistent fashion than her sister. Jane Austen teaches us that judgments of 'major' and 'minor' – like Forster's delightful 'flat' and 'round' – are misleading so far as they suggest only referential significance.

The lesson has large implications. Jane Austen's characters are 'vivid,' 'impressive,' even 'life-like' not because they are conceived or executed as 'real' people (who, unlike fictional people, are born and do die), but because they are rendered so consistently in terms of their function in the verbal structure of the novel. Jane Austen organizes her characters rather as phonemes are organized into language: the characters are effectively realized because focused by their discriminatory relations. They seem 'real,' paradoxically, because their representational validity is not allowed to interfere with their vitality as inter-defining forces in the verbal coherence of a fiction. This comment may seem strange to the point of perversity. But what do we mean by 'literary imagination' except the ability to conceive in linguistic form realities which for the less gifted are not so transposable? We would err should we treat any worthwhile novel only as a verbal organization. But criticism of fiction more often than not is vitiated by judgments too exclusively referential, even if unconsciously so. The novel, as Northrop Frye has insisted, operates in the ironic mode; its intrinsic nature is a shifting adjustment of existences, existence as a linguistic ordering and existence as an ordering of sociocultural actualities.[8] The chief problem in criticizing fiction is to remain alert to its moving balances, not to reduce a novel either to a mere pattern of language or to a mere representation of reality.

That the novel is necessarily both is revealed by plot. Sequence of events in a novel is less important than pacing of the sequence, purposeful variations in the speed with which events are reported. A novel is always in some essential fashion a story told rather than enacted. The form of a fictional plot, therefore, needs to be defined in terms of how the reader responds. A fine illustration of how fictional plot works is the account of Elizabeth's re-encounter with Darcy, a crucial event in *Pride and Prejudice.* From the time of Darcy's letter, the reader has been sure that Darcy and Elizabeth will meet again, but few hints have been given as to how they will be brought together. They meet by 'accident.' The Gardiners are unexpectedly forced to give up their Lake Country trip; finding themselves near Pemberley, they decide to visit it; by chance Darcy returns home a day early. At the beginning of Volume III, then, the reader's anticipations are realized by a random falling out of events, though he learns later that the force of Darcy's desire made such a meeting 'inevitable.' Jane Austen's narrative reveals the logic within social coincidence.[9] When the Gardiners plan to visit Derbyshire, necessarily for readers as well as Elizabeth 'there were many ideas connected.' It is as impossible for us as for her 'to see the word without thinking of Pemberley and its owner.' *Her* words crystallize *our* anticipations, so that we feel the self-deception in her next remark: '"But surely," said she, "I may enter his country with impunity, and rob it of a few petrified spars without his perceiving me"' (p. 239). It is not unfair to imagine Elizabeth 'saying' this to the disbelieving reader, for in the following pages suspense arises from Elizabeth's increasing assurance that she will not meet Darcy working against the reader's diminishing hopes that she will. That primary tension should thus be between character and reader is in accord with the circumstance that this narrative pivot is also a linguistic–thematic crux, exactly the point at which 'love' and 'property' begin to come together, that is, to create newly complex meanings in the mind of the reader.

Near the end of the novel Elizabeth replies to Jane's inquiry as to how long she has loved Darcy: 'It has been coming on so gradually, that I hardly know when it began. But I believe I must date it from my first seeing his beautiful grounds at Pemberley' (p. 373). Like all funny statements this one is fundamentally true, as we know from the first pages of the third volume. However fortuitous the falling out of social events, it is no verbal accident that Darcy and Elizabeth re-encounter amid the beauties of his magnificent estate. There, at first, Elizabeth 'saw and admired every remarkable spot and point of view . . . At that moment she felt, that to be mistress of Pemberley might be something!' Inside the house, she looks out of the drawing-room window (an owner's vantage-point) with delight. And 'as they passed into other rooms, these objects were taking different positions; but from every window there were beauties to be seen . . . "And of this place," thought she, "I might have been mistress!"' (p. 246). Verbal repetition set off by changes in tense helps us to experience the gradual transformation in Elizabeth's feelings toward Darcy. Having examined his land, then his home, she turns finally to his portrait, which we see her seeing 'with such a smile over the face, as she remembered to have sometimes seen, when he looked at her.' In the complex intensity of this development both her fearful and our pleasant expectations of Darcy's re-appearance are lost – until: 'As they walked across the lawn toward the river, Elizabeth turned back to look again; her uncle and aunt stopped also, and while the former was conjecturing as to the date of the building, the owner of it himself suddenly came forward from the road' (p. 251).

It is, as Elizabeth will later tell her sister, the owner of Pemberley she has learned to love. Mr Darcy is handsome, well-connected, and rich – fine attributes which would more than satisfy Miss Bingley, but 'insufficient' for 'a woman worthy of being pleased.' The owner of Pemberley is Mr Darcy – but more, a man of elegant yet robust taste, active in fulfilling social and personal responsibilities, admired and respected by worthy dependents; in fine, one capable of complementing Elizabeth's very different 'liveliness,' a vitality of personality not unconnected with her being the owner of nothing tangible.

Because referentially 'Fitzwilliam Darcy' and 'the owner of Pemberley' are the same, the linguistic distinction can be important. The dynamics of the novel's verbal design are finally to subsume one in the other, the union urging us to reconsider our understanding of realities to which the novel's key words refer. A successful fictional plot works through language to modify how we perceive reality. The chief ground of their interaction is character, or 'psychology,' the logic of inner motive a novel can reveal without theatrical exteriorizations. It is no accident that in *Pride and Prejudice* the culmination of events which begin Volume III and bring Darcy and Elizabeth together again turns on the emergence of her feeling of 'gratitude,' an emotion of appreciating awareness toward another: 'Gratitude, not merely for having once loved her, but for loving her still well enough, to forgive all the petulance and acrimony of her manner in rejecting him, and all the unjust accusations accompanying her rejection' (p. 265). From gratitude grows Elizabeth's love, a reasonable process in real life – though not in bad fiction, Jane Austen reminds us (p. 279). But reasonableness and social actualities aside, 'gratitude' and associated terms constitute the texture of a verbal interplay in Darcy's and Elizabeth's evolving relations throughout the book. To his first proposal she is forced to reply: 'It is natural that obligation should be felt, and if I could *feel* gratitude, I would now thank you. But I cannot – I have never desired your good opinion' (p. 190). This is a revelatory shock to a male protagonist (as we discover only much later) who must learn that the possessions of the owner of Pemberley are insufficient to overcome the repulsiveness of a Mr Darcy too confident of their potency. He learns because for the first time his selfishness (of 'practice' not 'principle') does not work, fails to fulfill his desire. The change initiated by this lesson precipitates his actions which draw forth the gratitude Elizabeth expresses to elicit his second proposal: 'I have been most anxious to acknowledge to you how gratefully I feel it. Were it known to the rest of my family, I should not have merely my own gratitude to express' (p. 365). 'If you *will* thank me,' he replies, 'let it be for yourself alone,' and he renews his offer. Elizabeth is now able to respond that 'her sentiments had undergone so material a change . . . as to make her receive with gratitude and pleasure, his present assurances' (p. 366). Because 'gratitude' is the mode of their interpersonal transactions, the culmination of their giving and receiving can be free admission of mutuality of authority. Darcy and Elizabeth finally depend on one another because each has come to respect the complementarity of the other's personality.

Darcy's and Elizabeth's final interdependence seems, however, to highlight an irreconcilable difference between her and our assumptions as to the nature of individual personality. The difference is not solely that for her individuality exists within a society pervasively hierarchical. For us, personality means, primarily, uniqueness, how one person exists separately, establishes an existential independence. This is one reason our novelists stress the sensory, useful for identifying peculiarity: each of us has his own smell.[10] For Jane Austen a personality exists only interactively. Or if we examine 'individuality' from a sociological point of view, we notice that our 'identity crises' never occur in her fiction. The question 'who am I?' arises when society does not comfortably answer it before it can be asked. While the societies depicted in Jane Austen's novels are neither so static nor so idyllic as is sometimes suggested, it is true that she does not (as we tend to) conceive social relations to be inherently in crisis. If our psychological and sociological presuppositions are so distinct from hers, and, as is obvious, if not enough of the cultural context of her art survives to permit a direct aesthetic (as distinct from antiquarian) appreciation of it, Jane Austen's twentieth-century popularity is, indeed, a wonder.

One ought probably to distinguish between 'meaning' and 'significance,' what a literary work determinately *is* from how it relates to something else, the distinction permitting discriminations between what a work meant to its author as opposed to how we choose to judge it.[11] There is reason for thinking that appreciation of literary art of another epoch is historical, including consciousness of how an earlier artist's beliefs and experiences differ from our own. Thus we can account for devout Christians admiring the *Iliad*, or latter-day atheists praising the *Divine Comedy*. But it seems difficult for many (particularly students knowing no history) to generate this aesthetic historicism in reading, for example, the historical fiction of Jane Austen's famous contemporary, Sir Walter Scott. We may need another kind of explanation for lasting success in a genre whose very name implies the fleeting interest of novelty.

To define what Jane Austen's works possess that Scott's do not, we might compare her fiction to the creations of the French mime, Marcel Marceau. He comes to mind because his performances are, like Jane Austen's, so bereft of all but the human performer. Yet Marceau, though always on stage alone, never represents a particular personality. He displays categories, occupation (mask-maker), physical size (Goliath), activity (walking), or biological condition (old age). But he does not present a category *as* a type: for the moment of the performance a class exists for us in individualized embodiment. This paradoxical realization depends, first, on the absence of everything but Marceau from the stage, but also on our knowledge of the 'cultural language' out of which an individuality is specified so 'abstractly.'[12] Unless you know, for example, what tight-rope walking is, Marceau's hilarious mime of an incompetent highwire man makes little sense. Marceau speaks to us of what we already know. Yet without his performance, we might not know that we know. Marceau's genius lies not so much in accurate imitating of human actions as in imitating them so that we may at least tacitly recognize their uniqueness. Anybody can pretend to lean on an invisible counter; Marceau pretends to lean so that we 'understand' how such leaning differs from other bodily actions.

Jane Austen's narrow subject-matter, genteel courtship, may be thought of as a Marceau-like 'abstract specification' not of gestures but of *forms* of civilized intercourse, modes of social transaction. Little of the etiquette of her society is portrayed in her novels: from them one could not learn how to behave faultlessly in early-nineteenth-century England. But one can learn from them much about the distinction, for instance, between genuine politeness and formalized courtesy. Her fiction enables us to discriminate underlying principles of personal relations. This is why, like so many fine novelists, she will appear to some readers 'immoral.' Her ethics cannot be comprehended within the prevailing code of conduct of her time. But because she uncovers ideal possibilities of relationship beneath specialized manifestations constituting a particular etiquette, her fiction persists as means for judging all kinds of manners, including those (inconceivable to her) of our time.

Jane Austen's characters are admirable or despicable depending on their accord with an essential system, which the actual etiquette of her time but imperfectly reflects. An anthropologist or social historian, so far as he sticks to his profession, reports how a specific group of people behave. A novelist reports their behavior as more or less revealing, and therefore defining, of an ideal of civilized intercourse. This is why referential elements in a novel must be integrated into a controlling verbal design: the combining permits evocation of a possible better order of civil intercourse through the medium articulating the inadequacy of actual social manners. The narrative of Darcy's courtship of Elizabeth embodies an ideal whose nature is indicated by the story's *failure* to confirm the hierarchical separations enunciated through the structure of early-nineteenth-century British society. Not revolutionary, the marriage of Darcy to Elizabeth nonetheless implies how class stratifications may for individuals be rendered liberative and fulfilling, not restrictive (as Lady Catherine would have them), without any yielding to the impulse for reductive levelling championed by Lydia, Wickham, and Mrs Bennet.

In sum, what is fictional in *Pride and Prejudice,* what is untrue to the life of Jane Austen's time, enables us a century and a half later to find new pleasure and value in her dead metaphors. Their order, the primary order of fictional art, allows us to escape simple referentiality, to respond to the novel with more than antiquarian interest. This is why one needs some such analogue as Marceau's performance to explain the novel's verbal form.[13] For what happens in *Pride and Prejudice* is not alone what happens to the characters, but also what happens – because of the novelist's word-arrangements – to those reading of the events.[14] *Pride and Prejudice* alerts us to this second tier of action because its primary adventures are so unspectacular. As pulp fiction proves that plots of violence may have little lasting effect, Jane Austen's gentility proves how an unexciting story may affect generations of readers.

Although it is impossible to illustrate briefly the enduring possibility of new pleasures preserved by the tidiness of Jane Austen's fictional structuring, the fame of *Pride and Prejudice*'s opening sentence allows a sketch not too misleadingly crude: 'It is a truth universally acknowledged, that a single man in possession of a good fortune, must be in want of a wife.'[15] That *we* thus begin in irony cannot be overemphasized. There are as yet no characters in the novel, and the first action of the fiction affects the reader by dislocating his expectations.[16] The disturbance initiated here is re-echoed at every level of the narrative and throughout determines the quality of the reader's experience. The sententious assurance of the first six words, seeming to prepare for a wise heartiness of traditional morality, is incongruous with the subsequent concern for marital status and income. But the sentence's conclusion with satisfying humor redeems the 'philosophic' promise of the opening words. Prefigured here is the pattern of the book's plot, which does not follow the simple contour of amusing anticlimax. Beautifully balanced – 'single man' and 'wife' are exquisitely placed, founded upon fine subordinate ironies (e.g., 'must') – the sentence as a *whole* resonates. For its periodicity, as critics have observed, displays genuine truth, though not the kind promised by the first phrase, and never likely to be 'universally acknowledged,' however generally applicable.

Not only substantively does *Pride and Prejudice* expand upon its originating sentence, reverberating between the verbal polarity/identity of 'good fortune'/'wife,' but also formally the novel's macrostructures recapitulate its genesis. Thus the totality of chapter 1, the discussion between Mr and Mrs Bennet – characteristically introducing Mr Bingley through an argument about the impossibility of getting to know him – is shaped analogously. What begins as 'normal,' expectable conversation quickly produces anomalies in relation: ' "Do not you want to know who has taken it?" cried his wife impatiently. "*You* want to tell me, and I have no objection to hearing it." ' (p. 3) The amusing triviality of this exchange evolves in the course of the novel into upsetting reversals of 'accepted' truths. Mr Bennet's humor at the expense of his wife's appearance and of his daughters' intelligence – 'They have none of them much to recommend them . . . they are all silly and ignorant' (p. 5) – will create ramifying implications until, in contrast to the dominant semantic association of 'land' with 'gentility,' Mr. Gardiner, though in trade in London and living in sight of his warehouses, will seem more a 'gentleman' than his land-holding brother-in-law. Mr Bennet's gentlemanliness is poisoned by psychological self-injury: his manner of speaking to his wife and his treatment of his daughters betrays profound self-disgust. Told that Elizabeth 'had never been blind to the impropriety of her father's behaviour as a husband' (p. 236), we understand that at issue is no mere quirk in Mr Bennet but the recurring human dilemma of multiple roles – adumbrated in the novel's first sentence – which points to the transctional problems of gifts and choices which make up social existence. We are fascinated by Mr Bennet's 'impropriety' as a husband because it consists less in public violations of formalized nineteenth-century etiquette than in a subtler subversion of rules of 'conjugal obligation and decorum' so as destructively to indulge his bitterness at 'the disappointment which his own imprudence had brought on' (p. 236).

It is through such complicating, amplifying, and intensifying of originating disequilibria set up in the reader's mind (e.g., the suggestion of a potential for incompatibility between 'good fortune' and 'wife') that *Pride and Prejudice* fictionalizes into visibility what I have called essential or ideal relations, such as true politeness. Enrichment of our apprehensive powers occurs through a continuously developing interaction between referential and verbal vectors, our perception of the distinction between the two being necessary to our recognition of the work's truth as 'fictional' truth, a truth different in kind, not degree, from non-fictional truth. That is why it takes imagination to enjoy fiction, not only to write it, and why, finally, it is not enough to praise, as we all must, Jane Austen's irony. More wonderful, so more exemplary, is her adroit use of verbal irony to make us aware of language's relation to persisting ironies inherent in the performances constituting social reality.

NOTES

1 Evidence for Jane Austen's critical esteem is the recent spate of books about her, amongst which I have found most helpful: Lloyd W. Brown, *Bits of Ivory: Narrative Techniques in Jane Austen's Fiction* (Baton Rouge: Louisiana State University Press, 1973); Alistair M. Duckworth, *The Improvement of the Estate* (Baltimore: Johns Hopkins Press, 1971); Darrel Mansell, *The Novels of Jane Austen* (London: Macmillan, 1973); Stuart M. Tave. *Some Words of Jane Austen* (Chicago: University of Chicago Press, 1973).

2 My remark is in no way intended to denigrate Auerbach's masterful work.

3 See 'Linguistics and Poetics,' *Style in Language*, ed. Thomas A. Sebeok (Cambridge, Mass.: Massachusetts Institute of Technology Press, 1960), pp. 350–77.

4 *The Ambassadors*, Book I, 3, ed. S. P. Rosenbaum (New York: W. W. Norton, 1964), p. 39.

5 I am using *Pride and Prejudice* as exemplary of Jane Austen's art because it appears to be the most widely known and frequently taught of the novels. All quotations are from *The Novels of Jane Austen*, ed. R. W. Chapman, 3rd ed., Vol. II (London: Oxford University Press, 1933).

6 My specific reference is to Schorer's introduction to *Pride and Prejudice* (Boston: Houghton-Mifflin, 1956), pp. xv-xvi, though this essay is dependent on his 'Fiction and the "Analogical Matrix," ' *Critiques and Essays on Modern Fiction*, selected by John W. Aldridge (New York: Ronald Press, 1952), pp. 83–98.

7 That Jane Austen is concerned with a phenomenon of widespread significance to her age can be illustrated by a comparison of her novels with Goethe's *Elective Affinities*. For example, after observing that 'opposite dispositions are the best basis for a very close union,' one of Goethe's characters immediately observes that 'affinities really become interesting only when they bring about separations.' See *Elective Affinities*, trans. Elizabeth Mayer and Louise Bogan (Chicago: Henry Regenery, 1963), ch. 4, p. 40.

8 Northrop Frye, *Anatomy of Criticism*, revised ed. (New York: Atheneum, 1966), pp. 33–52, 60–6, 248–50, 303–14. It should be clear by now that, unlike Frye, I use 'novel' and 'fiction' as synonymous terms in this essay.

9 The great Marxian critic George Lukács has identified this as a crucial issue. 'The key question is: what is meant by "chance" in fiction? Without chance all narration is dead and abstract. No writer can portray life if he eliminates the fortuitous. On the other hand, in his representation of life he must go beyond crass accident and elevate chance to the inevitable.' See *Writer and Critic*, trans. Arthur Kohn (London: Merlin, 1970), p. 112.

10 Because a reader must deal with a novel's specific language-structure on its own terms, since there are no others, we do not in *Pride and Prejudice* 'miss' sensory details. By the same token we do not regret the absence of Jane Austen's elegantly formalistic diction from *Lady Chatterley's Lover*. The coherence of Lawrence's novel is built up in one fashion, of Austen's

in another. But *neither* Lawrence nor Jane Austen holds up actual
manners as a model for posterity's admiration. Each reveals through a
verbal structure *potentialities* of civilized behavior.

11 On this distinction consult E. D. Hirsch, Jr, *Validity in Interpretation*
(New Haven: Yale University Press, 1967), especially pp. 140–3.

12 On the complexities of such specification, see two articles in the *Times
Literary Supplement*: Tzvetan Todorov, 'Artistic Language and Ordinary
Language,' 5 October 1973, 1169–70; and Hubert Damisch, 'Semiotics
and Iconography,' 12 October 1973, 1221–2.

13 In the sense in which I use the term, 'performance' is equally important to
all of Jane Austen's novels, though Howard S. Babb in his fine *Jane
Austen's Novels: The Fabric of Dialogue* (Columbus: Ohio State
University Press, 1962) uses 'performance' to distinguish *Pride and
Prejudice*.

14 To a degree I simply develop the point of Ronald S. Crane in his
remarkable essay, 'The Concept of Plot and the Plot of "Tom Jones"';
e.g.: 'For a plot, in the enlarged sense here given to the term, is not merely
a particular synthesis of particular materials of character, thought, and
action, but such a synthesis endowed necessarily, because it imitates in
words a sequence of human activities, with a power to affect our opinions
and emotions in a certain way.' See *Critics and Criticism*, abridged ed.
(Chicago: University of Chicago Press, 1957), p. 67.

15 Among the many who have commented on the first sentence, I might
single out Robert A. Donovan, *The Shaping Vision* ((Ithaca: Cornell
University Press, 1966), pp. 18–19, because this excellent critic so
unnecessarily (it seems to me) restricts his commentary to content.

16 Psychological reasons for, and constraints upon, fictional 'dislocating' are
brilliantly set forth by Simon O. Lesser, *Fiction and the Unconscious*
(New York: Random House, Vintage Ed., 1962 [1957]). 'Dislocating' raises
issues of theoretical importance, being related, for example, to
Shklovsky's 'defamiliarization' – see *The Theory of the Novel: New
Essays*, ed. John Halperin (New York and London: Oxford University
Press, 1974), especially p. 380. Halperin on p. 387, n. 10, links
Shklovsky's concept to Ortega, and I think the parallel would be worth
developing – e.g., 'we do not consider real what actually happens but a
certain manner of happening that is familiar to us . . . not so much what
we see as what we know.' See Ortega y Gasset, *Meditations on Quixote*,
trans. Evelyn Rugg and Diego Marín (New York: W.W. Norton and Co.,
1961), p. 132.

R. F. BRISSENDEN

Mansfield Park:
freedom and the family

I

For those who have succumbed to its unique power and fascination,
Mansfield Park is if not the greatest at least the most interesting of
Jane Austen's novels. As Alistair M. Duckworth has recently argued, it
is 'fundamental to Jane Austen's thought.'[1] Yet there exists a healthy
and respectable tradition of sceptical and unsympathetic criticism of
the work; and even its staunchest supporters must admit that the task
of defending the book, of explaining just *why* it should strike them as
such a great novel, is not simple or easy. Fanny Price clearly poses a
problem. She appears, at least to begin with, to be shy, weak, frail and
rather solemn – and it is impossible to believe that the novelist who
created characters so sparkling, brilliant and energetic as Elizabeth
Bennet and Emma Woodhouse did not realize this. Jane Austen was
an unusually gifted parodist – so, clearly, she must have known what
she was doing when she allowed her heroine to moralize over the
beauties of nature in the accents of Hannah More or Ann Radcliffe.[2]
Just as clearly she must have realized that, in outline at least, the plot
is almost glibly sentimental: when Fanny marries Edmund and
moves into the parsonage at Mansfield Park, virtue appears to be
rewarded as unequivocally as it is in Richardson's *Pamela*. And in the
allocation of punishments to the guilty and foolish – Julia and Maria,
the Crawfords and aunt Norris – poetic justice is scrupulously
observed.[3]

156

One would expect that the dénouement of a novel structured according to this formula would seem distressingly flat and artificial. On the contrary, there is something profoundly and strangely satisfying about the conclusion of *Mansfield Park*: despite the formulaic patness with which everything is wound up, there is a sense in which it 'finishes' more strongly than any of the other novels. And it is generally agreed – even by many of those who are unhappy with the book as a whole – that the penultimate section of *Mansfield Park*, the Portsmouth episode in which Fanny returns for a period to her family, is an unusually powerful piece of writing. Indeed there is, I think, no other passage in Jane Austen's fiction of comparable length in which the physical setting is so important or in which it is rendered with such vivid and sensuous concreteness. And the depiction of the vulgar realities of the Price household is not simply an exercise in naturalism for its own sake: Fanny's involvement with and response to the house and her family are deeply felt and intense – all the more intense, perhaps, because they are only imperfectly understood by Fanny herself. Psychologically the experience is distressing to the point of torment – and this is the main reason why her return from Portsmouth to Mansfield Park and Edmund should bring with it such an authentic sense of release and fulfilment. But neither the Portsmouth episode nor the conclusion stands alone: they have been prepared for by everything that has gone before and can be properly read only in the context of the novel as a whole. An examination of these later sections of the book would seem at any rate to offer a way to account in part for the sense of power, coherence and range of significance with which a reading of the novel finally leaves us.[4]

II

It is the combination of detailed physical realism and complex psychological response that gives the Portsmouth scenes their peculiar quality. It is not merely the Price house and family we are presented with, but these as perceived and experienced by Fanny. Her every sense is assaulted by the noisy, constricted, slovenly chaos in which her parents and the other children live; while at the same time the news she continually receives – through letters, visitors and even the newspaper – of the other world of Mansfield and London shocks her into a fresh sense both of herself and of the people with whom, over the last few years and months, she has been most intimately associated. The grubby particularity with which Jane Austen depicts the late afternoon scene in the Price parlor, for instance, is immediately striking. What makes it especially interesting, however, is the way in which it is related to the developing action of the novel:

157

The sun's rays falling strongly into the parlour instead of cheering, made her still more melancholy; for sun-shine appeared to her a totally different thing in a town and in the country. Here, its power was only a glare, a stifling, sickly glare, serving but to bring forward stains and dirt that might otherwise have slept. There was neither health nor gaiety in sun-shine in a town. She sat in a blaze of oppressive heat, in a cloud of moving dust; and her eyes could only wander from the walls marked by her father's head to the table cut and knotched by her brothers, where stood the tea-board never thoroughly cleaned, the cups and saucers wiped in streaks, the milk a mixture of motes floating in thin blue, and the bread and butter growing every minute more greasy than even Rebecca's hands had first produced it.[5]

The physical sordidness of the scene in Portsmouth is matched almost immediately by the moral sordidness of the scene in London; as Fanny watches the sunlight 'bring forward stains and dirt that might otherwise have slept', her father comes upon the paragraph in his newspaper which reveals that Henry Crawford has eloped with Maria Rushworth. The parallel between the exposure of the grease and dirt in the Portsmouth parlor and the exposure of the 'matrimonial *fracas* in the family of Mr R. of Wimpole Street'[6] may not have been consciously intended by the author, but it is beautifully congruous; and it evidences, if nothing else, the intensity with which Jane Austen's imagination is working at this point.

Although Fanny is profoundly shocked by the news (if not, in her innermost heart, altogether surprised), she has already reached and passed through the real climax of her Portsmouth experiences. This occurs when she acknowledges first to herself and then, more or less by default, to her parents, that her true home is Mansfield Park. Her return there was supposed to have taken place after Easter – a significant season in view of the novel's central concern with religious values – but Easter comes and goes, the spring approaches, and Fanny continues to pass her days 'in a state of penance,'[7] longing to be back with the people she loves and who she now knows love her.

Her eagerness, her impatience, her longings to be with them were such as to bring a line or two of Cowper's Tirocinium for ever before her. 'With what intense desire she wants her home,' was continually on her tongue . . . When she had been coming to Portsmouth, she had loved to call it her home, had been fond of saying that she was going home; the word had been very dear to her; and so it still was, but it must be applied to Mansfield. *That* was now the home. Portsmouth was Portsmouth; Mansfield was home.[8]

The coming of spring makes her absence from her true home even more agonizing: 'She had not known before, how much the beginnings and process of vegetation had delighted her. – What animation both of body and mind, she had derived from watching the advance of that season . . . from the earliest flowers, in the warmest divisions of her aunt's garden, to the opening of leaves of her uncle's plantations, and the glory of his woods.'[9] Mansfield Park, where Fanny – and the reader – now realize she belongs, is here firmly associated with all the processes of life and growth. Even more significantly the advance of spring – and specifically of spring at Mansfield – is seen as the signal for Fanny's own *'animation* both of body and mind.' Since the most noticeable thing about Fanny has been her inactivity – 'Fanny is almost totally passive . . . [she] triumphs by doing nothing,' Tony Tanner observes[10] – the choice of the word 'animation' in this context is of singular importance. And it is followed soon after by another word which, earlier in the novel, we should have been surprised to find associated with either Fanny or Mansfield Park, although in this context, like 'animation,' it seems perfectly appropriate. The word is 'liberty': 'To be losing such pleasures was no trifle; to be losing them, because she was in the midst of closeness and noise, to have confinement, bad air, bad smells, substituted for liberty, freshness, fragrance, and verdure, was infinitely worse.'[11] For the greater part of the novel Mansfield Park under the firm hand of Sir Thomas Bertram has seemed to exemplify the sort of restricted and rigid order that can be maintained only through the exercise of strict authority. Liberty, just as clearly, would appear to have been represented by the Crawfords – energetic, lively, always on the move and with no responsibility to anyone but themselves. And yet as the novel works towards its conclusion it becomes patent that the freedom enjoyed by Mary and Henry Crawford is illusory – they and the people with whom they have been so ruinously associated are trapped, while Fanny and Edmund are liberated.

III

Mansfield Park concludes with its heroine attaining two things – her rightful place as a member of her true family, and her freedom. In this it resembles that otherwise very different novel, *Emma.* Emma Woodhouse, of course, is her own mistress from the beginning – what she has to learn is how to exercise her freedom responsibly. Only when she has done this can she be considered worthy to marry Knightley. And her marriage, like Fanny's, it is worth noting, is very much within the family – Knightley is Emma's brother-in-law; and their relationship for much of the novel is more like that of brother and sister than that of lovers. At the beginning of *Mansfield Park* Fanny appears to have very little freedom – she is certainly far from being her own mistress. Yet in the most important matters – matters of principle, integrity and self-respect – she demonstrates as the novel develops that she has more real freedom than any of the other characters. When she eventually marries Edmund, and thus becomes a member of the Mansfield family, we feel that like Emma – though by a different process and by starting from a very different position – she too has earned the right to be where she is. We feel also, and are meant to feel, that a principle has been demonstrated in action, tested and vindicated. The struggle in Fanny's case, however, has been much sterner and more distressing than it is to be in Emma's.

In permitting Fanny to reconcile so successfully her desire to preserve her liberty of moral choice and her desire to remain the member of a family, Jane Austen succeeds in resolving a conflict that, in one guise or another, forms a centrally significant source of the life and action of many of the major novels of the eighteenth century. It is, of course, of fundamental importance in the work of Samuel Richardson. Each of his three heroines is concerned to a greater or lesser degree with the question of personal freedom; and there is a perceptible development from *Pamela* through *Clarissa* to *Sir Charles Grandison* in the subtlety and sophistication with which Richardson explores the issue. Pamela, as a servant, is in the lowliest and most helpless position – yet she is still a member of Mr B.'s 'family.'[12] And she succeeds in remaining a member of that family, at a much higher level, and on her own terms, only because, like Fanny, she pleads for the right to exercise her freedom: 'Whatever you have to propose, whatever you intend by me, let my assent be that of a free person, mean as I am, and not that of a sordid slave who is to be threatened and frightened into a compliance.'[13] At the other end of the scale Harriet Byron, rich and independent, is at the beginning of *Sir Charles Grandison* in a position very similar to that of Emma; and the manner in which she exercises her freedom is clearly meant to demonstrate that she deserves to become the wife of Richardson's Christian hero.

In *Clarissa* the issues are presented more starkly and are explored in tragic depth. The crucial word 'family' occurs in the very first sentence of the novel – and it is the word with which the long story is concluded.[14] Enclosed within the circle of the family, Clarissa endeavors to preserve her moral freedom – even if it is merely the freedom to say 'No.' All she wants, she tells her mother, is 'the liberty of *refusal,* which belongs to [her] sex.'[15] When this is denied her both by her family and by Lovelace, who rapes her, Clarissa's only course is to die: with her moral freedom intact she forsakes the earthly family for the heavenly one, going, as she ambiguously tells Lovelace, to wait for him at 'her father's house.'

It is well recognized both that Jane Austen writes in the tradition initiated and established by Richardson and that there are some particularly close parallels between Fanny Price's situation and those in which Pamela and Clarissa find themselves: Fanny clearly belongs to the sisterhood of virtuous and distressed heroines. But although in her case as in Pamela's virtue is triumphant, the relationship between Fanny and Clarissa – or between *Mansfield Park* and Richardson's novel – is the more interesting of the two, and this as much for the differences as for the similarities. To begin with, Fanny Price is not just another Clarissa Harlowe – initially at least she is both physically and psychologically a much frailer character. But she is subject to very similar pressures, and her response to these pressures is basically the same as that of Richardson's heroine: she insists merely on 'the liberty of *refusal*,' and the longer she insists on this right the stronger she becomes. Unlike Clarissa, however, she is permitted, after a struggle, to enjoy this liberty; and the moral validity of her stand is thoroughly vindicated by the outcome of events. When Edmund intervenes on her behalf over her refusal to take part in the play, for instance, he speaks more prophetically than he realizes: 'Do not urge her, madam . . . it is not fair to urge her in this manner. – You see she does not like to act. – Let her choose for herself as well as the rest of us. – Her judgment may be quite as safely trusted.'[16] As the action of the novel eventually demonstrates, no one's judgment can be safely trusted except Fanny's: she should indeed have been allowed to choose – not merely for herself, but for all of them.

Whether Jane Austen intended it or not, *Mansfield Park* reads at times as if it is meant to be taken as the comic, or at least non-tragic, version of *Clarissa*. The real terrors of Clarissa's situation are constantly invoked only to be dispelled by Fanny's determination to persist in her right to refuse to be pushed around unjustly. Sir Thomas's anger and displeasure at her rejection of Crawford's proposal are expressed in terms that echo the language of Harlowe Place – but once he sees that she cannot be shaken he treats Fanny humanely and with sympathy and respect. The spirit she shows here in fact earns her the right to be received as a true member of the Mansfield family.

The parallels between *Clarissa* and *Mansfield Park* are in some places remarkably close. The misrule both at Harlowe Place and at Mansfield Park, for example, occurs partly because the children are able to usurp the authority of an ineffectual father – ineffectual through illness in the one case and absence in the other. And the situa-

161

tion is made worse in each instance through the interference of an agent who represents thoroughly libertine principles. Henry Crawford, though charming, is as subtly sadistic and as mischievous as Lovelace, and his actions follow a surprisingly similar pattern. Like Lovelace he plays with the formalities of precedence in courtship. By rights he should offer himself to Julia – instead he courts Maria, who is engaged to Rushworth. Then in true Lovelace fashion, after leading Maria on, he disappoints her, forces her into a loveless marriage, courts her again and finally destroys her. He again flouts convention by paying court to Fanny instead of to Julia. And his flirtation with Fanny is initiated in a spirit of idle, *rational* mischief-making: 'I must take care of my *mind*,' he tells his sister; 'my plan is to make Fanny Price in love with me.'[17] Like Lovelace and Laclos's Valmont, another libertine villain, he tries to win her by assuming the appearance of generosity and benevolence – he arranges for her brother's advancement in the navy and he ostentatiously assumes his responsibilities as landlord. And in the end – again following the well-established pattern – he finds that he has been snared in his own net: he is the one who falls in love, who finds that his freedom is illusory; it is the girl who resists, and in this case retains her liberty. Crawford is not such a calculating villain as Lovelace; but he is an irresponsible and selfish man, and his actions lead directly to the ruin of Julia and Maria. His villainy also threatens Fanny, but it is deflected before it can harm her: true to the non-tragic spirit of the novel, the heroine is permitted to exercise the freedom of choice which she feels to be her right, and to survive. Not only does she survive, but she survives both as a free individual and as a member of her true family.

Crawford, of course, does not work alone: he is partnered and assisted in his libertinism by his sister. And the two of them are shown always – if for the most part lightly and amusingly – as offering a licentious threat to the established order and stability of the family. On the visit to Sotherton, for instance, there is a direct confrontation in the chapel between Fanny's vision of the family and Mary's mockery of it:

> 'There is something in a chapel and chaplain so much in character with a great house, with one's ideas of what such a household should be! A whole family assembling regularly for the purpose of prayer, is fine!' 'Very fine indeed!' said Miss Crawford, laughing. 'It must do the heads of the family a great deal of good to force all the poor housemaids and footmen to . . . say their prayers here twice a day.'[18]

The whole chapel scene consists in a delicately complex series of encounters between true and false (or traditional and sceptical) views of the family, of feeling, and of religion. The climax comes when Henry Crawford blatantly flirts with Maria as she stands beside her intended husband. His whispered comment, 'I do not like to see Miss Bertram so near the altar,'[19] is as resonant with implications and over-tones as is his sister's remark to Edmund later in the garden: 'We have taken such a serpentine course . . . since we left the first great path.'[20]

This whole chapter, and particularly the episode in the garden, is one of the richest and most brilliant passages in Jane Austen's fiction. With a touch at once light and supremely assured, she sets the immediate problems that beset the Bertram family in the context of the Edenic myth – the locked gates, the garden, the wilderness, the innocent and helpless heroine: all these evoke without over-empha-sizing the larger implications of the situation. And it is the wit and tact with which Jane Austen has achieved this that impresses us most. There was nothing particularly new in providing such a frame of refer-ence for a contemporary situation: the fall of man and the expulsion from paradise stand somewhere in the background of many of the most substantial works of literature produced during the century and a half preceding *Mansfield Park*. And the garden of Eden legend, of course, lends a particularly illuminating significance, and a religious and historical dimension, to any treatment of the conflict between the individual and the family. 'In leaving her "father's house" by way of the garden,' Mr Duckworth observes, 'Clarissa is clearly, in some sense, repeating the expulsion of man from Eden.'[21] In *Tom Jones* the parallel is drawn even more directly: Tom has his freedom thrust upon him when he is thrown out of Paradise Hall. Once he has learnt to temper his liberty with responsibility, however – to act with 'prudence' – he is restored to the family. And for Tom, his ideal family and his real family turn out to be the same: he is recognized as the legitimate heir and blood-relative of Allworthy, his foster father. In contrast to Clarissa, he is thus enabled to re-enter 'Paradise' and be reunited with his 'heavenly' father while still on earth.

The significance of the concepts of individual freedom and the family extended far beyond the domestic circle: they could be made to carry the widest of social, political and religious connotations. According to traditional Christian social theory, the family was the microcosm of society: the duty owed by the child to its parents was analogous to the duty owed by the citizen to priests, judges, governors and kings, and they in turn were seen as owing a similarly filial duty to God the heavenly father. In seventeenth-century works of piety such as Jeremy Taylor's *Holy Living and Holy Dying* this hierarchical and familial structure was set forth in rigidly formal terms. Conduct books such as *The Whole Duty of Man* and Defoe's *Family Instructor* examined the role of the family much more realistically – but they still firmly advocated the view that a proper understanding of what Richardson termed 'the SOCIAL and RELATIVE DUTIES' in the domestic sphere must inevitably lead to a proper understanding of the same duties in the larger social sphere: a good and obedient child must make a good and obedient citizen.[22]

The period during which the conduct book flourished and the novel was born also saw the emergence of libertiné and pornographic literature: *Clarissa, Tom Jones* and *Fanny Hill* were published within a few months of each other. And it is interesting that the authors of some of the most significant works in this *genre* also looked on the family as the microcosm of society – although they saw it not as a structure which needed to be defended and maintained but as one to be subverted, completely transformed or utterly destroyed. 'Libertinism,' as David Foxon has pointed out, became throughout Europe 'a fashionable and pervasive mode of thought whose freedom related to religion, politics and society as well as to sexual life.'[23] In Nicolas Chorier's *Satyra Sotadica* (c.1660) 'all perversions are welcome if they gratify the senses . . . Lesbian love, seduction of the young and innocent, multiple copulation, flagellation and more subtle forms of sadism. But above all, these take place within a tightly knit family, with the shocking suggestion that all the conventional relationships of society are merely a façade for personal gratification.'[24]

The prohibition of incest is one of the most powerful, if not the most powerful, of all taboos. An obvious reason for its strength is that the urges it seeks to control are themselves extremely powerful. The taboo against incest prevents us from expressing in full, adult, physically sexual terms our love for those very people with whom from childhood we have had the strongest emotional ties. It also forces us to put the other members of the family into separate, hierarchically distinct compartments. Conversely, the effect of breaking the taboo is to place the incestuous members of the family on an absolutely equal footing – the sexual relationship takes them out of the family hierarchy and establishes them as adult peers. (Pamela acknowledges this transforming effect of the sexual bond when she asserts – and eventually asserts successfully – her right to be treated as an individual human being by Mr B. when he approaches her as a lover, and not as a servant or even, ultimately, as a woman. Mr B., as head of the household, stands, of course, initially in a *paternal* relationship to his servants.) In the fantasy of the thoroughly bisexually incestuous family, therefore, we have the ultimate resolution of the conflict between familial order and authority and the urge to individual freedom. In the anarchic fantasies of Sade, writing nearly a century and a half after Chorier, there is no compromise between the family and the individual. For him the attainment of individual freedom depends on the utter desecration and destruction of all family ties. One of the high points in the career of his libertine heroine Juliette, for instance, comes when she succeeds in making her father have intercourse with her, then murders him and finally aborts the child she has conceived during the encounter.[25]

One may well ask what the nightmare world of the pornographic novel has to do with the relatively sunlit normality of most eighteenth- and early-nineteenth-century fiction – and especially with *Mansfield Park*. But incest is a recurring theme in literature;[26] and it plays a particularly significant role in some of the major novels of the period. (It also adds an extra *frisson* of horror to a number of minor Gothic and sentimental novels.) The possibility of incest temporarily thwarts the lovers in *Joseph Andrews*, for instance; and in *Tom Jones* it occupies a central and thematically relevant position in the whole action of the novel. The sexual adventure in which Tom acts at once with the greatest freedom, the greatest honor and the most unthinking generosity is his liaison with Mrs Waters. This is also the adventure which carries with it the threat of the most terrible punishment – and which leads directly to the happy transformation of Tom's fortunes at the conclusion of the novel. Mrs Waters is Tom's putative mother; and when, some time after their sexual encounter, he learns her identity he touches the depths of misery and horror. But she turns out, of course, not to be his mother at all – and more significantly it is she who, by revealing the truth, magically restores him to his birthright. Thus by at once invoking the possibility and evading the reality of incest, Tom brings about the conditions necessary for the happy and triumphant resolution of his difficulties.

In *Mansfield Park*, too, incest plays an extremely significant though less immediately obvious role. The alliance between Edmund and Fanny has distinctly incestuous overtones; and it is these, I believe, that give the relationship between these two rather ordinary people its underlying power. Not only does *Mansfield Park* have a wider range of social significance than any of Jane Austen's other novels, but it also has much greater psychological depth and complexity. This is why the marriage of Edmund to Fanny is something more than a conventional happy ending: it is a union which affords satisfaction at a number of levels, not all of which are directly apparent.

Fanny's strongest overt feelings are for her blood-brother William, who, although he appears only briefly, is also the most lively and the most likable of the male characters in the novel. And from the very beginning Edmund is closely linked with William in the minds of both Fanny and the reader. When Edmund discovers Fanny sobbing on the stairs soon after her arrival at Mansfield, he learns that of all her family it is William she misses most – and Edmund's first kindness to his cousin is to make it possible for her to send a letter to her brother. Later on Crawford also realizes the importance of William in Fanny's life – and he finally becomes 'an interesting object' to her when he arranges for William's advancement in the navy.

If William were not her brother he would make an ideal husband for Fanny – and they do in fact take great delight in talking of the time when William will have enough prize money 'to make the little cottage comfortable, in which he and Fanny [are] to pass all their middle and later life together.'[27] She cannot marry him, of course, and it would be absurd to suggest that she would consciously think of doing so. It is not surprising, however, that she should fall in love with Edmund, who, when she moves to Mansfield Park, assumes the part in her life played at Portsmouth by William. Edmund's role as her surrogate brother is confirmed by Fanny's acknowledgement of Mansfield as her 'true' home and Sir Thomas and Lady Bertram as her 'true' parents. And Edmund himself adds further confirmation when, after the scandal has broken, he calls for Fanny at Portsmouth: 'She found herself pressed to his heart with only these words, just articulate, "My Fanny – my only sister – my only comfort now."'[28] The marriage thus can be seen as fulfilling the forbidden incestuous dream of giving complete sexual expression to the feelings of love and affection we have for the closest members of our own family. When she marries Edmund, Fanny really does come 'home' to Mansfield Park.

And the incestuous significance of the relationship is openly pointed to in the first chapter of the novel. When Sir Thomas hesitates before finally agreeing to take Fanny into the household, Mrs Norris has no doubts at all about what is bothering him – nor about what will happen:

> 'You are thinking of your sons – but do not you know that of all things upon earth *that* is the least likely to happen; brought up as they would be, always together like brothers and sisters? It is morally impossible . . . It is in fact the only sure way of providing against the connection. Suppose her a pretty girl, and seen by Tom or Edmund a few years hence, and I dare say there would be mischief . . . But breed her up with them from this time, and suppose her even to have the beauty of an angel, and she will never be more to either than a sister.'[29]

Fanny, of course, becomes much more than a sister to Edmund. But her marriage to her cousin, like Tom Jones's affair with the woman assumed to be his mother, invokes the taboo of incest without in fact breaking it. Fanny is allowed to have her cake and eat it too: the incestuous freedom of her action is sanctified, and serves to confirm and strengthen her position within the family. (Also within the schematic polarization of the characters which eventually takes place Edmund and Fanny assume the role of the good brother and sister in opposition to the bad brother and sister, Henry and Mary.)

And the significance of the marriage, with which the book concludes, is heightened when it is set beside the central episode in the novel – the abortive theatrical. The performance of *Lovers' Vows*, as a number of people have pointed out,[30] threatens to subvert the established domestic arrangements at Mansfield – to disrupt the basic family order. Edmund initially opposes the scheme because he realizes it may have this effect; and when he finally agrees to take part it is to prevent the intrusion into the family circle of a comparative stranger. He is distressed, he tells Fanny, at the thought of

> 'the mischief that *may*, of the unpleasantness that *must* arise from a young man's being received in this manner – domesticated among us – authorized to come at all hours – and placed suddenly upon a footing which must do away all restraints. To think only of the license which every rehearsal must tend to create.'[31]

Despite Edmund's participation in the play, every rehearsal does in fact lead to licence – the lovers, Henry Crawford and Maria Bertram, make their vows, or at least begin the relationship which is to culminate in their tragically foolish elopement, an act which effectively damages two families – the Rushworths and the Bertrams. And, significantly, Crawford carries on the flirtation in a dramatic situation which invokes the specters of illicit sexuality and of incest. In the role of Frederick he plays the illegitimate son of Agatha, the part in the play taken by Maria. Under the eyes of her sister Julia (whose affections he has publicly trifled with) and of her intended husband, Rushworth, Crawford begins his seduction of Maria. The 'son,' indeed, is flagrantly wooing the 'mother' at the very instant when Julia 'with a face all aghast' bursts in with the news that Sir Thomas (the real father) has unexpectedly arrived home – the moment which marks the crucial turning point in the action of the novel:

> At the moment of [Julia's] appearance, Frederick was listening with looks of devotion to Agatha's narrative, and pressing her hand to his heart, and as soon as she could notice this, and see that, in spite of the shock of her words, he still kept his station and retained her sister's hand, her wounded heart swelled again with injury,
> and . . . she turned out of the room saying 'I need not be afraid of appearing before him.'[32]

For Maria, however, 'the very circumstance which had driven Julia away, was to her the sweetest support. Henry Crawford's retaining her hand at . . . a moment of such proof and importance, was worth ages of doubt and anxiety. She hailed it as an earnest of the most serious determination.'[33] Henry's flirtation with Maria is the fulcrum upon which the action of *Mansfield Park* is poised: from this moment the fortunes of Maria and Julia begin to decline and those of Fanny to rise; the ideally true Bertram family takes over from the flesh and blood 'false' family; and the licentious freedom of the Crawfords is exposed and contrasted with the authentic liberty represented by Fanny. And it is interesting if nothing more that just as in *Tom Jones* this central pivotal action should consist in a sexual encounter (though at a very different level) between a 'son' and his 'mother.'

IV

Mansfield Park may excite our admiration but it does not always arouse our affection. Edmund is a dull stick and Fanny – no matter how much we may come to sympathize with her – is something of a prig. 'To invite Mr and Mrs Edmund Bertram round for the evening,' as Kingsley Amis says, 'would not be lightly undertaken.'[34] One can understand even whilst one does not in any way endorse his condemnation of Edmund and Fanny as 'morally destestable' and of *Mansfield Park* as an 'immoral book.'[35] Yet the savagery of Amis's response is an index of the novel's quality: 'its greatness,' as Lionel Trilling says, '[is] commensurate with its power to offend.'[36] This greatness depends, I would suggest, both on its range of social and moral significance and on the complex, dynamic and vital web of motivations, desires, compulsions and affections by which the main characters are linked to each other – in other words, on its psychological depth. What makes the book offensive to some readers, I suspect, is that there appears to be a discrepancy between the dramatic power which it generates, especially in its concluding sections, and the personal and moral stature of the heroine and hero. Yet this discrepancy is part of the novel's final meaning. Fanny *is* a slight, frail, mainly passive character, one who for the most part responds to pressure from other people rather than one who initiates action; Edmund has sound ideas and good intentions but lacks robustness and clarity of vision. They may be admirable, but they are also limited. Jane Austen is clearly aware of their limitations – yet just as clearly she intends them to be the moral centers of the novel. They belong, indeed, to a well-established moral tradition: together they embody, though in an etiolated and fragile form, that blend of sensibility and principle, of feeling and rationality, which had been advocated by Christian apologists and by the British moral philosophers of the preceding century and celebrated and explored by its major novelists. Fanny is, in the best sense of the word, a *sentimental* heroine: she exemplifies both the belief that it is the right and the duty of the individual to follow freely the dictates of his or her own conscience and benevolent instincts, and the hope that in a properly ordered society it will be possible for the individual to do so. But by the time *Mansfield Park* came to be written neither the continuing existence of the established structure of society nor the notion of man's innate benevolence could be taken for granted. The values represented by Fanny and Edmund are under attack; and although Mansfield Park escapes improvement and the Bertram family is revitalized by its taking in Fanny as a member, these things happen in the midst of a restless, changing and threatening world. It is a world, moreover, which is seen by Jane Austen with a very clear and unsentimental eye. Although there can be no doubt as to her moral assessment of the Crawfords, she does not altogether condemn them: their charm is genuine, and although they are dangerous and irresponsible it is difficult to see them as deliberately evil.[37] Yet they pose an unmistakable threat to the continuing life and stability of the world that Mansfield Park represents; and it is a mark of the clarity of Jane Austen's vision that both the strength of the threat and the frailty of the defenses are seen so honestly for what they are. The mood of *Mansfield Park* is nostalgic and elegiac; and if Fanny succeeds in preserving both her freedom and her place within the family it is not done without cost: a certain gaiety, liveliness, sophistication and independence are sacrificed – and sacrificed knowingly. Perhaps the most significant thing about this complex, compassionate and deeply felt work is that although the heroine triumphs in the end, the triumph is not altogether of this world. Fanny finds her rightful place in her true family and lives out, we can assume, a happy life 'within the view and patronage of Mansfield Park';[38] but she has married the younger son and not the heir, and, unlike Pamela, will never be mistress of the estate.

NOTES

1 See *The Improvement of the Estate: A Study of Jane Austen's Novels* (Baltimore and London, 1971), p. ix. Every reader of Jane Austen who is interested in *Mansfield Park* must be indebted to this richly informed, enlightening and stimulating book.

2 See Kenneth L. Moler's *Jane Austen's Art of Allusion* (Lincoln, Neb., 1968), especially pp. 124–5 and 146–9.

3 The language Jane Austen employs reinforces the notion that justice is being observed. She comments, for instance, on the decision of Mrs Norris and Maria to live together, that 'their tempers became their mutual punishment' (p.450); and says of Henry Crawford: 'That punishment, the public punishment of disgrace, should in just measure attend *his* share of

the offence, is, we know, not one of the barriers, which society gives to virtue. In this world, the penalty is less equal than could be wished' (pp. 452–3). (All quotations from *Mansfield Park* are taken from the Penguin English Library edition, eḍ. Tony Tanner (Harmondsworth, 1966).

4   The 'range of significance' of *Mansfield Park* is particularly well brought out by Duckworth in *The Improvement of the Estate* and Tanner in his Introduction to the Penguin edition.

5   *Mansfield Park.* pp. 427–8.

6   *Ibid.*, p. 428.

7   *Ibid.*, p. 420.

8   *Ibid.*, pp. 420–1.

9   *Ibid.*, p. 421.

10 *Ibid.*, Introduction. p. 10.

11 *Ibid.*, p. 421.

12 The original meaning of the word, now obsolete though in use until the end of the eighteenth century, is 'the servants of a house or establishment; the household' (*OED*). The English word derives through the Latin *familia*, household, from *famulus*, servant.

13 *Pamela* (Everyman edition, London, 1914), I, 123.

14 The novel begins: 'I am extremely concerned, my dearest friend, for the disturbances that have happened in your family.' It concludes: 'The worthy widow LOVICK continues to live with Mr Belford; and by her prudent behaviour, piety, and usefulness, has endeared herself to her lady, and to the whole family.'

15 *Clarissa* (Everyman edition, London, 1932), I, 226–7.

16 *Mansfield Park*, p. 169.

17 *Ibid.*, p. 239. Italics mine.

18 *Ibid.*, p. 115.

19 *Ibid.*, p. 116.

20 *Ibid.*, p. 122.

21 *The Improvement of the Estate*, p. 15.

22 *The Whole Duty of Man* (1659), *The Family Instructor* (1715, 1718) and *The New Family Instructor* (1727) all went through numerous editions and remained in print throughout the eighteenth century. They were widely read. The phrase 'social and relative duties' comes from Richardson's Preface to his *Letters written to and for particular Friends, on the most important occasions (Familiar Letters*, 1741).

23 *Libertine Literature in England, 1660–1745* (New York, 1965), p. 49.

24 *Ibid.*, p. 48.

25 *La Nouvelle Justine, ou les Malheurs de la Vertu, suivie de l'Histoire de Juliette, sa Soeur* (Paris, 1797), VII, pp. 109–18.

26 Two novels in which both the incest and the changeling themes are used in ways that could bear comparison with *Mansfield Park* are *Wuthering Heights* and *The Vivisector*, by Patrick White. In every case the incest is not physically realized but symbolically played out with surrogate figures. In *The Vivisector* the transition of the hero from his flesh-and-blood family to his ideal one also functions as a means of illuminating a wide area of cultural and social significance. (I discuss this

in my essay, 'Art and Science: Patrick White's Vivisector' in *The Australian Experience*, ed. W.S. Ramson [Canberra, 1974].)

27 *Mansfield Park*, p. 369.

28 *Ibid.*, p. 432.

29 *Ibid.*, p. 44.

30 Lionel Trilling discusses this in his influential essay *'Mansfield Park'* (*The Opposing Self*, New York, 1955), included in *Jane Austen: A Collection of Critical Essays*, ed. Ian Watt (Englewood Cliffs, N.J., 1963). See also A. Walton Litz, *Jane Austen: A Study of Her Artistic Development* (London, 1965), pp. 117–27, and Alistair M. Duckworth, *The Improvement of the Estate*, pp. 55–60 (the note on p. 59 lists other articles dealing with the theatricals).

31 *Mansfield Park*, p. 175.

32 *Ibid.*, p. 192.

33 *Ibid.*, p. 193.

34 'What became of Jane Austen? [*Mansfield Park*]' in *Spectator*, 6745 (4 October 1957), 439–40. Included in *Jane Austen: A Collection of Critical Essays*, pp. 141–4.

35 *Ibid.*

36 *'Mansfield Park,'* in *Jane Austen: A Collection of Critical Essays*, p. 127.

37 Mary's character in particular seems to have been distorted by the pressures of the plot in the concluding section: she has, after all, shown considerable sensitivity and kindness to Fanny, in particular earlier in the novel. It is perhaps significant of Jane Austen's uneasiness here that we are no longer permitted to see Mary directly at this point.

38 *Mansfield Park*, p. 457. From the concluding sentence.

KENNETH L. MOLER

The two voices of Fanny Price

One of the most controversial issues that *Mansfield Park* raises concerns Jane Austen's attitude toward the troublesome heroine, Fanny Price. The assumption that Fanny embodies the novel's moral ideals, coupled with dissatisfaction with her personality and character, has led a rather large group of readers to respond negatively, in varying degrees, to the novel; some critics have even seen Fanny and Jane Austen as fellow hypocrites. Another group has held that while Fanny has her flaws, Jane Austen is aware of them: that Fanny is not a morally normative figure for *Mansfield Park* but a character whose failings, as well as virtues, are important to the novel's moral scheme.[1]

It seems to me clear that Jane Austen does see, and intends her readers to become aware of, at least two significant shortcomings in Fanny Price. In the first place, as I have argued elsewhere, Fanny displays a sort of 'poor relation' mentality that blinds her to much that is worthy in the Bertram family.[2] As a defense mechanism that is readily understood, considering her circumstances, she has availed herself of the traditional consolation of the underdog, the association of social superiority with moral inferiority. The refinements of the wealthy are suspect. The 'poor relation' mentality is shown in the manner in which Fanny cherishes, quite unrealistically, an image of her paternal home at Portsmouth as a paradise in which true affection makes the artificial 'manner' of Mansfield unnecessary. It is corrected by her visit to Portsmouth, where Fanny's illusions are dispelled as she discovers that the Price family is not more loving and considerate than the Bertrams, and that, in the absence of any deeper motivations, the

172

The two voices of Fanny Price

Bertrams' code of good manners makes them far pleasanter to live with. Fanny's acknowledgment that 'Portsmouth was Portsmouth; Mansfield was home' is as crucial to the novel's moral pattern as is the self-knowledge to which Sir Thomas Bertram is brought by his daughters' elopements.

I think that Fanny is also the dupe of what might be described as a 'schoolroom' outlook on life. She is out of touch with social realities, she tends to overlook or drastically minimize the hard social and economic facts of life that Jane Austen never allows one to forget for long. While others in the novel – Sir Thomas, Mary Crawford – are overly worldly, attaching excessive importance to such things as money, rank and their appurtenances, Fanny goes to an opposite extreme, and in the naïveté of a too-cloistered virtue closes her eyes to the socio-economic complexity of real life. It is no accident that her favorite *retreat* at Mansfield is the old schoolroom. This aspect of Fanny's mind is revealed in the tendency to overreact to worldliness in others. In envisioning her own future, Fanny is able (with her brother William's help) to ignore so many realities and probabilities. William's virtues are sure to have their reward in the Navy – despite a situation in which 'interest' is of very great importance in securing a man's promotion, and Sir Thomas Bertram's comparative lack of such 'interest.' With increasing rank, and the increasing prize-money that is also sure to come, there will be a competence sufficient to set up housekeeping in the charming little cottage in which Fanny and William will live happily ever after. Such things as the probability of William's marrying and the possibility of the little cottage filling up with children in the manner of the Price home at Portsmouth do not enter into her thinking.

Fanny's 'schoolroom' mentality is also revealed, as characters' moral makeups so often are in Jane Austen, by manipulation of conversational style – in particular, I believe, by the phenomenon that I have called Fanny's 'two voices.' Jane Austen so manages Fanny's talk that two distinctive conversational styles run through her speeches. Neither of them is attractive *per se*; both work together to define one of the principal areas of Fanny's moral inadequacy.

One of the 'voices' that the reader associates with Fanny Price is what might be described as her 'bookish' voice.[3] Fanny is often made to talk in a manner that sounds artificial and out of place in the real-life conversations in which her speeches occur. Her rhetoric sounds stilted and excessively 'literary,' and she often seems to be echoing uncomfortably closely literature – particularly educational and didactic literature – with which an early-nineteenth-century audience would have been familiar. Her rhapsody on the beauties of a starry night observed from the windows of the Mansfield drawing-room is a case in point.

> 'Here's harmony!' said she, 'here's repose! Here's what may leave all painting and all music behind, and what poetry only can attempt to describe. Here's what may tranquillize every care, and lift the heart to rapture! When I look out on such a night as this, I feel as if there could be neither wickedness nor sorrow in the world; and there certainly would be less of both if the sublimity of Nature were more attended to, and people were carried more out of themselves by contemplating such a scene.'⁴

Here Fanny's overdone rhetoric, with its elaborate use of exclamation and asyndeton, suggests second-rate speech-making or the poorly handled written word rather than normal discourse. The description of the elevating effects of the sublime in natural scenery is a commonplace into which one constantly stumbles in all sorts of literature of the period. The conscious moralizing of the conclusion recalls Gisborne, Hannah More and other educators and edifiers of young ladies. The effect of the whole is that of 'schoolmarmish' parroting of exemplary texts. Similar rhetoric and the same sententiousness give an artificial and derivative tone to the lecture on the evergreen that Fanny delivers to Mary Crawford in the garden of Mansfield Parsonage.

[handwritten marginal note: Omission of conjunctions]

> 'The evergreen! – How beautiful, how welcome, how wonderful the evergreen! – When one thinks of it, how astonishing a variety of nature! – In some countries we know the tree that sheds its leaf is the variety, but that does not make it less amazing, that the same soil and the same sun should nurture plants differing in the first rule and law of their existence. You will think me rhapsodizing; but when I am out of doors, especially when I am sitting out of doors, I am very apt to get into this sort of wondering strain. One cannot fix one's eyes on the commonest natural production without finding food for a rambling fancy.' (p. 209)

And in fact there is a suspiciously close resemblance between this speech and a similar reflection in Hannah More's *Strictures on the Modern System of Female Education*.⁵ Other examples of Fanny's artificial, derivative, 'bookish' style are found in her lecture on memory (pp. 208–9), in her reflections on Mr Rushworth's decision to cut down an avenue of trees at Sotherton (p. 56) and in her initial response to the disappointing chapel at Sotherton (pp. 85–6).

But Fanny has another distinctive way of talking. Let us consider, for example, the scene in which she and Edmund discuss Henry Crawford's proposal, and Fanny's refusal of Crawford, during a walk in the shrubbery at Mansfield. Edmund, while honoring Fanny's feelings and principles, is an advocate for Crawford: 'let him succeed at last, Fanny, let him succeed at last,' he says. Fanny's impulsive reply is 'Oh! never, never, never; he never will succeed with me,' to which she adds, after a mild reproof from Edmund on her being 'so very determined and positive,' 'I mean . . . that I *think*, I never shall, as far as the future can be answered for – I think I never shall return his regard' (p. 347). The conversation progresses and Fanny reaches her most important objection to Crawford.

> 'It is not merely in *temper* that I consider him as totally unsuited to myself; though in *that* respect, I think the difference between us too great, infinitely too great; his spirits often oppress me – but there is something in him which I object to still more. I must say, cousin, that I cannot approve his character. I have not thought well of him from the time of the play. I then saw him behaving, as it appeared to me, so very improperly and unfeelingly, I may speak of it now because it is all over – so improperly by poor Mr Rushworth, not seeming to care how he exposed or hurt him, and paying attentions to my cousin Maria which – in short, at the time of the play, I received an impression which will never be got over.' (p. 349)

Here, in contrast to the elaborately arranged phrasing of Fanny's 'bookish' speeches, sentences are often loosely structured. Thought is lost and caught up with by means of repetition, left incomplete, revised in mid-sentence. And the frequent interjections and hasty qualifications add to the spasmodic quality of the passage's speech rhythms. The exclamation is still conspicuous – it appears in so much of Fanny's talk – but here its effect is quite different from the effect it produces in the 'bookish' speeches.

The subject here is an agitating one for Fanny; but a similar style can sometimes be observed in passages that are emotionally low-keyed. Shortly after the return of Sir Thomas Bertram from Antigua, Edmund and Fanny comment on the decreased liveliness of the Bertram fireside since his return. 'You are one of those who are too silent in the evening circle,' Edmund remarks; and he goes on to add that on the previous evening Sir Thomas would have been gratified if Fanny had followed up a question on the slave trade with other remarks. 'It would have pleased your uncle to be inquired of farther.' Fanny replies:

> 'And I longed to do it – but there was such a dead silence! And while my cousins were sitting by without speaking a word, or seeming at all interested in the subject, I did not like – I thought it would appear as if I wanted to set myself off at their expense, by shewing a curiosity and pleasure in his information which he must wish his own daughters to feel.' (p. 198)

The same unevenness, the same hesitancy, are present to a lesser degree.

In a really difficult situation for Fanny, such as a conversation with Sir Thomas regarding Henry Crawford's determination to persist in his courtship, disorganization of thought and unevenness of rhythm increase; interjection and qualification bring her speech to the brink of inarticulateness.

> 'Indeed, Sir . . . I am very sorry that Mr Crawford should continue to – I know that it is paying me a very great compliment, and I feel most undeservedly honoured, but I am so perfectly convinced, and I have told him so, that it never will be in my power – ' (p. 330)

Henry's proposal, and Sir Thomas's proposal of Henry, reduce her to stuttering incoherence.

> 'No, no, no . . . This is all nonsense. Do not distress me. I can hear no more of this. Your kindness to William makes me more obliged to you than words can express; but I do not want, I cannot bear, I must not listen to such – No, no, don't think of me. But you are *not* thinking of me. I know it is all nothing.' (pp. 301–2)

> 'Oh! no, Sir, I cannot, indeed I cannot go down to him. Mr. Crawford ought to know – he must know that – I told him enough yesterday to convince him – he spoke to me on this subject yesterday – and I told him without disguise that it was very disagreeable to me, and quite out of my power to return his good opinion.' (p. 314)

Her talks with Henry during his post-proposal attempt at courtship (see p. 342) and her reply to Mary Crawford's note on the subject of William's promotion and Henry's love (p. 307) are also masterpieces of schoolgirlish inarticulateness.

The word 'schoolgirlish' brings us to the point. Of the two conversational styles the reader chiefly associates with Fanny Price, one is that of the schoolbook; the other, that of the schoolgirl. Jane Austen combines Fanny's excessively 'bookish' style with her girlish tendency to become incoherent in 'real-life' situations to point up an aspect of her heroine's moral inadequacy: her failure to come to grips with the world of social reality that lies outside of the East Room. Fanny needs to come out of the schoolroom. And she does shed some of her 'schoolroom' mentality, just as she loses some of her 'poor relation's' outlook on life during her visit to Portsmouth.

There she learns that the question of the importance of worldly goods is not so simply answered as she had wished to believe. Economics can turn a potential Lady Bertram into a Mrs Price. With a disposition 'naturally . . . like Lady Bertram's,'

a situation of similar affluence . . . would have been much more
suited to [Mrs Price's] capacity, than the exertions and self-denials
of the one, which her imprudent marriage had placed her in. She
might have made just as good a woman of consequence as Lady
Bertram, but Mrs Norris would have been a more respectable
mother of nine children, on a small income. (p. 390)

The absence of a decent amount of the things of this world is seen to
be a very real evil at Portsmouth. And Fanny is impressed enough by
what she finds there that, although she is far from being turned into a
Charlotte Lucas, she is brought to consider the advantages that a
socially and economically advantageous marriage to Henry Crawford
might bring to her and her family – something that has never entered
into her thinking on the matter before (p. 419). Sir Thomas had
predicted that a visit to Portsmouth might help to revise Fanny's
excessively 'unworldly' outlook on life. And wrong as he has been
about so many other things. Sir Thomas is right about this one. Portsmouth marks a big step toward maturity on Fanny's part.

Fanny's increasing maturity is reflected, I believe, in some rather
significant voice-changing that takes place during and after the Portsmouth episodes. Unfortunately, she does not talk very much in the
latter part of the novel. But I think that what is probably her most
memorable speech from this part of the book – her comments on
receiving Edmund's letter describing the state of his relations with
Mary in London – represents an interesting departure from the
language in which many of her earlier responses to emotional situations was couched.

'He is blinded, and nothing will open his eyes, nothing can, after
having had truths before him so long in vain. – He will marry her,
and be poor and miserable. God grant that her influence do not
make him cease to be respectable . . . Finish it at once. Let there
be an end of this suspense. Fix, commit, condemn yourself.' (p. 424)

While the passage is emotional in tone, it has a balanced, almost
epigrammatic quality that might even remind one of Elizabeth
Bennet. Certainly the firm control of language here does not suggest
the schoolgirl. And some of Fanny's reflections upon receiving Mary's
transparent inquiries about Tom Bertram's health show a similar
departure from her earlier girlish voice.

Edmund would be forgiven for being a clergyman, it seemed, under
certain conditions of wealth; and this, she suspected, was all the
conquest of prejudice, which he was so ready to congratulate
himself upon. She had only learnt to think nothing of consequence
but money. (p. 436)

It is possible, too, that some of the reflections upon nature in the latter part of *Mansfield Park* may be designed to contrast with Fanny's earlier 'bookish' responses to natural beauty. Let us compare with the rhapsodies on evergreens and starlit nights the passage in which Fanny, amidst the squalor of Portsmouth, thinks of spring in the country.

> She had not known before what pleasures she *had* to lose in passing March and April in a town. She had not known before, how much the beginnings and progress of vegetation had delighted her. – What animation both of body and mind, she had derived from watching the advance of that season which cannot, in spite of its capriciousness, be unlovely, and seeing its increasing beauties, from the earliest flowers, in the warmest divisions of her aunt's garden, to the opening of leaves in her uncle's plantations, and the glory of his woods. To be losing such pleasures was no trifle; to be losing them, because she was in the midst of closeness and noise, to have confinement, bad air, bad smells, substituted for liberty, freshness, fragrance, and verdure, was infinitely worse. (p. 432)

Clichés and too-obvious rhetoric are replaced with detailed, rather precise references to observed phenomena. And when Fanny returns to Mansfield she sees its natural beauty not with the eyes of essayists of the period, but with her own:

> when they entered the Park, her perceptions and her pleasures were of the keenest sort. It was three months, full three months, since her quitting it; and the change was from winter to summer. Her eye fell everywhere on lawns and plantations of the freshest green; and the trees, though not fully clothed, were in that delightful state, when farther beauty is known to be at hand, and when, while much is actually given to the sight, more yet remains for the imagination. (pp. 446–7)

It is perhaps *apropos* to recall that in *Pride and Prejudice* Jane Austen had used Mary Bennet's overly 'bookish' speeches as a comic device. She had also made the loosely structured, gushing conversation of Lydia Bennet a reflection of Lydia's arrested mental and emotional development. Fanny Price, like several other Austen heroines, is a young lady who needs to be introduced to the world; and Fanny's introduction to social reality is an important part of *Mansfield Park*'s moral scheme. The novel is, in part, about Fanny's growing up.

NOTES

1 The views of the first group of critics are represented in rather extreme form in the chapter on *Mansfield Park* in Marvin Mudrick's *Jane Austen:*

Irony as Defense and Discovery (Princeton, New Jersey: Princeton University Press, 1952), and in Kingsley Amis's 'What Became of Jane Austen?', *Spectator*, 4 October 1957, 439–40. The ideas that Fanny is in some respects morally inadequate and that she needs to mature are presented in Margaret Kennedy's 'How Ought a Novelist,' *Fortnightly Review*, 172 (1952), 337–44; in the chapter on *Mansfield Park* in my *Jane Austen's Art of Allusion* (Lincoln, Nebraska: University of Nebraska Press, 1968); and in Ann Banfield's 'The Moral Landscape of *Mansfield Park*,' *Nineteenth-Century Fiction*, 26 (1971), 1–24.

2 *Jane Austen's Art of Allusion*, pp. 146–54.

3 For further discussion of this, see *Jane Austen's Art of Allusion*, pp. 111–27.

4 *The Novels of Jane Austen*, ed. R. W. Chapman, Vol. III (London: Oxford University Press; 3rd ed., 1933), p. 113. All subsequent references to *Mansfield Park*, henceforth included parenthetically in my text, are to this edition.

5 See *Jane Austen's Art of Allusion*, pp. 115 and 125. Hannah More, discussing the study of geography and natural history, remarks that observation of the varieties of trees can and should lead to wonder at the workings of Nature's God. A pupil should be 'led to admire the considerate goodness of Providence in having caused the spiry fir, whose slender foliage does not obstruct the beams of the sun, to grow in the dreary regions of the north, whose shivering inhabitants could spare none of its scanty rays; while in the torrid zone, the palm-tree, the plantain, and the banana, spread their umbrella leaves to break the almost intolerable fervours of a vertical sun.' See *The Works of Hannah More* (New York, 1884), Vol. I: *Strictures on the Modern System of Female Education*, Ch. 9, p. 349.

BARBARA HARDY

The objects in *Mansfield Park*

Dickens fixes his narrative inspiration in *The Old Curiosity Shop* in a vision of Nell surrounded by the curiosities. His narrator observes:

> We are so much in the habit of allowing impressions to be made upon us by external objects, which should be produced by reflection alone, but which, without such visible aids, often escape us, that I am not sure I should have been so thoroughly possessed by this one subject, but for the heaps of fantastic things I had seen huddled together in the curiosity-dealer's warehouse. These, crowding my mind, in connection with the child, and gathering round her, as it were, brought her condition palpably before me. (ch. i)

This comment on the power of objects emphasizes the world of things in which Nell has her fictional existence. The surrounding objects determine the social shape of her experience and also act as symbols to enlarge her innocence and the corruptions that threaten it. Analysis and symbol alert us to an important aspect of life and novels, about which novelists have spoken more than critics. We inhabit a world of social objects and personal symbols. Inheritances, earnings, purchases, presents and remembrances are determined by class, wealth and culture, and determine us. We make and take impressions in the object-world according to our taste, temperament and mind. Morandi's object-world would not exist without the life of the kitchen, but it is coloured, shaped, animated and grouped by his imagina-

180

tion. The novelist's concern with society, morality and psychology must lead him to objects, but he will recreate them.

Every personal history includes a collection of the 'expressive things' discussed by Madame Merle in Henry James's *The Portrait of A Lady*. She rebukes Isabel Archer's dangerous belief in her freedom and independence but draws her own values too exclusively from connoisseurship, predatoriness, and possession. Isabel has to discover the discomfort of being weighed down, impeded and enclosed in a world of objects, and struggles against being reduced to an object. James creates conflicts out of the powers of objects to express, enlighten and support, and also to restrict, deceive, corrupt and imprison. The objects in his world are Jamesian objects, visible to our eye through his eye, appreciated and placed, beautiful and dangerous.

The same can be said of Jane Austen, quiet initiator of so much in nineteenth-century fiction. Her novels use visible aids, because her characters need them. Jane Austen regards her expressive things with a muteness that comes to seem typical and fitting. Her objects are not endowed with a very conspicuous sensuous life, and accrete their symbolic significances slowly, piecemeal, unobtrusively. They are rendered quietly, items in the domestic world that exists outside novels, a world in which novels themselves are subdued or conspicuous presences. The Gothic novels enjoyed by Catherine Morland and Isabella Thorpe in *Northanger Abbey* are more conspicuous than the books in the other novels but none of them is given covers, colours, or bibliographical details. Objects seem to assert themselves more, and are more numerous, in Jane Austen's later novels, but their life is usually sunk below the surface, seldom loud or flaunted even when playing an important part as a personal or social symbol, or a dramatic property, useful tools in the craft of fiction. We can only come to understand the role of things in these novels if we look at a large number of them, because they work through accumulation. No one object is described with the detail or force of James's golden bowl but the prints, piano, music, books, and china in *Sense and Sensibility* play their unobtrusive part in defining culture and passion. Jane Austen's rare descriptions of nature stand out as sensuously vivid, unlike her descriptions of man-made objects. Those are hardly ever visualized, though we often see the characters looking at them hard enough. Fanny Price's possessions are scarcely differentiated, and when she thinks of airing a geranium it takes us by surprise. A few of her books are mentioned, but casually, in the course of conversation with Edmund. Tom's work-boxes and netting-boxes appear *en masse,* because that is what is wrong with them as presents. Fanny's 'works of charity and ingenuity' are also unspecified, like the unnamed object

in *The Ambassadors,* modestly self-effacing, still, timid. The books in
Fanny's collection never glow with colour, like James's lemon-
coloured volumes; her jewels are so rarely described that the two gold
necklaces and the amber cross[1] stand out crucially in the drama of
donation.

The stillness or invisibility of the objects seems to go with a certain
reticence about the human experience of objects. Like Jane Austen,
George Eliot likes to place her heroines in solitary rooms, and the
rooms contain their possessions. Dorothea Brooke looks round her
boudoir, in *Middlemarch,* and we are made to see and feel the room
and its objects through her profound affective experience:

> Her blooming full-pulsed youth stood there in a moral
> imprisonment which made itself one with the chill, colourless,
> narrowed landscape, with the shrunken furniture, the never-read
> books, and the ghostly stag in a pale fantastic world that seemed to
> be vanishing from the daylight.
>
> Each remembered thing in the room was disenchanted, was
> deadened as an unlit transparency, till her wandering gaze came to
> the group of miniatures, and there at last she saw something which
> had gathered new breath and meaning: it was the miniature of Mr
> Casaubon's aunt Julia, who had made the unfortunate marriage – of
> Will Ladislaw's grandmother. Dorothea could fancy that it was
> alive now – the delicate woman's face which yet had a head-strong
> look, a peculiarity difficult to interpret. Was it only her friends who
> thought her marriage unfortunate? Or did she herself find it out to
> be a mistake, and taste the salt bitterness of her tears in the merciful
> silence of the night? What breadths of experience Dorothea seemed
> to have passed over since she first looked at this miniature! She felt
> a new companionship with it, as if it had an ear for her and could
> see how she was looking at it. Here was a woman who had known
> some difficulty about marriage. Nay, the colours deepened, the lips
> and chin seemed to get larger, the hair and eyes seemed to be
> sending out light, the face was masculine and beamed on her with
> that full gaze which tells her on whom it falls that she is too
> interesting for the slightest movement of her eyelid to pass
> unnoticed and uninterpreted. The vivid presentation came like a
> pleasant glow to Dorothea: she felt herself smiling, and turning
> from the miniature sat down and looked up as if she were again
> talking to a figure in front of her. (ch. xxviii)

I quote at length in order to show what Jane Austen does not do.
When she sets her heroine to gaze at a portrait which is full of meaning she says nothing about its details and little about the emotions of
the scrutiny. We watch Elizabeth Bennet looking at Darcy's likeness,

and response is tellingly withheld. Appearances and feelings are diffused through Jane Austen's action, and significances are often muted. When Elinor Dashwood realizes that the ring, the miniature, and the letter are proofs of Lucy Steele's engagement to Edward Ferrars, nothing is made vivid or concrete, no details given of her painful memory of the ring with the hair she has taken for her own, or the picture which is eagerly thrust at her by her rival. Yet we do not feel that there is any doubt about what is happening. The neutrality of these objects is telling.

There are exceptions, which mostly occur in the descriptions of objects whose actual appearances are important in the plot or the theme, like the modern furniture and the japanned chest in *Northanger Abbey*, or the details of the seaside resort in *Sanditon*. We might be tempted to agree with Graham Hough[2] that material objects are suspect in Jane Austen, and she certainly takes pains to show that her heroines are not concerned, in general, with such particulars. Mrs Allen's ruling passion is wholly sartorial, but she is rendered fairly harmless. Mrs Jennings runs on about the felicities of Colonel Jennings's estate, but she lists particulars with relish, and her kind offer of dried cherries and old Constantia wine as a cure for heartbreak is made sympathetically, even touching off a warm recollection of her dead husband. Her daughter, Mrs Palmer, shows her lack of seriousness as she rattles off particulars, but she is kind-hearted, if stupid. Jane Austen will not let us depreciate Miss Bates, whose domestic trivialities are ramblingly recalled, but who is genuinely grateful for family affections and favours received. Jane Austen often shows an over-attentiveness to surfaces and trivialities as evidence of a want of mind, but less often of a want of heart. The worst materialists in Jane Austen are condemned for their attention to cash, not goods.

Jane Austen is decidedly unaesthetic in her feeling for objects, and those characters who yearn for elegance, colour, dash and beauty are in danger. Frank Churchill's present of the piano was as reckless and self-indulgent as his alibi of the London haircut. Marianne Dashwood has to learn to replace Willoughby's shooting-jacket with Colonel Brandon's flannel waistcoat. Catherine Morland needs to learn to love a hyacinth, but Mr Rushworth's enthusiasm for the blue dress, pink satin cloak, and 'fine fancy suit by way of a shooting dress', is as mindless as his pride in the never-mastered two-and-forty speeches of Count Cassel. Some treasured objects are intrinsically valuable, like William's amber cross and Edmund's plain gold chain, but they are never valued just for beauty and price. It seems right that William's present should be incomplete, having nothing to hang on, and that Edmund's present, like all his presents, should be valued chiefly for its thoughtful suitability. Jane Austen knows that human beings treasure all sorts of odds and ends, a scrap of paper with a few words in the beloved handwriting, a stub of pencil, or a court plaster. Emma marvels at Harriet, and makes the matter-of-fact suggestion that the ritual burning might spare the useful plaster. The trivial object saturated in private feeling can seem ridiculous to outside eyes. Jane Austen smiles at Fanny's eager pouncing on the unfinished note, and is amused as well as sympathetic as she chronicles that sad breakfast table in Mansfield Park, where Sir Thomas leaves Fanny to cry in peace, 'conceiving perhaps that the deserted chair of each young man might exercise her tender enthusiasm, and that the remaining cold pork bones and mustard in William's place, might but divide her feelings with the broken egg-shells in Mr Crawford's' (Vol. II, ch. xi).[3] Whether Fanny sighed over William's relics we do not know, because the specificity of the table is one of Jane Austen's gentle jokes.

In another novelist such details might solidify or swell the scene, but objects hardly ever do this, or only this, in Jane Austen. The glance Sir Thomas gives, by candlelight, to the ceiling and stucco of the billiard-room is a mute witness of a more than physical vandalism. Mary Crawford notices the size of the chairs in the east room when she comes to rehearse with Fanny: 'We must have two chairs at hand for you to bring forward to the front of the stage. There – very good school-room chairs, not made for a theatre, I dare say; much more fitted for little girls to sit and kick their feet against when they are learning a lesson' (Vol. I, ch. xviii). Her speech briefly glances at the past, at education, and at learning, but mentions the chairs as properties, filling in the furnishings of the east room as Jane Austen best likes to do, casually, mentioning things as they naturally come up in the course of conversation or action. We know what Fanny's hair looks like because of William's ingenuous praise of its odd fashion, and see the glossy spots on her dress because they remind Edmund of something Mary wore. Things are kept in their place.

Mansfield Park contains no accessory as visible as Robinson Crusoe's hairy hat and umbrella, the writing materials of Richardson's heroines, Oliver Twist's porridge bowl, or the sticks and bicycles of Beckett's people. But Fanny Price also has her survival kit. Letters, books, plants, work-boxes and ornaments furnish her room and her progress. Like everyone, she begins as a recipient and must learn to give. She begins as a pupil and must learn to teach. Like everyone in a monied society, she has to learn to spend money. Like everyone under a roof, she has to furnish a space for herself. She has to live in a world where other people use objects too, in similar and dissimilar ways, for loving and hating, nourishing and starving, freeing and imprisoning, giving and taking.

Fanny Price anticipates the Victorian heroine. Dickens images Nell in her innocent sleep amongst the grotesque things in her grandfather's shop, George Eliot images Maggie Tulliver and Dorothea Brooke in their lonely rooms, and Jane Austen constantly recurs to the east room in Mansfield Park. Key episodes recur in that room, to make it potent for several people; but it is Fanny's room, taking her stamp and re-forming that stamp:

> It had been their school-room; so called till the Miss Bertrams would not allow it to be called so any longer, and inhabited as such to a later period. There Miss Lee had lived, and there they had read and written, and talked and laughed, till within the last three years, when she had quitted them. The room had then become useless, and for some time was quite deserted, except by Fanny, when she visited her plants, or wanted one of the books, which she was still glad to keep there, from the deficiency of space and accommodation in her little chamber above; but gradually, as her value for the comforts of it increased, she had added to her possessions, and spent more of her time there; and having nothing to oppose her, had so naturally and so artlessly worked herself into it, that it was now generally admitted to be her's . . . Mrs Norris, having stipulated for there never being a fire in it on Fanny's account, was tolerably resigned to her having the use of what nobody else wanted, though the terms in which she sometimes spoke of the indulgence, seemed to imply that it was the best room in the house. (Vol. I, ch. xvi)

In every sense, this is the heart of Mansfield Park. It is under-heated, until Sir Thomas rescinds Mrs Norris's orders, but its temperature is right for Fanny. She has the advantage of not being born in a hothouse, but is transplanted from an exposed ground which ensured her hardiness. It is not a large room, though when she goes back to her parents' house in Portsmouth she appreciates its comparative spaciousness. Moreover, the reception rooms of Mansfield Park had first astonished her, 'too large for her to move in with ease' (Vol. I, ch. ii). Jane Austen uses the word 'nest' with very great precision. Mrs Norris is well-named, as the bad nurse, and arranged that Fanny should be given the little white attic, which she outgrows, to build for herself. Like other people, she makes a place where she can feel at home and be herself. The 'comforts' are her materials for nest-building, as well as the shelter, warmth and nourishment that a nest should provide.

The contents of nests tell us a lot about the builders, and Fanny's contains several different classes of objects. First on Jane Austen's careful list are solaces which George Eliot was to commend to Gwendolen Harleth, the means of going out of oneself:

> The comfort of it in her hours of leisure was extreme. She could go there after any thing unpleasant below, and find immediate

consolation in some pursuit, or some train of thought at hand. – Her
plants, her books – of which she had been a collector, from the first
hour of her commanding a shilling – her writing desk, and her
works of charity and ingenuity, were all within her reach;

Next come remembrances of things past:

Every thing was a friend, or bore her thoughts to a friend; and
though there had been sometimes much of suffering to her – though
her motives had been often misunderstood, her feelings
disregarded, and her comprehension undervalued, though she had
known the pains of tyranny, of ridicule, and neglect, yet almost
every recurrence of either had led to something consolatory; her
aunt Bertram had spoken for her, or Miss Lee had been
encouraging, or what was yet more frequent or more dear – Edmund
had been her champion and her friend; – he had supported her
cause, or explained her meaning, he had told her not to cry, or had
given her some proof of affection which made her tears delightful.
(Vol. I, ch. xvi)

Many of these potent things are unnamed and invisible, but some are
tangible reminders of things that have been given, by her brother
William and her cousin Tom. The things given by her cousin
Edmund, who is the prime donor in the novel, are not mentioned.
Some of them are too big, like the horse he buys for her use, and some
of them too transient, like the writing materials he first gave her when
she needed to write to William, or the glass of wine for her headache.
On this first survey of the room we hear only of Edmund's 'proof of
affection which made her tears delightful'. Fanny builds with books,
paper, needles, and plants. Her possessions are described as friends
and the reminders of friends. The signs, instruments, and souvenirs of
her personal growth, education, virtue and charity are not all the room
contains.

It is the archive of Mansfield Park, and its objects are the cast-offs of
childhood, cared for by no one but Fanny. She is the nestling, the
builder, and a brooding maternal presence. She is qualified for brooding by her powers of memory, like the hero of Wordsworth's *Prelude*,
David Copperfield, Henry Esmond, Maggie Tulliver, Stephen Deda-
lus, and Proust's Marcel. Like them, she preserves the past with love,
care, and imagination, willing life, never death. The east room
contains much more than her personal survival kit. The discarded
childhoods of Mansfield Park are preserved in the relics, the kicked
chairs, and the miscellaneous objects unfit for social or aesthetic
show:

The room was most dear to her, and she would not have changed its
furniture for the handsomest in the house, though what had been

originally plain, had suffered all the ill-usage of children – and its greatest elegancies and ornaments were a faded footstool of Julia's work, too ill done for the drawing-room, three transparencies, made in a rage for transparencies, for the three lower panes of one window, where Tintern Abbey held its station between a cave in Italy and a moonlight lake in Cumberland; a collection of family profiles thought unworthy of being anywhere else, over the mantel-piece, and by their side and pinned against the wall, a small sketch of a ship sent four years ago from the Mediterranean by William, with H.M.S. Antwerp at the bottom, in letters as tall as the main-mast. (Vol. I, ch. xvi)

The novel's themes radiate out from this centre.[4] Fanny's education depends on objects, and the reminder of Edmund's kindness takes us back to his gifts of paper, pen, help, and a promise of his father's frank. The books recall the earlier and later stages in reading in a novel where books are beloved and dangerous. A volume of Shakespeare, happily falling open at the right page, or thereabouts, is an aid to the seductive Henry Crawford. Fanny has to learn to be a teacher as well as a pupil, and helps to form her sister Susan's taste in literature as Edmund helped to form hers. When they are together in their small, cold room in Portsmouth, it reminds Fanny of the east room, emphasizing her changed and expanded role. The east room is like old nurseries where the children's heights are recorded on the wall in sad signs of mutability and happy signs of growth. Fanny's arrival in Mansfield Park, amongst the valuable and fragile objects ('whatever she touched she expected to injure') is the beginning of a journey outwards.

When Edmund observes that she will soon be with Macartney in China, he draws attention to the capacity of her room. Books about China and the drawing of William's ship remind us of Fanny's wide sensibilities and knowledge. She questions her uncle about the slave trade, and knowledge joins enthusiasm in her rhapsody on the evergreen. She has a sense of the larger world, past and present, even though she shocks her cousins by not knowing how to get to Ireland, only thinking of the Isle of Wight. She has a room of her own, a centre of a large and expanding sphere.

At Sotherton Fanny sighs for the doomed avenue, and misses the trappings and trophies of a medieval past in the modern chapel. Her interest in geography and botany is of no interest to Mary Crawford and her sense of history is faintly priggish, though imperfect, and in need of correction from Edmund. Her thoughtful and bookish broodings over the romantic past are contrasted with Mary's accomplished, self-regarding, and femininely charming quotation from Louis XIV, and with her cousin's early boast about repeating 'the chronological order of the kings of England, with the dates of their accession, and most of the principal events of their reigns' (Vol. I, ch. ii). Jane Austen knew how hard it was for women to be educated. Unlike Catherine Morland's, Fanny's interest in the public world involves past and present, history and literature, and is grounded in personal experience. Her laments at Sotherton against the prospects of heartless modernization do not spring from a Gothic sentimentality, which she might have imbibed from Scott and Cowper. She gains from coming after those antiquarians, Marianne Dashwood and Catherine Morland. Jane Austen thoroughly expressed, exercised, and released her critical sense of romantic historicism in her early novels, leaving herself free to appreciate the imaginative sense of the past in *Mansfield Park* and *Persuasion*. Both Fanny and Anne Elliot cultivate a personal and familiar sense of the Past, Anne's being devastatingly contrasted with Sir Walter's false pride, and Fanny's, more quietly, with that of her uncle and Mrs Norris. Fanny asks about the world as questions become relevant, starting with the Isle of Wight, following the voyages of her brother and her uncle, then travelling beyond.

Fanny must take the credit of stepping out of a long line of antiquarians going back through the heroines of Mrs Radcliffe, who looked back to the past somewhat fitfully, to Don Quixote. George Eliot's Dorothea Brooke is made more explicitly Quixotic than any of Jane Austen's heroines, but I like to think that she may owe something of her sense of the world to Fanny Price. Dorothea's imagination is less aesthetic than Fanny's, but Fanny is never merely aesthetic. Their sense of the world is made up of an acknowledgment of past and present. The wider world starts at home, in 'the island', or at Tipton. Dorothea knows that a knowledge of the past may help her to do something, 'Now – in England', though she makes the vast, if understandable, error of taking Casaubon as her authority. His sterile pedant's imagination can tell her nothing about great men of the past, nor about Raphael, nor about Rome, nor even about the bad housing conditions in ancient Egypt. Jane Austen's young ladies are taught the same futile and fragmentary 'toybox history of the world' as George Eliot's,[5] but her author provides Fanny with a more imaginative teacher than Casaubon, as George Eliot did for Esther Lyon and Gwendolen Harleth.

Memory, gratitude, charity and learning are joined in the east room, 'so blended together, so harmonized by distance, that every former affliction had its charm' (Vol. I, ch. xvi). Despite the harmony, or because of it, there are difficulties in Fanny's role as keeper of a personal and domestic culture. The allure of the past is not criticized in *Mansfield Park*. Like *Persuasion,* it shows Jane Austen's mature and melancholy emphasis on the continuity and unity of individual and family life. She comes to cherish the personal history. Fanny's personal possessions have to be seen in the context of her early displacement in the large rooms amongst the grand objects, and also in the light of later progress. Tom's word 'creepmouse', used just before the first examination of her feelings in the east room, reminds us of her timidity and self-effacement. The nest is the place where she recovers self-possession.

The collection of objects carries her back to pain as well as pleasure, though the nest of comforts blends discomforts with elations. Some of the souvenirs demand her active gratitude, and she looks at a table 'covered' with Tom's presents, 'the work-boxes and netting-boxes' whose very numerousness and sameness are mutely eloquent. She is 'bewildered as to the amount of the debt which all these kind remembrances produced'. Weighed down by benefaction, she asks, before Dorothea Brooke, 'what she ought to do'. Fanny asserts her personality as well as Mary Crawford, and more bravely and spiritedly. She is not too timebound or too creepmouse to find in her nest what we should find in all proper nests, the strength to fly away. This is something that neither Maggie Tulliver nor Dorothea Brooke finds, and though their circumstances are admittedly rather different there is no doubt that Jane Austen's Fanny is endowed with a more urgently liberated imagination.[6] The consultation of the sacred objects is done with some humour, as Fanny turns to the oracular work-boxes and to Edmund's profile and her geraniums. She hopes to inhale 'a breeze of mental strength' as she airs the plants, for which she cares. Like Fanny, they need air. Like her they flourish in the cool east room, to grow sturdily and fragrantly at the heart of Mansfield Park. Fanny becomes distressed rather than inspired, has to face people as well as objects, cannot retreat to Macartney as Edmund suggests, but the room does its work. Her refusal to act rejects Tom's image of the 'creepmouse'.

Gratitude is carefully discriminated by Jane Austen. Fanny is not so grateful that she forgoes her sense of self, though where she owes proper gratitude she gives it gladly. In a novel where gratitude is so important, the drama of donation plays a large part, and the presents in the east room, like the plant and the pictures, also reach out to past and future. Fanny has to become a teacher, a donor and a creditor. And she has to be recognized and respected in these adult responsibilities. The objects in the room show her care for what is personal and for what is impersonal, suggesting that it can be heartless to care too much or too little for objects. It would be wrong to be too grateful for the massed work-boxes. Fanny's feeling for the geranium which she airs is an almost buried instance of her lovingness. In a more rhapsodic mood, she moves naturally from the praise of human memory to the praise of the evergreen, that related symbol, but the need for an inspiring breeze seems to be placed in her own imaginative need for the green world for which she thirsts in Portsmouth, and for which Anne Elliot (and probably Jane Austen) longed in the 'white glare of Bath'. Fanny recognizes in nature the things that are beyond self, though she feels a connection between them, shown with that faint humour with which Jane Austen sharpens her solemnity.

Fanny's feeling for things shows her ability to make symbols to recognize the world of things beyond self, and so ultimately to extend the sphere of the self. She begins life as a recipient of presents, each stage in her progress being represented through the drama of donation. The east room is Fanny's solitary theatre for scenes of other giving and taking. She goes there to deposit the Crawfords' chain in her box 'of smaller treasures', to find Edmund with his more suitable, plain and unequivocal chain, a present which is fitting both literally and morally:

> Almost unconsciously she had now undone the parcel he had just put into her hand, and seeing before her, in all the niceness of jeweller's packing, a plain gold chain perfectly simple and neat, she could not help bursting forth again. 'Oh! this is beautiful indeed! this is the very thing, precisely what I wished for! this is the only ornament I have ever had a desire to possess. It will exactly suit my cross. They must and shall be worn together. It comes too in such an acceptable moment. Oh! cousin, you do not know how acceptable it is.' (Vol. II, ch. ix)

When she is in distress about Henry Crawford's proposal the room is the scene of further indebtedness, as Sir Thomas heaps coals of fire in the empty grate.

She has to grow out of being a mere recipient. In Portsmouth, she finds herself in the new position of power and responsibility, and heals a breach by giving:

> It had very early occurred to her, that a small sum of money might, perhaps, restore peace for ever on the sore subject of the silver knife, canvassed as it now was continually, and the riches which she was in possession of herself, her uncle having given her £10 at parting, made her as able as she was willing to be generous. But she was so wholly unused to confer favours, except on the very poor, so unpractised in removing evils, or bestowing kindnesses among her equals, and so fearful of appearing to elevate herself as a great lady at home, that it took some time to determine that it would not be unbecoming in her to make such a present. It was made, however, at last. (Vol. III, ch. ix)

She finds herself able to use money, to buy the knife, to buy food, to order books; 'she became a subscriber – amazed at being any-thing *in propria persona*, amazed at her own doings in every way' (Vol. III, ch. ix). Jane Austen dares to put the word 'creepmouse' in Tom's mouth because she had so thoroughly known the special temptation of her heroine's modesty and dependence. The word plainly ceases to be appropriate. Fanny is subdued by heavy debts of gratitude but learns to give. Her education in taking and giving works through the receipt of many gifts, good, indifferent and poisonous, as well as through her shift of environment, a change of objects.

Like Henry James after her, Jane Austen knew that possessions could be both over-valued and under-valued. Fanny does not thoroughly appreciate the comforts of Mansfield until deprived of them in the squalors of Portsmouth. The comforts of Mansfield are equivocal. Fanny's room is cold in winter, though its aspect makes it bearable. If a headache makes her for once lie on the sofa, Mrs Norris's nagging injustice soon gets her off. Lady Bertram's fringes and carpet-work are useless, Pug is fat and spoiled. The warmth of the drawing-room is discovered by Mary Crawford's wit to be 'too hot' for comfort. Lady Bertram congratulates herself for sending her maid to help Fanny, but too late. The rooms are too large, their objects daunting. She returns to her parents' house in Portsmouth for the purposes of Sir Thomas's interesting experiment in environment to find the rooms too small, the house too noisy, the light bad, the food half-cooked, the cutlery and dishes sticky, the maids hopeless. The quiet fastidiousness of Fanny perhaps suggested to James the scene in *The Wings of the Dove* where Kate Croy delicately opens a window to banish the odours of the children's luncheon, and is aware of the stickiness of objects and surfaces. Fanny becomes homesick and learns that Mansfield is home – though not exactly as Sir Thomas has planned. But she also learns to spend, buy, teach, and slightly improve the bad housekeeping. The lesson is a subtle one, but it is learned.

The geranium is not the only natural object in Mansfield Park. Fanny's enthusiasm is directed to its gardens, woods and skies, as well as to the unobtrusive elegance and comforts which are appreciated through absence. Fanny praises nature above all, looking at the stars with Edmund, though losing him to the luxuries of the drawing-room and to Mary's music. She exclaims at the beauty of the evergreen in a rhapsodic tribute for which she apologizes. Her appreciation of natural objects is an essential part of her ardent and informal sensibility. Objects are loved as friends or reminders of friends, and so is nature. It is valued for its sublimity, which can carry people 'more out of themselves', and Fanny can distinguish constellations, trees, and weather. Mary cannot be carried out of herself, and Henry Crawford's feeling for Fanny is acutely grounded on his sense of her capacity for ardour. But the natural objects have human associations. Her enthusiasm for the stars is unpriggishly bound up with Edmund: 'You taught me to think and feel on the subject, cousin' (Vol. I, ch. xi). It contrasts with the items in the young ladies' syllabus automatically rattled off by Maria – containing, amongst other things, 'all the metals, semi-metals, Planets, and distinguished philosophers' (Vol. I, ch. ii). The grounds of Mansfield are missed in Portsmouth: 'She had not known before, how much the beginnings and progress of vegetation had delighted her' (Vol. III, ch. xiv). Despite the headache that began in the rose-garden, the gardens have a changed aspect in the memory of losses, but the gardens are 'her aunt's', the woods 'his woods'. It is a personal Nature.

The chief contrast of the novel is drawn between Fanny's two homes, Mansfield and Portsmouth, and depends on the moral significance of objects and the responses and uses of people. The affinity between Fanny and Edmund is revealed in their common feeling for objects, natural and man-made, as the drama of donation proceeds. The other characters in the novel misuse or misvalue objects, either devouring them or regarding them as ornaments or mere accessories. Edmund himself is temporarily guilty of infidelity as a donor, as he diverts to Mary Crawford the use of the horse he has bought for Fanny's use. And he is in danger of being attracted by the surfaces and comforts that indecorously characterize the parsonage. Houses cannot be separated from their objects, and Jane Austen makes them expressive of the owner, in a way which may have impressed George Eliot and Henry James. At the Parsonage Mrs Grant's diversions of pretty furniture, plants and poultry are what must be expected of a childless woman, and her horticultural improvements are approved and appreciated by Fanny's rhapsody in the shrubbery. Less innocent are the objects associated with her husband's epicureanism. His ruling passion is even rebuked by Mary, and fixed through such objects as the 'great round table', the turkey in danger of not keeping, the green goose which disappoints him, a tough pheasant which keeps Mrs Grant from the play, and the Moor Park apricot, despised by him, diplomatically complimented by his wife, and originally paid for by Sir Thomas. The accessory objects of the Parsonage combine in a seductive harmony to which Edmund is not indifferent:

> A young woman, pretty, lively, with a harp as elegant as herself; and both placed near a window, cut down to the ground, and opening on a little lawn, surrounded by shrubs in the rich foliage of summer, was enough to catch any man's heart. The season, the scene, the air, were all favourable to tenderness and sentiment. Mrs Grant and her tambour frame were not without their use; it was all in harmony;

and as every thing will turn to account when love is once set going,
even the sandwich tray, and Dr Grant doing the honours of it, were
worth looking at. (Vol. I, ch. vii)

The touch is light that unmistakably blends the objects and their
bland charms. Mary's outside does charm Edmund, and the description just assimilates the various objects – Mary, harp, window, and
sandwich tray – to each other to explain, and rebuke, the charm.
Mary's attitude to her accessories is carefully revealed as unimagina-
tive, careless of the life around, whose routines make it amusingly
inconvenient for a farmhouse to transport a young lady's harp. Mary's
worldliness is insensitive to the facts and qualities of the larger world,
to which Fanny is sharply responsive.

Mary is indifferent to remembrances and presents. She laughs away
her brother's presents:

> 'Its being a gift of my brother's need not make the smallest
> difference in your accepting it, as I assure you it makes none in my
> willingness to part with it. He is always giving me something or
> other. I have such innumerable presents from him that it is quite
> impossible for me to value, or for him to remember half.' (Vol. II,
> ch. viii)

She amusingly invents facts about distances and time, or the direction
of the wind, as suits her purpose, offering her feminine illogicalities to
flatter and tease, in all the self-centredness of conscious charm. Fanny
moves out of herself, to fix the object. This can be priggish, to be sure,
though her apology for rhapsody shows an awareness of response not
found in prigs. When she praises the evergreen it is because she sees
that Mary is 'untouched and inattentive' to her praise of human
memory, and is changing the subject to praise Mrs Grant's garden.
Her tactfulness is untutored and heavy, including lines like 'In some
countries we know the tree that sheds its leaf is the variety', but touching and amusing. Jane Austen is perfectly aware that knowledge can
be boring and playful feminine ignorance appealing: 'I see no wonder
in this shrubbery equal to seeing myself in it'; and 'South or North, I
know a black cloud when I see it.' But Fanny has ardour as well as
knowledge, unlike Mary Bennet.

Her relation to objects carefully contrasts with the other women's
attitudes. Mrs Grant is harmlessly and typically concerned to cultivate
her garden and feed her husband. Mrs Price struggles helplessly with
the things around, insolent like Lady Bertram, but less happily placed
on a sofa, with Pug and a useless piece of needlework, which Fanny
will sort out when it gets troublesome. (But it is a mark of Lady
Bertram's Humour and of her moral breadth that she offers Fanny a

puppy.) Fanny has trouble with the objects that surround the three Ward sisters – Lady Bertram's work, the half-clean dishes at Portsmouth, the unprepared outfits of the boys, and the Mansfield roses she picks and then carries over to Mrs Norris's house where they will be dried. Objects are too much for Mrs Price, no trouble at all to Lady Bertram, and spoils for Mrs Norris – who 'spunges' the roses, the 'supernumerary jellies' after Fanny's first ball, the green baize of the undrawn curtains for *Lovers' Vows,* a cream cheese, a little heather, and some pheasants' eggs from Sotherton. Whenever there is a party, Mrs Norris is there to carry off the left-overs. Since the feasts in Jane Austen's novels are almost as frequently spoiled as the comic and weary feasts in Thackeray, Mrs Norris is often carrying off loot from a battlefield. Whatever the occasion, there is almost always something in it for her. Jane Austen's materialists are finely discriminated and must not be lumped together. Mrs Norris has no feeling for the objects she scrounges but likes saving money. Even those pheasants' eggs that she talks about in her false self-pitying style as giving her 'a few living creatures' to care for in her 'lonely hours' will give her no trouble. Like Fanny, they will be hatched at Mansfield.

The spoils of Sotherton get in the way on the journey home – to irritate, but gratify, Maria, and to be put on Fanny's willing lap. They are only a part of Maria's richer spoils, to which Mrs Norris helps her, and for which they both pay so dearly. Sotherton is a highly expressive place, like Mansfield and the Parsonage, the east room and the White House. It is heavy like its owner, badly in need of improvement, facing the wrong way, marked by iron palings, a significantly locked gate, a tantalizing ha-ha and a little wilderness. Its chapel is well-furnished but unoccupied, its altar misused by the clandestine actors, Henry and Maria, and joked about by Julia. Mrs Rushworth shows them round, repeating her 'lesson' without any feeling for history or things. Fanny is always a witness to other people's abuse of things.

We perceive the import of Jane Austen's objects as we may perceive the import of things in life, realizing the significance of conspicuous consumption, the weight of benefactions, the responsibilities of purchase, or the importance of knowing and feeling about things through the accretions of experience. Her method is not to highlight these significances, and many of them she may have taken for granted, or not classified in the ways that will occur to our modern minds. There are local symbols which make themselves felt as they occur, but even these tend to be assimilated to the experience within the novel, striking the imagination of the characters first and foremost. Henry James mixes the methods; we feel that the characters in *The Wings of the Dove* or *The Golden Bowl* are perceiving, analysing, and even manipulating the symbolic objects, but that behind their analysis lies the larger authorial irony. Jane Austen seems to prefer not to go behind her characters. Fanny is sufficiently explicit about gratitude and presents to be able to understand the potlatch. Henry Tilney, Marianne, Elinor, Emma – all have their own views, as Emma's parody of Miss Bates's old petticoat makes clear, but there is an intellectual comprehension which rises to its author's insights. There is also usually someone in the novel who would understand her own total moral view. It is Fanny's wit and perception which see the larger indecorum of Maria's impatient, reckless refusal to wait for Rushworth's key: 'you will certainly hurt yourself against those spikes, – you will tear your gown – you will be in danger of falling into the ha-ha' (Vol. I, ch. x). Fanny, like Edmund, shows her imagination only in such grasp of serious significances, while Mary's entertaining wit and perception are fanciful, playing with resemblances without seeing implications, turning wilderness, the vices and rears, and the game of 'Speculation' into amusing *double entendres*: 'There, I will stake my last like a woman of spirit. No cold prudence for me.' Fanny's game of cribbage with her aunt is by contrast one-dimensional, but she fully understands the relevance of the geranium's need for an inspiring breeze.

Jane Austen's method is not to set objects in a carefully prepared social scene, like many of Thackeray's, in which the details of pictures, ornaments, carpet, furniture and food are sociologically exact. Nor is it to make the objects totally resonant, like the cruel, small, jealous windows of Osmond's house in *The Portrait of A Lady,* or the smooth grey stone, 'polished a little by life', of the house where Chad Newsome lives in Paris. Nor does she combine the two methods, as George Eliot does in *Middlemarch.* Jane Austen sets her characters in action, in a world naturally filled with things. As they take their way through the streets of Bath, the promenade at Portsmouth, dirty lanes, drawing-rooms, dining-rooms, parties of pleasure, or solitary rooms, their path is strewn with objects. They tend not to be dwelt on, in their accidentals, unless the characters choose to dwell on them, which they will do from time to time for a variety of good and bad reasons. Some of the characters seem to regard the objects in their lives with a sense of proportion which does not force itself upon us as an imperative, but simply seems to resemble the implicit attitude of the author. The spirit, solidity and stillness of the characters, as of their surroundings, is created in a world of things.

NOTES

1 This was based on an actual cross given to Jane Austen by her brother Frank.

2 'Narrative and Dialogue in Jane Austen', *Critical Quarterly* (Autumn 1970).

3 All references to *Mansfield Park* are taken from *The Novels of Jane Austen*, ed. R. W. Chapman, 3rd ed. (London: Oxford University Press, 1933).

4 Tony Tanner has an excellent discussion of the room in his Penguin English Library edition of *Mansfield Park*.

5 It was this disjointed factual learning which was attacked by early feminists in the first half of the nineteenth century.

6 For Jane Austen, the vicarious light may have represented a personal need, as for George Eliot the imagined return became imperative. The most potent images of liberation are not always those supplied by the most liberated people.

JOHN HALPERIN

The worlds of *Emma*:
Jane Austen and Cowper

In his 'Biographical Notice of the Author' prefixed to the posthumous first edition of *Northanger Abbey* and *Persuasion* (1818), Henry Austen tells us that his sister's 'favourite moral writers were Johnson in prose, and Cowper in verse'; while J. E. Austen-Leigh, in the 1870 *Memoir* of his aunt, says that among her most admired writers were 'Johnson in prose, Crabbe in verse, and Cowper in both.'[1] Even without these clues, Jane Austen's devotion to Cowper is easily discernible.

Her letters mention him often. In a 1798 letter to her sister Cassandra, then visiting her brother and his family in Kent, Jane Austen writes: 'We have got Boswell's "Tour to the Hebrides," and are to have his "Life of Johnson"; and, as some money will yet remain . . . it is to be laid out in the purchase of Cowper's works.'[2] Cowper's works apparently being purchased soon afterwards, she writes just three weeks later to the same correspondent that their father 'reads Cowper to us in the evening' at Steventon.[3] In an 1807 letter to Cassandra, written from Southampton, Jane Austen announces that the gardener, at her request, has procured some syringas: 'I could not do without Syringa, for the sake of Cowper's Line. – We also talk of a Laburnum.'[4] The reference here is to Book VI of *The Task* (1785):

Laburnum, rich
In streaming gold; syringa, iv'ry pure. (ll. 149–50)[5]

197

In an 1813 letter to Cassandra, written from her brother's home in Kent, Jane Austen says: 'I am now alone in the Library, Mistress of all I survey – at least I may say so & repeat the whole poem if I like it, without offence to anybody.'[6] The poem referred to here clearly is Cowper's *Verses on Alexander Selkirk* (1782), the first line of which is 'I am monarch of all I survey.' In another 1813 letter to Cassandra from Kent, Jane Austen refers to the resignation from domestic service of one William, her brother Henry's servant, in these terms: 'I am glad William's going is voluntary, & on no worse grounds. An inclination for the Country is a venial fault. – He has more of Cowper than of Johnson in him, fonder of Tame Hares & Blank verse than of the full tide of human Existence at Charing Cross.'[7] The reference to 'Tame Hares & Blank verse' recalls *The Task* (written in blank verse) once again: extolling the advantages of rural solitude and contemplation, Cowper in Book VII speaks of

> The timorous hare,
> Grown so familiar with her frequent guest. (ll. 305–6)

There are as well several other possible and perhaps more likely sources in Cowper for Jane Austen's reference. One is 'Epitaph on A Hare' (1783), an account (in ballad stanzas) of the poet's attempt to tame 'a wild Jack-hare'; still another is his prose 'History of My Three Hares,' an anti-hunting piece which appeared in the *Gentleman's Magazine* in June 1784 and which speaks specifically of his having tamed to the point of household domestication two of three hares he adopted. Both of these pieces would have been available to Jane Austen in the set of Cowper's works bought by her father.

Cowper is also either mentioned or quoted or in some way alluded to in four of Jane Austen's novels. In *Sense and Sensibility,* while the poet is not directly named, the novelist probably had him in mind when she wrote the scene in which the proposed 'improvements' at Barton are being discussed.[8] Elinor is appalled by the idea of knocking down trees in order to construct a greenhouse and a flower garden. She, and Jane Austen, may well be reacting here against Cowper for once. The poet, taking an uncharacteristically tolerant view of the earlier eighteenth century's passion for subjugating the natural to the artificial, had said – again in *The Task* (Book III) – the following:

> Who loves a garden, loves a green-house too.
> Unconscious of a less propitious clime
> There blooms exotic beauty, warm and snug,
> While the winds whistle and the snows descend.
>
> Strength may wield the pond'rous spade,
> May turn the clod, and wheel the compost home;

But elegance, chief grace the garden shows
And most attractive, is the fair result
Of thought, the creature of a polish'd mind. (ll. 566–9 and 636–40)

On the subject of imposing artificial order on nature, at least, Elinor
and Marianne agree (p. 226), and one suspects that Jane Austen, a
devotée of Gilpin, is in the same camp. In this she shares a prejudice
common to many of her late-eighteenth-century counterparts. In any
case, Cowper seems to be present here, if only as a straw man. It could
also be that Jane Austen is thinking of a very different passage from
The Task, one in the first Book which takes a view similar to her own
(cited by Fanny in *Mansfield Park* – see below); but the language
here, especially the references to gardens and greenhouses, suggests
that the passage I have quoted is the one she has in mind.

Cowper is also mentioned several times by name in *Sense and
Sensibility,* though again not quoted directly. Marianne, in a conversation with her mother early in the novel, castigates Edward for his
inert reading of Cowper:

'I could hardly keep my seat. To hear those beautiful lines which
have frequently driven me wild, pronounced with such impenetrable calmness, such dreadful indifference!' –

'He would certainly have done more justice to simple and elegant
prose. I thought so at the time; but you *would* give him Cowper.'

'Nay, mama, if he is not to be animated by Cowper! – but we must
allow for the difference of taste.'[9]

Later, Marianne happily discovers that Willoughby shares her delight
in Cowper and Scott and admires Pope 'no more than is proper.'[10]
Had she a fortune, as Edward says in a subsequent scene, she would
fill the house with Thomson, Cowper and Scott: 'she would buy up
every copy, I believe, to prevent their falling into unworthy hands.'[11]
Marianne's enthusiasms often blind her to the true nature of those
who share or fail to share them with her; but her taste *per se* is not
condemned here – Jane Austen too was an admirer of Cowper and
Scott.

Cowper is twice quoted directly in *Mansfield Park*. Fanny, discussing with Edmund and Mary some proposed alterations at Sotherton,
deprecates the suggested destruction of an avenue of trees: 'Cut down
an avenue! What a pity! Does it not make you think of Cowper? "Ye
fallen avenues, once more I mourn your fate unmerited."'[12] The reference here once again is to *The Task* (Book I):

Ye fallen avenues! once more I mourn
Your fate unmerited: once more rejoice
That yet a remnant of your race survives. (ll. 338–40)

Again Jane Austen and her heroine take the side of nature and look upon 'improvements' with a jaundiced eye. Later in the novel, when Fanny at Portsmouth yearns for Mansfield, she thinks of Cowper's *Tirocinium* (1785): ' "With what intense desire she wants her home," was continually on her tongue.'[13] The poem itself is a long harangue in heroic couplets denouncing the practice of sending children off to boarding schools at an age at which homesickness is inevitable. The passage in question reads thus:

> Th' intended stick that loses day by day
> Notch after notch, till all are smooth'd away,
> Bears witness, long ere his dismission come,
> With what intense desire he wants his home. (ll. 559–62)

Jane Austen quotes yet again from Cowper in the first chapter of *Sanditon*.

> 'Why, in truth Sir, I fancy we may apply to Brinshore, that line of the Poet Cowper in his description of the religious Cottager, as opposed to Voltaire – "*She*, never heard of half a mile from home." '[14]

The reference here is to Cowper's *Truth* (1782), where the poet, praising the virtues of rural simplicity over those of citified rationalism, says in part:

> Oh happy peasant! Oh unhappy bard!
> His the mere tinsel, hers the rich reward;
> He prais'd perhaps for ages yet to come,
> She never heard of half a mile from home;
> He lost in errors his vain heart prefers,
> She safe in the simplicity of hers. (ll. 246–51)

(It is tempting to see in Jane Austen's fastening upon this particular passage some suggestion of a connection in her mind between her own obscurity and that of Cowper's virtuous but uncelebrated cottager.)

Jane Austen's most interesting quotation from Cowper, however, is that which occurs in *Emma* (III, v). Mr Knightley, rightly suspecting a secret attachment between Frank Churchill and Jane Fairfax and distressed at Emma's apparently willful blindness to this possibility, wonders to himself whether he is only suspiciously conjuring up something with no basis in fact:

> he could not help remembering what he had seen; nor could he avoid observations which, unless it were like Cowper and his fire at twilight,

'Myself creating what I saw,'

brought him yet stronger suspicion of there being a something of
private liking, of private understanding even, between Frank
Churchill and Jane.[15]

The quotation is again from *The Task,* this time from Book IV. The
passage cited reads thus:

Me oft has fancy, ludicrous and wild,
Sooth'd with a waking dream of houses, tow'rs,
Trees, churches, and strange visages, express'd
In the red cinders, while with poring eye
I gaz'd, myself creating what I saw. (ll. 286–90)

The Task, written in 1783–4 and first published in 1785, is a blank-
verse poem in six books.[16] Proclaimed a masterpiece by the critics, the
poem rescued Cowper from obscurity and made him, virtually over-
night, the most famous poet in England. *The Task* addresses itself to
the question of how man should live, and it ultimately concludes that
rural solitude and leisure are most conducive to the acquisition of
piety and virtue.[17] What Cowper values most in pastoral ease is the
way it inspires the solitary individual to contemplate nature and its
objects – and, in doing so, to re-examine his own thoughts as well.
Such re-examination often leads him, in *The Task,* to make instructive
comparisons between rural and urban habits of contemporary life.
The poem is both descriptive and didactic, emphasizing as it does the
poet's ideas about man's situation, morally speaking, in his world. Of
particular interest to readers of Jane Austen are Books IV and VI.

It is not an accident that Mr Knightley's distress about Emma's
solipsistic state of mind finds expression in a quotation from Book IV
of *The Task.* In that section of the poem from which the quotation is
taken, Cowper comments at some length (ll. 282–307) on the propen-
sity of the mind to create images which take on for it the assumption
of reality, of truth. His subject here is the capacity of the mind for self-
deception, for the subjection of the imagination to fancy and self-
created truths. The phrase 'myself creating what I saw' is central, and
by extension it becomes so in *Emma* too when we remember that it is
Emma's inability to subject fancy to reason that causes most of her
problems and forms the core of the novel's dramatic structure. Her
perception of the world and of the people in it is clouded by her
imagination, by misplaced faith in her own powers of deduction, until
the final resolution. She actually does what Mr Knightley hopes he is
not doing – that is, she creates what she sees by perceiving what is not
there and not perceiving what is. She sees less with her eyes than with
her imagination, and in doing so constructs a series of realities which

201

have no basis in fact. Thus she sees Mr Elton falling in love with Harriet, Frank Churchill falling in love with Harriet, Mr Knightley falling in love with Harriet; and so she does not see Mr Elton pursuing herself, Frank Churchill and Jane Fairfax executing together their dance of deception, or even the true nature of the relationship between herself and Mr Knightley. Her 'reality' is of her own making – until Mr Knightley's proposal and her own sudden self-revelation.

Indeed, almost all of the major characters in *Emma* live within a reality of their own devising; the world they see is often a function of their own selfish egoism. Jane Austen's theme is ubiquitous; there are worlds and worlds in *Emma*. In Mr Woodhouse's world everyone as a matter of course prefers bad food to good and lives in mortal fear of draughts. In Frank Churchill's world the deception of others is of more constant importance than any consideration of their feelings. In Miss Bates's world everyone is dying for news not of their own relations, but of hers alone. In the world of the Eltons, social *éclat* and surface charm are always sufficiently endearing to others, no matter how virulent the vulgarity beneath. Harriet's world is one which may be conveniently created for one by a friend and handed over intact for one's own use and habitation – a pleasant world indeed, in which an illegitimate pauper of bovine intellect may sit back and wait for proposals of marriage, in rapid succession, from such men as Messrs Elton, Churchill, and Knightley. Even Mr Knightley's world is slightly askew, colored as it is by jealousy of a rival in love masquerading as intellectual and moral antipathy – Mr Knightley fails to see that his uncompromising dislike of Frank Churchill is a direct result of his passionate jealousy of him while it is generally assumed that Frank is courting Emma. All of these people, to varying extents, live in self-created, autonomous worlds – separate tables of the mind. Hugh Blair's 'Lectures on Rhetoric,' which Jane Austen is known to have read, tells us that 'We create worlds according to our fancy, in order to gratify our capacious desires.'[18] This is also what Cowper is telling us. The phrase from *The Task* quoted in *Emma* could well have been the novel's epigraph.

Cowper plays variations on this theme throughout much of Book IV of *The Task*:

Man in society is like a flower
Blown in its native bed. 'Tis there alone
His faculties expanded in full bloom
Shine out, there only reach their proper use. (ll. 659–62)

We find out what we are only through intercourse with others; alone we stagnate, feeding only on ourselves. One of Emma's problems is that she is too much alone, too far removed from the social intercourse of equals who would challenge her intellect and her judgment. She is so used to having her opinions accepted as law that she has come to think that she must always be right. There is no one, except on occasion Mr Knightley, to cause self-questioning in her, to start in her a searching assessment of her own powers of discrimination.

The phenomenon of self-imposed blindness is of course not confined to *Emma* among Jane Austen's novels. Elizabeth Bennet too has an unwarranted confidence in her own judgment, which is so often faulty. She does not take suggestions easily. And so she too fails to perceive reality accurately throughout much of *Pride and Prejudice,* basing her assessments of others upon erroneous perceptions which are the result, once again, of images of reality self-created rather than objective. Thus she fancies Wickham in the right and Darcy in the wrong merely because Wickham has flattered her and Darcy has insulted her. Perception becomes a function of ego rather than of reason; vision reproduces and imposes outward upon reality the images and shadows of the mind. Like Emma, Elizabeth is made to undergo a process of social intercourse which forces a rearrangement of her perceptions of the world and of herself. First impressions, she discovers, are often inaccurate because they are often self-indulgent.

Marianne Dashwood in *Sense and Sensibility* and Catherine Morland in *Northanger Abbey* also get into trouble because they find themselves at the mercy of a romantic imagination, a way of perceiving things that is a function of fancy rather than of discriminating judgment. This way of looking at things Jane Austen always condemns. The failure to *see,* the human capacity for self-deception, is her constant theme.

At the end of Book IV of *The Task,* Cowper suggests that meaningful social intercourse will ultimately teach the sentient being where he belongs among the various hierarchies of the world. An openness to experience can be instructive.

> Some must be great. Great offices will have
> Great talents. And God gives to every man
> The virtue, temper, understanding, taste,
> That lifts him into life, and lets him fall
> Just in the niche he was ordained to fill. (ll. 788–92)

He goes on to praise the 'unambitious mind,' content with its own proper sphere of activity, its own 'offices.' Emma's attempt to play God to her world must end in failure, as such attempts always must. By the end of the novel, however, everyone has found his or her proper level, whether it be that of Mrs Elton, Robert Martin, Jane Fairfax, or Mr Knightley. To fancy that we can surmount or circumvent our 'niche' or function at variance with our God-given 'talents' is merely to remain self-deceived.

Book VI of *The Task* also stresses the importance of

> a mind well strung and tuned
> To contemplation (ll. 263–4)

and attacks him who is

> by his vanity seduced,
> And soothed into a dream. (ll. 283–4)

Again it is the fruitful agony of self-understanding that Cowper seems to be pleading for, an ordeal of knowledge whose reward is perception of the world cleansed of selfish concerns. Emma's ordeal, like Elizabeth Bennet's, is climaxed by the explosion of her 'dream,' of her inability to see herself and others as they are. Cowper's theme is central in both novels.

At the end of *The Task*, Cowper strings together some precepts which seem to have, once again, particular relevance for readers of Jane Austen, and especially for readers of *Emma*.

> He is the happy man, whose life even now
> Shows somewhat of that happier life to come;
> Who, doomed to an obscure but tranquil state,
> Is pleased with it, and, were he free to choose,
> Would make his fate his choice; whom peace, the fruit
> Of virtue, and whom virtue, fruit of faith,
> Prepare for happiness; bespeak him one
> Content indeed to sojourn while he must
> Below the skies, but having there his home.
>
> Stillest streams
> Oft water fairest meadows, and the bird
> That flutters least is longest on the wing.
> Ask him, indeed, what trophies he has raised,
> Or what achievements of immortal fame
> He purposes, and he shall answer – None.
> His warfare is within. There unfatigued
> His fervent spirit labours. There he fights,
> And there obtains fresh triumphs o'er himself,
> And never withering wreaths, compared with which
> The laurels that a Caesar reaps are weeds. (ll. 906–14 and 929–39)

Cowper suggests here that contentment's first prerequisite is inner peace, the fruit of an inner kind of 'warfare.' This warfare, this self-questioning, is the only possible road to that understanding of self which is the chief condition of human happiness. The unexamined life is not worth living. Man must strive *within* himself – the only kind of 'worldly' striving worthwhile; only then will he be ready to make his fate his choice. There can be no tranquility in self-ignorance, and there can be none in self-conceit. Clearly these are central lessons of *Emma*. Until Emma finds that she must look within to see without, until she discovers that she cannot play God to her world, her existence is merely an exercise in solipsism.

It is an unimpeachable fact that Jane Austen read and admired Cowper. Her novels and letters reveal a real familiarity with his work – indeed, they suggest at times that she committed a goodly amount of it to memory. She is able to quote him facilely and off-handedly whenever she chooses. How much of her own work derives specifically from her reading of Cowper we may never know, both because so much of that phenomenon we call literary influence is unconscious and unrecorded and unrecordable, and also because we are missing, courtesy of the timorous Austen family, so much documentary evidence needed to answer such questions. What is clear, however, is that she was reading him, or hearing him read, as early as 1798, and perhaps earlier than that; that he was always one of her favorite writers; that her themes and his are sometimes the same themes; and that *Emma* specifically focuses on particular evils – self-imposed blindness, self-deception in relation to others – from a moral perspective similar to Cowper's. The influence itself may have been great, or it may have been small; but the two writers undeniably intersect in Jane Austen's surviving volumes, perhaps more significantly than a dozen quotations might indicate. For even a single chance phrase remembered suggests a substantial intellectual or philosophical imprint beneath, upon which it rests.

NOTES

1 *The Novels of Jane Austen,* ed. R. W. Chapman, Vol. v (London: Oxford University Press, 1923; 3rd ed, 1933), p. 7; and J. E. Austen-Leigh, *A Memoir of Jane Austen* (London: Richard Bentley, 1870), p. 110.

2 *Jane Austen: Selected Letters 1796-1817,* ed. R. W. Chapman (London: Oxford University Press, 1955), p. 17.

3 *Jane Austen's Letters to Her Sister Cassandra and Others,* ed. R. W. Chapman (London: Oxford University Press; 2nd ed., 1952), p. 39. I am indebted throughout to Chapman's helpful annotations.

4 *Ibid.,* p. 178.

5 My quotations from Cowper, here and throughout, are taken from *Cowper: Poetry and Prose,* ed. Brian Spiller (London: Rupert Hart-Davis, 1968). Further references will be identified in the text by line number. I

wish to express here my gratitude to Professor Donald Greene for putting his knowledge of Cowper at my disposal.

6 *Jane Austen's Letters*, p. 335.

7 *Ibid.*, p. 368.

8 *The Novels of Jane Austen*, Vol. I, p. 226. The connection was first called to my attention by Everett Zimmerman's essay in this volume, 'Admiring Pope no more than is proper: *Sense and Sensibility.*'

9 *Ibid.*, p. 18.

10 *Ibid.*, p. 47.

11 *Ibid.*, p. 92.

12 *The Novels of Jane Austen*, Vol. III, p. 56.

13 *Ibid.*, p. 431.

14 *The Works of Jane Austen*, ed. R. W. Chapman, Vol. VI: *Minor Works* (London: Oxford University Press, 1954; rev. ed., 1965), p. 370.

15 *The Novels of Jane Austen*, Vol. IV, p. 344.

16 By an odd coincidence, Cowper apparently wrote it at the instigation of one Lady Austen (1738–1802), an evangelical widow (of Sir Robert Austen, d. 1772) whom Cowper met in 1781 and who ultimately became a close friend of the poet for several years before she remarried and moved to France. One version of the genesis of *The Task* has it that Lady Austen (no relation of the novelist, nor was her husband) assigned to Cowper, when he complained to her that he could think of nothing to write about, the 'task' of writing about a sofa, and *The Task* was the result (Book I of the poem is entitled 'The Sofa'). See *English Prose and Poetry 1660–1800*, ed. Frank Brady and Martin Price (New York: Holt, Rinehart, and Winston, 1962), p. 422n, and Spiller, 'Introduction,' and pp. 393 and 624n. Cowper tells us more about the composition of the poem in a 1786 letter to Lady Hesketh; see Spiller, pp. 768–75.

17 Spiller, pp. 393–4. Cowper summarizes the meaning of the poem in these terms in a letter to William Unwin. *The Task,* as Spiller points out here, with its stress on the necessity of man's putting himself into right relations with God, was of incalculable importance to the Evangelicals in their work of bringing about a revolution in the field of morals.

18 See *Lectures on Rhetoric and the Belles Lettres*, ed. Harold F. Harding (Carbondale: Southern Illinois University Press, 1965), Vol. I, p. 391. I am indebted to the essay in this volume by Katrin Ristkok Burlin, '"The pen of the contriver": The four fictions of *Northanger Abbey*,' for alerting me to this passage. Jane Austen alludes to Blair in *Northanger Abbey*. See *The Novels of Jane Austen*, Vol. V, pp. 108 and 296.

JOSEPH WIESENFARTH

Emma: point counter point

It is a rare pleasure to read a fugue, and *Emma* is the rare novel that provides that pleasure.[1]

The subject of *Emma* is match-making. It catches the tone of mind, emotion, and spirit of every character in the novel, and it develops the novel's theme of 'virtue overcoming selfishness and self-centeredness' and 'establishes the principle that happy relations are good' – much better indeed than being nothing more than 'handsome, clever, and rich.'[2] The subject is introduced by the narrator, who says quite simply of Miss Taylor's marriage to Mr Weston that 'Emma had always wished and promoted the match.' It is developed in a series of expositions, the first of which, in three voices, is a conversation between Emma, Mr Knightley, and Mr Woodhouse that takes place the evening of the Weston wedding. In this conversation Mr Knightley introduces a countersubject, which Mr Woodhouse ludicrously echoes, by cautioning against match-making.[3] 'Every friend of Miss Taylor must be glad to have her so happily married,' says Mr Knightley. 'And you have forgotten one matter of joy to me,' replies Emma; 'I made the match myself.' Mr Knightley, however, doesn't believe a word of Emma's claim:

'A straight-forward, open-hearted man, like Weston, and a rational unaffected woman, like Miss Taylor, may be safely left to manage their own concerns. You are more likely to have done harm to yourself, than good to them, by interference.'

'Emma never thinks of herself, if she can do good to others,'

207

rejoined Mr Woodhouse, understanding but in part. 'But, my dear, pray do not make any more matches, they are silly things, and break up one's family circle grievously.'

'Only one more, papa; only for Mr Elton . . .'

'But if you want to shew him any attention, my dear, ask him to come and dine with us some day . . . I dare say Mr Knightley will be so kind as to meet him.'

'With a great deal of pleasure, sir, at any time,' said Mr Knightley laughing . . . 'Invite him to dinner, Emma . . . but leave him to chuse his own wife. Depend upon it, a man of six or seven-and-twenty can take care of himself.' (I, 1)[4]

This first exposition is followed by the episode of Harriet Smith's introduction to Hartfield and by a second and more dramatic exposition of the subject as Emma tries to make a match between Harriet and Mr Elton. Subsequent episodes bring Jane Fairfax to Highbury, introduce Frank Churchill to Randalls, reacquaint Harriet with Abbey-Mill farm, and transport her to Brunswick Square, the John Knightleys' residence in London, where she meets Robert Martin once again. The Coles' dinner party, the Crown Inn ball, the Donwell strawberry party, and the Box Hill excursion form another set of similar episodes that alternate with the expositions while also being derived from them. The major expositions of subject and countersubject occur with Emma projecting marriages between Harriet and, successively, Mr Elton, Mr Knightley, and Frank Churchill, and with Harriet on her own accepting and marrying Robert Martin; with Mrs Weston projecting a marriage between Jane Fairfax and Mr Knightley, and with Jane on her own accepting and marrying Frank Churchill; and with Mr and Mrs Weston projecting a marriage between Emma and Frank, and with Emma on her own accepting and marrying Mr Knightley. Motifs within the expositions and episodes emphasize the importance that society gives to a bride; link reason and fancy to nature and artificiality; and develop the various meanings of the word *elegance*. A stretto occurs when the subject and countersubject appear at shorter intervals: between chapters 10 and 19 of the last volume, Harriet and Robert Martin are engaged, and they marry in September; Emma and Mr Knightley are engaged, and they marry in October; and Jane Fairfax and Frank Churchill announce their engagement, and they set their wedding for November. The novel ends with a coda,[5] which extends everything that has already been fully developed, concluding with a pedal-point of perfect happiness sounding beneath discordant notes given off *piano* by Highbury's turkey-thieves and *fortissimo* by Mrs Elton's vanity: 'Very little white satin, very few lace veils; a most pitiful business! – Selina would stare when she heard of it' (III, 19).[6]

Emma's taking the likeness of Harriet Smith is a particularly rich and satisfying passage of exposition, having echoes and counter-echoes throughout the novel. We see immediately that the portrait of Harriet is Emma's attempt to create an image of the girl that corresponds to Mr Elton's flattering suggestion that Emma has improved Harriet:

> 'You have given Miss Smith all that she required,' said he; 'you have made her graceful and easy. She was a beautiful creature when she came to you, but, in my opinion, the attractions you have added are infinitely superior to what she received from nature.'
> 'I am glad you think I have been useful to her; but Harriet only wanted drawing out, and receiving a few, very few hints . . .'
> 'Skilful has been the hand.' (I, 6)

The 'drawing out' by the 'skilful hand' produces the portrait. Harriet appears with 'a little improvement to the figure,' 'a little more height,' and 'considerably more elegance.' Looking at the portrait, Mrs Weston notices that 'Miss Smith has not those eye-brows and eye-lashes. It is the fault of her face that she has them not.' Mr Knightley tells the artist, 'You have made her too tall, Emma.' Mr Elton contradicts the critics and praises the artist. Emma knows that she is wrong and they are right. She has forced Harriet into a mold of elegance. When a thoroughly vulgar woman later appears in Mrs Elton – 'neither feature, nor air, nor voice, nor manner, were elegant' (II, 14) – Emma begins to see the danger of making people appear by art what they are not by nature.

The portrait is a product of Emma's cleverness, and cleverness is a negative aspect of character in the novel. 'Emma,' says Mr Knightley, 'is spoiled by being the cleverest of her family.' He tells Mrs Weston that Emma 'will never submit to any thing requiring industry and patience and a subjection of the fancy to the understanding' (I, 5). Mr Knightley illustrates his judgment by pointing to Emma's failure in 'any course of steady reading,' and the narrator substantiates it by saying that Emma 'was not much deceived as to her own skill either as an artist or a musician, but she was not unwilling to have others deceived, or sorry to know her reputation for accomplishment often higher than it deserved' (I, 6). Mr Knightley tells Mrs Weston that Emma can only give Harriet 'a little polish'; and he tells Emma that she has cured Harriet of 'her school-girl's giggle,' but nothing more. He sees Emma in effect as having made a change in Harriet's manner but not in what Harriet substantively is – the natural daughter of somebody, a girl with a good heart but a bad head. Emma has tried to make Harriet appear what she is not. The portrait does exactly the same thing. Like Emma herself, it is too clever by half.

Mr Knightley consistently looks to the substance of things while

Emma looks to their appearance. She tries to make Harriet appear
elegant to society although the girl is inherently incapable of
elegance. The words *elegance* and *elegant* are derived from the Latin
word *eligere,* to choose out or to select, and they occur in *Emma* more
frequently than they do in any other Austen novel.

Elegance emphasizes beauty without grandeur, beauty that is
soothing rather than striking.[7] The soothing qualities of elegance are
'those which are appropriate, accurate, exact in some respect.'[8] *Emma*
is a novel that demands such qualities because it is filled with
charades, conundrums, enigmas, and word-puzzles. These in small
raise larger issues: the *Courtship* charade raises the issue of who is
courting whom; the *Dixon* word-puzzle, the issue of whom Jane Fairfax loves; the *M* and *A* conundrum, the issue of what perfection really
is. The word BLUNDER runs like a discord through the novel, indicat-
ing mistakes that are made in the games of words as well as in the
more serious and dangerous games of match-making. Life as depicted
in *Emma* demands accuracy and exactness, which are qualities of
elegance, to perceive correctly, to act appropriately, and to achieve the.
perfection of love that the end of the novel celebrates. Elegance in
Emma then is the enemy not only of the simplicity of a Harriet Smith
and of the vulgarity of a Mrs Elton but also of mystery and disguise –
of the gallantry of Mr Elton and of the amiability of Frank Churchill,
for instance – that make right judgment and good conduct more difficult for all. True elegance in *Emma* is inherent in Mr Knightley's keen
judgment of character, genuine English amiability, and straightforward humane action.

Both Emma and Jane Fairfax achieve such true elegance after they
repudiate their mistakes and misconduct – the one her judgment that
Harriet is suitable to be a gentleman's wife, the other her toleration of
a secret engagement that is not consonant with moral obligation.
Emma and Jane, with faculties capable of refinement, can achieve
complete elegance. This is not the case, however, with Harriet Smith
and Augusta Elton. Physically, Harriet is below the stature of true
elegance, or middle height.[9] Mentally, Harriet, hopelessly ungrammatical, must employ Emma to write her refusal to Martin's offer of
marriage. Morally, Harriet can be led into wrong action (witness her
submission to Emma) or into right action (witness her dependence as
a wife on Martin's judgment). Emotionally, Harriet is a votary of
Martin, Elton, Knightley and Martin once again. Harriet is a sweet-
tempered, good-natured girl, but not an elegant woman.

Mrs Elton is characterized by an overlay of elegance that opulently
exhibits her vulgarity. This is especially evident in her dress, speech,
and manner. Mrs Elton, who is only 'as elegant as lace and pearls
could make her' (II, 16), arrives at Donwell Abbey 'in all her apparatus

of happiness, her large bonnet and her basket,' talking 'strawberries, and only strawberries' (III, 6). Her speech is characteristically larded with the Sucklings, Maple Grove, and the barouche-landau, which indicates that her standards of judgment are formed by wealth; therefore, she finally sees the thoroughly satisfying wedding of Emma to Mr Knightley as a poor affair. Her manners have 'ease but not elegance' (II, 14), that is, she is facile but not refined. Mrs Elton presents the façade of the elegant woman but is actually inelegant: she is rude to Harriet, patronizes Mr Woodhouse ('this dear old beau of mine'), tries to expropriate Mr Knightley's guests, insists on Jane's becoming a governess, and sets up as Emma's rival. She is 'self-important, presuming, familiar, ignorant, and ill-bred' (II, 15), the epitome of inelegance.

Jane Fairfax, on the other hand, is a paragon of womanly elegance:

> Jane Fairfax was very elegant, remarkably elegant; and she had herself the highest value for elegance. Her height was pretty, just such as almost everybody would think tall, and nobody could think very tall; her figure particularly graceful . . . Her eyes, a deep gray, with dark eye-lashes and eye-brows, had never been denied their praise . . . It was a style of beauty, of which elegance was the reigning character, and as such, she [Emma] must, in honour, by all her principles, admire it: – elegance, which, whether of person or of mind, she saw so little in Highbury. (II, 2)

If one thinks about this description of Jane Fairfax and compares it with the portrait of Harriet Smith, it becomes evident that Emma tries to make a Miss Fairfax of a Miss Smith. Jane has a graceful figure; Emma gives 'a little improvement' to Harriet's figure. Jane is not tall but is thought tall; Emma gives Harriet 'a little more height.' Jane's eyebrows and eyelashes are much praised; Emma improves Harriet's eyebrows and eyelashes. Jane's style of beauty is distinguished by elegance; Emma gives Harriet's person 'considerably more elegance' than it possesses. Mr Knightley and Mrs Weston immediately see the flaws in Emma's likeness of Harriet. The inaccuracy of Emma's portrait is therefore a tribute to what Jane Fairfax represents, elegance, not to what Harriet is, nature in a relatively unrefined state. But there is indeed more to it than this. The portrait of Harriet is also the portrait of moral aspiration in Emma, however misguided it may at the moment be.

Emma's not being 'sorry to know [that] her reputation for accomplishment [was] often higher than it deserved' is a left-handed confirmation of the value she places on elegance. But it is clear that Emma cannot associate with Jane Fairfax without losing her reputation for accomplishment and without being seen for what she more

truly is. When Jane plays the pianoforte, Emma is second fiddle at
best. Emma's invention of a liaison between Jane and Mr Dixon, then,
is simply a way of giving herself a spurious sense of moral superiority
while Jane is in Highbury to overshadow her in other ways.

Emma's invention of a lover for Jane in Mr Dixon is also an extension of her invention of lovers for Harriet. This suggests another
dimension of meaning in the portrait. Harriet serves as a surrogate for
Emma's emotional life. At Box Hill, Frank Churchill asks Emma:

> 'Will you choose a wife for me? – I am sure I should like any body
> fixed on by you . . . Find somebody for me. I am in no hurry.
> Adopt her, educate her.'
>   'And make her like myself.'
>   'By all means, if you can.'
>   'Very well, I undertake the commission. You shall have a
> charming wife.' (III, 7)

While Emma herself is not available to be made love to, she creates
the elegant Harriet of the portrait for the specific purpose of making
her *disponible* to gentlemen like Frank Churchill. It is no accident of
the plot that of the three men whom Emma wishes Harriet to marry,
one makes 'violent love' to Emma, a second is thought of as a husband
for Emma, and the third marries Emma. So another aspect of Emma's
making Harriet an elegant lady in her portrait is Emma's need to make
Harriet someone like herself. For if we once again return to the lines
of the portrait of Miss Smith, we see this time traces of the likeness of
Miss Woodhouse.

> 'Such an eye! – the true hazel eye – and so brilliant! regular features,
> open countenance, with a complexion! oh! what a bloom of full
> health, and such a pretty height and size; such a firm and upright
> figure . . . She is loveliness itself.' (I, 5).

The more closely Harriet approximates the elegance of Jane Fairfax,
the more closely she approximates the features of Emma. The portrait
has as much to do with the unconscious emotional life of Emma as it
does with her unconscious moral aspirations. When one thinks of Karl
Kroeber's statement that in *Emma* 'happy relations are good,' one sees
how appropriate a moral–emotional axis is in a healthy, elegant
woman.

The portrait shows the reader, then, that Emma has fallen in love
with society's image of what a lady suited to be a gentleman's wife
should be, and it shows that she tries to create Harriet in that image.
Emma is trying to make Harriet, by clever drawing, what she has not
been able to make herself by good judgment and the steady perfection
of her own natural abilities. In Harriet's portrait one side of Emma's

character is shown in her neglect of what she truly respects – superiority of mind, talent, and character. Harriet's portrait represents Emma's control over society's adherence to appearances and her lack of control over herself. Her neglect of Jane represents Emma's fear that although she is handsome, clever and rich and looks like a lady – having herself what she gives Harriet – she may not be as thorough a lady as she ought to be.

In that resonant and vibrating passage in which Emma draws a Harriet who does not exist, we see Emma creating out of society's norms and out of her unconscious self an image that she falls in love with. (Harriet is, after all, invested with Emma's emotional needs and is a symbol of her power.) Emma re-enacts with Harriet elements of the myth of Pygmalion and Galatea. The celibate king, who thought women eminently wanting in perfection, created the statue of a woman, which he perfected so painstakingly that he fell hopelessly in love with it. Finally his love brought his art to life through the intercession of Venus and he espoused the beauty he created.[10]

Lloyd Brown has recently indicated the variety of parody in Jane Austen's novels,[11] and Emma's taking the likeness of Harriet and investing herself entirely in it seems to be a parody of Ovid's famous story. But the most significant element of the parody is that Emma cannot bring her portrait of Harriet to life. The ungrammatical girl with her relics of a court plaister and an old pencil stub is simply incapable of becoming an elegant woman. On the one occasion that she thinks herself so she decides that Mr Knightley would not be a match too good for her: 'If he does choose me, it will not be any thing so very wonderful.' At this moment Pygmalion *manqué* repudiates Galatea *manquée* decidedly: 'Oh God! that I had never seen her!' Emma, like Pygmalion, tries to bring to life an artifical Harriet, but cannot do so save for this one horrible moment which Harriet's delusion concerning Mr Knightley brings about. Emma tries to create an elegant woman and produces only a dangerous one.

Insofar as the novel concerns Emma's growth into responsible womanhood by immersing her in the process of match-making, her embarrassing entanglement with Harriet is a necessary evil. That Harriet is Emma living vicariously is evident from Emma's enjoying and suffering the emotional and moral complexities of Harriet's multiple courtships more than the girl herself does. Harriet affords her sponsor the most intense moments of pleasure and pain until Emma decides that she really has to live her own life or lose Mr Knightley and every best thing along with him. Instead of creating a Galatea through whom she can live more fully, Emma creates in Harriet, at least momentarily, a vain woman who threatens to destroy her.

Emma's failure with Harriet is also a failure of her wish to dominate everybody and everything in Highbury. She repeats this perversity in the case of Frank Churchill, who has not yet paid a wedding-visit to Randalls. Mrs Weston sketches a picture of Frank's character which exonerates him, but Emma refuses to see it as a likeness of Churchill: 'If he could stay only a couple of days, he ought to come; and one can hardly conceive a young man's not having it in his power to do as much as that' (I, 16). When Mr Knightley and Emma discuss the same problem, he says: 'I cannot believe that he has not the power of coming, if he made a point of it' (I, 18). Emma refuses, however, to admit the probability of this argument – the very argument she used against Mrs Weston – and she proceeds to sketch a likeness of Churchill that she very well knows is different from what she believes him to be. Right or wrong is not the issue here for Emma with Frank's likeness, nor was it the issue for her earlier with Harriet's. The issue is Emma's having her own way.

Now this desire on Emma's part to dominate, more than anything else, threatens her well-being. She has everything at her command and is at the command of no man alive. Though she sees marriage as woman's best good, she does not see it as her own. Though she calculatingly promotes the marriages of others, she has to be surprised into her own: 'It darted through her, with the speed of an arrow, that Mr Knightley must marry no one but herself!' (III, 11). Emma's manipulation of Harriet is simply the primary example of her love to dominate. Harriet's portrait is an image of Emma's 'disposition to think a little too well of herself.' The creating of an elegant eligible Harriet is the comedy of Emma's narcissism. This excessive love of self is given its grotesque features in the character of Augusta Elton.

Emma is characterized by an elegant appearance – face, figure, height – which, as we have seen, complements Jane Fairfax's. But Emma is also characterized by a vulgarity of mind that complements Augusta Elton's. Each insists on the adequacy of her inner resources – the 'many resources within myself' – that make the 'world' unnecessary to one and marriage unnecessary to the other. Like Mrs Elton, Emma has a reputation for accomplishment, but both scant their crayons and pianoforte. We suspect Mrs Elton of little reading, and we never see Emma open a book – though she has reading lists aplenty. And like Mrs Elton, Emma loves to dominate. When Emma is told that the Crown Inn ball – which 'she had always considered . . . as peculiarly for her' – must be begun by Mr Elton's bride, 'Emma heard the sad truth with fortitude . . . It was almost enough to make her think of marrying' (III, 2). When during the Box Hill excursion Frank Churchill announces that Emma presides wherever she is, 'Mrs Elton swelled at the idea of Miss Woodhouse's presiding' (III, 7). When Mr Knightley suggests a strawberry party at Donwell Abbey, Mrs Elton insists on inviting the guests; but he replies that only a Mrs Knightley can 'invite what guests she pleases to Donwell' (III, 6). When Emma becomes his bride and by virtue of that title supercedes Mrs Elton, the latter is outraged: 'No more exploring parties to Donwell made for *her.* Oh! no; there would be a Mrs Knightley to throw cold water on every thing' (III, 17). Though Miss Woodhouse finally wins this contest with Mrs Elton by repudiating her most Augusta-like qualities in becoming Mrs Knightley, she is too much like Mrs Elton for too long for comfort.

Mrs Elton's patronage of Jane Fairfax, for instance, is a mirror in which we see Emma's patronage of Harriet. Jane Fairfax, however, is as much Mrs Elton's superior as Harriet is Emma's inferior. Emma fails to educate Harriet's simplicity, and Mrs Elton fails to break down Jane's elegance. Emma's solicitude to get Harriet the right husband is mirrored in Mrs Elton's solicitude to get Jane the right position as governess. Emma avoids Jane because she cannot patronize her, and Mrs Elton avoids Emma because she cannot patronize her. What Mrs Elton wants to be, she tells Mr Knightley, is 'Lady Patroness.' She takes up Jane to be superior to her, just as Emma takes up Harriet to be superior to her. What Emma and Mrs Elton show each other each in her own way is the vulgar mind of self-important people. Emma wins out over Mrs Elton because she is intelligent enough finally to see that her own mind has been vulgar. Save for her affection for Mr Knightley, she finds that 'every other part of her mind was disgusting' (III, 11). When Emma visits Jane subsequent to their engagements, Jane says to Emma: 'I know that I must have disgusted you' (III, 16). Jane and Emma finally find themselves one in repenting their misdeeds. 'Mystery; Finesse – how they pervert the understanding!' says Mr Knightley (III, 15). There is to be no more mystery and finesse for Emma and Jane. In finding themselves disgusting they achieve precise judgment, which is the mark of an elegance of mind that finally matches their elegance of person.

That Emma achieves elegance of mind by the shaping abrasiveness of experience is undeniable. But equally undeniable is the shaping force of Mr. Knightley's love on her character.

Till now that she was threatened with its loss, Emma had never known how much her happiness depended on being *first* with Mr Knightley, first in interest and affection . . . She had herself been first with him for many years past. She had not deserved it; she had often been negligent or perverse, slighting his advice, or even wilfully opposing him, insensible of half his merits, and quarrelling with him because he would not acknowledge her false and insolent estimate of her own – but still, from family attachment

215

and habit, and thorough excellence of mind, he had loved her, and watched over her from a girl, with an endeavour to improve her, and an anxiety for her doing right, which no other creature had at all shared. (III, 12)

The counterpoint to Emma's failure as Pygmalion is Mr Knightley's success. Emma is in a real way his Galatea. He has been at work on her for at least eight years, since she was thirteen. He has half-consciously loved her that length of time, and he has been jealous of her affection from the moment Frank Churchill arrived in Highbury. Mr Knightley's aim has ever been to bring to perfection what is substantial in Emma. He does not agree with Mr Weston's conundrum that *M* and *A* are two letters that equal perfection (Emma). Mr Knightley cures Emma's vanity, corrects her judgment, moves her to repentance, and frees her of the crippling notions that her good depends upon her independence as an unmarried aunt and upon her need independently to mother her father. He helps her to become an elegant woman. Jane Austen allows her true Pygmalion to succeed where the possibilities of Galatea's nature give intelligent direction to his art. Such art has of course positive moral implications.

'Teach us to understand the sinfulness of our own hearts, and bring to our knowledge every fault of temper and every evil habit in which we have indulged to the discomfort of our fellow-creatures, and the danger of our own souls' – this was Jane Austen's own prayer at the day's end.[12] For Emma that prayer is answered in the person of Mr Knightley, who teaches her to understand, corrects her faults of temper, and warns her about harming Harriet Smith and herself. The pattern of the Pygmalion story in *Emma*, with its point (Emma as Pygmalion) and its counterpoint (Mr Knightley as Pygmalion), is the most complex rendering of this myth in Jane Austen's novels. It is the most delightful elaboration of a story that appears in *Northanger Abbey, Sense and Sensibility,* and *Mansfield Park* – in Henry Tilney's shaping of Catherine Morland, in Colonel Brandon's shaping of Marianne Dashwood, and in Edmund Bertram's shaping of Fanny Price. The hard truth in these novels is that Pygmalion is inevitably male.

Pride and Prejudice and *Persuasion,* however, redress the balance in favor of women, employing the more radical story of Cinderella as an underlying pattern to do so. The Cinderella story appeals to the rightness of personal merit achieving social recognition as well as to the fitness of genuine love finding happy marriage. *Mansfield Park* shows the pattern of Cinderella's story colliding with the pattern of Pygmalion's. With Mrs Norris as a stepmother, Maria and Julia as stepsisters, and Henry Crawford as Prince Charming, Fanny Price refuses to be Cinderella. Edmund Bertram made her, and it is

Edmund Bertram she loves. The possibilities of Cinderella's world are destroyed as its characters disintegrate under the pressure of moral existence. When Edmund realizes that he loves Fanny, Pygmalion marries Galatea and the old myth is affirmed, along with the positive values of gentry life.

Emma is Jane Austen's last and most lively rendering of this pattern and theme. In finally having Emma repudiate the role of Pygmalion for that of Galatea, Jane Austen does not present the triumph of male society. She celebrates the education of a woman who has become the equal of the good and intelligent man who has been anxious for her. Emma Woodhouse is no less a heroine than Elizabeth Bennet. Darcy's second proposal is an affirmation of Elizabeth's moral and intellectual excellence, and it is her due as his equal. Mr Knightley's proposal to Emma is the same. But Emma and Elizabeth come to their engagements by different paths, with that of Cinderella emphasizing the greater need for perception on the part of the man and that of Galatea emphasizing the greater need for perception on the part of the woman. In finally having Darcy affirm Elizabeth as Cinderella, Jane Austen repudiates all that is unreasonable and unnatural in her society. In finally having Emma repudiate the role of Pygmalion for that of Galatea, Jane Austen affirms all that is reasonable and natural in a society that withstands fanciful delusions and snobbish willfulness.

No matter which pattern is emphasized in her novels – the Cinderella or the Pygmalion and Galatea – Jane Austen adheres to a norm of clear thinking enunciated by Samuel Johnson: a man ought to endeavor 'to distinguish nature from custom, or that which is established because it is right, from that which is right only because it is established.'[13] Jane Austen's Cinderella novels show the force of nature displacing customs that are considered right only because they are established. Jane Austen's Pygmalion novels show the force of nature preserving customs that are established because they are right. The radical and conservative tendencies that the myths in Jane Austen's novels emphasize are based on nature as interpreted by man's reason. In all her novels the final triumph of the natural order as interpreted by intelligent people – whose self-searching leads to mortification and then rebirth in understanding and affection – shows that the stories of Cinderella and Pygmalion and Galatea are part of an all-encompassing mythos of comedy.

One of the inevitable delights of comedy comes from its rendering of the complexities and pitfalls of life without allowing them to overcome the order of affection and intelligence which makes life joyful. The delight of a comedy is akin to that of a complex musical form – the form of a fugue, for instance – which sets in harmony the dissonance of counterpoint as well as its melody. For all the complications that develop in the course of its rendering, we know from the form itself that the ending will resolve them brilliantly and delightfully. The subjects of *Emma,* complexly developed in the counterpoint of the Pygmalion myth with its parody, are pleasantly resolved in the final harmonies of the novel:

> The wedding was very much like other weddings, where the parties have no taste for finery or parade; and Mrs Elton, from the particulars detailed by her husband, thought it all extremely shabby, and very inferior to her own. – 'Very little white satin, very few lace veils; a most pitiful business! – Selina would stare when she heard of it.' – But, in spite of these deficiencies, the wishes, the hopes, the confidence, the predictions of the small band of true friends who witnessed the ceremony, were fully answered in the perfect happiness of the union.

Only the Mrs Eltons of the world fail to delight in the complexities of Emma – *Emma* the novel, Emma the woman, and *M–A* the conundrum. One must finally suspect that in the absence of finery and parade, true elegance of any kind is beyond their comprehension – and say no more.

NOTES

1 Willi Apel suggests that there may be no such thing as 'fugue form' but only 'fugal procedure.' He does nevertheless provide a description of a 'student's fugue.' A fugue is always written in counterpoint, the combination of two or more melodic lines that produce harmony without losing their linear individuality. A fugue is based on a short melody called a *subject* introduced by one *voice* (an individual part) and then taken up by other voices in close succession. The first development of the subject by several voices is called an *exposition,* a name also given to subsequent developments of the subject. The second statement of the subject, which occurs in the exposition, can introduce a *countersubject,* a melody designed as a counterpoint to the subject, which is a continuation of the subject as well as a contrast to it. *Episodes* in a fugue do not completely restate the subject, but are usually related to it. They are frequently based on *motifs,* musical phrases derived from the subject. The 'over-all structure of a fugue,' says Apel, 'is an alternation of expositions and episodes.' A fugue frequently includes a *stretto* towards its ending; the *stretto* consists of rapid entries of the subject after very short intervals of time. A *coda* with a *pedal-point* often ends the fugue. The *coda,* or tail, extends into a satisfying conclusion what has already been logically developed. The *pedal-point* within the coda is a note that is held while harmonic progressions, sometimes discordant with it, continue above it.
    In this exposition of 'fugue form' I have followed Willi Apel, *Harvard*

Dictionary of Music, 2nd ed. (Cambridge: Belknap Press, 1970), 'Fugue,' pp. 335–7. See also J. A. Westrup and F. L. Harrison, *The New College Encyclopedia of Music* (New York: Norton, 1960), 'Coda,' p. 146; 'Countersubject,' p. 163; 'Episode,' p. 225; 'Pedal Point,' p. 492; 'Stretto,' p. 629. The definitions supplied in this note are meant to limit the meaning of the words defined as they are used in the text.

2 Karl Kroeber, *Styles in Fictional Structure: The Art of Jane Austen, Charlotte Brontë, George Eliot* (Princeton: Princeton University Press, 1971), pp. 22–3.

3 Because of the equal importance of the countersubject, the form of *Emma* is analogous to that of a *double fugue:* 'a fugue in which the countersubject has an individual character and is consistently used throughout the piece, combined with the main subject' (Apel).

4 *Emma,* Vol. IV in *The Novels of Jane Austen,* ed. R. W. Chapman (1st ed., 1923; London: Oxford University Press, 3rd ed., 1933). Quotations are cited by volume and chapter. In editions of *Emma* that number chapters consecutively, Vol. II, ch. 1 is 19, and Vol. III, ch. 1 is 37.

5 On the ending of *Emma,* see Lloyd W. Brown, *Bits of Ivory: Narrative Techniques in Jane Austen's Fiction* (Baton Rouge: Louisiana State University Press, 1973), p. 224.

6 This analysis of *Emma* in terms of the structure of a fugue is not meant to insist that Jane Austen modeled her novel on the form of a fugue, though it seems that she could have because her knowledge of music was considerable, as the music books at Chawton cottage transcribed by her own hand show; it is meant to suggest a way of conceptualizing the form of the novel that seems apt and satisfying. One may want to say that I am here giving fuller exposition to an analogy that critics of Austen have more or less consciously hinted at in the metaphors they use to describe her novels. Karl Kroeber, for instance, talks about resolving ' "discrepancies" into harmonies' in *Emma,* and about an 'emerging theme . . . counterpointed by a structural movement.' See *Styles in Fictional Structure,* pp. 20–3. A. Walton Litz, writing of *Pride and Prejudice,* says the novel provides 'a final pleasure unique in Jane Austen's fiction, a sense of complete fulfillment analogous to that which marks the end of some musical compositions.' See *Jane Austen: A Study of Her Artistic Development* (New York: Oxford University Press, 1965), p. 102. Other modes of conceptualizing the form of *Emma* are discussed in Joseph Wiesenfarth, *The Errand of Form: An Assay of Jane Austen's Art* (New York: Fordham University Press, 1967), pp. 182–3, n. 16. Jane Nardin's excellent analysis of *Emma* (pp. 107–28) has one defect: it equates elegance with conventional propriety, which is defined as impeccable manners devoid of feeling. Just as a conventional propriety is distinguished from true propriety, conventional elegance can be distinguished from true elegance; indeed, Nardin hints at this distinction when she tells us that Emma's word for the concept of true propriety (the kind esteemed by Elinor in *Sense and Sensibility*) is 'elegance' (p. 116). See *Those Elegant Decorums: The Concept of Propriety in Jane Austen's Novels* (Albany: State University of New York Press, 1973). Stuart M.

Tave provides a more flexible discussion of the meanings of elegance in *Some Words of Jane Austen* (Chicago and London: University of Chicago Press, 1973), pp. 222–9.

7 Jean H. Hagstrum, *Samuel Johnson's Literary Criticism* (Minneapolis: University of Minnesota Press, 1952), p. 130.

8 Patricia Ingham, 'Dr Johnson's "Elegance,"' *Review of English Studies,* 19 (1968), p. 278. Nardin's restricted application of elegance 'to the more superficial aspects of social convention only,' allowing it 'no moral overtones whatsoever,' is too limited to satisfy as a definition of the word as it is used in *Emma; see Those Elegant Decorums,* p. 12; see also p. 14.

9 Writing of his sister, Henry Austen remarks, 'Her stature was that of true elegance. It could not have been increased without exceeding the middle height.' See 'Biographical Notice of the Author' in *The Novels of Jane Austen,* Vol. v, p. 5.

10 Ovid, *The Metamorphosis,* 110: 243–97. Ovid is not on R. W. Chapman's general index of literary allusions in Austen's works (*Novels of Jane Austen,* Vol. v, pp. 295–306, 311). But one can reasonably assume that the daughter of George Austen would know the story either from her classicist father or from the translations of Golding (1567) and Sandys (1632) or from Dryden's rendering of it in 'Pygmalion and the Statue,' *Fables Ancient and Modern* (1700). That the essential pattern of the Pygmalion–Galatea story exists in Jane Austen's novels is, on the evidence, unquestionable; the immediate source of the pattern is more of a problem to establish.

11 *Bits of Ivory,* pp. 199–235.

12 *The Novels of Jane Austen,* Vol. vi: *Minor Works,* ed. R. W. Chapman (1st ed., 1954; London: Oxford University Press, 1958), p. 453.

13 Samuel Johnson, *The Rambler,* ed. W. J. Bate and Albrecht B. Strauss (New Haven and London: Yale University Press, 1969), p. 70. *Rambler* No. 156, from which this quotation comes, is devoted to the rules of tragedy, but generalizations of more universal application are found within it. Its epigraph from Juvenal is one of them: 'For wisdom ever echoes nature's voice' (p. 65). Another statement of such universal application is the following: 'The accidental prescriptions of authority, when time has procured them veneration, are often confounded with the laws of nature, and those rules are supposed coeval with reason, of which the first rise cannot be discovered' (p. 66).

A. WALTON LITZ

Persuasion: forms of estrangement

Virginia Woolf, in her essay on Jane Austen in *The Common Reader* (1925), found that *Persuasion* was characterized by 'a peculiar beauty and a peculiar dullness.'

> The dullness is that which so often marks the transition between two different periods. The writer is a little bored. She has grown too familiar with the ways of her world; she no longer notes them freshly. There is an asperity in her comedy which suggests that she has almost ceased to be amused by the vanities of a Sir Walter or the snobbery of a Miss Elliot. The satire is harsh, and the comedy crude. She is no longer so freshly aware of the amusements of everyday life. Her mind is not altogether on her object. But, while we feel that Jane Austen has done this before, and done it better, we also feel that she is trying to do something which she has never yet attempted.

Most readers will agree with Virginia Woolf's response, whether or not they care to use the term 'dullness': Jane Austen has her eye on new effects in *Persuasion,* and situations or characters which yielded such rich comic pleasures in previous novels are given summary treatment. Most readers would also agree that there is a 'peculiar' beauty in *Persuasion,* that it has to do with a new allegiance to feeling rather than prudence, to poetry rather than prose, and that it springs from a deep sense of personal loss. As Virginia Woolf phrases it, Jane Austen 'is beginning to discover that the world is larger, more mysterious, and more romantic than she had supposed.'

221

We feel it to be true of herself when she says of Anne: 'She had been forced into prudence in her youth, she learned romance as she grew older – the natural sequel of an unnatural beginning.' She dwells frequently upon the beauty and the melancholy of nature, upon the autumn where she had been wont to dwell upon the spring. She talks of the 'influence so sweet and so sad of autumnal months in the country.' She marks 'the tawny leaves and withered hedges.' 'One does not love a place the less because one has suffered in it,' she observes. But it is not only in a new sensibility to nature that we detect the change. Her attitude to life itself is altered . . . the observation is less of facts and more of feelings than is usual. There is an expressed emotion in the scene at the concert and in the famous talk about woman's constancy which proves not merely the biographical fact that Jane Austen had loved, but the aesthetic fact that she was no longer afraid to say so.

Persuasion has received highly intelligent criticism in recent years, after a long period of comparative neglect, and the lines of investigation have followed Virginia Woolf's suggestive comments. Critics have been concerned with the 'personal' quality of the novel and the problems it poses for biographical interpretation; with the obvious unevenness in narrative structure; with the 'poetic' use of landscape, and the hovering influence of Romantic poetry; with the pervasive presence of Anne Elliot's consciousness; with new effects in style and syntax; with the 'modernity' of Anne Elliot, an isolated personality in a rapidly changing society. Many of these problems were discussed in my own earlier study,[1] but I would like to consider them again, I hope with greater tact and particularity. Of all Jane Austen's major works, *Persuasion* suffers the most from easy generalizations, and requires the most minute discriminations. For example, my own remark that 'more than has been generally realized or acknowledged, [Jane Austen] was influenced by the Romantic poetry of the early nineteenth century'[2] has been frequently quoted with approval, but I now feel that it needs severe definition: What are the qualities of Romantic poetry reflected in Jane Austen's new attitudes toward nature and 'feeling'? How do these new effects in *Persuasion* differ from those in the earlier novels? The following pages offer no startlingly new perspectives, but rather a refinement of several familiar points of view.

In spite of Jane Austen's warning to a friend 'that it was her desire to create, not to reproduce,'[3] readers from her own day to the present have delighted in identifying Anne Elliot with Jane Austen. Anne is twenty-seven years old, a dangerous age for Jane Austen's young women; Charlotte Lucas is 'about twenty-seven' when she accepts the foolish Mr Collins, and Marianne in *Sense and Sensibility* laments that a 'woman of seven and twenty . . . can never hope to feel or inspire affection again.'[4] Jane Austen's own broken 'romance,' the details of which are hopelessly obscure, seems to have taken place around 1802, when she was twenty-seven, and Virginia Woolf was probably justified in her belief that *Persuasion* confirms 'the biographical fact that Jane Austen had loved.' Other passages from Jane Austen's life are obviously driven deep into the life of the novel: the careers of her sailor brothers, and the pleasant days at Lyme Regis in the summer of 1804, when she explored the area with Cassandra and her brother Henry. These facts give a certain sanction to biographical speculation, if one cares for that sort of thing, but they do not explain the intensity with which readers have pursued the 'personal' element in *Persuasion*. That intensity comes from the fiction, not from a curiosity about the writer's life, and has to do with the lost 'bloom' of Anne Elliot.

If asked to summarize Jane Austen's last three novels in three phrases, one might say that *Mansfield Park* is about the loss and return of principles, *Emma* about the loss and return of reason, *Persuasion* about the loss and return of 'bloom.' To make these formulations, however crude they may be, is to appreciate the deeply *physical* impact of *Persuasion*. The motif words of the earlier novels are the value terms of the eighteenth century – sense, taste, genius, judgment, understanding, and so forth – and their constant repetition is a sign of Jane Austen's rational vision. But there is something idiosyncratic and almost obsessive about the recurrence of 'bloom' in the first volume of *Persuasion*. 'Anne Elliot had been a very pretty girl, but her bloom had vanished early,' while Elizabeth and Sir Walter remained 'as blooming as ever,' at least in their own eyes (p. 6). The word occurs six times in the first volume, culminating in the scene on the steps at Lyme where Anne, 'the bloom and freshness of youth restored by the fine wind,' attracts the admiration of Wentworth and Mr Elliot (p. 104). It then disappears from the novel, only to return in the 'blushes' which mark Anne's repossession of her lost love: 'Glowing and lovely in sensibility and happiness, and more generally admired than she thought about or cared for, she had cheerful or forebearing feelings for every creature around her' (p. 245).

But 'bloom' is only one of many physical metaphors which make the first half of *Persuasion* Jane Austen's most deeply felt fiction. A sense of the earth's unchanging rhythms, confined in earlier works to an occasional scene and usually presented in the 'picturesque' manner, provides a ground-rhythm for the first half of *Persuasion*.

> Thirteen years had seen [Elizabeth] the mistress of Kellynch Hall, presiding and directing with a self-possession and decision which could never have given the idea of her being younger than she was.

For thirteen years had she been doing the honours, and laying down the domestic law at home, and leading the way to the chaise and four, and walking immediately after Lady Russell out of all the drawing-rooms and dining-rooms in the country. Thirteen winters' revolving frosts had seen her opening every ball of credit which a scanty neighbourhood afforded; and thirteen springs shewn their blossom, as she travelled up to London with her father, for a few weeks annual enjoyment of the great world. (pp. 6–7)

This marvellous passage, which acts out the progress of time and exposes the static lives of Kellynch Hall, would have been cast in a very different form in the earlier fictions. Narrative summary and authorial commentary have given way to a poetic sense of time's changes that commands the first volume of *Persuasion*. The chapters set in Somerset are pervaded with references to the autumnal landscape, which dominates Anne's emotions as she waits with little hope for 'a second spring of youth and beauty' (p. 124); while the scenes at Lyme are softened by the romantic landscape and the freshening 'flow of the tide' (pp. 95–6, 102). This poetic use of nature as a structure of feeling, which not only offers metaphors for our emotions but controls them with its unchanging rhythms and changing moods, comes to a climax in the scene where Anne's mind, depressed by the recent events at Lyme and her imminent departure for Bath, becomes part of the dark November landscape.

An hour's complete leisure for such reflections as these, on a dark November day, a small thick rain almost blotting out the very few objects ever to be discerned from the windows, was enough to make the sound of Lady Russell's carriage exceedingly welcome; and yet, though desirous to be gone, she could not quit the mansion-house, or look an adieu to the cottage, with its black, dripping, and comfortless veranda, or even notice through the misty glasses the last humble tenements of the village, without a saddened heart. – Scenes had passed in Uppercross, which made it precious. It stood the record of many sensations of pain, once severe, but now softened . . . She left it all behind her; all but the recollection that such things had been. (p. 123)

Such a passage fully justifies Angus Wilson's reply to those who say 'that there is no poetry in Jane Austen.' The poetry is there in 'the essential atmosphere of her novels – an instinctive response to those basic realities of nature, the weather and the seasons.' All of Jane Austen's heroines, whether declining like Fanny and Anne, or flourishing like Emma and Elizabeth, are acutely conscious of their physical lives. The fact of 'being alive,' as Wilson says, 'is never absent from the texture of the thoughts of her heroines.'[5]

Most readers of Jane Austen would agree with Wilson's claims, and would also agree that *Persuasion* represents her most successful effort to build this sense of physical life into the language and structure of a novel. If asked for proof, they would point to the frequent allusions to the Romantic poets, especially Byron and Scott, and to the famous passage (pp. 84–8) where Anne's autumnal walk is permeated with poetic 'musings and quotations.' But here they would be, I think, demonstrably wrong. Most of Jane Austen's direct references to the Romantic poets in *Persuasion* are associated with Captain Benwick, and have the same satiric intent – although they are gentler in manner – as the references to contemporary poetry in *Sanditon*. When Anne and Captain Benwick talk of 'poetry, the richness of the present age,' his enthusiasm for Scott and Byron is so emotional that Anne ventures to 'recommend a larger allowance of prose in his daily study' (p. 101), and her caution is confirmed when Benwick's raptures on Byron's *The Corsair* are interrupted by Louisa's rash jump to the Lower Cobb. Jane Austen has no place in her world for the Byronic hero, and Wentworth is not – as one recent critic has claimed – a successful recreation of Byron's Corsair.

Surely Angus Wilson is right in implying that Jane Austen's assimilation of the new poetry is most profound when least obtrusive. 'If we seek for any conscious concern for nature, we get either the Gilpin textbook stuff of *Northanger Abbey* or the "thoughts from the poets" of Fanny or Anne Elliot.'[6] A good example of Jane Austen's conscious concern for nature would be the scene in *Mansfield Park* where Edmund joins Fanny at the window to view the stars:

> his eyes soon turned like her's towards the scene without, where all
> that was solemn and soothing, and lovely, appeared in the
> brilliancy of an unclouded night, and the contrast of the deep shade
> of the woods. Fanny spoke her feelings. 'Here's harmony!' said she,
> 'Here's repose! Here's what may leave all painting and all music
> behind, and what poetry only can attempt to describe. Here's what
> may tranquillize every care, and lift the heart to rapture! When I
> look out on such a night as this, I feel as if there could be neither
> wickedness nor sorrow in the world; and there certainly would be
> less of both if the sublimity of Nature were more attended to, and
> people were carried more out of themselves by contemplating such
> a scene.' (p. 113)

This is a set-piece out of eighteenth-century aesthetics, in which Fanny responds to the natural landscape with appropriate emotions of 'sublimity' and transport. Even the descriptive details are heavily literary, drawn from Shakespeare and Ann Radcliffe.[7] A different and more intimate sense of landscape is displayed by the famous autumnal walk in *Persuasion:*

Her *pleasure* in the walk must arise from the exercise and the day, from the view of the last smiles of the year upon the tawny leaves and withered hedges, and from repeating to herself some few of the thousand poetical descriptions extant of autumn, that season of peculiar and inexhaustible influence on the mind of taste and tenderness . . . After one of the many praises of the day, which were continually bursting forth, Captain Wentworth added:

'What glorious weather for the Admiral and my sister! They meant to take a long drive this morning; perhaps we may hail them from some of these hills. They talked of coming into this side of the country. I wonder whereabouts they will upset to-day. Oh! it does happen very often, I assure you – but my sister makes nothing of it – she would as lieve be tossed out as not.'

'Ah! You make the most of it, I know,' cried Louisa, 'but if it were really so, I should do just the same in her place. If I loved a man, as she loves the Admiral, I would be always with him, nothing should ever separate us, and I would rather be overturned by him, than driven safely by anybody else.'

. . . Anne could not immediately fall into a quotation again. The sweet scenes of autumn were for a while put by – unless some tender sonnet, fraught with the apt analogy of the declining year, with declining happiness, and the images of youth and hope, and spring, all gone together, blessed her memory. She roused herself to say, as they struck by order into another path, 'Is not this one of the ways to Winthrop?' But nobody heard, or, at least, nobody answered her.

Winthrop . . . was their destination; and after another half mile of gradual ascent through large enclosures, where the ploughs at work, and the fresh-made path spoke the farmer, counteracting the sweets of poetical despondence, and meaning to have spring again, they gained the summit of the most considerable hill, which parted Uppercross and Winthrop, and soon commanded a full view of the latter, at the foot of the hill on the other side. (pp. 84–5)

Fanny Price has three transparencies on the panes of her window, depicting Tintern Abbey, a cave in Italy, and a moonlit lake in Cumberland; the subjects may suggest Wordsworth, but her tastes are strictly for the picturesque and the academic sublime. The presentation of Anne Elliot's autumnal walk is much closer to a Wordsworthian view of nature, emphasizing as it does the responsive ego, yet it would be a mistake to identify Anne's thoughts on autumn with the powerful reactions of the great Romantic poets. Her 'poetical descriptions' are, most likely, culled from the popular magazine poets, and her literary taste is not necessarily superior to that of Fanny Price.

What is different in *Persuasion* is the way in which two views of nature, both conventional, have been internalized to provide a complex and original impression. Whereas in *Sense and Sensibility* Marianne's sentimental effusions on nature are dramatically counterpointed to Edward's practical view, her sense of the picturesque set against his sense of the ordinary, the autumnal scene from *Persuasion* locates both responses within Anne's mind. After she has fallen sentimentally and self-indulgently into quotation, the sight of the farmer ploughing, 'meaning to have spring again,' rescues Anne from 'poetical despondence,' and restores her emotional composure. This passage is infused with a sense of immediate feeling absent from the description of Fanny's rapture, but it remains a consciously 'literary' construction, closer to Cowper than to Wordsworth. In the final scene at Uppercross already quoted, however, the effects are truly Wordsworthian. The cottage viewed on a 'dark November day' is a stockpiece of the picturesque, with its irregular shape and misty appearance, yet it is transformed by memory, by 'reflection' and 'recollection,' into a complex symbol of what 'had been.' In the opening chapters of *Persuasion* Jane Austen is most 'poetic,' most Wordsworthian, when she is willing to abandon the literary allusion and give herself to a direct passionate rendering of nature's changing face.

Our discussion of the romantic dimensions of *Persuasion* has been confined to the first half of the novel, the opening twelve chapters, and for good reason: the latter half of the novel is radically different in style and narrative method. Any census of the metaphors of natural change will find that they are concentrated in the first half, suggesting that *Persuasion* has a deliberate two-part structure that has been often overlooked. *Northanger Abbey*, its companion in the posthumous four-volume edition, was always intended as a two-part romance: the original version sold to the publisher Crosby in 1803 was described as 'a MS. Novel in 2 vol. entitled Susan.' All of Jane Austen's other novels were published in three parts, and designed to fit that pattern. Thus the three-part division of *Pride and Prejudice* follows the three-act structure of a stage comedy, and the three parts of *Emma* correspond to three successive stages in a process of self-discovery. But Jane Austen deliberately chose to construct *Persuasion* in two parts (the numbering of the cancelled last chapters proves this), and much of the apparent unevenness or 'dullness' of the novel is explained by this artistic decision.

The first half of *Persuasion* portrays Anne Elliot against a natural landscape, and it is there that Jane Austen's new-found Romanticism is concentrated. Once the action has moved to Bath a claustrophobic atmosphere descends, and the external world becomes insubstantial: Anne, without a human confidante but sustained by nature in the first volume, is left terribly alone in the second volume – only the reconciliation with Wentworth can save her from anonymity. The language of the second volume, although less satisfying to our modern taste, is deliberately fashioned to express this sense of personalities moving in a vacuum. The rich metaphors of Volume One are replaced by the eighteenth-century value terms of earlier novels, but – as Virginia Woolf noted – with a sense of perfunctory ritual. It is as if Jane Austen, hurrying to the final reunion, were at long last impatient with those weighty terms of judgment and admonition that had served her so well in earlier years. In a space of seven pages (pp. 140–7) the word 'sensible' occurs six times along with 'pride,' 'understanding,' 'decorum,' 'candid,' 'amiable,' 'sensibility,' and 'imaginations.' This is an aggressive return to the abstract language of the earlier fictions, but it is difficult to tell whether Jane Austen does so out of boredom – as Virginia Woolf seems to imply – or out of a desire to convey the eighteenth-century stasis of Bath. In any case, the contrast between the first and second volumes of *Persuasion* is profound in the realm of language and metaphor, reflecting the radical dislocation of Anne Elliot. And there are differences in narrative method as well. The first half of the novel presents Anne as the commanding center. As Norman Page has shown, the 'slanting of the narrative through the mental life of the principal character,' already developed in *Emma*, is the dominant mode in *Persuasion;* narrative, authorial comment, dialogue, and interior monologue merge into one another.[8] 'Free indirect speech,' in which lengthy dialogue is compressed and located within the central consciousness, is combined with more conventional narrative methods to give a sense of the entire novel taking place within the mind of the heroine. But this complex method of internalized presentation is most evident in the first volume, and in Volume Two – as Anne Elliot enters the alien environment of Bath – Jane Austen reverts to earlier and more objective methods. It is a sign of Anne's isolation that the revelation of William Elliot's true nature, and even of Wentworth's love, must come to her through letters, one of the most 'external' of fictional devices.

Another aspect of style in *Persuasion,* present in both volumes but more characteristic of the first, is a rapid and nervous syntax designed to imitate the bombardment of impresions upon the mind. A fine example occurs when Anne, a victim of the rambunctious child Walter, is rescued by Captain Wentworth.

In another moment, however, she found herself in the state of being released from him; some one was taking him from her, though he had bent down her head so much, that his little sturdy hands were unfastened from around her neck, and he was resolutely borne away, before she knew that Captain Wentworth had done it. (p. 80)

Here the passive construction, the indefinite pronouns, and the staccato syntax all imitate the effect of the incident upon Anne's mind. Page is certainly right when he says that such passages, common in *Persuasion*, do not make statements about an emotional situation but suggest the quality of the experience through the movement of the prose.[9]

When we examine these details of sentence structure and punctuation, however, a certain caution is necessary. The sentences of *Persuasion* do, for the most part, move away from the Johnsonian norm, and in the revisions of the cancelled chapters one can see Jane Austen struggling toward a more expressive form. But one should remember that all of Jane Austen's manuscripts display a greater flexibility of sentence structure than her printed works, and although the cancelled chapters of *Persuasion* and the manuscript of *Sanditon* exhibit an extraordinary freedom, many of the same qualities are present in the manuscript of *The Watsons* (c. 1803–4). The printer of Jane Austen's day had great license with punctuation, paragraphing, and even sentence structure, and part of the 'flowing' quality of *Persuasion* may derive from a printer (T. Davison) whose standards and tastes differed from those of the printers who handled the earlier manuscripts. This does not affect the general import of Page's argument, but the dangers of relying too heavily on details of punctuation and sentence structure are evident in Page's comparison of a passage in the cancelled Chapter Ten with the revised version:[10]

He found that he was considered by his friend Harville an engaged man. The Harvilles entertained not a doubt of a mutual attachment between him and Louisa; and though this to a degree was contradicted instantly, it yet made him feel that perhaps by *her* family, by everybody, by *herself* even, the same idea might be held, and that he was not *free* in honour, though if such were to be the conclusion, too free alas! in heart. He had never thought justly on this subject before, and he had not sufficiently considered that his excessive intimacy at Uppercross must have its danger of ill consequence in many ways; and that while trying whether he could attach himself to either of the girls, he might be exciting unpleasant reports if not raising unrequited regard.

He found too late that he had entangled himself [cancelled version, p. 260 of Chapman's edition].

'I found,' said he, 'that I was considered by Harville an engaged man! That neither Harville nor his wife entertained a doubt of our mutual attachment. I was startled and shocked. To a degree, I could contradict this instantly; but, when I began to reflect that others might have felt the same – her own family, nay, perhaps herself, I was no longer at my own disposal. I was hers in honour if she

wished it. I had been unguarded. I had not thought seriously on this
subject before. I had not considered that my excessive intimacy
must have its danger of ill consequence in many ways; and that I
had no right to be trying whether I could attach myself to either of
the girls, at the risk of raising even an unpleasant report, were there
no other ill effects. I had been grossly wrong, and must abide the
consequences.'

He found too late, in short, that he had entangled himself . . .
[final version, pp. 242–3].

Page's comments upon the improved 'personal and dramatic form' of
the revised version are just, but his observation that three long sentences have been broken up into nine shorter sentences falls away
when we realize that the cancelled version, as Page quotes it, is actually reprinted from the 1870 *Memoir*, where Jane Austen's lively manuscript had been 'regularized' by the Victorian editor and printer. The
actual passage from the manuscript, reproduced below, shows the
nervous energy of Jane Austen's first draft, and reminds us that the
relationship between Jane Austen's first drafts and the printed texts
must often have been that of sketch to varnished canvas.

> He found that he was considered by his friend Harville, as an
> engaged Man. The Harvilles entertained not a doubt of a mutual
> attachment between him & Louisa – and though this to *a degree,*
> was contradicted instantly – it yet made him feel that perhaps by *her*
> family, by everybody, by *herself* even, the same idea might be held
> – and that he was not *free* in honour – though, if such were to be the
> conclusion, too free alas! in Heart. – He had never thought justly on
> this subject before – he had not sufficiently considered that his
> excessive Intimacy at Uppercross must have it's danger of ill
> consequence in many ways, and that while trying whether he c^d
> attach himself to either of the Girls, he might be exciting unpleasant
> reports, if not, raising unrequited regard! – He found, too late, that
> he had entangled himself – [11]

Persuasion reveals an author who is unusually sensitive to the
forces of her time. Of all the novels, it is the only one where the action
is precisely dated, and that date is 'the present' (1814–15). The other
novels are slightly retrospective in their treatments of manners and
events, but *Persuasion* is filled with references to contemporary history ('This peace will be turning all our rich Navy Officers ashore') and
the most recent publications of the Romantic poets. These topical
references are matched by certain passages in the novel which seem to
reflect the events of 1815–16, when *Persuasion* was a work-in-prog-
ress. The description of the 'green chasms between romantic rocks'

near Lyme may echo *Kubla Khan,* first published in 1816, although
the chronology is doubtful and the whole passage strikes me as more
picturesque than Coleridgean;[12] more likely is the influence of Scott's
famous review in the *Quarterly* upon Jane Austen's retreat from
'prudence.' In Scott's review, which Jane Austen had read by 1 April
1816 (*Persuasion* was not completed until the summer), Jane Austen
was characterized as anti-sentimental and anti-romantic, her novels
bearing the same relation to those of the 'sentimental and romantic
cast, that cornfields and cottages and meadows bear to . . . the
rugged sublimities of a mountain landscape.' Scott then went on to
deplore the neglect of Cupid and romantic feelings, implying that
Jane Austen coupled 'Cupid indivisibly with calculating prudence.'[13]
This must have stung the creator of Anne Elliot, and we may take her
passionate statement on 'romance' as a covert reply.

> How eloquent could Anne Elliot have been, – how eloquent, at
> least, were her wishes on the side of early warm attachment, and a
> cheerful confidence in futurity, against that over-anxious caution
> which seems to insult exertion and distrust Providence! – She had
> been forced into prudence in her youth, she learned romance as she
> grew older – the natural sequel of an unnatural beginning. (p. 30)

Unlike Jane Austen's other major works, *Persuasion* is filled with a
sense of the moment – both historical and personal – at which it was
written.

It is not these particular signs of contemporaneity, however, but
Jane Austen's powerful response to a changing relationship between
society and the self that gives *Persuasion* its hold on the modern reader. In *Pride and Prejudice* the old order of Darcy and Pemberley can
be accommodated to the new forces represented by the middle-class
Gardiners; in *Persuasion* there seems little hope of accommodation
between stasis and unpredictable change. 'The Musgroves, like their
houses, were in a state of alteration, perhaps of improvement' (p. 40),
and this tension between old ways and 'more modern minds and
manners' divides the novel. Sir Walter has retreated into a wilderness
of mirrors, the Baronetage his favorite looking-glass, and Jane
Austen's sympathies are firmly on the side of the new natural aristocracy represented by the Navy; but in giving her allegiance to them
Jane Austen knows that Anne must 'pay the tax of quick alarm' (p.
252). The ending of *Persuasion,* unlike that of the other novels, is
open and problematic. One could glean from *Persuasion* a list of
terms which would make it sound like a textbook in modern sociolo-
gy: 'estrangement,' 'imprisonment,' 'alienations,' 'removals.' The
heroine is 'only Anne' (pp. 5–6), and the word 'alone' echoes through
the novel. *Persuasion* is filled with a sense of what time can do, with

its 'changes, alienations, removals': it can lead to 'oblivion of the past' (p. 60) and even annihilation of the self. Anne has painfully learned 'the art of knowing our own nothingness beyond our own circle' (p. 42), and at the end of the novel that circle, so lovingly restored and enlarged, has no permanence beyond the moment. Virginia Woolf might have said that *Persuasion* is marked by a peculiar terror as well as a peculiar beauty.

NOTES

1 *Jane Austen: A Study of Her Artistic Development* (New York, 1965).
2 *Ibid.*, p. 153.
3 J. E. Austen-Leigh, *Memoir of Jane Austen*, ed. R. W. Chapman (Oxford, 1926), p. 157.
4 *Sense and Sensibility*, p. 38. All page references for the novels are to *The Novels of Jane Austen*, ed. R. W. Chapman (London: Oxford University Press; 3rd ed., 1933.
5 Angus Wilson, 'The Neighbourhood of Tombuctoo,' in *Critical Essays on Jane Austen*, ed. B. C. Southam (London, 1968), p. 191.
6 *Ibid.*
7 In *Jane Austen and Her Predecessors* (Cambridge, 1966), pp. 78 and 107–8, Frank W. Bradbrook points out the allusions to *The Merchant of Venice* and *The Mysteries of Udolpho*.
8 Norman Page, *The Language of Jane Austen* (Oxford, 1972), pp. 48–53 and 127–36.
9 *Ibid.*, p. 50.
10 *Ibid.*, pp. 51–2.
11 *Two Chapters of Persuasion*, ed. R. W. Chapman (Oxford, 1926), pp. 20–1.
12 See Alethea Hayter, 'Xanadu at Lyme Regis,' *Ariel*, 1 (1970), 61–4.
13 *Jane Austen: The Critical Heritage*, ed. B. C. Southam (London, 1968), p. 68. Jane Austen refers to Scott's review in a letter of 1 April 1816.

III
Views and reviews

MARY LASCELLES

Jane Austen and the novel

My motto is taken from Professor Sutherland's *Preface to Eighteenth Century Poetry*. 'All through the eighteenth century', he says, 'poetry was regarded as an art: the art of making poems. Coleridge and Shelley, you might almost say, wrote poetry: Dryden and Pope wrote poems.'[1] It is my contention that, whereas Scott, you may fairly say, wrote fiction, Jane Austen wrote novels. As a truism, this would be readily accepted. To maintain it as truth is another matter.

No one who has been long engaged in the precarious business of criticism would undertake to prove anything. A modest endeavour to verify particular intuitions may be acknowledged; but even this requires, if not evidence, tokens which will pass for critical currency, and currency requires agreement. 'The eighteenth-century poet', Professor Sutherland continues, 'invariably thought in terms of the poem, the thing to be made; and the critics were always ready to tell him how it should be (or more often, perhaps, how it should have been) written.' Neither poet nor critic felt any hesitation in framing an agreed notion of the artifact in terms they both understood. But, beyond a few pleasantries in letters to scribbling nephew or niece, a few asides to Cassandra, Jane Austen has left little indication of the scope and aim of the novel as she saw it, while its earliest critics are mainly concerned with moral issues – an enquirer from another civilization could not hope to frame a critical theory out of their praise or censure. What I am seeking has to be inferred from Jane Austen's practice – alike what she does and what she refrains from doing; together with certain delicate allusions to the convention within

235

which she was working. For there is an artistic convention which she discernibly accepts – which she would no more despise and ignore than a poet would propose to write a sonnet and produce eleven lines of irregular verse ending in the middle of a sentence. This convention is clearly distinguishable from the conventional artifices and false values of the transient, the merely fashionable novels of her own day, to which she reacted in hilarious mockery. Having written about that long ago,[2] I now forbear, except in so far as some point of comparison seems unavoidable.

The convention *within* which Jane Austen writes belongs to a distinct species of novel. Walter Raleigh, looking at it from a masculine point of view and calling it the novel of 'domestic satire', laid down this condition: 'Man is stripped of the public trappings on which he prides himself, he is bereft of all wider social relations, and appears simply and solely as a member of a family, – by that let him stand or fall.'[3] This will allow a little amplification: man, in these novels, signifies what woman expects, or hopes she may expect, of life; love, courtship and marriage are the themes; marriage is on the horizon, and what should follow is admitted only by implication: Edmund and Fanny, though undemanding, come to need a larger income than Thornton Lacey can yield.[4] Under the influence of Richardson and Fanny Burney, this theme of courtship had hardened and contracted: man appeared as wolf or sheep-dog, predator or mentor, threat of perdition or promise of reward. Jane Austen, who commands as many variations on a theme as the great musicians, frames a pattern of story which transcends these limitations even while remaining constant to itself: the centre holds, the rim does not constrain.

With the exception of *Sense and Sensibility,* which often defies inclusion in generalizations about her novels, this is the pattern to which they conform: in its very centre she develops the discovery of love by a young woman, and a man not much older; and this proves a kind of self-discovery, a growing up into self-knowledge. Catherine Morland opens like a bud – a tight, unpromising little bud – in the warmth of her love for Henry Tilney. Elizabeth Bennet learns the hard way, through discovery of her own error, that it is marriage with Darcy she needs for her fulfilment; but it is here that the pattern begins to show more subtle possibilities, for Darcy himself must find that love is stronger than pride. In *Mansfield Park* a finer equilibrium is achieved: Edmund has to discover, what Fanny has long known, the nature of their mutual need; meanwhile, Fanny must watch the course of his self-deception, fearful lest knowledge come too late. Emma Woodhouse has to learn her own fallibility, and, at a deeper level, her hitherto unguessed incompleteness; but Mr Knightley also has to discover the quality of his affection for her: were it the elder-brotherly concern he supposes, his reaction to Frank Churchill's attentions and her apparent acceptance of them might have been quite as strong, but it would' have taken another direction. Anne Elliot's self-knowledge is of long standing; she is poignantly aware of the nature and strength of her own love, but she must abide Frederick Wentworth's resistance to the renewal of his, and his efforts to translate resentment into indifference; and time is an even more formidable adversary for her than for Fanny.

No matter how this delicate balance is adjusted, nor how variously and intricately other characters and events contribute to the outcome, these lovers remain central to every one of the six novels: their centre of gravity. Such a nice balance is rare in English fiction, while an undisputed concentration on love and courtship (or seduction) is hardly to be found in the hundred years stretching between *Clarissa Harlowe* and *Jane Eyre*. Scott accords his lovers just so much absent-minded benignity as a preoccupied man may spare for his children's friends; the tragedy and comedy, the smoke and flame, of Scotland's history are his magnetic north.[5]

Evelina may be cited as an exception: here, surely, the state of the heroine's heart was meant to be our main concern, and is it our own willfulness that prefers the social satire? But I suspect that Fanny Burney's novels and their numerous offspring provoke a question not so simply answered. The domestic novel is of necessity heroine-centred. Thackeray can only have been teazing when he called *Vanity Fair* 'a novel without a hero', as though that were a contradiction in terms. It is the heroine who is indispensable. But what, in this context, *is* a 'heroine'? Heroism without fortitude would indeed be a paradox. Certainly the conventional heroine is prompt to put herself at risk; and, as an element of terror enters, and the fear of committing social blunders yields to the fear lest she may suffer violence, she grows more daring – but it is the daring of a flustered goose. Emotional hazards likewise beset her, and she responds in a strain of high-pitched sentiment which might be hard to sustain in common life. Jane Austen glances towards this extravagance, more than once and in a diversity of moods: most sedately in *Emma*. Although Emma has cast Harriet for the part of heroine in a little play of love and courtship, she underrates its demands: having to confess her own misjudgment of Mr Elton's intentions, she chooses the time when Harriet, having got over her cold, should be prepared for 'getting the better of her other complaint' – unrequited love.[6] Shocked to discover its ravages, she nevertheless expects the few weeks of Mr Elton's absence to undo the harm she has done, merely on the ground of his indifference. By a nice irony, when she finds herself in an apparently similar situation, her reaction is impulsive: 'It darted through her, with the speed of an arrow, that Mr Knightley must marry no one but herself.'[7] And the outcome of that impulse will disqualify her as a heroine: she learns that poor Harriet is yet again mistaken and that she herself is Mr Knightley's choice, and acquiesces, 'for as to any of that heroism of sentiment which might have prompted her to entreat him to transfer his affection from herself to Harriet, as infinitely the most worthy of the two – or even the more simple sublimity of resolving to refuse him at once and for ever, without vouchsafing any motive, because he could not marry them both, Emma had it not'.[8]

All in all, it is perfectly appropriate – though some may find the proposition surprising – that Fanny Price, the least like a conventional heroine of all in the novels, should be the most heroic. The significant phrase is 'heroism of principle',[9] at odds with 'many of the feelings of youth and nature'. Since she is not sustained by Elinor Dashwood's stoicism of temperament nor Anne Elliot's maturity, only this principle of self-control can account for her conduct. She withstands her beloved Edmund's plea for approval of a course they both think wrong; only his preoccupation with Mary Crawford prevents him from realizing that she has not yielded an inch.[10] She stands up even to Sir Thomas Bertram, whom she fears and on whom she is entirely dependent, and offers no word of that defence which must have vindicated her at Maria's expense: 'Her ill opinon of [Mr Crawford's principles] was founded chiefly on observations, which, for her cousins' sake, she could scarcely dare mention to their father. Maria and Julia – and especially Maria – were so closely implicated in Mr Crawford's misconduct, that she could not give his character, such as she believed it, without betraying them.'[11] Mary Crawford's confidences as to her resolution against marrying a younger son are inviolably safe with Fanny.[12] So are those letters in which Mary, with heartless self-interest, tries to find out whether Edmund is likely to remain a younger son. Only when Edmund has declared his irrevocable alienation from Mary Crawford does Fanny feel 'more than justified in adding to his knowledge of her real character, by some hint of what share his brother's state of health might be supposed to have in her wish for a complete reconciliation'.[13] Here is no rhetorical heightening. Indeed, it is characteristic of the *presentation* that this interchange should take place in the presence of Lady Bertram, 'who, after hearing an affecting sermon, had cried herself to sleep'.[14]

We are now in the proper key for the author's own voice: 'I purposely abstain from dates on this occasion, that every one may be at liberty to fix their own, aware that the cure of unconquerable passions, and the transfer of unchanging attachments, must vary much as to time in different people. – I only intreat every body to believe that exactly at the time when it was quite natural that it should be so, and not a week

earlier, Edmund did cease to care about Miss Crawford, and became
as anxious to marry Fanny, as Fanny herself could desire.'[15] Besides
the valedictory gesture with which novelist or dramatist may choose
to dismiss the persons of his tale, there is here a smiling reminder of
Edmund's reiterated assertion – 'I cannot give her up.' But that is not
all. The double theme of time and constancy has been twisted into the
third volume of *Mansfield Park*. Latterly, it has carried reassurance:
Fanny fears that Edmund will not be able to speak to her of his disappointment – 'Long, long would it be ere Miss Crawford's name passed
his lips again . . . It *was* long. They reached Mansfield on Thursday,
and it was not till Sunday evening that Edmund began to talk to her
on the subject.'[16] We hear again the playful tones of *Northanger
Abbey*: 'Anxiety . . . can hardly extend to the bosom of my readers,
who will see in the tell-tale compression of the pages before them, that
we are all hastening together to perfect felicity.'[17] And still the score is
not complete: filaments fine as gossamer connect time and constancy;
time might have vanquished Fanny. She is at the vulnerable age, the
proper age for a heroine: 'although there doubtless are such unconquerable young ladies of eighteen (or one should not read about them)
as are never to be persuaded into love against their judgement . . . I
have no inclination to believe Fanny one of them.'[18] Jane Austen
declares outright that, supposing Edmund married to Mary, Henry
Crawford's constant suit would have won Fanny. But his constancy is
in question. Fanny hopes that he will desist: 'She could not, though
only eighteen, suppose Mr Crawford's attachment would hold out for
ever.'[19] Sir Thomas fears that he may: assured by Edmund that Fanny
needed only time, 'he could not help fearing that if such very long
allowances of time and habit were necessary for her, she might not
have persuaded herself into receiving his addresses properly, before
the young man's inclination for paying them were over'.[20] Romantic
time and natural time do not move to the same rhythm.

'Exactly at the time when it was quite natural' – there you hear the
rhythm of *Persuasion*, the one novel from which a significant passage
of revision has been preserved.[21] Here alone we can watch Jane
Austen deciding not to do something; and we should be the more
grateful for this because it is the novel in which she least often shows
her hand. Though narration is explicit and explanation of circumstances ample, all is carried in the same tone: the narrator never stands
aside to invoke comparison with the way things happen in fiction.[22]
Thus the greater part of *Persuasion*, from Wentworth's appearance to
the end, may be reckoned a simple, straightforward expansion of that
one assertion in *Mansfield Park*: 'Exactly at the time when it was quite
natural that it should be so, and not a week earlier' Wentworth discovered his own love and found it returned. The outcome is natural in so

far as it springs directly from the characters of the two concerned. As
Anne reflects, when it seems that a mistake may separate them, she
will do well to 'let things . . . take their course . . . "Surely, if there
be constant attachment on each side, our hearts must understand each
other ere long." '23 And so, in the revised version, they do, without
conscious interference by anyone else. Admiral Croft's intervention,
which precipitated this understanding in the first draft, may or may
not be out of character (as I formerly questioned); it certainly spoils
this delicate intimation of a drawing together, almost insensibly, quite
invisibly. Like Herrick's lovers,

> So silently they one to th'other come,
> As colours steale into the Peare or Plum.24

This privacy in a crowd is nicely pointed by the very misunderstand-
ing which threatens their meeting on a crucial occasion: Mrs
Musgrove's supposition that it is Captain Harville whom Anne is
anxious to see at her father's house that evening.25 Thus the part of
Persuasion which Jane Austen rewrote (as distinct from that which
she recopied with improvements) can be observed approximating
still more closely to that ideal pattern towards which her earlier novels
have tended.

So far, good – or at least, not bad. Allusion and revision are recognized objects of critical attention, though we may not agree as to the
outcome. I must now advance onto ground which is less firm – so soft
indeed that I fear quaking sands. The surface, however, is not uninvit-
ing. Although a negative generalization is not likely to yield proven
fact, I may surely look for unanimity of impression when I say that
Jane Austen is, to all appearance, not concerned with power. And yet
power is a major concern among the novelists of her century, and with
at least one of her predecessors. I intend no disparagement: it is natural and may be right that any novelist intent on social criticism should
exult in the power at his disposal – this new power of the serious
popular novel. I am a little troubled by the elation that vibrates in
Richardson's letters, a ferment of the spirit in Dickens, a growing
appetite in both. There can be no doubt, however, that they were
convinced of the absolute goodness of their aims. Why is Jane Austen,
of whose fundamental seriousness no attentive reader can be in doubt,
indifferent to power?

I offer two suggestions to account for this – distinct, but not mutually exclusive. If we look for common ground among those novelists
who enjoy the *feel* of power, we shall find that they are all exclaiming
to the reader, in tones of varying intensity: 'If I could but make you
see!' Scott wants us to see the predicament of Scotland; Mrs Gaskell,
the state of Manchester in the hungry forties; Dickens, a mounting
tale of wrong. This means that their function is that of interpreters.

They speak from the people of one country to those of another; they translate from one language into another. This office of interpreter is not confined to the novel of broad social criticism: Richardson, speaking for the soul beset (in *Pamela* and *Clarissa*), George Eliot for the soul perplexed, perform a similar function. But Jane Austen speaks the language of the country about the people of the country to the people of the country – or so it seems. It is not that she never explains – Elliot family history, for example; or the faulty upbringing of the young Bertrams. (Edmund's immunity must be credited to Oxford.) But she maintains unshaken confidence not only in the validity but also in the intelligibility of her explanations. Perhaps that is why Henry James, one of the Interpreters, appears to be climbing, with ice-axe, rope and brandy-flask, a slope which she ascends unencumbered, not having noticed how steep it is. This raises the question: what is she doing there?

I suggest that Jane Austen regarded the making of a novel as an end, not the means to an end. She was as deep in love with the novel as a poet is in love with poetry. Most novelists came to it from other ways of writing, which may be presumed their first choice – notably, from journalism. It has been the sequel or alternative to history, diaries, voluminous correspondence, even verse. Jane Austen seems never to have contemplated writing anything else; and how much she wanted to write *this* must be evident from her early career: rejection, suppression, shabby treatment at the hands of her earlier publishers never stopped her writing, or rewriting, novels. And for this persistence she could not put forward the plea which had become traditional among scribbling women: a thriftless husband and helpless children. She was merely engrossed in making an artifact which pleased her.

This brings me squarely to the question which is hardest of all to answer: how is it that a novelist who makes no pretence of writing anything but novels, lays no claim to have discovered letters, memoirs or other documents, who even has the effrontery to mention 'the pen of the contriver',[26] creates this extraordinary illusion of actuality? It has outlasted the world which she took for granted. It operates, not only in a world which I remember, one which a ghost returning from the nineteenth century would at least recognize, but also in one which such a spirit would find both unrecognizable and unintelligible, the world of today. To this I can testify, alike on the strength of many years' teaching and the reports of younger teachers still at work. Readers remarkably various in every other respect become engrossed in her story, lend credence to her characters and take delight in both. (True, I have failed to satisfy an enquirer who wished to know why Henry Tilney bore so little resemblance to her Lutheran pastor; but perhaps she expected too much.)

For the theme of her inaugural lecture at Bedford College,

London,[27] Mrs Tillotson took the effect of personal intervention by the novelist, throughout the nineteenth century and in a wide literary context. Mine is the way it works in Jane Austen's novels, and even there within a relatively narrow context. I may therefore, without the least disparagement of that admirable argument, press interrogation further, returning to two passages which the lecturer chose for comment, and which I have already quoted. When Jane Austen *purposely abstains from dates,* she is, as Mrs Tillotson points out,[28] using a time-honoured device, one familiar to Chaucer under the term *dubitatio.* Yes, but Chaucer was giving his own version of a story already current, and his hesitation on a point of fact was used to fortify the impression that, whereas all this *happened,* his information about it was of variable quality. Will the device hold with a tale told for the first time – one, moreover, that had never happened?[29]

Scott, among nineteenth-century novelists, affords the nearest counterpart to Chaucer, in that he is telling (in his greatest novels) a known story, about people of whose characters and intents he has formed his own opinion; but his manner towards both is so different from that of the traditional rhetorician that he seems at times to be saying: 'I may not know how to make the most of a story, but just listen to this!' – and into a note goes a favourite anecdote. His Victorian successors, whatever the factual framework of their tales, seem to me a little heavy-handed in their protestations of authenticity. To win our assent, more delicate signalling is required.

I return to Mrs Tillotson's argument. Quoting that passage from *Northanger Abbey* in which the reader is reminded that the happy ending cannot now be long delayed, she comments: '"All hastening together" is a key phrase; writer, characters, and readers, are all within the same charmed circle.'[30] I maintain that this invitation to enter the charmed circle has *pervaded* the Chawton novels. It is not merely valedictory; nor, as in *Northanger Abbey,* has it been expressed in an opening pleasantry: the reader has not been invited to speculate on those circumstances calculated to produce 'all the desperate wretchedness of which a last volume is capable'.[31] In the mature novels, Jane Austen will make her presence known only when it is called for, but it is *felt* throughout, even in chapters consisting almost wholly of dialogue. Captain Harville, teasing Anne, claims: '"I do not think I ever opened a book in my life which had not something to say upon woman's inconstancy . . . But perhaps you will say, these were all written by men."' To which Anne rejoins: '"Perhaps I shall. – Yes, yes, if you please, no reference to examples in books . . . I will not allow books to prove any thing."'[32]

It is ironical that Captain Harville should call to witness his friend's reading, only to capitulate as another consideration forces itself upon him: ' "When I think of Benwick, my tongue is tied." ' Does the threat of some ironic reversal lurk in the enigmatic fragment we know as *Sanditon?* Here the double vision – of life interpreted according to books, and life observed – is given to the sensible, reflective Charlotte Heywood, who 'had not *Camilla's* youth, and had no intention of having her Distress'.[33] She is agreeably conscious of the gift, and of the entertainment it may afford: 'Perhaps it might be partly owing to her having just issued from a circulating Library – but she cd not separate the idea of a complete Heroine from Clara Brereton. Her situation with Lady Denham so very much in favour of it! – She seemed placed with her on purpose to be ill-used.'[34] Further observation of their relationship does not entirely confirm this expectation. It is shaken, in quite a different way, by the glimpse of Clara which Charlotte catches just as the fragment breaks off.[35] What the future held for Charlotte herself we shall never know.

Thus between the author's conception and the measure of perception she allows to her most observant character, a steady balance is held, and a pervasive sense of *this* author's presence unobtrusively sustained. Balance, as the athlete and the dancer know, may be lost through wayward impulse – of which the intellectual counterpart must surely be irrelevance. The English novelist is often tempted by the uncalled-for comic or pathetic episode, and sometimes by the loose finery of stylistic display. Such temptations have so little force for Jane Austen that those who regard her temperament with respectful antipathy will not credit her with self-denial. My present concern, however, is with the outcome, not the origin, of her notable manifestations of equipoise, especially the last of the three I have mentioned. There was the nice balance in the parts assigned to her lovers, neither of whom is there merely to give occasion for what the other must undergo;[36] one between the outer world of happenings and that inner world of expectancy – of hope and apprehension – whose forms and colours are often borrowed from imaginative literature; and there is that between the story-teller and the imagined circle whom his tale charms to attention.

To say how this charm operates would require a book on the nature of narrative illusion; but I will offer a suggestion designed for the present context. Johnson wrote to Richardson on the publication of *Sir Charles Grandison:*

> I have no objection but to the preface in which you mention the letters as fallen by some chance into your hands, and afterwards mention your health as such that you almost despaired of going

through your plan. If you were to require my opinion which part should be changed, I should be inclined to the suppression of that part which seems to disclaim the composition. What is modesty if it departs from truth? Of what use is the disguise by which nothing is concealed?[37]

As R. W. Chapman points out, Richardson does not quite commit himself to either position; but he shilly-shallies – and so forfeits trust. Like so many of Johnson's literary judgments, this one appears at first sight to be simply moral; but, further considered, reveals close and curious penetration into the workings of the imagination. Inconsistency can set a barrier between narrator and reader.

If I return to Mrs Tillotson's image of the charmed circle – which may possibly have arisen in talk between us long ago – I seem to see the story-teller as one assailed by a peculiar doubt. Whereas the dramatist, if it falls to his lot to attend or take part in a performance, will be moving among forms as substantial as his own, the novelist moves among phantoms. 'There', he may well exclaim, 'are the people I have conjured into being; there, no more corporeal than they, the people I have called into a circle solely to watch what becomes of *those others* – but where, in this shadowy world, am I?' He may, however, think it better to keep this question to himself, lest it bring upon his readers a sense of alienation.

Johnson's large consciousness of human solidarity would not admit any difference of kind between the writer and the common reader. Preoccupied, as so often in his essays, with the problem of communication, he regards this supposedly average person as a more or less articulate fellow-being, alternately delighted and tormented by the challenge of language, its inherent problems and those which convention has imposed upon it. Catherine Morland's 'I cannot speak well enough to be unintelligible'[38] is a capital piece of Johnsonian satire, from the children's end of the table.

Even without Henry Austen's assurance, we should be able to recognize Johnson as Jane Austen's 'favourite moral writer . . . in prose'.[39] It is surely clear that the morality she accepted from him included literary good manners, the foundation of a just and happy relationship between writer and reader.

Here the novelist enjoys one advantage, if he chooses to consider it such. As Walter Raleigh says, 'Novelists generally have been insatiable novel-readers.'[40] It is in many ways a companionable art – too companionable, some of them may think: it seems that every reader is ready to tell them how fiction should be written. The great novelists will seldom demur: after all, they alone know where that faint line runs between illusion and delusion – what the novel is, and is not.

1 James Sutherland, *A Preface to Eighteenth Century Poetry* (Oxford, 1948), p. 120.
2 *Miss Austen and Some Books* (*London Mercury*, April 1934), and *Jane Austen and her Art* (Oxford, 1939).
3 Walter Raleigh, *The English Novel* (London, 1907), p. 255.
4 *Mansfield Park*, p. 473, in *The Novels of Jane Austen*, ed. R. W. Chapman (London: Oxford University Press, 1923, subsequently revised). All further references to the texts of Jane Austen's novels are to this edition.
5 Smollett, having no benignity to spare, treats this element in his novels either as broad comedy or as a concession to a taste he does not share.
6 *Emma*, p. 141.
7 *Ibid.*, p. 408.
8 *Ibid.*, p. 431.
9 *Mansfield Park*, p. 265. To anyone seeking certainty in computation, I commend the number of times the word *principle* occurs in *Mansfield Park*.
10 *Ibid.*, pp. 153–5.
11 *Ibid.*, pp. 317–8.
12 *Ibid.*, p. 211. Mary and Fanny are talking at cross purposes here, Mary objecting to the customary designation of a younger son, Fanny as a reader of poetry hearing heroic overtones in the name *Edmund*; but the purport of Mary's references can hardly have escaped Fanny.
13 *Ibid.*, p. 459.
14 *Ibid.*, p. 453.
15 *Ibid.*, p. 470.
16 *Ibid.*, p. 453.
17 *Northanger Abbey*, p. 250.
18 *Mansfield Park*, p. 231.
19 *Ibid.*, p. 331.
20 *Ibid.*, p. 356.
21 What can be learnt from Jane Austen's verbal revision in manuscripts of unpublished writing is insignificant by comparison with this.
22 Anne's likening of herself to Fanny Burney's Miss Larolles is quite another sort of allusion – see *Persuasion*, p. 189.
23 *Ibid.*, p. 221.
24 *Lovers, how they come and part.*
25 *Persuasion*, p. 239. This incident, occurring at the White Hart, makes no part of the first draft.
26 *Northanger Abbey*, p. 232. Not her own pen, but that of certain fellow-novelists.
27 Kathleen Tillotson, *The Tale and the Teller* (London, 1959); reprinted in Geoffrey and Kathleen Tillotson, *Mid-Victorian Studies* (London, 1965) – from which I quote.
28 *Ibid.*, p. 10.
29 I hold unshakeably to my conviction that Jane Austen never used fragments of family history, legend or gossip in composing the stories of her published work.

30 *Mid-Victorian Studies,* p. 10.
31 *Northanger Abbey,* p. 20.
32 *Persuasion,* p. 234.
33 *Sanditon,* in Jane Austen's *Minor Works,* ed. R. W. Chapman (London: Oxford University Press, 1954), p. 390. Sir Edward Denham's infatuation seems incongruously like a return to the mood of *Northanger Abbey,* but the setting in both is a resort, a place of busy idleness.
34 *Ibid.,* p. 391.
35 *Ibid.,* p. 426.
36 With the possible exception of *Sense and Sensibility.*
37 *Letters,* ed. R.W. Chapman (London: Oxford University Press, 1952), Letter 49, 26 September 1753.
38 *Northanger Abbey,* p. 133.
39 *Biographical Notice* prefixed to *Northanger Abbey* and *Persuasion.*
40 *The English Novel,* p. 256.

MARVIN MUDRICK

Jane Austen's drawing-room

The case against Jane Austen never quite blows away. It was drawn up in 1850 by Charlotte Brontë, who thought *Pride and Prejudice* 'an accurate daguerrotyped portrait of a commonplace face' and Jane Austen a monster of prudence: 'the Passions are perfectly unknown to her. . . . Jane Austen was a complete and most sensible lady, but a very incomplete, and rather insensible (*not senseless*) woman.'[1] Almost a century passed before the case got stated with whole-hearted exasperation: 'this old maid,' snarled D.H. Lawrence, 'is, to my feeling, thoroughly unpleasant, English in the bad, mean, snobbish sense of the word'[2] (ranked patterns of correctness obliviously sitting out the Industrial Revolution and the Napoleonic wars); though even devotées come round to wondering, sooner or later, how far her example announced and legitimized and perhaps predetermined that imperturbable conspiracy of prudence, the nineteenth-century English novel. Can we forgive her? Angus Wilson doesn't: deplores that cautionary and provincial conspiracy and the writer he holds responsible for it; taxes 'Anglo-Saxon critics' with keeping Jane Austen's reputation artificially high; suavely taxes them with uniting in a conspiracy of their own, tight little islanders,

> to canonize the foundress of the religion of the English novel, meaning by that religion a regard for all the qualities which the English novel does not share with the great novels of other countries. Not that I should care to deny the justification of this canonization, for through Jane Austen was transmitted to her

247

English heirs Richardson's brilliant Grandisonian care for minutiae
and mistrust of worldliness; while foreigners preferred Clarissa,
Lovelace and passion; to be fair to the English tradition, the loss, I
should say, was only a shade less theirs than ours.[3]

Jane Austen is, then, practical, prosaic, prissy and overrated. Wilson
seems to be saying that, overrated as she is, she nonetheless somehow
managed to impose her personal and artistic shortcomings on three or
four generations of English novelists ('the English tradition': i.e.,
Dickens, Trollope, Hardy, Lawrence, *et al.*) as well as (why stop
now?) on the world they lived in and wrote about – an imputation
which, if true, would make her the most influential artistic second-rat-
er in history. But Jane Austen might be as superb as some think she is
and she would still have had no power to retard or deflect or, for that
matter, accelerate the rise of the middle class. Victorianism preceded
Queen Victoria; in 1821 Sir Walter Scott used a family anecdote to
illustrate a moral change that had been going on over the previous
sixty years and more (the period included Jane Austen's entire lifetime) – a massive and irresistible ossifying of inhibitions against
explicitness:

It is very difficult to answer your Ladyship's curious question
concerning change of taste; but whether in young or old, it takes
place insensibly without the parties being aware of it. A grand-aunt
of my own, Mrs Keith of Ravelstone, who was a person of some
condition, being a daughter of Sir John Swinton of Swinton – lived
with unabated vigour of intellect to a very advanced age. She was
very fond of reading, and enjoyed it to the last of her long life. One
day she asked me, when we happened to be alone together, whether
I had ever seen Mrs Behn's novels? – I confessed the charge. –
Whether I could get her a sight of them? – I said, with some
hesitation, I believed I could; but that I did not think she would like
either the manners, or the language, which approached too near that
of Charles II.'s time to be quite proper reading. 'Nevertheless,' said
the good old lady, 'I remember them being so much admired, and
being so much interested in them myself, that I wish to look at them
again.' To hear was to obey. So I sent Mrs Aphra Behn, curiously
sealed up, with 'private and confidential' on the packet, to my gay
old grand-aunt. The next time I saw her afterwards, she gave me
back Aphra, properly wrapped up, with nearly these words: – 'Take
back your bonny Mrs Behn; and, if you will take my advice, put her
in the fire, for I found it impossible to get through the very first
novel. But is it not,' she said, 'a very odd thing that I, an old woman
of eighty and upwards, sitting alone, feel myself ashamed to read a
book which, sixty years ago, I have heard read aloud for the

amusement of large circles, consisting of the first and most
creditable society in London.'

'This, of course,' Scott concluded with a smugness that sets off all the
more distinctly his beautiful picture of the alert, troubled, and philosophical old gentlewoman, 'was owing to the gradual improvement of
the national taste and delicacy.'[4]

Jane Austen wasn't responsible for the Industrial Revolution or the
Albert Memorial. As to 'the gradual improvement of the national taste
and delicacy,' so far was she from being responsible for it that, by the
time she began writing her novels, it had very nearly finished off the
residue of eighteenth-century candor in Jane Austen and everybody
else writing books: her *juvenilia* (1790–3) can still be cheekily receptive to drunkenness, thievery, adultery, illegitimacy; by the date of
Northanger Abbey (*c.* 1803), John Thorpe is barely allowed to swear
with a tactful dash ('oh, d— it!'); in *Sense and Sensibility* (revised and
published in 1811), Marianne can still exclaim 'Good God!' fully
spelled out and remain a lady; but none of Jane Austen's characters
will ever after venture to take such liberties. Sixty years earlier, young
Mrs Keith of Ravelstone had listened comfortably while Aphra Behn's
novels were being read aloud in a respectable drawing-room, and
Richardson (in *Clarissa*, 1748) hadn't scrupled to transcribe for
posterity Lovelace's explicit appraisal of the 'neatness' and 'elegance'
of the 'dairy-works' of the widow Sorlings' two pretty daughters.

So if Jane Austen doesn't have as liberal a vocabulary as Richardson, Sterne, Fielding, Smollett, neither will Dickens or George Eliot
or any of the Brontës and for the same reasons. Exactly, says Wilson,
that's why English novelists of the nineteenth century are inferior to
the French and Russian, who, making off across the Channel with
'Clarissa, Lovelace and passion,' leave to English fiction Richardson's
less valuable legacy, the 'Grandisonian care for minutiae and mistrust
of worldliness.' Charlotte Brontë, on the other hand, sister of Emily
and author of *Jane Eyre,* is in no position to concede the Continental
monopoly of passion. Jane Austen lacks it no doubt ('the Passions are
perfectly unknown to her'); but not every nineteenth-century English
novelist or her sister is deficient in men on horseback, nubile
governesses,[5] depressing scenery, locks and bolts, occasional moder-
ate to heavy rain, gigantic tantrums, *rigor mortis* (bite-me-to-death-I-
love-it) *à la* Heathcliff: 'I tried to close his eyes. . . . they would not
shut: they seemed to sneer at my attempts, and his parted lips and
sharp white teeth sneered too!' – if only, cried Herbert Read, quoting
the passage, if only Jane Austen could have felt and written like *that!*[6]
After all, as Mrs Bennet assures Darcy, 'there is quite as much of *that*
going on in the country [not only the Brontës' Yorkshire but the

Austens' Hampshire] as in town.' The case against Jane Austen always comes down, with slightly averted eyes, to country matters. What both Angus Wilson and Charlotte Brontë mean by passion, singular or plural, is sexuality, particularly the sexuality of women; the sexual precedence of women: erotic excitability and readiness (with the right partner, naturally), an eagerness for physical connection (sanctioned by love, it goes without saying), a desire and capacity for orgasm; coitus as the warmth of life.

Certainly *Clarissa* is, as Wilson suggests (lamenting its abduction by foreigners), the source and text. Richardson had already, with *Pamela,* made a false start by inventing the woman's novel or modern romance, in which the heroine sacrifices everything for the sake of a lifetime of unbounded self-satisfaction. With *Clarissa,* however, its earliest readers recognized at once, Richardson invented a new kind of adventure story; translated to the Continent, it became the modern novel – in which the heroine comes forward at last to take her chances and the subject is passion. Lovelace, archaic male, keeps imagining himself as the hero of an old-fashioned novel and Clarissa as his goal or prey; keeps so frantically busy playing Don Juan or the Marquis de Sade or Heathcliff or Rochester or Quetzalcoatl that, in a novel twice the length of *War and Peace,* he never notices Clarissa's unintimidated passion and readiness; and his distraction finally wrecks them both.

Clarissa is pristine and unique, but at least one of Jane Austen's women might have done almost as well as Clarissa captivating Lovelace and giving him fits: Marianne Dashwood. The anti-Austenites don't help their case when they fail to acknowledge that Marianne is an obvious exception to it. Indeed, as they might argue, *Sense and Sensibility* is itself an exception, a runaway great novel (like *Madame Bovary)* whose fussy moral scheme isn't proof against this or that intransigent character – an Emma Bovary or a Marianne Dashwood, for example. The first published novel 'By a Lady' (as the title page designated the author) who was one of the two spinster daughters of a rural clergyman, *Sense and Sensibility* is paved with good intentions: in her public début the author intends to avoid all risks, even with the title itself, which therefore turns out to be not an ironic balancing-act (like the title of her second novel, *Pride and Prejudice)* but a crude *a priori* judgment. Sense is right and sensibility is wrong: so she insists from the outset, as early as the scenes introducing Elinor and Marianne. The author proposes that sensibility (passion, flightiness, irrationality) has charms, but sense (prudence, keeping the lid on, calculating the odds) pays off; she is determined to prove what nobody ever doubted. Only, already in chapter II, the moral scheme gets scrambled quite a bit by those exhilarating flint-hearted philis-

tines Mr and Mrs John Dashwood, whose talent for reciprocal ration-
alization proves that though sense is shrewder than sensibility it's
crazier too. What the novel goes on to prove beyond a doubt, over the
author's protests, is that sense (not only the John Dashwoods' but
Elinor's) is mean and deadly, but sensibility – i.e., Marianne – is generous, responsive, frank, loyal, loving, passionate, tragically open to the
torment of rejected love:

> At that moment she first perceived him, and her whole countenance
> glowing with sudden delight, she would have moved towards him
> instantly, had not her sister caught hold of her.
>
> 'Good heavens!' she exclaimed, 'he is there – he is there – Oh!
> why does he not look at me? why cannot I speak to him?'
>
> 'Pray, pray be composed,' cried Elinor, 'and do not betray what
> you feel to every body present. Perhaps he has not observed you
> yet.'
>
> This however was more than she could believe herself; and to be
> composed at such a moment was not only beyond the reach of
> Marianne, it was beyond her wish. She sat in an agony of
> impatience, which affected every feature.
>
> At last he turned round again, and regarded them both; she
> started up, and pronouncing his name in a tone of affection, held
> out her hand to him. He approached, and addressing himself rather
> to Elinor than Marianne, as if wishing to avoid her eye, and
> determined not to observe her attitude, inquired in a hurried
> manner after Mrs Dashwood, and asked how long they had been in
> town. Elinor was robbed of all presence of mind by such an
> address, and was unable to say a word. But the feelings of her sister
> were instantly expressed. Her face was crimsoned over, and she
> exclaimed in a voice of the greatest emotion, 'Good God!
> Willoughby, what is the meaning of this? Have you not received my
> letters? Will you not shake hands with me? . . . Have you not
> received my notes?' cried Marianne in the wildest anxiety. 'Here is
> some mistake I am sure – some dreadful mistake. What can be the
> meaning of it? Tell me, Willoughby; for heaven's sake tell me, what
> is the matter?'[7]

Nobody admired Jane Austen more intelligently than George
Moore, and nobody has written better about this scene:

> the theme of the book is a disappointment in love. . . . Marianne
> cannot give up hope, and the Dashwoods go to London in search of
> the young man; and every attempt is made to recapture him, and
> every effort wrings her heart. She hears of him, but never sees him,
> till at last she perceives him in a back room, and at once, her whole

251

countenance blazing forth with a sudden delight, she would have moved towards him instantly had not her sister laid her hand on her arm, and in the page and a half that follows Miss Austen gives us all the agony of passion the human heart can feel; she was the first; and none has written the scene that we all desire to write as truthfully as she has; when Balzac and Tourguéneff rewrote it they wrote more elaborately, but their achievements are not greater. In Miss Austen the means are as simple as the result is amazing . . . it is here that we find the burning human heart in English prose narrative for the first, and, alas, for the last time.[8]

Moore and Angus Wilson remind us of a fact of literary history, that the French and Russian novelists took up passion from English fiction and carried it off for their own purposes; but Moore contends also that the only English novelist in whose work (in only one of whose novels, rather) they could have found the literary model of passion was, not Richardson, but Jane Austen! The notion, however historically unsound (and unfair to her later novels, which Moore admits not having read lately), begins to seem less fantastic when Moore describes what he considers Jane Austen's great and fundamental discovery:

> it was Miss Austen's spinsterhood that allowed her to discover the Venusberg in the modern drawing-room. . . . We do not go into society for the pleasure of conversation, but for the pleasure of sex, direct or indirect. Everything is arranged for this end: the dresses, the dances, the food, the wine, the music! Of this truth we are all conscious now, but should we have discovered it without Miss Austen's help? It was certainly she who perceived it, and her books are permeated with it, just as Wordsworth's poems are with a sense of deity in nature; and is it not this deep instinctive knowledge that makes her drawing-rooms seem more real than anybody else's? Marianne loves beyond Juliet's or Isolde's power; and our wonder at her passion is heightened by the fact that it wears out in drawing-rooms among chaperons.[9]

Richardson's Venusberg is a London brothel or a remote country-house (only the lovers are real). Jane Austen's is her own familiar drawing-room, which 'seems[s] more real than anybody else's' because the unregarded and attentive spinster,[10] lacking other diversions, observes what's really going on there – especially *that*, as Mrs Bennet would say:

> 'Lizzy,' cried her mother, 'remember where you are, and do not run on in the wild manner that you are suffered to do at home.'
> 'I did not know before,' continued Bingley immediately, 'that you were a studier of character. It must be an amusing study.'

252

'Yes; but intricate characters are the *most* amusing. They have at least that advantage.'

'The country,' said Darcy, 'can in general supply but few subjects for such a study. In a country neighbourhood you move in a very confined and unvarying society.'

'But people themselves alter so much, that there is something new to be observed in them for ever.'

'Yes, indeed,' cried Mrs Bennet, offended by his manner of mentioning a country neighbourhood. 'I assure you there is quite as much of *that* going on in the country as in town.'

Every body was surprised; and Darcy, after looking at her for a moment, turned silently away.

Everybody in this allegory of love, from Ungovernable Indelicacy to Scrupulous Correction, knows that winning is everything; but only those who win know how many different ways there are to lose:

Mrs Bennet, who fancied she had gained a complete victory over him, continued her triumph.

'I cannot see that London has any great advantage over the country for my part, except the shops and public places. The country is a vast deal pleasanter, is not it, Mr Bingley?'

'When I am in the country,' he replied, 'I never wish to leave it; and when I am in town it is pretty much the same. They have each their advantages, and I can be equally happy in either.'

'Aye – that is because you have the right disposition. But that gentleman,' looking at Darcy, 'seemed to think the country was nothing at all.'

'Indeed, Mama, you are mistaken,' said Elizabeth, blushing for her mother. 'You quite mistook Mr Darcy. He only meant that there was not such a variety of people to be met with in the country as in town, which you must acknowledge to be true.'

'Certainly, my dear, nobody said there were; but as to not meeting with many people in this neighbourhood, I believe there are few neighbourhoods larger. I know we dine with four and twenty families.'

Nothing but concern for Elizabeth could enable Bingley to keep his countenance. His sister was less delicate, and directed her eye towards Mr Darcy with a very expressive smile.[11]

Elizabeth, the 'studier of character,' does in fact perfectly understand Bingley, who is a faultless and predictable young man and therefore of no further interest to her. Foolish, touchy Mrs Bennet, still fascinated by country matters, knows very well what the drawing-room game is, and is indecorous enough to flaunt (if not actually name) what she knows. Bingley's sister knows that Mrs Bennet is a loser, but doesn't know that only losers solicit praise for recognizing losers. Everybody goes back to square one except Elizabeth and Darcy:

> 'Do you not feel a great inclination, Miss Bennet, to seize such an opportunity of dancing a reel?'
>
> She smiled, but made no answer. He repeated the question, with some surprise at her silence.
>
> 'Oh!' said she, 'I heard you before; but I could not immediately determine what to say in reply. You wanted me, I know, to say "Yes," that you might have the pleasure of despising my taste; but I always delight in overthrowing those kind of schemes, and cheating a person of their premeditated contempt. I have therefore made up my mind to tell you, that I do not want to dance a reel at all – and now despise me if you dare.'
>
> 'Indeed I do not dare.'
>
> Elizabeth, having rather expected to affront him, was amazed at his gallantry; but there was a mixture of sweetness and archness in her manner which made it difficult for her to affront anybody; and Darcy had never been so bewitched by any woman as he was by her. He really believed, that were it not for the inferiority of her connections, he should be in some danger.[12]

At first Darcy, like Lovelace too vain and masculine to know how to win by yielding, becomes merely passion's slave and blunders into the grotesque proposal that Elizabeth angrily rejects:

> In spite of her deeply-rooted dislike, she could not be insensible to the compliment of such a man's affection, and though her intentions did not vary for an instant, she was at first sorry for the pain he was to receive; till, roused to resentment by his subsequent language, she lost all compassion in anger . . . He concluded with representing to her the strength of that attachment which, in spite of all his endeavours, he had found impossible to conquer; and with expressing his hope that it would now be rewarded by her acceptance of his hand. As he said this, she could easily see that he had no doubt of a favourable answer . . . Such a circumstance could only exasperate farther, and when he ceased, the colour rose into her cheeks, and she said,
>
> 'In such cases as this, it is, I believe, the established mode to express a sense of obligation for the sentiments avowed, however unequally they may be returned. It is natural that obligation should be felt, and if I could *feel* gratitude, I would now thank you. But I cannot – I have never desired your good opinion, and you have certainly bestowed it most unwillingly. I am sorry to have occasioned pain to any one. It has been most unconsciously done,

however, and I hope will be of short duration. The feelings which, you tell me, have long prevented the acknowledgment of your regard, can have little difficulty in overcoming it after this explanation.'

Mr Darcy, who was leaning against the mantle-piece with his eyes fixed on her face, seemed to catch her words with no less resentment than surprise. His complexion became pale with anger, and the disturbance of his mind was visible in every feature . . . At length, in a voice of forced calmness, he said,

'And this is all the reply which I am to have the honour of expecting! I might, perhaps, wish to be informed why, with so little *endeavour* at civility, I am thus rejected. But it is of small importance.'

It's a remarkable scene, and in its furiously formal Johnsonian cadences it tells us more about love and marriage than we could learn from a secret diary or any number of Brontë manuals:

'I might as well enquire,' replied she, 'why with so evident a design of offending and insulting me, you chose to tell me that you liked me against your will, against your reason, and even against your character? Was not this some excuse for incivility, if I *was* uncivil? But I have other provocations. You know I have. Had not my own feelings decided against you, had they been indifferent, or had they even been favourable, do you think that any consideration would tempt me to accept the man, who has been the means of ruining, perhaps for ever, the happiness of a most beloved sister?'

As she pronounced these words, Mr Darcy changed colour; but the emotion was short, and he listened without attempting to interrupt her while she continued.

'I have every reason in the world to think ill of you. No motive can excuse the unjust and ungenerous part you acted *there.* You dare not, you cannot deny that you have been the principal, if not the only means of dividing them from each other. . . .'

She paused, and saw with no slight indignation that he was listening with an air which proved him wholly unmoved by any feeling of remorse. . . .

'Can you deny that you have done it?' she repeated.

With assumed tranquillity he then replied, 'I have no wish of denying that I did every thing in my power to separate my friend from your sister, or that I rejoice in my success. Towards *him* I have been kinder than towards myself.'[13]

Trying to sympathize with Charlotte Brontë, one can imagine why it would never have occurred to her that Elizabeth and Darcy are *roused* to this pitch of formal rhetoric; one can imagine why such a refinement and dramatization of the Johnsonian idiom would seem as mechanical and unexpressive to an impatient nineteenth-century sensibility as, say, Dr Johnson himself seemed to Wordsworth and Coleridge. Surely what bothers her is Elizabeth's (Jane Austen's) full and unapologetic articulateness: woman's province is feeling, and feeling ought to be inarticulate or at least convulsive and incoherent. But – like all of Jane Austen's other heroines (except those hole-and-corner anomalies, Elinor Dashwood and Fanny Price) – Elizabeth is as strong and brave in her talk as in her feeling. How else could she ever penetrate to the quick of an armored male ego like Darcy's? In *Mansfield Park* Mary Crawford, baffled by a comparable male ego, drops decorum altogether and goes so far as to transform Jane Austen's drawing-room into a boudoir:

> 'I had gone a few steps, Fanny, when I heard the door open behind me. "Mr Bertram," said she. I looked back. "Mr Bertram," said she, with a smile – but it was a smile ill-suited to the conversation that had passed, a saucy playful smile, seeming to invite, in order to subdue me; at least, it appeared so to me. I resisted; it was the impulse of the moment to resist, and still walked on. I have since – sometimes – for a moment – regretted that I did not go back; but I know I was right.'[14]

Mary is a century too early, and the author can't approve; but Elizabeth and Marianne and Catherine Morland and Emma Woodhouse would all of them have understood Mary's last choice and Edmund's lingering regret.

So, of course, would Anne Elliot. Can Charlotte Brontë or Angus Wilson or D.H. Lawrence have read *Persuasion?* (Herbert Read seems to have read it, because he cites the scene of Louisa's fall from the Cobb as evidence of the marionette-like unnaturalness of Jane Austen's characters.[15]) Suppose Charlotte Brontë, coming on the scene a generation earlier, had stated not in 1850 but in 1815 her reservations about the author of *Pride and Prejudice,* and Jane Austen had heard them and come to a decision: Well, if this literary lady considers Elizabeth or me (not to mention Marianne) such a cold fish, maybe I'd better invent a heroine who's warm enough for absolutely anybody – I'll invent Anne Elliot, of course. For instance, since Miss Brontë calls me 'a very incomplete, and rather insensible (*not senseless*) woman,' I'll use 'senseless' (minus italics, so she won't think I'm plagiarizing) as the very word to specify the kind of joy Anne feels at the moment when she can begin to hope again:

> No, it was not regret which made Anne's heart beat in spite of herself, and brought the colour into her cheeks when she thought of Captain Wentworth unshackled and free. She had some feelings

which she was ashamed to investigate. They were too much like joy, senseless joy![16]

As far as I can (resolves the penitent author of *Pride and Prejudice*) I'll model her in anticipation after – Jane Eyre! except she'll be open-eyed, clear-headed, unsentimental –

> Anne had not wanted this visit to Uppercross, to learn that a removal from one set of people to another, though at a distance of only three miles, will often include a total change of conversation, opinion, and idea. She had never been staying there before, without being struck by it, or without wishing that other Elliots could have her advantage in seeing how unknown, or unconsidered there, were the affairs which at Kellynch-hall were treated as of such general publicity and pervading interest; yet, with all this experience, she believed she must now submit to feel that another lesson, in the art of knowing our own nothingness beyond our own circle, was becoming necessary for her.[17]

– and she'll be loving, large-hearted, ready for delight, a wellspring of good feeling –

> Anne saw [the Crofts] wherever she went. Lady Russell took her out in her carriage almost every morning, and she never failed to think of them, and never failed to see them. Knowing their feelings as she did, it was a most attractive picture of happiness to her. She always watched them as long as she could; delighted to fancy she understood what they might be talking of, as they walked along in happy independence, or equally delighted to see the Admiral's hearty shake of the hand when he encountered an old friend, and observe their eagerness of conversation when occasionally forming into a little knot of the navy, Mrs Croft looking as intelligent and keen as any of the officers around her.[18]

– and she'll be intense, spontaneous, unpremeditatedly delightful –

> and Anne – but it would be an insult to the nature of Anne's felicity, to draw any comparison between it and her sister's; the origin of one all selfish vanity, of the other all generous attachment.
>
> Anne saw nothing, thought nothing of the brilliancy of the room. Her happiness was from within. Her eyes were bright, and her cheeks glowed, – but she knew nothing about it. She was thinking only of the last half hour, and as they passed to their seats, her mind took a hasty range over it. His choice of subjects, his expressions, and still more his manner and look, had been such as she could see in only one light.[19]

Unlike Elizabeth or Marianne, Anne won't be much of a talker, I'll see to that; she'll be nearly as introspective as scruffy little Jane Eyre: in her daily concerns she'll be the helpful, unobtrusive maiden aunt, nurse, confidante, companion, baby-sitter (I've done the whole routine myself); rather like a governess. But some readers just won't be fooled by the real thing, they'll keep holding out for the imitation.

For the real thing is sometimes almost too bare and painful to contemplate: so Jane Austen showed with Marianne and now devotes an entire novel to showing moment by moment with Anne, as when Anne braces herself to survive her first meeting with Wentworth after seven years:

> a thousand feelings rushed on Anne, of which this was the most consoling, that it would soon be over. And it was soon over. In two minutes after Charles's preparation, the others appeared; they were in the drawing-room. Her eye half met Captain Wentworth's; a bow, a curtsey passed; she heard his voice – he talked to Mary, said all that was right; said something to the Miss Musgroves, enough to mark an easy footing: the room seemed full – full of persons and voices – but a few minutes ended it. Charles shewed himself at the window, all was ready, their visitor had bowed and was gone; the Miss Musgroves were gone too, suddenly resolving to walk to the end of the village with the sportsmen: the room was cleared, and Anne might finish her breakfast as she could.
>   'It is over! it is over!' she repeated to herself again, and again, in nervous gratitude. 'The worst is over!'[20]

It isn't over, but she might as well take a breath while thinking so. Too much depends on the mistake she made years ago and can't imagine she'll ever have the chance to make again. *Persuasion* is about loneliness and growing old gracefully; about lost and last chances; about staying out of the way, perfecting 'the art of knowing our own nothingness'; and about passion, which covers with confusion, electrifies with senseless joy, stuns or transfixes or agitates – passion tried and true, which destroys the illusion of one's own insignificance and discloses as if on stone tablets the meaning of the past:

> It was in one of these short meetings, each apparently occupied in admiring a fine display of green-house plants, that she said –
>   'I have been thinking over the past, and trying impartially to judge of the right and the wrong, I mean with regard to myself; and I must believe that I was right, much as I suffered from it, that I was perfectly right in being guided by the friend whom you will love better than you do now. To me, she was in the place of a parent. Do not mistake me, however. I am not saying that she did not err in her advice. It was, perhaps, one of those cases in which advice is good

or bad only as the event decides; and for myself, I certainly never
should, in any circumstance of tolerable similarity, give such
advice. But I mean, that I was right in submitting to her, and that if
I had done otherwise, I should have suffered more in continuing the
engagement than I did even in giving it up, because I should have
suffered in my conscience. I have now, as far as such a sentiment is
allowable in human nature, nothing to reproach myself with; and if
I mistake not, a strong sense of duty is no bad part of a woman's
portion.'

Anne, learning how to occupy space again, may be excused this slight
case of conscience as she reclaims the past, especially when a moment
later she replies with all possible colloquial alacrity to Wentworth's
unnecessary question:

'Tell me if, when I returned to England in the year eight, with a few
thousand pounds, and was posted into the Laconia, if I had then
written to you, would you have answered my letter? would you, in
short, have renewed the engagement then?'
  'Would I!' was all her answer; but the accent was decisive
enough.[21]

Women know what they know but – as Anne, newly free to speak
out, is glad to be reminded by Captain Harville – it's men who write
the books:

'Well, Miss Elliot . . . we shall never agree I suppose upon this
point. No man and woman would, probably. But let me observe that
all histories are against you, all stories, prose and verse. If I had
such a memory as Benwick, I could bring you fifty quotations in a
moment on my side of the argument, and I do not think I ever
opened a book in my life which had not something to say upon
woman's inconstancy. Songs and proverbs, all talk of woman's
fickleness. But perhaps you will say, these were all written by men.'
  'Perhaps I shall. – Yes, yes, if you please, no reference to examples
in books. Men have had every advantage of us in telling their own
story. Education has been theirs in so much higher a degree; the
pen has been in their hands. I will not allow books to prove any
thing.'[22]

Because (Anne almost says, glorying in her exemplary role) no book,
until this one, has ever told the truth about *me*. Richardson could do
the great incendiary talker, Clarissa; but it took Jane Austen, in her
last novel, to do Anne Elliot, the great quiet incendiary, the unregarded lady in the drawing-room, who till she has all the reason in the
world leaves the talking to others, questions no arrangements while

noticing them all, never imposes, always assists, and keeps her heart and soul available for anybody – Captain Wentworth or the Crofts or the author or the reader – who might at some time or other have the good luck to accompany her on her unnoticed morning walk along the streets of Bath:

> Prettier musings of high-wrought love and eternal constancy, could never have passed along the streets of Bath, than Anne was sporting with from Camden-place to Westgate-buildings. It was almost enough to spread purification and perfume all the way.[23]

NOTES

1 *The Brontës: Their Friendships, Lives, and Correspondence*, ed. T. J. Wise and J. A. Symington (Oxford, 1932), Vol. III, p. 99.

2 *A Propos of Lady Chatterley's Lover* (London, 1930), p. 58.

3 'The Neighbourhood of Tombuctoo,' in *Critical Essays on Jane Austen*, ed. B. C. Southam (London, 1968), p. 185. But Continental writers adored *both* Richardsons: in 'The Portrait' (1841–2), Gogol eulogizes 'Prince R., one of the best and most honourable of all young noblemen of that time, handsome of face and of a noble, chivalrous character, the ideal hero of novels and women, a Grandison in every respect.' *The Overcoat and Other Tales of Good and Evil*, tr. David Magarshack (Norton, 1965) p. 145.

4 J. G. Lockhart, *Memoirs of the Life of Sir Walter Scott, Bart.* (2nd ed., Edinburgh and London, 1839), Vol. VI, pp. 406–7.

5 Regarding passion and *Jane Eyre*, Lawrence (cross-grained as ever) comments: 'I don't think any married woman would have written [it]. . . . In [*Jane Eyre*] . . . there is a certain naïve attitude to men which would hardly survive a year of married life.' *Phoenix* (New York, 1968), p. 337.

6 *English Prose Style* (Boston, 1955), pp. 109–12.

7 *The Novels of Jane Austen*, ed. R. W. Chapmen, Vol. I (3rd ed., London, 1933), II, vi.

8 *Avowals* (London, 1924), pp. 39–40.

9 *Ibid.*, pp. 57–8.

10 Making allowance for the dash of vitriol, Mary Russell Mitford's contemporary gossiping gives us an impression of the effect Jane Austen must have had on her neighbors once they knew exactly who was sitting there: 'a friend of mine, who visits her now, says that she has stiffened into the most perpendicular, precise, tactiturn piece of "single blessedness" that ever existed, and that, till *Pride and Prejudice* showed what a precious gem was hidden in that unbending case, she was no more regarded in society than a poker or a fire-screen, or any other thin upright piece of wood or iron that fills its corner in peace and quietness. The case is very different now; she is still a poker – but a poker of whom every one is afraid. It must be confessed that this silent observation from such an

observer is rather formidable . . . a wit, a delineator of character, who
does not talk, is terrific indeed!' *The Letters of Mary Russell Mitford*, ed.
R. B. Johnson (New York, 1925), p. 127 (Letter to Sir William Elford, 3
April 1815).

11 *The Novels of Jane Austen*, Vol. II (I, ix).
12 *Ibid.*, II, x.
13 *Ibid.*, II, xi.
14 *The Novels of Jane Austen*, Vol. III (III, xvi).
15 *Loc. cit.*
16 *The Novels of Jane Austen*, Vol. V (IV, vi).
17 *Ibid.*, III, vi.
18 *Ibid.*, IV, vi.
19 *Ibid.*, IV, viii.
20 *Ibid.*, III, vii.
21 *Ibid.*, IV, xi.
22 *Ibid.*, IV, xi.
23 *Ibid.*, IV, ix.

DONALD GREENE

Jane Austen's monsters

Monsters, as J.R.R.Tolkien has said, are not peripheral to *Beowulf*, but at its very center; and there may be many more of them in the poem than we first suspect.[1]

It is her ability to include the potential cruelty and nastiness of ordinary people together with their more admirable and pleasant qualities in one balanced image of humanity that in part makes Jane Austen a great novelist.[2]

Not many people now think of Jane Austen as the gentle, secluded spinster who gives us a picture of quiet, 'ordinary' uneventful life in a humdrum rural society, preaching the tired clichés of a conventional and superficial morality. Yet G. K. Chesterton's 'paradoxical' over-reaction to this kind of thing – '[Her] inspiration was the inspiration of Gargantua and of Pickwick; it was the gigantic inspiration of laughter. . . . She was the very reverse of a starched or a starved spinster; she could have been a buffoon like the Wife of Bath if she chose' – though a salutary corrective to the older view, hardly tells the whole truth either. It is interesting that what startled Chesterton into writing this was the recently recovered juvenilia, in particular *Love and Friendship*, written when Jane Austen was fourteen.[3] Since R. F. Brissenden's brilliant analysis of this satire and other juvenile pieces,[4] in which he audaciously links her with her contemporary Sade as a deflater of the sentimental 'image of man as a social, sympathetic, generous, benevolent, and good-natured being,' picturing him rather as 'an isolated, anarchic, selfish, cruel, violent, and aggressive being,'

262

we have become uneasily aware that there are depths of the knowledge of evil – as well as of good – in Jane Austen's writings for which perhaps none of Chesterton's illustrations provides a very exact parallel.

If the mention of Sade strikes the reader as going a little too far – though Brissenden has no difficulty demonstrating that 'sadistic' is an entirely accurate term for the utterly ruthless self-centered aggression of Laura and Edward and Augustus and Sophia, with their 'sensibility too tremblingly alive' to their own material welfare, at whatever expense to that of others – let us compromise, and associate her with the great nineteenth-century Russian writers – Tolstoy, Dostoevsky, Turgenev, Chekhov.[5] Like Jane Austen, they are all 'realists,' concerned to give a carefully observed picture of 'manners' in the here-and-now, adept at hitting on some significant small detail of appearance or behavior that gives us a clue to the inner make-up of a character. There is a wealth of comedy in their writings, even those of Dostoevsky – regarded, no doubt justly, as the 'grimmest' of the four. They are all intensely dedicated moralists, and they hold in common the same system of morality, that of orthodox Christianity, which recognizes that man is far from the 'social, sympathetic, generous, benevolent, good-natured being' that sentimentalists would like to believe in, but that he retains a hard core of original sin, which not even the greatest human saint can completely rid himself of, yet the existence of which has to be recognized if it is to be mitigated. The great climactic scenes in Tolstoy and Dostoevsky, as in Jane Austen,[6] are those of self-recognition, where a central character reaches the stage of being able to confess, as Jane Austen's Book of Common Prayer put it, 'I have left undone those things which I ought to have done, and I have done those things which I ought not to have done, and there is no health in me.' If it be argued that Tolstoy and the others are 'tragic' writers in a way that Jane Austen is not, because those of their characters who fail to reach such self-recognition suffer seemingly harsher fates – Anna Karenina's suicide, the murder of Fyodor Karamazov, the destruction of Ranevskaya's cherry orchard – it might be replied that the fate of Jane Austen's unconverted, that of having to go on living with themselves, or with one another – Lydia Bennet with Wickham, Maria Rushworth with Mrs Norris, to mention some notable examples – are probably quite as productive of misery in the long run. Jane Austen's 'Let other tongues dwell on guilt and misery. I quit such odious subjects as soon as I can, impatient to restore everybody not greatly in fault themselves to tolerable comfort, and to have done with all the rest'[7] has bothered some critics; and yet Dante's title for his great work, *The Divine Comedy,* has implications not entirely irrelevant to Jane Austen's work.

Mr Brissenden has demonstrated beyond question the insight into the depths of human perversity revealed in Jane Austen's juvenile pieces. It has been pointed out more than once that her upbringing as the daughter of a country parson, far from handicapping her in obtaining such insight, provided her with at least as good an opportunity as any modern urban 'social worker' for acquiring it. One thinks of Agatha Christie's spinster detective, Miss Jane Marple (her given name is surely no coincidence), to whom a 'sophisticated' friend observes:

> 'You've always been a sweet innocent looking creature, Jane, and all the time underneath nothing has ever surprised you, you always believe the worst.'
>
> 'The worst is so often true,' murmured Miss Marple.
>
> 'Why you have such a poor idea of human nature, I can't think – living in that sweet peaceful village of yours, so old world and pure.'
>
> 'You have never lived in a village, Ruth. The things that go on in a pure peaceful village would probably surprise you. . . . Human nature, dear, is very much the same everywhere. It is more difficult to observe it closely in a city, that is all. . . . Very nasty things go on in a village, I assure you.'[8]

There is as much scope for a would-be Raskolnikov or Anatol Kuragin in a Yasnaya Polyana or the country estate of the Karamazovs (or a Chawton or Steventon) as in St Petersburg. The shocked horror with which H.W. Garrod and others have deplored the 'cynicism' in Jane Austen's letters – as a relatively mild instance, 'Yesterday came a letter to my mother from Edward Cooper to announce, not the birth of a child, but of a living . . . Staffordshire is a good way off; so we shall see nothing more of them till, some fifteen years hence, the Miss Coopers are presented to us, fine, jolly, handsome, ignorant girls'[9] – is perhaps testimony to how much better a preparation for a realistic novelist is a life spent in such places than in an academic quadrangle.

I should like, in this essay, to trace a little farther than Brissenden does – that is to say, in her later works – Jane Austen's constant awareness of the many grotesque forms which the perversion of native human potential can take, and the dangers inherent in that perversion. Her works indeed, it can be argued, present as manifold and nightmarish a zoo of distortions of human nature as Pope's Cave of Spleen (which, in turn, it has been suggested, owes something to the iconographic tradition of Hieronymus Bosch and other medieval portraitists of human psychological and moral distortion):

Here stood *Ill-Nature* like an ancient maid,
Her wrinkled form in black and white array'd;

With store of pray'rs, for mornings, nights, and noons,
Her hand is filled; her bosom with lampoons.
There *Affectation* with a sickly mien
Shows in her cheek the roses of eighteen,
Practised to lisp and hang the head aside,
Faints into airs, and languishes with pride . . .
Unnumber'd throngs on ev'ry side are seen.
Of bodies chang'd to various forms by *Spleen.*
Here living teapots stand, one arm held out,
One bent; the handle this and that the spout:
A pipkin there like Homer's tripod walks;
Here sighs a jar, and there a goose-pye talks;
Men prove with child, as pow'rful fancy works,
And maids turn'd bottels, call aloud for corks.[10]

'Spleen' has had many synonyms, ranging from the 'acedia' of the Middle Ages, through the 'melancholy,' 'hypochondria,' 'vapours,' and so forth of the sixteenth to eighteenth centuries, to the 'neurasthenia' and 'weak nerves' of the nineteenth and the 'neurosis' of the twentieth.[11] It and its manifold harmful effects have always been with us. Moralists of the eighteenth century and earlier did not, I think, subscribe to the later dichotomy of 'reason' and 'emotion' as separate parts of human nature: in the victim of 'spleen' both intellectual and emotional awareness are dulled. 'Dulness' is, of course, Pope's and Swift's favorite word for the condition, and Pope superbly sums up the effect on the individual of the systematic course of stultification in the educational institutions of his day (and later):

First slave to Words, then vassal to a Name,
Then dupe to Party; child and man the same.
Bounded by Nature, narrow'd still [continually] by Art,
A trifling head and a contracted heart.[12]

In spite of the growing popularity of the dichotomy in the later eighteenth century – the notion that a sufficient quota of emotional 'sensibility' will compensate for any amount of intellectual inadequacy, that 'reason' is perhaps even the enemy of 'sensibility' (cf. Rousseau's first *Discours,* 'O vertu! science sublime des âmes simples, faut-il donc tant de peine et d'appareil pour te connaître? Tes principes non sont-ils pas gravés dans tous les coeurs?' Or, later, the Reverend Charles Kingsley's 'Be good, sweet maid, and let who will be clever') – it seems dubious that Jane Austen subscribed to it.[13] The hero and heroine of *Pride and Prejudice,* Elizabeth and Darcy, are not only the most intelligent, best educated, and wittiest of the cast of characters, but, like Millamant and Mirabel in *The Way of the World,* are also the most capable of genuine and deep feeling. Those of its characters who are the most stupid – Mrs Bennet, the Reverend Mr Collins, Lady Catherine de Bourgh – are also emotionally the most obtuse, unable to feel concern for anyone's welfare outside their own.

The most egregious example of this combined intellectual and emotional obtuseness – perhaps the most thoroughgoing 'monster' of the six published novels of Jane Austen's maturity – is Mary Bennet, who esteems herself the 'intellectual' of the family, and whose intellectualism displays itself in such ludicrous exhibitions as, when Elizabeth proposes to walk through the mud to visit their ailing sister Jane,

> 'I admire the activity of your benevolence,' observed Mary, 'but every impulse of feeling should be guided by reason; and, in my opinion, exertion should always be in proportion to what is required,'[14]

and

> [Mr Bennet] 'What say you, Mary? For you are a young lady of deep reflection, I know, and read great books, and make extracts.'
> Mary wished to say something very sensible, but knew not how.
>
> They found Mary, as usual, deep in the study of thorough bass and human nature.
>
> [Mary on Mr Collins' letter] 'The idea of the olive branch perhaps is not wholly new.'

Mary contributes nothing whatever to the plot of the novel, except to add her quota to the collective folly of the Bennet family. Her infrequent and inconsequential appearances, however, have something of the function of a death's head at a feast, reminding us that under the 'light, bright, and sparkling' surface of the story there lurks great danger.[15] Mary, fortunately, is without much power to affect the lives of those around her. But the juxtaposition of one of her first with one of her last appearances in the novel is hair-raising in its implication that lip-service to moral precepts may co-exist with the most astounding emotional callousness:

> 'Pride,' observed Mary, who piqued herself upon the solidity of her reflections, 'is a very common failing, I believe. By all that I have ever read, I am convinced that it is very common; indeed, that human nature is particularly prone to it, and that there are very few of us who do not cherish a feeling of self-complacency on the score of some quality or other, real or imaginary.'

This pomposity is beautifully placed in perspective when it is followed by a 'reflection' which is, by implication, of equal importance, given the speaker: ' "If I were as rich as Mr Darcy," said a young Lucas, ". . . I would keep a pack of foxhounds, and drink a bottle of wine every day." ' It is when Mary has an opportunity to apply what she has read to a practical situation that one is staggered: when she gives us her reaction to her sister Lydia's downfall, saying, 'with a countenance of grave reflection,'

> 'This is a most unfortunate affair; and will probably be much talked of. But we must stem the tide of malice, and pour into the wounded bosoms of each other the balm of sisterly consolation. . . .
> Unhappy as the event must be for Lydia, we may draw from it this useful lesson: that loss of virtue in a female is irretrievable – that one false step involves her in endless ruin . . . and that she cannot be too much guarded in her behaviour towards the undeserving of the other sex.'

It is no wonder that 'Elizabeth lifted up her eyes in amazement, but was too much oppressed to make any reply.' In Mary we sense with a shudder those future German intellectuals, professors of ethics or theology, who failed to notice anything untoward in the charnel-houses of Auschwitz and Buchenwald. Somehow even the Reverend Mr Collins's 'You ought certainly to forgive them as a Christian, but never to admit them in your sight, or allow their names to be mentioned in your hearing' is not quite so shocking: Mary and Lydia are sisters, close in age, who have grown up together; Mr Collins is only a distant cousin who has seen little of them.

If one were to undertake a full catalogue (this essay can be only a sampling) of the human freaks in Jane Austen's writings, one could perhaps do no better than to use the old medieval classification of the seven cardinal sins. As a Protestant, Jane Austen did not of course believe that sin is so neatly divisible. Yet she would surely have agreed with the older moralists that pride – egocentricity, the over-estimation of one's own importance in the scheme of things, the in-ability to love, to feel emotion for, anyone or anything beyond the status of one's own ego – is the primary sin, of which the others are merely variations. As the utterly cold and self-centered – and stupid – Mary Bennet wisely remarks, 'Human nature is particularly prone to it.' It is pride that causes the downfall (temporarily) of Jane Austen's heroines. Although it is usually said that in *Pride and Prejudice* it is Darcy who represents the first quality and Elizabeth the second, the fact is that both are equally guilty of both: of the emotional unreceptivity that is the product of an unrealistically high opinion of oneself, and of the intellectual blindness (prejudice) that is its consequence. At the beginning of the novel, Elizabeth must be well aware, before many sentences have been exchanged between them, that Darcy is the only man she has ever met, or is likely to meet, who has an intelligence equal to her own, and is therefore a fit match for her; one assumes that the example she has lived with, and of which her father specifically warns her, of the danger of marrying beneath one's I.Q. is not lost on her. Yet she allows her (deservedly) high opinion of her own shrewdness to be flattered by Wickham. The words in which she repents are significant:

> 'How despicably have I acted! . . . I, who have *prided* myself on my discernment! – I, who have valued myself on my abilities! . . . How humiliating is this discovery! – Yet, how just a humiliation! – had I been in love, I could not have been more wretchedly *blind!*'

Likewise Emma: self-complacency results in both emotional and intellectual obtuseness: 'How could you be so *unfeeling* to Miss Bates?' Knightley reproaches her. 'You whom she had known from an infant . . . to have you now, in *thoughtless* spirits and the *pride* of the moment, laugh at her, humble her.' And Emma, like Elizabeth, is forced to acknowledge the charge, and undergo her own agony of salutary self-humiliation: 'How to understand the deceptions she had been thus practising on herself, and living under! The blunders, the *blindness* of her own *head* and *heart!*'[16] The two are inseparable.

Perhaps the least dangerous form of pride is the simple and absurd snobbery which Jane Austen knows so well how to depict. In themselves, the *grande-damerie* of Lady Catherine de Bourgh and the Debrett-worship of Sir Walter Elliot are made to seem so transparently ridiculous that it is hard to imagine anyone's taking them seriously and being hurt by them. (And yet even they are in a position to control and injure other people's lives: Lady Catherine's daughter is by this time probably beyond help though there must have been a time when she could have been saved.) As for the Reverend William Collins, Jane Austen even allows us to feel a certain compassion for him. Like a good modern psychiatrist, she is well aware that an inflated sense of one's own importance and the need constantly to assert it are often the product of a deep inner insecurity, usually the product of childhood trauma: Mr Collins

> had been but little assisted by education or society; the greatest part of his life having been spent under the guidance of an illiterate and miserly father. . . . The subjection in which his father had brought him up had given him originally great humility of manner, but it was now a good deal counteracted by the self-conceit of a weak head.

There is an explanation even for the repellent Mary Bennet, who, 'in consequence of being the only plain one in the family, worked hard for knowledge and accomplishments' and 'was always impatient for display.'[17]

In the medieval tradition, Sloth is often placed next to Pride in the hierarchy of the sins: Spenser puts him at the head of the procession that drags Pride's chariot along.[18] Its victim feels that he is so important in the scheme of things that he need not put forward effort of his own: it is for other, inferior beings to provide for him. Jane Austen presents us with a fine gallery of the slothful. Curiously, her male examples, notably Mr Bennet and Mr Woodhouse, are, when we first meet them, and for some time afterwards, not unattractive. Yet it gradually dawns on us that Mr Bennet and Mr Woodhouse are monsters, after all. Their sloth is not so harmless as their loving daughters Elizabeth and Emma would at first like to think. Elizabeth's final judgment on her father – after she herself, by suffering, has acquired some insight into the problems of human relationships – is severe and just. She

> had never been blind to the impropriety of her father's behaviour as a husband. She had always seen it with pain; but respecting his abilities, and grateful for his affectionate treatment of herself, she endeavoured to forget what she could not overlook, and to banish from her thoughts that continual breach of conjugal obligation and decorum which, in exposing his wife to the contempt of her own children, was so highly reprehensible. But she had never felt so strongly as now, the disadvantages which must attend the children of so unsuitable a marriage, nor ever been so fully aware of the evils arising from so ill-judged a direction of talents; talents which rightly used, might at least have preserved the respectability of his daughters, even if incapable of enlarging the mind of his wife.[19]

Mr Bennet's abdication of his responsibilities, it is easy to see, stems from his too high opinion of himself. He is a clever man; he has made one stupid mistake, in his marriage: he therefore feels that he is being unjustly punished by heaven, and, in revenge, as it were, refuses in future to exert his cleverness again, except in the form of what, finally, seem rather cheap wisecracks at the expense of his wife. In the end, he is presented to us as an object of contempt, not pity:

> To his wife he was very little otherwise indebted, than as her ignorance and folly had contributed to his amusement. This is not the sort of happiness which a man would in general wish to owe to his wife; but where other powers of entertainment are wanting, the true philosopher will derive benefit from such as are given.[20]

This last is surely one of the most acid of Jane Austen's many acidities. It is gratifying, on one occasion, to find Mrs Bennet, in her own way, giving him as good as she gets: 'I wish you had been there, my dear, to have given him one of your set-downs.'[21] There is indeed something perverted in an intelligent and well-educated man using his talents for nothing better than to give his wife and younger daughters 'set-downs.' Mrs Bennet is incorrigibly stupid, and can (with an effort) be forgiven her sillinesses: there is something more ominous in Mr Bennet.

We learn little about the causes of Mr Woodhouse's 'valetudinarianism' (except of course, as always, self-gratification at the expense of others), though the consequences of his neglect of his paternal duties are as harmful to Emma as Mr Bennet's to his daughters. Jane Austen is apparently prepared to forgive him, presumably on the same grounds as Mrs Bennet may be forgiven – unlike Mr Bennet, he is stupid, and could have done little to help in Emma's development even if he had wanted to make the effort.[22]

Of other examples of sloth in the novels, the two younger Ward sisters in *Mansfield Park* are perhaps the most memorable. It is as though the eldest, Mrs Norris, had monopolized all the energy in the trio. Lady Bertram is let off lightly;[23] but Jane Austen's (or Fanny Price's) treatment of Mrs Price has awakened some protest. Fanny's verdict on her mother is indeed harsh: 'a dawdle, a slattern, who neither taught nor restrained her children, whose house was the scene of mismanagement and discomfort from beginning to end.'[24] She is, to be sure, the victim of circumstances: had her lot fallen in Lady Bertram's easy ways, we are told, she might have dawdled as satisfactorily as her sister. But it is a severe judgment, after we have come to know the malignant Mrs Norris, to say that even she 'would have been a more respectable mother of nine children on a small income' than Mrs Price.

There is no question that Jane Austen has high standards for mothers as well as fathers; not many of those in her writings live up to these standards. Perhaps the only really satisfactory parent in all the novels is Mrs Gardiner in *Pride and Prejudice*. One thinks of the charming vignette when Mr and Mrs Gardiner and Elizabeth return from their trip to Derbyshire:

> The little Gardiners, attracted by the sight of a chaise, were
> standing on the steps of the house as they entered the paddock; and,
> when the carriage drove up to the door, the joyful surprise that
> lighted up their faces, and displayed itself over their whole bodies,
> in a variety of capers and frisks, was the first pleasing earnest of
> their welcome.[25]

Clearly this is a far different relationship from that between Fanny Price and her mother, who, after many years of separation, had 'no affection towards herself [Fanny]; no curiosity to know her better, no desire of her friendship, and no inclination for her company.'[26] As always, in Jane Austen's unpleasant people, it boils down finally to a lack of capacity for feeling.

Money, it has often been pointed out, is of great importance in Jane Austen's novels – as in those of many other great novelists – since it is always of great importance to the ubiquitous avarice of the human race. Like the others, the sin of Avarice is the permeation of a natural and, in itself, not sinful human emotion, the enjoyment of the material things of life, by pride, by an irrationally exaggerated need for security of the ego – one thinks of the recurrent newspaper accounts of ragged old men and women, whose poverty-stricken quarters are discovered, after their deaths, to be overflowing with secreted wealth. Jane Austen is well aware of the desirability of a modicum of the material goods of the world and satirizes the shallowness of Marianne Dashwood's 'romantic' contempt for mere money ('What have wealth and grandeur to do with happiness!' she exclaims – she will settle for a mere 'competence' of two thousand pounds a year),[27] as well as that of Edward and Laura and Sophia and Augustus in *Love and Friendship,* who, fortified by the consciousness of their virtue, plunder their friends and relations without scruple.

Yet no more hair-raising illustration of avarice has been penned – unless it be the debate between Goneril and Regan as to how many attendants their father can get along without ('What need one?' 'O reason not the need!') – than the scene of Mr and Mrs John Dashwood discussing how to carry out the late Mr Dashwood's dying request that they assist his widow and daughters:

> 'Well, then, *let* something be done for them; but *that* something need not be three thousand pounds. . . . Five hundred pounds would be a prodigious increase to their fortunes. . . . I do not know whether upon the whole it would not be more advisable to do something for their mother while she lives . . . something of the annuity kind, I mean. . . . A hundred a year would make them all perfectly comfortable. . . . But then, if Mrs. Dashwood should live fifteen years, we shall be completely taken in. . . . A present of fifty pounds, now and then, will prevent their ever being distressed for money; and will, I think, be amply discharging my promise to my father. . . . As to your giving them more, it is quite absurd to think of it. They will be much more able to give *you* something';[28]

and they end by making designs on the widow's set of breakfast china, which is 'twice as handsome as what belongs to this house.' By contrast with such monstrosity, Aunt Norris's little meannesses in *Mansfield Park* and General Tilney's frank acquisitiveness in *Northanger Abbey* seem trifling.

Lust, in Jane Austen, is often closely linked with avarice. This is certainly the case with such professional seducers as Wickham in *Pride and Prejudice* and Willoughby in *Sense and Sensibility,* though for Lydia Bennet, Wickham's willing 'victim,' it seems to be little more than thoughtless adolescent fun – Lydia is perhaps the most easily forgivable of Jane Austen's 'villainesses.' In the case of Henry Crawford, his adultery with Maria Rushworth – since he has an income of £4,000 a year and nothing to gain by the action – seems rather to be the product of vanity (like Pope's Philomedé, who 'sins with poets thro' pure love of wit').[29] And perhaps *invidia* too enters into it, a word inadequately translated as 'envy': maliciousness, the desire to hurt others, better expresses it; very often, as with Henry Crawford, it may be the product of wounded vanity. The best exponent of *invidia* in the novels is probably Mrs Norris: Susan Price 'came perfectly aware that nothing but ill humour was to be expected from Aunt Norris.'[30] But this kind of pointless fretfulness, constantly looking for an opportunity to make life unpleasant where it could be pleasant, turns up innumerable times among the lesser characters. Wrath – not the clean anger Jane Austen and her major heroines are capable of feeling at genuine wrongdoing, but the ludicrous outrage of the self-inflated when they are deflated – appears in the shape of Lady Catherine de Bourgh's ridiculous tirade against Elizabeth, and General Tilney's 7 a.m. expulsion of Catherine from the sacred precincts of Northanger Abbey (is the name 'north *anger*' only a coincidence?). Of the traditional seven, perhaps it is Gluttony which comes off most lightly in the novels – I can think of only one genuine gourmand, the Reverend Dr Grant in *Mansfield Park.*[31] One can hardly dignify as *gourmandise* Mr Woodhouse's insistence that 'Serle understands boiling an egg better than anybody. I would not recommend an egg boiled by anybody else.' There is little excess drinking – perhaps only the famous case of 'Mr Weston's good wine' and the Reverend Mr Elton.[32]

There is a legend that Jane Austen 'mellowed' as she grew older; and it is perhaps true that if we tried to trace a curve showing the incidence of 'monstrosity' in her writing, beginning with *Love and Friendship,* through *Pride and Prejudice* (formerly *First Impressions*), with the other novels in chronological order, ending with *Persuasion,* it would on the whole be a descending one. The satire in *Pride and Prejudice* is sharper than in *Mansfield Park* and *Emma;* the preposterous Sir Walter and Elizabeth Elliot, the scheming Mrs Clay and the double-dealing William Elliot in *Persuasion* are certainly milder and less dangerous 'villains' than the Bonnie-and-Clyde-like quartet of *Love and Friendship.*

But this thesis is at once demolished by a glance at the twelve completed chapters of her last novel, called by its editor *Sanditon*. She began writing it shortly after she had seen *Persuasion* through the press, and ceased during her last illness. Next perhaps to *Love and Friendship* it contains the largest quantity of freaks, all depicted with her most mature skill.

There is the 'enthusiast,' Mr Parker, with his obsession of making the obscure seaside village of Sanditon a popular resort: 'Sanditon was a second wife and four children to him – hardly less dear and certainly more engrossing. . . . It was his mine, his lottery, his speculation, and his hobby horse [Jane Austen knew her Sterne]; his occupation, his hope, and his futurity.'[33] In pursuit of it, he has moved his family from their comfortable old home in the valley to a newly built, windswept hilltop mansion, Trafalgar House (though he now laments that he had not waited a few years and given it the even more 'with-it' name of Waterloo). He defends his choice with logic equal to that of Walter Shandy:

> '*We* have all the grandeur of the storm, with less real danger, because the wind meeting with nothing to oppose or confine it around our house, simply rages and passes on – while down in this gutter [the sheltered situation of the old home] nothing is known of the state of the air, below the tops of the trees – and the inhabitants may be taken totally unawares by one of those dreadful currents which do more mischief in a valley, when they *do* arise, than an open country ever experiences in the heaviest gale.'[34]

There are his hypochondriac and self-doctoring sisters. Miss Diana finds a visit to Sanditon 'quite an impossibility. I grieve to say that I dare not attempt it, but my feelings tell me too plainly that in my present state, the sea air would probably be the death of me.' As for her sister,

> 'I doubt Susan's nerves would be equal to the effort. She has been suffering much from the headache, and six leeches a day for ten days together relieved her so little that we thought it right to change our measures – and being convinced that much of the evil lay in her gum, I persuaded her to attack the disorder there. She has accordingly had three teeth drawn, and is decidedly better, but her nerves are a good deal deranged. She can only speak in a whisper – and fainted away twice this morning on poor Arthur's trying to suppress a cough.'[35]

Jane Austen's attitude toward feminine fainting fits has not changed since the time of Laura and Sophia, who 'fainted alternately on a sofa.'[36]

273

There is the great lady of Sanditon ('Every neighbourhood should have a great lady,' the third chapter begins, with the sententiousness of the opening of *Pride and Prejudice*), the wealthy widow of Mr Hollis and later of Sir Harry Denham, who

> had succeeded in removing her and her large income to his own domains, but he could not succeed in the views of permanently enriching his family, which were attributed to him. She had been too wary to put anything out of her own power – and when on Sir Harry's decease she returned again to her own house at Sanditon, she was said to have made this boast to a friend 'that though she had *got* nothing but her title from the family, still she had *given* nothing for it.'[37]

Lady Denham beautifully sums up her philosophy of life: 'I am not the woman to help anybody blindfold. I always take care to know what I am about and who I have to deal with before I stir a finger. I do not think I was ever overreached in my life; and that is a good deal for a woman to say that has been married twice.'[38] 'She is thoroughly mean,' Charlotte Heywood, the incipient heroine of the story, passes judgment on her. 'I had not expected anything so bad. . . . And she makes everybody mean about her.'[39]

Finally, we have perhaps the most egregious ass in the whole of Jane Austen's writings – young Sir Edward Denham, the would-be but financially handicapped Byronic hero.[40] His intellectual and moral pretensions surpass even those of Mary Bennet, his 'sensibility' even those of Marianne Dashwood, and Laura, Edward, and the rest in *Love and Friendship*.

> Sir Edward's great object in life was to be seductive. With such personal advantages as he knew himself to possess, and such talents as he did also give himself credit for, he regarded it as his duty. He felt that he was formed to be a dangerous man – quite in the line of the Lovelaces. The very name of Sir Edward, he thought, carried some degree of fascination with it.[41]

Clara Brereton, the immediate object of this duty, 'saw through him, and had not the least intention of being seduced – but she bore him patiently enough to confirm the sort of attachment which her [?his] personal charms had raised.'

> A greater degree of discouragement indeed would not have affected Sir Edward. He was armed against the highest pitch of disdain and aversion. If she could not be won by affection, he must carry her off. He knew his business. Already had he had many musings on the subject. If he *were* constrained so to act, he must naturally wish to

strike out something new, to exceed those who had gone before him, and he felt a strong curiosity to ascertain whether the neighbourhood of Tombuctoo might not afford some solitary house adapted for Clara's reception; but the expense, alas! of measures in that masterly style was ill-suited to his purse, and prudence obliged him to prefer the quietest sort of ruin and disgrace for the object of his affections to the more renowned.[42]

Sir Edward as a literary critic is worth attending to:

'I am no indiscriminate novel-reader. The mere trash of the common circulating library, I hold in the highest contempt. . . . The novels which I approve are such as display human nature with grandeur – such as show her in the sublimities of intense feeling – such as exhibit the progress of strong passion from the first germ of incipient sensibility to the utmost energies of reason half-dethroned – where we see the strong spark of woman's captivations elicit such fire in the soul of man as leads him (though at the risk of some aberration from the strict line of primitive obligations) to hazard all, dare all, achieve all, to obtain her.'

And much more in this vein. 'If I understand you aright,' Charlotte says, with brilliant understatement, 'our taste in novels is not at all the same.'[43]

It is interesting that though this was written in the heyday of Byronism, Jane Austen does not lay the blame on Byron (whom she never seems to have taken very seriously: there are references in *Persuasion* to his current popularity, but in the *Letters* he receives one cursory mention, 'I have read the Corsair, mended my petticoat, and have nothing else to do'[44] – a 'set-down' worthy of Mr Bennet); but on her favorite Richardson, for providing Sir Edward with his ideal: 'With a perversity of judgement, which must be attributed to his not having by nature a very strong head, the graces, the spirit, the sagacity, and the perseverance of the villain of the story [*Clarissa*] outweighed all his absurdities and all his atrocities with Sir Edward.' As well as misreading 'all the Essays, Letters, Tours, and Criticism of the day' with equal perversity, Sir Edward 'gathered only hard words and involved sentences from the style of our most approved writers.'[45] The comic climax of *Sanditon* was surely intended to be an attempted abduction and rape by Sir Edward, in Lovelace fashion, of Clara (or, failing her, Charlotte); it would have been one of Jane Austen's most hilarious scenes. But it was not to be.

One could go on almost indefinitely. There are complex and fascinating perversities in characters who have not even been mentioned in the above sketch – Frank Churchill, the Steeles, Mrs

Elton – as well as those in such early or fragmentary works as *Lady Susan, The Watsons* and *Catherine*. But enough has been said to demonstrate that Jane Austen is no mean psychopathologist. One needs to remember that she grew up in the great age of English caricature, when Hogarth's engravings were on every wall, and Gillray, Rowlandson and the Cruikshanks were producing their twisted, grotesque distortions of the human frame. 'Hogarth's moralizing, Gillray's irony, Rowlandson's comedy, Newton's burlesque,' Mrs George, the greatest scholar of the genre, characterizes some of them.[46] All those terms could be applied to Jane Austen's vast zoo of monstrosities – as could such more recent ones as 'surrealism,' 'black humor,' and 'the absurd.'

NOTES

1 Stephen C. Bandy, 'Cain, Grendel, and the Giants of *Beowulf*,' *Papers on Language and Literature*, IX, 3 (Summer 1973), p. 235. The Tolkien reference is to his famous essay in Proceedings of the British Academy, 1936, '*Beowulf*: The Monsters and the Critics.'

2 R. F. Brissenden, '*La Philosophie dans le boudoir*; or, A Young Lady's Entrance into the World,' *Studies in Eighteenth-Century Culture*, II (1972), 128 (Proceedings of the American Society for Eighteenth-Century Studies).

3 In his 'Preface' to Jane Austen, *Love and Freindship and Other Early Works* (New York, 1922), p. xv. Here as elsewhere in quoting from works edited from Jane Austen's MSS, I have corrected her erratic spelling and done some normalizing of 'accidentals' – as she clearly expected her own publishers to do.

4 See note 2.

5 Of course one of the great sources of modern Continental fiction generally was Jane Austen's mentor Richardson, the influence of whose great contemporary popularity in France and Germany was far-reaching.

6 C. S. Lewis, in 'A Note on Jane Austen,' *Collected Literary Essays* (Cambridge, 1969, pp. 175–6) quotes a number of these. I refer to two of them (Elizabeth Bennet's and Emma Woodhouse's) below.

7 *The Novels of Jane Austen*, ed. R. W. Chapman, 3rd ed. (5 vols; London 1932–4 and often reprinted), III, 461 – the famous opening of the last chapter of *Mansfield Park*. It is noteworthy that, in spite of this disclaimer, the chapter *is* in fact largely a description of guilt and misery.

8 Agatha Christie, *They Do It with Mirrors* (London, 1952; American title, *Murder with Mirrors*), ch. 1.

9 *Jane Austen's Letters to Her Sister Cassandra and Others*, ed. R. W. Chapman, 2nd ed. (London, 1952), p. 55. Jane Austen's cousin, the Reverend Edward Cooper, and his wife were prolific. Jane Austen later apologizes (sardonically?) for failing to keep track of their progeny: 'It was a mistake of mine, my dear Cassandra, to talk of a tenth child at Hamstall. I had forgot there were but eight already' (*Letters*, p. 280).

10 *The Rape of the Lock*, Canto IV, 11. 26–34, 47–54.

11 In my 'From Accidie to Neurosis: *The Castle of Indolence* Revisited' (in *New Perspectives on Eighteenth-Century Literature*, ed. Maximillian E. Novak, Berkeley and Los Angeles, 1974), I try to trace some of these changes in nomenclature.

12 *The Dunciad* (1743), IV, 501–4.

13 I offer this theory subject to correction. It is true that, in *Sense and Sensibility*, the title itself suggests the acceptance of such a dichotomy, with the implication that sensibility (emotion) should be subordinated to sense (reason). But this may be an over-simple reading both of the terminology and the novel.

14 This and the following quotations from *Pride and Prejudice* are from *Novels*, II, 38, 7, 60, 64, 20, 289, 364. Careful readers will notice that, in the spirit of R. W. Chapman, I have tampered somewhat with the received punctuation of the quotation from II, 20, in an attempt to improve the meaning. I have used this and the quotation from III, 289, as the starting-point for an article, 'The Sin of Pride' (*New Mexico Quarterly*, 34 [Summer 1964], 8–30).

15 In somewhat the same way as, in Evelyn Waugh's *Decline and Fall* (London, 1928), the fate of little Lord Tangent is narrated in a few casual asides at distant intervals. He is accidentally shot through the foot by the drunken starter at a school foot race. ' "That won't hurt him," says his mother, Lady Circumference. "Am I going to die?" said Tangent, his mouth full of cake.') A little later, *apropos* of nothing in particular, ' "Tangent's foot has swollen up and turned black," said Beste-Chetwynd with relish.' Still later, at Grimes' wedding, 'Everybody else, however, was there except little Lord Tangent, whose foot was being amputated at a local nursing home.' Several chapters later, Lady Circumference, who disapproves of the highly publicized wedding of the hero to Mrs Beste-Chetwynd, exclaims, ' "It's maddenin' Tangent having died just at this time. . . . People may think that that's my reason for refusin' to attend the ceremony." ' Such is the complete biography of Lord Tangent.

16 The last three quotations are from *Novels*, II, 208; IV, 374–5, 411–12. I have added some emphasis.

17 *Novels*, II, 70, 75.

18 *The Faerie Queene*, Book I, Canto IV, Stanza 18.

19 *Novels*, II, 236–7.

20 *Novels*, II, 236.

21 *Novels*, II, 13.

22 See *Novels*, IV, 7.

23 Her 'other side' is the subject of E. M. Forster's well-known discussion in *Aspects of the Novel* (Cambridge, 1927; ch. 4), where he uses her as his illustration of the 'round,' as opposed to the 'flat,' character. He might perhaps have cited another 'indolent' character, Lady Middleton, in *Sense and Sensibility*, whom we have become used to seeing seated on a sofa in 'cold insipidity' – 'The chief of the songs which Lady Middleton had brought into the family on her marriage . . . perhaps had lain ever since in the same position on the pianoforte' – and 'roused to enjoyment' only by the sight of her spoiled children. She too shows an unexpected side,

when Marianne is in trouble, by rousing herself, abandoning her rubber of whist, and taking her home (*Novels*, I, 34–5, 178).

24 *Novels*, III, 389.

25 *Novels*, II, 286.

26 *Novels*, III, 390.

27 *Novels*, I, 91.

28 *Novels*, I, 9–12.

29 *Moral Epistle* II, 'To a Lady,' line 76.

30 *Novels*, III, 449.

31 See, for example, *Novels*, III, 54.

32 Professor John Halperin calls my attention to Mr Price, Fanny's father, in *Mansfield Park*. But it might be argued that his drinking is not, like Dr Grant's love of his dinner and Mr Elton's intoxication, something out of the ordinary, but merely part of his general slovenliness: 'He read only the newspaper and the navy-list; he talked only of the dockyard, the harbor, Spithead, and the Motherbank; he swore, and he drank, he was dirty and gross' (*Novels*, III, 389).

33 *The Works of Jane Austen*, Vol. VI, ed. R. W. Chapman (London, 1954), p. 372.

34 *Works*, VI, 381.

35 *Works*, VI, 387.

36 *Works*, VI, 86.

37 *Works*, VI, 376.

38 *Works*, VI, 399.

39 *Works*, VI, 402.

40 Both the turgidity of his style and the appreciation of his own 'sensibility' remind one of the writings of Jane Austen's putative cousin, Sir Egerton Brydges (cf. my 'Jane Austen and the Peerage,' *PMLA*, 68 [December 1953], 1022–4).

41 *Works*, VI, 405.

42 *Works*, VI, 405–6.

43 *Works*, VI, 403–4.

44 *Letters*, p. 379.

45 *Works*, VI, 404–5.

46 M. Dorothy George, *Hogarth to Cruikshank: Social Change in Graphic Satire* (New York, 1967), p. 13.

ALISTAIR M. DUCKWORTH

'Spillikins, paper ships, riddles, conundrums, and cards': games in Jane Austen's life and fiction

Games of skill, games of chance, games with words were familiar features of Jane Austen's life from first to last. A few months before her death she began to write a rather gloomy letter to Fanny Knight: 'I must not depend upon being ever very blooming again. Sickness is a dangerous Indulgence at my time of Life.' But in the evening, realizing she 'was languid & dull & very bad company when I wrote the above,' she makes an effort to be more 'agreable.' Her thoughts turn to the troubles of others, to her mother worried (with reason as it turned out) that her expectations from Leigh Perrot's will would be disappointed, to an acquaintance whose young daughter was seriously ill, to Fanny's brother William suffering from a cough: 'Tell William . . . I often play at *Nines* & think of him.'[1] Her thoughts might have included memories of other games, of Battledore and Shuttlecock, for example, played with William at Godmersham in 1805: 'he & I have practiced together two mornings, & improve a little; we have frequently kept it up *three* times, & once or twice *six*' (*Letters*, p. 161). Or she might have remembered bilbocatch, at which she was an acknowledged expert, or spillikins, which she considered as 'a very valuable part of our Household furniture' (*Letters*, p. 179), or any number of card games: whist, commerce, casino, loo, cribbage, but especially Speculation, whose usurpation by Brag and other games at Godmersham during Christmastide 1808–9 'mortified' her deeply, because 'Speculation was under my patronage' (*Letters,* p. 247).

Equally, she could have recalled the word games – riddles, conundrums and charades – which occupied her relatives and 'excessively' delighted her (*Letters,* p. 298). Clearly, games were not simply 'intervals of recreation and amusement . . . desirable for every body' (p. 87), as Mary Bennet sententiously concedes in *Pride and Prejudice,*[2] but an integral part of the Austen family life. Jane Austen could sympathetically anticipate the completion of one of Cassandra's journeys by writing: 'In a few hours you will be transported to Manydown & then for Candour & Comfort & Coffee & Cribbage' (*Letters,* p. 302). She could also understand the consolatory function games could serve at times of sadness, as when, soon after the death of Elizabeth Bridges Knight in October 1808, she took care of the two oldest Knight boys in Southampton. She writes to Cassandra: 'We do not want amusement: bilbocatch, at which George is indefatigable, spillikins, paper ships, riddles, conundrums, and cards' (*Letters,* p. 225). In the evening, she finds it perfectly natural, after Psalms, Lessons and a sermon at home, that the boys should immediately 'return to conundrums.'

Given the delight in recreation of all kinds that is often manifest in the letters, we may be unprepared for the negative uses to which Jane Austen puts games in her fiction. Seldom are games unambiguously ratified in the novels. One thinks of the 'merry evening games' (p. 28), reminiscent of those in *The Vicar of Wakefield,* that Harriet plays at the Martins' until Emma teaches her to play a new and more dangerous sport. In *Emma,* too, the geriatric amusement Mrs Bates and Mrs Goddard get from picquet and quadrille at Hartfield seems harmless enough. Like age, youth may be exempt from serious criticism. Catherine Morland's preference for 'cricket, base ball, riding on horseback, and running about the country at the age of fourteen' (p. 15) is perfectly suited to her unheroic debut, the carefree childhood prelude to more dubious recreational involvement with Gothic fiction. Such positive uses are slight, however, compared with Jane Austen's normal mode. Lovers of games in the novels, or of field sports, an outside and exclusively masculine form of games, are more often than not selfish, irresponsible or empty-headed characters whose pursuit of a favorite pastime labels them in various ways as morally or socially deficient.

Card games, especially, are suspect in the early novels, often becoming emblems of a vacuous and despicable society. Examples could be multiplied. For the moment, a description of a typical evening at Lady Middleton's in *Sense and Sensibility* will suffice:

They met for the sake of eating, drinking, and laughing together,
playing at cards, or consequences, or any other game that was
sufficiently noisy . . . The insipidity of the meeting was exactly
such as Elinor had expected; it produced not one novelty of thought
or expression. (p. 143)

Not surprisingly, the anti-social Marianne Dashwood 'detests' cards:
while Lady Middleton and others play at the table, and Elinor and
Lucy exchange information over the work basket, Marianne is at the
pianoforte, 'wrapt up in her own music and her own thoughts' (p.
145).

The game-playing societies of the Middletons and the John
Dashwoods in *Sense and Sensibility,* which reveal 'no poverty of any
kind, except of conversation' (p. 233), may remind us that Jane Austen
did not always endorse games in the letters. Outside the family
(though occasionally inside it, too) games could be viewed negatively.
Jane Austen could share Elizabeth Bennet's distrust of 'playing high':

> We found ourselves tricked into a thorough party at Mrs.
> Maitland's . . . There were two pools at Commerce, but I would
> not play more than one, for the Stake was three shillings, & I cannot
> afford to lose that, twice in an evenᵍ. (*Letters,* p. 215)

She could go beyond Elinor Dashwood's recognition of social
mediocrity to something like Marianne's misanthropy, as when she
wrote to Cassandra from Bath in May 1801 about 'another stupid
party':

> there were only just enough to make one card table, with six people
> to look on, & talk nonsense to each other . . . I cannot anyhow
> continue to find people agreable . . . Miss Langley is like any
> other short girl with a broad nose & wide mouth, fashionable dress,
> & exposed bosom. (*Letters,* pp. 128–9)

She could combine protest against the banal monotony of card-play-
ing with her rather unlikeable fondness for obstetrical humor.
Elizabeth Knight had just given birth to her eleventh child at
Godmersham (the confinement from which she would not recover,
though Jane did not know it) when the novelist wrote to Cassandra in
October 1808:

> at seven o'clock, Mrs. Harrison, her two daughters & two Visitors,
> with Mr. Debarry & his eldest sister walked in; & our Labour was
> not a great deal shorter than poor Elizabeth's, for it was past eleven
> before we were delivered. – A second pool of Commerce, & all the
> longer by the addition of the two girls, who during the first had one

corner of the Table & Spillikens to themselves, was the ruin of us.
(*Letters,* p. 211)

And in other letters her attitude to card-playing, as well as to field
sports, could be severe.[3]

When such passages in the letters are set against the novels it is
possible to argue for a continuity of ironic criticism directed against
sterile social settings, to talk of a discharge of aggression on Jane
Austen's part against social conventions that is often overt in the
letters and ineffectively disguised in the novels. In such a view, the
important distinction to be made is not that between letter-writer and
novelist but between Jane the family member and Jane the ironic
critic of her society. Both as sister, or aunt, in the letters, and as
author, she separates family (the unit of meaning in which games have
value) from society outside (the discredited arena in which games
become the expression of inconsequential or repugnant behavior).

One reason may immediately be given for not accepting this
plausible and common view. Not infrequently, Jane Austen exposes
in her novels conduct of which, as we learn from the letters, she
herself had been guilty in life. Like Emma, for example, she was a
match-maker, in a context which suggests that the boredom of
card-playing drove her to this trivial form of imaginative play (*Letters,*
p. 210), and elsewhere she shows herself to be as keen as Anne Steele
to price the lace and muslin of an acquaintance (*Letters,* p. 105). Nor
is this simply a matter of moral wisdom coming in maturity. Rather, it
may be suggested, in her fiction, she, or her 'second self,' could be
'better' than she was in life. Not that her life ever exhibited quite the
hatred and vulgarity of which she has been accused; but she could, for
example, display in one of her last letters precisely the kind of
actuarial calculation satirically exposed much earlier in the despicable character of Mrs John Dashwood in chapter two of *Sense and
Sensibility.*[4] We have, as E. M. Forster long ago suggested, to
distinguish between the 'Miss Austen' who (he felt) mainly wrote
trivial, ill-bred and sententious letters and the 'Jane Austen' who
composed the novels.[5]

Forster's review gives some support to those who view the difference between letters and fiction simply in terms of the structural
complexity of the ironic vision presented. The family, he suggests,
was of supreme importance to her, 'the unit within which her heart
had liberty of choice; friends, neighbours, plays and fame were all
objects to be picked up in the course of a flight outside and brought
back to the nest for examination.' But Forster's main point in the
review is to distinguish generically between letters and novels in

terms of their unequal ability to deal with her limited subject matter. In the novels, he proposes, 'Meryton may reproduce the atmosphere of Steventon because it imports something else – some alignment not to be found on any map.' What this extraordinary 'alignment' is the review does not tell us, and we are left a little troubled by Forster's easy faith in the alchemical powers of her art to transmute an original poverty of material into enduring and memorable aesthetic form. It is in his own fiction, and especially in *Howards End* that Forster's meaning is clear, for there he not only shows that he has learned a lesson in the 'possibilities of domestic humor,' but he also uses inconsequential motifs like 'games' or 'garden improvements' to define social values and dangers in ways that reveal his debt to Jane Austen. We may agree, therefore, that her letters do not constitute significant cultural analysis but go on to argue that they do provide an expressed awareness of social triviality and imperfection which, rhetorically structured through her art, moves from local and undirected criticism to the articulation of the best society she can envisage. From the fragmentary exposures of inadequate social behavior in the letters, from her own occasionally deficient personal responses, she weaves a fictional pattern in which ironical exposure is raised to a higher degree, but in which, too, the 'alignment' of a good society, never perhaps to be found in real life, is discernible.[6]

In *Pride and Prejudice,* for example, card games, like the motifs of laughter, piano-playing, letters and books, are deftly integrated into the novel's antithetical structure so as to expose extremes of social conformity and individual freedom and to define a normative marriage of the moral self to a worthy society. Thus, balanced against the 'nice comfortable noisy game of lottery tickets, and a little bit of hot supper afterwards' (p. 74) promised by Mrs Philips, there is the 'superlatively stupid' evening of quadrille and casino at Rosings, during which 'scarcely a syllable was uttered that did not relate to the game' (p. 166). Not only are the particular games chosen fitted to the families that play them, but noise is appropriate to the underbred vulgarity of Mrs Philips as silence is to the sterile formality of Lady Catherine. Between vulgar 'trade' and arrogant aristocracy the social-climbing Bingleys at Netherfield play games that recall their origins in trade and announce their aspirations: commerce, picquet, loo, vingt-un.[7] Even Mr Collins sees cards as his entrée to better prospects, proud to be sent for by Lady Catherine 'to make up her pool of quadrille in the evening' (p. 66), but equally willing, when the card tables are placed at Mrs Philips', to sit down to whist. Earlier at Longbourn, offended by Lydia's vulgar interruption of his reading from Fordyce, Collins nevertheless offers himself as Mr Bennet's antagonist at backgammon, turning from serious sermons to frivolous play as easily as he changes his matrimonial intentions from Jane to Elizabeth during his morning tête-à-tête with Mrs Bennet (p. 71).

Other characters are also exposed by the motif. Lydia, naturally, is 'extremely fond of lottery tickets' (p. 76), and, though Wickham 'did not play at whist' on the same occasion at the Philips', we can assume that gambling contributed to the loss of the £3,000 which Darcy gave him on his resignation of the 'valuable family living' bequeathed to him by Darcy's father. Significantly, neither Elizabeth nor Darcy is a noted card-player. Elizabeth certainly has no Puritanical objection to cards, but she declines to play loo at Netherfield, 'suspecting them to be playing high' (p. 37). Her refusal causes Mr Hurst, 'an indolent man, who lived only to eat, drink, and play at cards' (p. 35), to think her 'singular,' and Miss Bingley to insinuate that she is a blue-stocking who 'despises cards' (p. 37). When Mr Hurst reminds Miss Bingley of the card table a little later, it is of no avail: 'She had obtained private intelligence that Mr. Darcy did not wish for cards . . . She assured [Mr Hurst] that no one intended to play' (p. 54). True, a chastened Darcy, seeking to propose a second time to Elizabeth, will permit himself to fall victim to Mrs Bennet's 'rapacity for whist players' at Longbourn (p. 342), but after the marriage to Elizabeth it is unlikely that the shades of Pemberley will be too often polluted by noisy lottery tickets or commerce – at least in the form of cards; when Mr Gardiner comes from Cheapside to fish in the Pemberley pond the Darcys and the Gardiners may occasionally play at vingt-un – for Elizabeth has 'pleasure in many things' (p. 37) – but they are more likely to listen to Georgiana play the piano.

In the perfectly articulated plot of *Pride and Prejudice* Jane Austen uses card games to expose inadequate behavior much in the way she does in the letters, but she also creates a fictional world of her own – a far superior version, it might be suggested, of the word games her family and she enjoyed – in which by skillfully 'aligning' various motifs she gives both aesthetic and moral shape to her experience. Her interest lies not in condemning cards as such but in evaluating social performance in any area. Simply to be able to play the piano well, for example, does not necessarily mean much, as Mary Bennet sufficiently shows.

The skill and success with which Jane Austen accommodates terms inherited from eighteenth-century ethical and aesthetic debate so as to propose confidently in *Pride and Prejudice* a reciprocally satisfying relation between self and society, innovation and culture, have often been described. Many readers are, however, less happy with her treatment of opposing terms in *Sense and Sensibility,* and it may therefore be useful to see this novel, too, *sub specie ludi.*

Games in Jane Austen's life and fiction

Sense and Sensibility describes a world whose intellectual poverty is everywhere apparent, where selfishness appears in such obsessive recreational activities as hunting and shooting (Sir John Middleton), exaggerated maternal devotion (Lady Middleton), billiards (Mr Palmer), or collectively in the ubiquitous playing of cards. In such a society repudiation and withdrawal into the self may seem natural, even commendable responses. Marianne is 'of no use on these occasions, as she would never learn the game' (p. 166). (In her 'good-humoured' solicitude, Mrs Jennings will seek in vain to console her: 'She hates whist I know; but is there no round game she cares for?' [p. 195].) As a heroic individualist, Marianne abhors the 'common-place' in language (p. 45), decorum (pp. 48 and 53), and the aesthetic appreciation of landscape (pp. 96–98); as with her mother, 'common sense, common care, common prudence [are] all sunk in . . . romantic delicacy' (p. 85); she detests 'jargon' and seeks a personal utterance beyond what is 'worn and hackneyed out of all sense and meaning' (p. 97). But the novel will not permit her to discover an individual language outside of society, one of Jane Austen's points being that 'communication' and 'community' are necessarily corresponding terms. The man with whom she wishes to escape from 'every common-place notion of decorum' (p. 48) betrays her – while Lady Middleton and her guests are playing casino – and in so doing betrays 'the common decorum of a gentleman' (p. 184). Married to his heiress, Willoughby will regret his betrayal, but he does not end in domestic misery, as has been suggested: 'in his breed of horses and dogs, and in sporting of every kind, he found no inconsiderable degree of domestic felicity' (p. 379).

There can be no doubt that in aligning games with a trivial and opportunistic society Jane Austen brought to *Sense and Sensibility* the critical disgust often displayed in her letters, and the extent to which her fictional resolution succeeds in this novel in defining the grounds of a good society whose rules can be enthusiastically accepted, whose 'game' can be willingly played, is debatable. Unlike Darcy and Knightley in later novels, Brandon and Ferrars are unconvincing representatives of social values even as they play to the rules of the gentlemanly code. It can be said, too, that in Marianne's sickness and near suicide Jane Austen personally explores the grief and pain that are, she has discovered, the inevitable consequences of attempting to liberate the 'natural' self from both inner and outer restrictions. Perhaps this makes *Sense and Sensibility* a novel about civilization and its discontents.[8] Certainly we hear Marianne's as well as Elinor's voice in the letters. Taken together, however, the experiences of Marianne and Elinor reveal that for Jane Austen society is the only conceivable context of individual behavior and that, while capitula-

tion to the 'commonplace' is to be avoided, participation in a
'common' system of language and manners is both a necessary and –
where language and manners exist in an improved rather than a
debased condition – an authentic response.

We should stay with the word 'common,' for it contains an
ambiguity at the heart of Jane Austen's fiction which gives meaning to
her conception of play and performance in public places. Common
can mean commonplace – the banal, the hackneyed, the stale, the trite:
this is Marianne's constant recognition. But it can also refer to that
which belongs equally to an entire 'community,' as in common sense,
a common language, the common law, the Book of Common Prayer.
Jane Austen's constant fictional search is for a proper mediation
between these terms, for individual performance which both
invigorates and respects inherited systems of value, for a 'playfulness'
that vitalizes without distorting or destroying conventions. Wickham
is a negative example in this as well as in other respects. His ability to
make Elizabeth feel that 'the commonest, dullest, most threadbare
topic might be rendered interesting by the skill of the speaker' (p. 76)
seems unexceptionable until we remember the context: he is just
about to slander Darcy under the cover of a game of lottery tickets in
Meryton. After re-reading Darcy's letter, Elizabeth will realize 'the
impropriety of such communications to a stranger' (p. 207). Another
negative character is Tom Musgrave in *The Watsons,* who, we are
told, 'had a lively way of retailing a commonplace . . . that had great
effect at a Card Table' (*Minor Works,* p. 359). In contrast, Mr Howard,
'tho' chatting on the commonest topics . . . had a sensible, unaffected, way of expressing himself, which made them all worth hearing' (p.
335). Significantly, Mr Howard also 'reads extremely well, with great
propriety & in a very impressive manner' (p. 343); in the pulpit he is
without 'any Theatrical grimace or violence.' The distinction between
Musgrave and Howard, as well as between cards and sermons, takes
us forward to the more serious debate over sermon delivery between
Edmund Bertram and Henry Crawford in *Mansfield Park* (pp.
339–41). Both men agree that there has been a 'too common neglect' of
reading aloud in the ordinary school system, but their proposals for
'improvement' are very different. Crawford sees the preacher's role to
be that of bringing 'new or striking' delivery and interpretation to
'subjects limited, and long worn thread-bare in all common hands';
Edmund is much more restrained, arguing that 'distinctness and
energy may have weight in recommending the most solid truths.'

The whole debate exists within the larger metaphor of estate improvements, an instrument permitting Jane Austen in *Mansfield Park*
to bring her fictional concern for a proper 'communication' between a
cultural heritage and individual performance to its most serious pitch.

Crawford, the 'pre-eminent' card-player and 'capital improver' (p. 244), not only finds fault with commonplace biblical texts and 'redundancies' in the liturgy, but with the structure of houses and the dispositions of landscapes, and it is clear that in his role as fashionable London preacher or as landscape improver he would, if permitted, radically alter many common 'grounds' of social existence. In *Sense and Sensibility,* Marianne's 'systems have all the unfortunate tendency of setting propriety at nought' (p. 56), but as the victim of a manipulative society her social performance is more of a threat to herself than to culture, and in any case, as Elinor predicts, she finally settles 'her opinions on the reasonable basis of common sense' (p. 56). By contrast, the recreational 'systems' of Henry and Mary Crawford – their play-acting, card-playing, 'improvements' and other 'manoeuvre[s] against common sense' (p. 212) – carry subversive cultural implications. Games, in *Mansfield Park,* are a very serious matter.

In this recognition, Forster's remarks about the poverty of her subject matter which harmed the letters but mysteriously aided the novels are open to further question. Landscape improvement, after all, was an issue of the day. We can no longer accept Jane Austen's own valuation of her fiction as pictures of domestic life in country villages. The social substance of her work, as Raymond Williams has most recently argued, far from being trivial, is remarkably intricate and complex.[9] Responding in her own fictional mode to the highly fluid social process observed, more censoriously and from a more mobile and radical point of view, by Cobbett in *Rural Rides,* she records and evaluates an era of speculative interaction between landed and trading wealth which, exacerbated by the wars and the 'paper system,' resulted in what Cobbett saw as the invasion of a relatively stable rural structure by 'nabobs, negro-drivers, generals, admirals, governors,' and the like. The mobility she observes bears, of course, upon her own class interests and concerns.[10] Nevertheless, what she 'sees' – improvements to houses and landscapes, for example – is the direct result of profits made from an improved agriculture and reflects fundamental economic changes in her society. In this context, the important questions are: what is the nature of her cultural analysis? and how is it conveyed and defined by often trivial fictional metaphors?

Williams argues, rightly in my view, that her irony is not directed against the base of her culture, which she accepts as given. Though her experience is of a changing society, she assumes that the visible improvements in society resulting from profits should be accompanied by commensurate improvements in moral behavior. Since her experience contradicts this assumption, however, since 'cultivation' and 'civilization,' in Coleridge's terms, are frequently at variance, critical irony results, and her moral analysis is so insistent that it tends to become separable from its social base and to serve as an independent value.

This is a ponderable argument which I find especially applicable to *Persuasion*, where Anne Elliot, with 'no Uppercross-hall before her, no landed estate, no headship of a family' (p. 250), is in the end literally separated from her cultural inheritance. But the argument seems to me much less descriptive of *Mansfield Park* and *Emma*, novels whose value systems remain, in my view, firmly connected to a social base. The matter may be pursued by the consideration of one of her techniques of cultural definition in *Persuasion, Mansfield Park* and *Emma*, the motif of games.

A brief examination of forms of recreation in *Persuasion* supports Williams' proposition. On being forced to leave Kellynch on account of her father's vanity and extravagance, Anne nowhere finds a society commensurate with her sense of duty or intelligence. Her brother-in-law at Uppercross 'did nothing with much zeal, but sport; and his time was otherwise trifled away, without benefit from books, or anything else' (p. 43). Later at Bath, having witnessed Benwick's 'indulgence' in romantic poetry at Lyme and Louisa's stupid and selfish jumping game on the Cobb, she discovers a society marked by 'the elegant stupidity of private parties' (p. 180) and the 'nothing-saying' of its inhabitants (p. 189). It is a society whose 'manoeuvres of selfishness and duplicity must ever be revolting' to Anne (p. 207), but are accepted by Elizabeth and Mr Elliot, not to mention Mrs Clay, as a 'game' (p. 213). Mr Elliot plays the role of gentleman with consummate skill, his 'manners' becoming an 'immediate recommendation' to the rank-conscious Lady Russell (p. 146), but in the end even she must recognize 'how double a game he had been playing' (p. 250).

In some ways, the speculative society of *Persuasion* reminds us of *Sense and Sensibility*, but the heroines are significantly different. Unlike Marianne, whose refusal to play card games was at least in part selfish repudiation, Anne is the most 'perfect' of the heroines, always in search of a 'useful' social role. That she should be 'no card-player,' should find that 'the usual character' of evening parties has 'nothing' for her (p. 225) becomes, then, a severe indictment of the 'civilization' manifest in the last novel. The same indictment could only have been served in *Sense and Sensibility* if Elinor, too, had refused to play the game. Anne's marriage to Wentworth and the navy, in this context, is a kind of 'intra-social' union new in Jane Austen's fiction, akin to that of the Harvilles in Lyme, poor but sufficient in themselves, or to the Crofts, who 'go shares . . . in every thing' (p. 168) whether on land or sea, and whose way of life is 'not endurable to a third person' (p.

73). At the end of the novel the separation of morality from its basis in society is marked, appropriately for this theme, when Anne, secretly happy in her engagement to Wentworth, attends a last social gathering in Bath: 'It was but a card-party, it was but a mixture of those who had never met before, and those who met too often – a common-place business, too numerous for intimacy, too small for variety' (p. 245). Here, as distinguished from *Sense and Sensibility,* Jane Austen's dislike of the 'common-place' is not off-set by her fictional affirmation of the valuable 'systems' society provides in 'common' for its members.

Moreover, if we go from *Persuasion* to *Sanditon,* further grounds may be found for arguing that in the last works morality is separate from class, and culture, in its limited and human sense, from society. *Sanditon* describes a hyperactive Regency world in which the desire to 'improve' an inherited society, successfully qualified in *Mansfield Park* so as to guarantee cultural continuity, becomes the manic recreation of Mr Parker and Lady Denham, his principal 'Colleague in Speculation' (*Minor Works,* p. 375), whereby 'a quiet Village of no pretensions' is 'planned & built, & praised & puffed, & raised . . . to a something of young Renown' (p. 371). The card game at Godmersham whose patroness Jane Austen considered herself to be, and in whose honor she wrote mock-elegaic verses (*Letters,* pp. 252–3), has left the drawing-room and become the expressive emblem of a fervently 'speculative' world in which inherited estates are exploited in the form of bathing places to make fortunes for 'projectors' and 'enthusiasts.' Experiencing this 'striking' world, Charlotte Heywood, in the fragment, lacks even Anne's consolation in love. She finds her world 'very amusing – or very melancholy, just as Satire or Morality might prevail' (p. 396), the point being, in the context of this argument, that satire (or irony) can no longer be written on culture's behalf but has become the expression of an independent and separatist vision.

The same proposition does not, however, apply to Jane Austen's two greatest novels where, I would argue, 'cultivation' in its human sense cannot be considered separately from 'civilization,' and where, while exposing alternative 'systems' of many kinds, Jane Austen is still able 'to discover the "organic" in an existing society.'[11]

In *Mansfield Park* 'speculation,' like 'improvements' of a radical kind, is kept under social control, even as its social threat is revealed. The relevant scene is in chapter vii of the second volume, precisely at the center of the work, where the 'round' game of Speculation not only serves as a symbolic synecdoche of the novel's characterization and themes but permits Jane Austen, in distinguishing between good and bad card players, to suggest, inversely, a distinction between socially responsible and irresponsible individuals. It is a subtle and complex chapter in which the motif of card-playing is more fully integrated into the fictional fabric than ever before. All of the major characters are brought together at the Mansfield parsonage except Rushworth and Maria, who are honeymooning at Brighton (a suitably suspect locality). There are, in fact, two card games played: whist, engaging Sir Thomas and Mrs Norris, and Dr and Mrs Grant; and Speculation, involving Fanny, Edmund, the Crawfords, Lady Bertram and William Price. As elsewhere in *Mansfield Park* (on the carriage trip to Sotherton, before the altar in the chapel, and during the walk through the wilderness), spatial groupings are superbly illuminating, casting light before and after. Sir Thomas, for example, does not play with his wife but with Mrs Norris, a comment both upon Lady Bertram's intelligence and on his own misguided 'partnership' with Mrs Norris throughout. (At the end, he is relieved to be rid of her, for 'she seemed a part of himself' [p. 465].) When Sotherton is mentioned during the whist game, Mrs Norris responds with 'high good-humour,' having just won 'the odd trick by Sir Thomas's capital play and her own' (p. 245). We are reminded of an earlier 'capital play' they effected together: while it was Mrs Norris who was 'most zealous in promoting the match' between Maria and Rushworth during Sir Thomas's absence in Antigua (p. 39), it was the baronet who, on his return and anxious for an alliance with a rich neighbouring estate, permitted it. Now, at the Grants', he entertains another 'speculation,' even while pretending not to, concerning a 'most advantageous matrimonial establishment' for Fanny with Crawford (p. 238).

The evening of cards at the Grants' does not, however, simply reveal Sir Thomas in a bad light. He shows good sense in vetoing Mrs Norris's enthusiastic attempts to coerce William into visiting his cousins at Brighton and, in a later conversation with Edmund and Crawford concerning the importance of a parson's residency in his parish, he demonstrates his fundamental commitment to religion as a vocation (pp. 247–8). What the evening of cards does show, in brief compass, is the ambivalence surrounding Sir Thomas throughout the novel, a man theoretically committed to worthy concepts of stewardship who, under the pressures of a failing West Indian venture and an extravagant elder son, compromises his principles and gives way to venal speculation. He wins his 'game' when Maria marries Rushworth, but loses it when Maria, carrying the stage role she plays in *Lovers' Vows* into real life, runs off with Crawford, bringing disgrace on herself and her family.

Mansfield Park is saved from his 'grievous mismanagement' (p. 463) not by Sir Thomas's children but by his niece, 'indeed the daughter . . . he wanted' (p. 472). It is therefore appropriate that at the Mansfield parsonage Fanny 'had never played the game [of Speculation] nor seen it played in her life' (p. 239). Opposed to the play-acting, which endangers the physical fabric and moral 'system' of the Mansfield house, and to Crawford's improvements, which will alter Sotherton beyond recognition if adopted, she has no desire to play or win at cards, preferring to 'cheat herself' for her brother's benefit (p. 244). The only 'speculation' she allows herself during the evening is of William's future as an Admiral. Fanny's real antagonist is, of course, Henry Crawford, 'pre-eminent in all the lively turns, quick resources, and playful impudence that could do honour to the game' (p. 240). Even while helping her to bid ('the game will be yours,' he says), he engages in an imaginative play of the mind which, no less than his views on sermon delivery later, reveals to Fanny the cultural threat he poses. His speculation takes the form of detailed plans for the 'improvement' of Edmund's future parsonage. But Thornton Lacey is in no need of the transforming Reptonian 'scheme' he proposes. Like Sanditon *before* Mr Parker's improvements, it is 'a retired little village' (p. 241), and Edmund shows responsibility when he bluntly tells Crawford that 'very little of your plan for Thornton Lacey will ever be put in practice' (p. 242).

Mary Crawford's own interest in the transformation of Thornton Lacey stems from her wish to 'improve' Edmund's profession and prospects. Thus she is disturbed by Edmund's refusal to consider making his future home the 'occasional' residence of 'a man of education, taste, modern manners, good connections' (p. 244). Characteristically, her response takes the form of *double entendre,* as she uses the vocabulary of the card game to announce to Edmund secretly her determination to raise him from his clergyman's profession, which, as she informed him in the chapel at Sotherton, she considers 'nothing': 'There, I will stake my last like a woman of spirit. No cold prudence for me. I am not born to sit still and do nothing. If I lose the game, it shall not be from not striving for it' (p. 243). Still later, when 'the picture she had been forming of a future Thornton' is destroyed by Sir Thomas's insistence on the need for Edmund's residency there, we are told that 'all the agreeable of *her* speculation was over for that hour. It was time to have done with cards if sermons prevailed' (p. 248).

The association of cards with the speculators and improvers in *Mansfield Park* is a major shift in emphasis in the use of the motif. True, cards may still serve to expose stupidity and indolence. Thus Lady Bertram will complain: 'Fanny, you must do something to keep me awake. I cannot work. Fetch the cards, – I feel so very stupid' (p. 283). But more often than not cards are connected with the active manipulators of people and situations. Mrs Norris, for example, who plays Perissa to Lady Bertram's Elissa throughout the novel, is 'occupied' in making up card-tables at the Mansfield Ball (p. 277). Like Mary Crawford, she was not born to sit still but is described (the present participle is appropriate to her as the adjective is to Lady Bertram) as 'dictating,' 'promoting,' 'contriving,' 'manoeuvring,' 'always planting and improving,' and so on. The Crawfords are more intelligent, vital and witty than she, but they share the same physical and linguistic hyperactivity and pose a similar threat to cultural order. Only when the active speculators and improvers are expelled from Mansfield, and Fanny marries Edmund, can the right mediation between 'nothing-doing' and 'bustle,' 'yawns' and 'restlessness,' old-fashioned Sotherton and 'completely altered' Compton, be achieved.

The expulsion of vitality from Mansfield culture is problematic – an unacceptable feature of the novel to many readers. Yet in *Emma,* so different in tone from *Mansfield Park,* there is, if not the same ostracism, still a serious qualification of the vitality that takes on a manipulative character. By transforming, rather than eradicating, false wit and vitality, however, Jane Austen makes *Emma* a far more generally palatable affirmation of culture.

There is a curious split in *Emma* between card games such as whist, picquet and quadrille, whose function at first seems to be to provide harmless and trivial amusement for the superannuated and valetudinarian characters, and the word games such as riddles, charades, enigmas, conundrums, anagrams and acrostics, which involve the youthful and lively Emma in dubious relations with Harriet, the Eltons and Churchill. The importance of the card games as a motif should not be dismissed. Complete with a 'vast deal of chat, and backgammon' (p. 329), evenings at Hartfield define the second childhood of Mr Woodhouse, his abrogation of all connection with progress or generation, his wish to live cossetted from draughts, marriages and time itself, supported by his diet of thin gruel and endless 'rounds' of cards. On one level, cards suggest that society and identity alike are endlessly repetitive, not subject to dynamic change or the decay that leads to death. On another, they announce Jane Austen's belief in the fifth commandment: Emma's attempts 'by the help of backgammon, to get her father tolerably through the evening' (p. 9) are of a different order from her 'courtship' games with Elton and Churchill.[12]

Card games serve in other ways in *Emma:* to permit an evaluation and comparison of Mr Weston's gregarious, indiscriminate bonhomie and John Knightley's 'strong domestic habits' (pp. 96–7), for example; or to expose Mrs Elton's parvenu ambitions (p. 290); or to emphasize Mr Knightley's strong sense of social responsibility, as on the occasion of the ball at the Crown. There Emma, seeing Knightley among the standers-by feels 'he ought to be dancing, – not classing himself with the husbands, and fathers, and whist-players, who were pretending to feel an interest in the dance till their rubbers were made up' (pp. 325–6). This is a resonant scene, which not only reveals Emma's unconscious love of Knightley, but sets 'cards' against 'dancing' as emblems of qualitatively different social orders. Knightley ought indeed to be dancing, that is, to be participating fully in Highbury society. Emma contrasts his 'firm upright figure' with the 'stooping shoulders of the elderly men' (i.e., the card-players), and as he moves a few steps nearer to her she recognizes 'in how gentlemanlike a manner, with what natural grace, he must have danced, would he but take the trouble.' Why, then, does he not? Partly because he is jealous of Churchill, Emma's 'own partner,' but mainly because here, as during the word games at Hartfield and on Box Hill, he will not participate in the games Emma plays in partnership with Churchill. Significantly, however, when Elton outrageously breaks all rules of decorum and considerateness by blatantly refusing to dance with Harriet, Knightley steps forward to lead her to the set (p. 328). More than a humane act, this demonstrates his own wish to be a 'dancer' rather than a 'whist-player' and his determination to participate in the right kind of social dance, one which will properly include within its formations natural daughters like Harriet and, from other evidence, orphans like Jane Fairfax and old maids like Miss Bates. By contrast, Emma's games pose threats to harmonious social continuity; it was her misguided and socially unreasonable match-making which led to Elton's insult in the first place. Moreover, when Knightley's noble gesture gives Harriet matrimonial ideas which even she knows to be out of the question, Emma will unwittingly foster them, to her own and the community's potential harm. Clearly, Highbury will only be restored to harmony and order when Emma and Knightley become partners in a proper social dance at the end of the novel. But this will require Emma to abandon the word games she first promotes and then engages in, in the insidious company of Churchill.

Even more than cards and dancing, word games have important structural and thematic functions in *Emma*, a fact which requires us to face again the paradox of a beloved family recreation becoming the aesthetic expression of dubious social behavior. True, lovers of word games may be simply childish like Mr Woodhouse who, try as he might, cannot remember beyond the first stanza of 'Kitty, a fair but frozen maid,' or Harriet whose 'only mental provision . . . for the evening of life, was the collecting and transcribing all the riddles of every sort that she could meet with' (p. 69). But word games are more than a technique used for the occasional exposure of deficient characters. Quite apart from the extraordinarily high frequency of 'games' words in the lexicon of *Emma* (e.g., trick, finesse, puzzle, mystery, connivance, speculation, double-dealing), words which are by no means always restricted to the playing of games, there is evidence that Jane Austen quite consciously structured her novel according to a 'system' of word games in order to reveal more dangerous threats to the social community than childish triviality. Consider the nature and sequence of games played. In the first volume the misunderstood charade leads to the fiasco of Elton's proposal and the failure of Emma's first matrimonial 'scheme' (chapter ix); in the third volume the anagrams at Hartfield (chapter v) and the conundrums on Box Hill (chapter vii) add negative tones to Emma's unadvised collusion with Churchill and mark the wide 'separation,' physical as well as moral, between her and Knightley, Frank and Jane, at this juncture; and in between the first crisis and the climax on Box Hill there are various games involving puzzles and secrets. Often these games are more or less complex riddles involving mysteries of personal identity: Who is the charade addressed to? Who is the mysterious donor of Jane Fairfax's piano? Who sent Churchill news of Perry's 'plan of setting up his carriage' (p. 344)? What two letters express perfection? Even where mystery is unnecessary it may be promoted anyway: thus, when Emma decides not to interfere in the matter of Harriet's new infatuation (p. 341), she instructs Harriet: 'let no name ever pass our lips' (p. 342). Emma's outrageous *Doppelgänger*, Mrs Elton, later seeks to capitalize upon her privileged knowledge of Jane's secret engagement by stage-whispering to Mrs Bates: 'I mentioned no *names,* you will observe' (p. 454).[13] By contrast, during the alphabet game at Hartfield, when Churchill passes the anagram of *Dixon* to Jane, she pushes away the letters 'with even an angry spirit,' saying only, 'I did not know that proper names were allowed' (p. 349).

A curious but instructive reversal has occurred: in real life, where names should be known, gifts acknowledged, and engagements made public, there is secrecy, whereas in children's games, which should be a recreation largely separate from normal life, 'proper names' (Miss Woodhouse, Dixon, Perry, Em-ma) keep appearing, in some instances in contravention of the rules of the game. Given the confusion between games and life, it is not perhaps surprising that Jane Fairfax should be 'a riddle, quite a riddle' to Emma, or that Jane's willingness to endure the 'mortification of Mrs. Elton's notice and the penury of her conversation' should appear as a 'puzzle' (p. 285). But what this 'system of secrecy and concealment' (p. 398) suggests in *Emma* is that a necessary and desirable contract between a perspicuous language and a properly functioning society has been broken.

Churchill, of course, is the games player, *par excellence.* It is he who promotes the confusion between games and life and introduces into Highbury 'guesses,' 'surprises,' 'tricks' far in excess of his need to set up a 'blind to conceal his real situation' with Jane Fairfax (p. 427). Unpredictable in his social existence – always arriving too early or too late, failing to write necessary letters, or writing them promptly and then forgetting to send them – Churchill is a traitor to certain common social rules. It is for this reason that Jane Austen uses strangely extreme language to describe him in the later chapters. Emma, no doubt comically exaggerating in her annoyance at being duped, accuses him of 'a system of hypocrisy and deceit, – espionage, and treachery' (p. 399). Hyperbolic as it is, the language is suggestive of his menace. Knightley, analyzing his letter of apology to Mrs Weston, sees that Churchill was 'playing a most dangerous game' (p. 445), and exclaims: 'Mystery; Finesse – how they pervert the understanding! My Emma, does not every thing serve to prove more and more the beauty of truth and sincerity in all our dealings with each other?' (p. 446). Knightley, of course, stands against Churchill throughout as a plain and 'open' man. He 'does nothing mysteriously' (p. 226); he feels that 'surprizes are foolish things' (p. 228). In his behavior 'community' and 'communication' are correspondent terms. So too are 'civilization' and 'cultivation.' Thus, during the alphabet game at Hartfield, he is separate from the 'system' Churchill promotes, seeing it as 'a child's play, chosen to conceal a deeper game on Frank Churchill's part' (p. 348).

Yet Churchill is not ostracized at the end of *Emma,* nor is Emma's vitality subdued: 'Serious she was, very serious in her thankfulness, and in her resolutions; and yet there was no preventing a laugh, sometimes in the very midst of them' (p. 475). For some readers, the sincerity of Emma's repentance is called into question by such passages and by her continued activity as an 'imaginist': when Mrs Weston gives birth to a girl, Emma's first thought, only half suppressed, is to make 'a match for her, hereafter, with either of Isabella's sons' (p. 461). Such a view, however, misrepresents the quality of Emma's playfulness following Box Hill. Now morally detached from Churchill, her love of games is ratified, as when she sympathetically imagines Mr Weston's 'fireside enlivened by the sports and the nonsense, the freaks and the fancies of a child never banished from home' (p. 461), or, 'laughing and blushing,' composes a last riddle as she promises to call Mr Knightley once by his Christian name 'in the building in which N. takes M. for better, for worse' (p. 463). Such games are very different from those played on Box Hill, where Perfection came too soon (p. 371). Only Mrs Elton could wish for a replay of that game (p. 455), though Churchill in his last meeting with Emma tries to start up the Dixon and Perry games again. Emma no longer plays with him, however, her sympathies, as distinguished from Box Hill, being with Jane (pp. 477–80). For her, games are no longer a threat. Married to Knightley and living at Hartfield with him and her father, she will participate in a 'vast deal of chat and backgammon,' not to mention 'Candour & Comfort & Coffee & Cribbage.' The triumph of *Emma*, in the end, is that it can require society to be the noblest game of all, exacting the most demanding of moral performances, and yet give space within this play for recreation in its most trivial guises. In *Emma* Jane Austen described not only a family but a society in which the Miss Austen of the *Letters* could feel at home.

NOTES

1 *Jane Austen's Letters to her sister Cassandra and others,* ed. R. W. Chapman, 2nd ed. (London: Oxford University Press, 1964), pp. 487–8. All subsequent citations in the text preceded by *Letters* will refer to this impression.

2 All page references to Jane Austen's novels included in the text will be to *The Novels of Jane Austen,* ed. R. W. Chapman, 5 vols., 3rd ed. (London: Oxford University Press, 1959–60). References to *The Watsons* and *Sanditon* will be to *The Works of Jane Austen,* ed. R. W. Chapman, Volume VI: *Minor Works* (London: Oxford University Press, 1963).

3 Cf. *Letters,* pp. 93, 113, 139, 294, 330–1, 338, 344.

4 'But still she [Mrs J. Austen] is in the main *not* a liberal-minded Woman, & as to this reversionary Property's amending that part of her Character, expect it not my dear Anne; – too late, too late in the day; & besides, the Property may not be theirs these ten years. My Aunt is very stout.' (Letter to Anne Sharp, 22 May 1817; *Letters,* p. 494). This is crude enough, but who would escape whipping if all private sentiments expressed in letters were to be made public? It is difficult to see more than a straining after effect when E. M. Forster hears 'the whinneying of harpies' in some of Jane Austen's letters.

5 Forster made the distinction in his review of Chapman's edition of the letters (1932); collected in *Abinger Harvest* (1936; reprinted New York: Harcourt Brace, 1964).

6 Forster acknowledges his debt to Jane Austen in 'The Art of Fiction, I: E. M. Forster,' *Paris Review,* 1 (Spring, 1953), 39. He is less elliptical about Jane Austen's successful aesthetic transformations of the trivial in *Aspects of the Novel* (1927), chapters 3 and 4 (both treating 'People'). His general distinction there between *Homo Sapiens* and *Homo Fictus,* as well as his specific discussion of Miss Bates as both a realistic portrait of a chatty spinster and a 'word-mass' inextricably bound to the fictional world of Highbury, provides supporting argument for his distinction later in his review of the letters between Miss Austen and Jane Austen and between Steventon and Meryton.

7 In *The Watsons* Tom Musgrave persuades the Watson family to give up Speculation, 'the only round game at Croydon' (p. 354), for vingt-un, the game played at Osborne Castle.

8 As Tony Tanner argues in his excellent introduction to the Penguin edition of the novel (Baltimore, 1969).

9 *The Country and the City* (New York: Oxford University Press, 1973), pp. 108–19. The argument here extends the discussion made in the introduction to *The English Novel: From Dickens to Lawrence* (London: Chatto and Windus, 1970).

10 Williams points out the limitations of her social awareness. Like Cobbett, she was not aware that the economic erosion of 'traditional' standards had been going on since the sixteenth century, and that the conflict between 'old' and 'new' wealth would result in the consolidation of an existing class and not in its destruction.

11 Raymond Williams applies this phrase to Burke in *Culture and Society: 1780–1950* (1958; reprinted New York: Harper, 1966), p. 140.

12 That these are trials endured for the sake of piety is shown when Emma, miserable following Knightley's rebuke on Box Hill, sets her present state in comparison to playing games with her father: 'A whole evening of back-gammon with her father, was felicity to it' (p. 377).

13 Mrs Elton more consciously mimics Emma on Box Hill following Mr Weston's complimentary conundrum: 'I had an acrostic once sent to me upon my own name, which I was not at all pleased with' (p. 372).

ANDREW WRIGHT

Jane Austen abroad

together with
Jaime Alazraki (Mexico), Raimonda Modiano (Romania), Jonathan
Saville (Russia), Cynthia Walk (Germany), Ulla Wohlleben (Sweden),
Wai-Lim Yip (China)

Jane Austen does not travel well, but she travels much. *Raison et
sensibilité, ou les deux manières d'aimer, La Nouvelle Emma, ou les
caractères anglais du siècle,* and *Le Parc de Mansfield, ou les trois
cousines,* all appeared in her lifetime; *La Famille Elliot, ou l'ancienne
inclination, Orgueil et Prévention* (and, in the same year, 1822,
Orgueil et Préjugé), and *L'Abbaye de Northanger* were issued within
half a dozen years of her death; and R. W. Chapman, from the second
edition of whose *Jane Austen: A Critical Bibliography* (Oxford, 1955) I
take this information, lists Spanish, Italian, German and Finnish translations of one or more of Jane Austen's works in the twentieth century.
But they are mere drops in the bucket. For her two-hundredth birthday
it seems appropriate to look at her more recent travels round the world,
and to sample the difficulties which *Pride and Prejudice* (the most frequently translated of her novels) has encountered as it has been recon-
stituted elsewhere. Within the last twenty years, *Pride and Prejudice*
has made its appearance – or reappearance – in Austria, Belgium, Bra-
zil, China, Czechoslovakia, Egypt, Finland, France, Germany, Hol-
land, Iceland, Italy, Japan, Mexico, Portugal, Romania, Spain, Sweden,
Switzerland, Turkey, the USSR and Yugoslavia. Furthermore at least
seven English versions – simplifications or abridgments or both – have

been issued since the second war, printed in such widely separated parts of the world as Hong Kong. Amsterdam and Huddersfield.

For purposes of the present survey, each of the foreign-language collaborators agreed to examine a translation with the modern reader in mind, to canvass the difficulties that a young and literate but not necessarily learned and certainly not bilingual Chinese, German, Mexican, Romanian, Russian or Swede would encounter in reading *Ao Man Yü P'ien Chien, Stolz und Vorurteil, Orgullo y prejuicio, Mindrie si prejudecata, gordost' i predubeždenie* or *Stolthet och fordom.* Each of the separate sections contains some general observations; and each touches – where appropriate – on three passages differing in narrative presentation: chapter 1 entire; the letter of Mr Collins to Mr Bennet in chapter 13; and the conversation between Elizabeth and Lady Catherine in chapter 56 (chapter 14 of the third volume). Finally, I examine three English versions of the novel.

CHINA

Pride and Prejudice has attracted little serious critical attention in China and yet Jane Austen's name is almost proverbial. Nearly every college student has read one of the five recent full or abridged translations of *Pride and Prejudice.* Though not without faults, they read felicitously in Chinese. But it is not so much the quality of the translations that has made *Pride and Prejudice* proverbial as the Chinese socio-cultural context and atmosphere, the general reader's readiness to absorb it in a certain way. In spite of the abundance of the belletristic tradition of poetry and such profound novels as *The Dream of the Red Chamber,* the sensibility of the audience of classical stories had been very much caught up in a middle-class mentality. Developed from the story-telling guilds of the twelfth and thirteenth centuries, the majority of stories and novels offered many stereotypes of sentimental love stories, dynastic histories of heroes and sensational ghost and crime stories that appealed to a semi-literate class of leisurely merchants whose ethical purposefulness and codes of conduct were those of blind compliance to established rules and whose value judgments were often mercenary and crudely materialistic.

During the May 4th Movement of 1919, the mushrooming of translations of poetry and novels and theories from the West ushered in a sentimental Romanticism (as opposed to epistemological Romanticism), Ibsenism and European critical realism, with the latter dominating the scene of the novels. Most of the readers were attracted by novels of social commitment and social protest (many of them assuming a proletarian stance). But as far as the change of taste is concerned, the traditional middle-class mentality, also the so-called 'novelistic tradition,' persisted in the consciousness of the readers at large. It was in this transition between the old and the new (Joyce, Eliot and Kafka were not yet known) that *Pride and Prejudice* was first introduced into China. Consequently, a curious fate befell this masterpiece. From a literary point of view and in spite of its popularity, it suffers from being too easily translated into a mentality which still has a strong grip upon a large audience, nevertheless an audience hardly aware of the destructive triteness of the stock images, dialogues and situations that are worked into the translations. From the English original, one can appreciate more fully the epigrammatic poignancy and the ironic manipulation of Jane Austen's art. Not that Chinese does not afford some happy epigrammatic sayings, irony and intellectual complexity in the translations, but that they are overwhelmed by the stock responses of the audience – partly inspired by their analogues in the original, partly by the ready-made rhetoric of the Chinese novelistic tradition. Hence, *Pride and Prejudice* is a *message* novel: a moral lesson is more strongly urged than in the original.

The silly garrulous Mrs Bennet's eagerness to make arrangements for her daughters to impress a rich young bachelor is a motif repeated in China endlessly in old stories, new novels, popular story-telling over the radio, folk dramas on the streets, soap-opera novels read by 'elderly maid servants' and so forth – a motif well encapsulated in one proverbial phrase and concept: 'To hook the golden turtle' (i.e., son-in-law from a wealthy or politically influential family).

William Collins' letter uses a rhetoric extremely circumlocutory and periphrastic to cover up an intention which cannot be directly spelled out without creating some injurious vexation. In Jane Austen's England, this rhetoric is highly developed. So is it in China. In fact, there are many books on this art – the Art of Expressing Disagreeable Emotions and Opinions – with a voluminous compilation of ready-made floral, musical, and, on the surface, sweet and pleasant epigrammatic phrases culled from the classics. Almost all the translators encounter no difficulty in transposing this art into Chinese – as if the Chinese phrases have been there waiting for Jane Austen. But these phrases also make the passage sound merely trite and merely dull. The only legitimate use of such phrases is for ironic effect, which is not the case with Mr Collins' letter: at least, *he* does not mean to be ironical.

'The engagement . . . from their infancy' as a pretext for Lady Catherine to reproach and repel Elizabeth Bennet has also a Chinese ring to it. One recurrent theme in Chinese stories and operas has been woven out of the conflict arising from the violation of a 'marriage agreement made during or upon pregnancy of the mothers of two families.' While the situation is not exactly the same and it is not the main plot of the novel, the manner (together with the snobbishness) with which Lady Catherine rails at Elizabeth conjures up in a Chinese reader many resemblances in popular stories. The complex witticisms of Elizabeth, her firmness in asserting herself, are exceptional: this is a most delightful and satisfying portrayal even in Chinese. Elizabeth appears as a combination of the witty heroine of a traditional comedy of manners and the emancipated Nora – prepared, anachronistically, by Ibsenism.

GERMANY

Published in Germany (Leipzig: List Verlag, 1965, 1967, 1969), Austria (Vienna: Die Buchgemeinde, 1967) and Switzerland (Lausanne: Rencontre, 1968), Werner Beyer's *Stolz und Vorurteil* represents the most recent and widely distributed German version of *Pride and Prejudice* now available on the Continent. Accordingly, the German today who encounters *Pride and Prejudice* in his native language will almost inevitably perceive the novel through the filter of this translation. *Stolz und Vorurteil* basically offers a competent literal reading of the text. Some difficulties are caused by the limitations of German vocabulary and syntax; others come from the use of the vocabulary of one century in the attempt to recapture a milieu buried by nearly two centuries of historical change; but the greatest limitation is inherent in the fact of translation itself: the language of the translator is not Jane Austen's. In each case the result is a distortion of the original stylistic intent and a loss or shift in meaning.

Jane Austen's prose style relies heavily on conceptual language, but Beyer's translation often fails to communicate the breadth of the English. Where an English noun has a number of connotations, Beyer may of necessity employ a word of narrower scope. The effect is to simplify the characters and the standards by which they are measured. Beyer's translation of the title is a primary example. The English terms are descriptive, the German normative or valuational. 'Pride and Prejudice' expresses, albeit ironically, the social attitudes of the gentry; 'Stolz und Vorurteil' implies a fault of moral character. Consequently from the outset the German version is more confined. At the end of chapter 1, Mrs Bennet is described as a woman of 'uncertain temper.' Beyer's translation is 'unberechenbare Launen' ('unpredictable moods'). Where the English connotes a general instability of character, the German refers exclusively to Mrs Bennet's emotional disposition. Again, the translation imposes a restriction of meaning and indicates a loss of conceptual complexity.

At the opening of the first chapter the juxtaposition of the grand announcement with what follows betrays the narrator's ironic attitude toward a provincial middle class that regards its customs and assumptions as something more than provincial truths. The aphorism becomes a *bon mot.* Syntactically the noun clause itself consists of a subject modified by two prepositional phrases linking any single man who has the desirable attribute of money with the intention of marriage. The subsequent paragraph makes it clear that this connection is assumed to be self-evident by families in the neighborhood with marriageable daughters.

> In der ganzen Welt gilt es als ausgemachte Wahrheit,
> dass ein begüterter Junggeselle unbedingt nach
> einer Frau Ausschau halten muss.

> (In the whole world it is an accepted truth that a propertied
> bachelor necessarily must be on the lookout for a wife.)

In Beyer's translation the aphorism loses its syntactical balance by the insertion of an adverb which is not found in the English. This addition overstates the connection ('necessarily must') and turns the phrase into an absolute moral imperative as opposed to a general observation of qualities that inhere in single men. The English sentence builds dramatically and ends concisely on the climactic word 'wife,' which corresponds to the hopes of the neighboring families. The German reaches its high point at the middle and dissipates itself in a cumbersome double verb construction which forfeits the irony of the conclusion.

The ironies in the exchange between husband and wife – lost on Mrs Bennet, but shared by Mr Bennet with the reader – are a hallmark of the first chapter. When Mrs Bennet complains that her husband has 'no compassion on my poor nerves,' he replies:

> 'You mistake me my dear. I have a high respect for your nerves. I
> have heard you mention them with consideration these twenty years
> at least.'

Beyer's translation of the last sentence reads:

> 'Mindestens seit zwanzig Jahren redest du mir von ihnen die Ohren
> voll.'

> ('For at least the past twenty years you have talked my ears off about
> them.')

Mr Bennet's sarcasm is understated in the English; in the German it is a direct insult. The overstatement makes Mr Bennet appear less tolerant of his wife and his marriage, more openly tempestuous.

Jane Austen's style is the cultivated idiom of her period. It seems almost too obvious to say that the English reader recognizes that her language does not belong to the twentieth century. The historical perspective is lost on the German reader since Beyer writes in a twentieth-century idiom replete with colloquialisms. Thus when Mrs Bennet is 'discontented' in the English, 'something goes against her grain' in the German ('Wenn ihr etwas gegen den strich ging'). In each case the German text accurately renders the sense of these lines, but the idiom is colloquial and up-to-date.

Beyer's tendency toward overstatement works to his advantage in William Collins' letter of introduction to Mr Bennet. For instance:

> and on these grounds I flatter myself that my present overtures of good will are highly commendable, and that the circumstance of my being next in the entail of Longbourn estate, will be kindly over-looked on your side, and not lead you to reject the offered olivebranch.

Here German syntax lends itself to elaborate phrasing. The displacement of verb and auxiliaries to the end of each clause extends the actual length of the sentences and exaggerates the impression of orotundity.

> und aus diesen Gründen schmeichle ich mir, es auszusprechen, dass meine hiermit unternommenen Annäherungsversuche ein höchst löbliches Unterfangen sind, und gebe der Hoffnung Ausdruck, dass die Tatsache, dass ich der nächste in der Erbfolge für Longbourn bin, von Ihnen gütigst übersehen werden und Sie nicht veranlassen möge den Ihnen entgegengestreckten Ölzweig zurückzuweisen.

What this letter gains in isolation, however, it loses in context. Since the whole translation is marred by overstatement the particular irony of this passage is obscured.

In Elizabeth's final conversation with Lady Catherine, dramatic irony is concentrated in the dialogue between the characters, while the narrator reports on their movements as an ostensibly neutral and detached observer. Thus when Lady Catherine is unable to intimidate Elizabeth, she is described as being 'highly incensed.' The German translation reads: 'Ihre Hochwohlgeborenen spie Gift und Galle' ('Her ladyship spewed poison and gall')! The German metaphor is startling. It is altogether too crude an expression for the carefully modulated tones of Jane Austen's narrative.

In other passages the German is simply careless and imprecise. Furious at the thought that Elizabeth may frustrate her marriage plans for Darcy, Lady Catherine castigates her as 'a young woman of inferior birth, of no importance in the world, and wholly unallied in the family.'

> Und jetzt . . . kommt ein junges Ding niederer Herkunft dazwischen, die in der Welt nicht das Geringste bedeutet und mit unserer Familie nichts zu tun hat.

> (And now . . . a young thing of low birth gets in the way who doesn't mean the slightest in the world and who has absolutely nothing to do with our family.)

Lady Catherine may lose her temper, but not her vocabulary. Curiously Jane Austen's characters, particularly those with aristocratic pretensions, become more articulate under stress. This is because language functions not only as a measure of character and intelligence but also of rank. In a novel where the characters and their milieu are specifically defined through language, any distortion of diction or syntax tends to blur such distinctions.

MEXICO

For each Spanish translation about which one may say that it improves on the original text – such as Borges' Spanish version of Virginia Woolf's *Orlando* – there are countless examples of poor, clumsy, coarse translations. Bitter about the quality of these translations, Cortázar has characterized their language as merely informative. He adds: 'Having lost its *originality,* this translated language deadens the euphonic, rhythmic, chromatic, sculptural, structural stimuli, and altogether the hedgehog of style pointing to the reader's sensitivity, striking and urging him through his eyes, his ears, his vocal chords and even his taste, in a play of resonances and correspondences and adrenalin which enters his blood to modify the system of reflexes and responses and to stir up a porous participation in that vital experience which a short-story or a novel is.' Regrettably, these remarks are wholly applicable to the Spanish translation of *Pride and Prejudice.* Published in Mexico City in 1959 by UNAM (National Autonomous University of Mexico), *Orgullo y prejuicio* is introduced with a fifteen-page essay on Jane Austen by Carlos Fuentes. It also includes a useful bio-bibliography of Jane Austen. The translator is not identified.

The first chapter offers a few instances of chromatic nuance missed by the translator. He uses a too familiar and informal language where the English is, to say the least, normative. Thus the Spanish colloquialisms *posma* (sluggish) and *pollos* (young guys) as the respective translations of 'tiresome' and 'young men' are objectionable on two accounts: first, they are stylistically wrong; second, for a Mexican or Latin American reader these words are meaningless since their usage, being regional, is restricted to Spaniards. The Spanish *pesado* (tiresome) and *jóvenes* (young men) would have supplied a much simpler and more accurate solution.

The same mistake occurs in the choice of personal pronouns. The translator chose, in the relations between the Bennets, the familiar *tú* over the formal *usted* for the second-person singular. Realizing that Mrs Bennet cannot address Mr Bennet in that familiar form and still keep the *Mr,* he dropped the title form throughout the entire book, thus changing the tone and distance which define a subliminal side of their relationship. The choice of the familiar form is even less fortunate in the letter of William Collins to Mr Bennet: it goes against the grain of its inflection. Once the familiar *tú* is adopted there is little room for the heading 'Dear Sir,' which the translator changes to *Querido primo* (Dear cousin).

The text is also plagued with mistranslation. 'Loan' is consistently rendered *pradera* (prairie), 'copse' becomes *breñal* (craggy ground), 'scandalous' is changed arbitrarily into *espantosa* (frightful), 'industriously' becomes *mañosamente* (craftily), 'I am entitled to know' produces the awkward sentence *poseo títulos para conocer* (I possess titles to know), 'presumption' engenders *pretension*, 'elopement' (for which Spanish has no exact translation other than the general *fuga* – flight) is translated as *rapto* (kidnapping) – creating a new story wherein Wickham has kidnapped Elizabeth's sister.

The translator also stumbles often over the use of verbal tenses, and there are several cases where the English text has been badly misread. Having failed to achieve correctness at these basic levels, the translator expectedly is generally insensitive to the subtleties and intricacies of Jane Austen's style. What is left is a hasty translation devoid of any effort to cast in a different language some of the major features which underline Jane Austen's art. If one of the greatest achievements of *Pride and Prejudice* is characterization by means of dialogue, inflection of voice, and in general handling of language, a translation such as the one offered to the Mexican reader blurs the characters to disfiguration. Of those 'euphonic, rhythmic, chromatic, sculptural and structural stimuli' which bring writing to the status of literature, very little has been preserved, thus reducing the value of the translation to its 'informative function.'

Almost matching the outlook of the translator, Carlos Fuentes' 'Introduction' approaches the novel as an informative document, or, as he says, as 'the typical expression of the new bourgeois class, intended *to consecrate* the new values: that is, intended to protect those values from criticism.' Beyond this, Fuentes grants to Jane Austen's novels the merit of 'bearing the responsibility for the subsequent respect towards the banal and well-made novel which limits for that very reason today's English fiction.' If this is Fuentes, why should an anonymous translator strive any further, and why should the helpless Mexican reader question a translation into a language which is more pastiche than Spanish?

ROMANIA

The Romanian translation offers difficulties in the very title *Mindrie si prejudecata* (translated by Ana Almageanu, Bucharest, 1969), since the Romanian language does not have a word for pride expressing both the notion of proper self-esteem and that of a vain arrogance symptomatic of the sin of pride. A translator must choose between two words, *mindrie* and *orgoliu*, each denoting the positive and negative meaning of 'pride' separately. The word *mindrie*, which is the one preferred by the translator, signifies primarily the virtues of dignity, honor, and self-respect, and has only secondary associations with the notion of vanity or arrogance. The word *orgoliu*, on the other hand, is straightforwardly negative; one could not render Mary's reflection on the difference between vanity and pride or speak of Darcy's 'proper' pride by using this word. The translator's choice of *mindrie* is justified because it is more readily susceptible of pejorative connotation and thus has a larger capacity to absorb the ambiguity of the English word than *orgoliu*, which cannot take on a positive sense. But, as is to be expected, the use of a word which is not the full semantic equivalent of 'pride' is bound to create difficulties. Because *mindrie* is essentially a complimentary term, in the title of the novel where the only referent is *prejudecata* ('prejudice') it implies a false opposition between quality and defect, the good and the bad. From the title alone, a Romanian reader might presume that the novel is about the struggle of a noble hero against the prejudices of society.

The choice of *mindrie* as the equivalent for the 'pride' of the novel presents a further difficulty. Given the fact that Romanian has a fully expressive term to communicate the negative sense of 'pride,' the word *orgoliu*, how does one translate 'pride' in contexts where it is clearly meant to convey disapproval? If a translator is to remain faithful to one of the major paradigms of the original novel, which involves the repetition of 'pride' until the word fixed in the title is gradually understood in all its complexity, then he could not employ two words, one of which is excluded from the title. The Romanian translator is quite aware of this problem; she decides to maintain the word *mindrie* consistently wherever 'pride' occurs in the English text. While preserving the verbal pattern of the original, however, this often violates the logic of the Romanian language. In such sentences as 'Some people call him proud; but I am sure I never saw anything of it' or 'Everybody is disgusted with his pride,' the noun *mindrie* and the adjective *mindru* make a compliment sound like a reproach and a reproach sound like a compliment. It would be like saying in English, 'Some people call him dignified; but I am sure I never saw anything of it.'

The opening statement of *Pride and Prejudice,* so much celebrated by critics, is spoiled in translation because of the improper use of the word *burlac,* which, besides being phonetically unpleasant, is pejorative, insinuating loose morals. When Mr Bennet asks his wife whether their prospective neighbor is 'married or single' and Mrs Bennet answers 'Oh! single, my dear, to be sure!', the word *burlac* conveys mockery, which is hardly what Mrs Bennet, at least, means to express.

In the same chapter the translator makes overt another neutral term of the original, a practice which again places the stigma of impropriety on a character where no such thing is meant by the author. Thus Mrs Bennet's description of Bingley as a 'single man *of large fortune'* becomes in Romanian 'Burlac si *putred de bogat,'* which in addition to the jarring word *burlac* contains a phrase that conveys exactly the English meaning of 'filthy rich.'

The blatant pomposity of the letter from Mr Collins is essentially a function of its convoluted syntax. In the Romanian text, however, syntax as such is less effective. Being a highly inflected language, Romanian has greater capacity to form subordinate sentences than English and thus what is ornate syntax in Collins' original letter is perfectly natural syntax in the Romanian translation. To achieve the affected tone of the letter one has to rely much more on lexical means in Romanian than on syntax, and that is where metaphor can be helpful. But the translator unfortunately renders Mr Collins' 'wish to heal the breach' as 'dorinta unei reconcilieri' ('the desire for a reconciliation'), which is ineffectual not only for the reason suggested but also because of the contrast which Jane Austen establishes between Mr Collins' metaphoric penchant and the non-figurative language preferred as the norm in *Pride and Prejudice.*

In addition to syntactical differences, the lack of morphological equivalence between the English and the Romanian languages further complicates the problems of translation. Romanian has a morphological category with no referent in English, namely the pronoun of politeness. In direct address a Romanian speaker has a choice of four pronouns – *tu, dumneata, dumneavoastra, domnia voastra* – depending on how intimate or distant he wishes to be with the interlocutor. Accordingly, Romanian has great flexibility in expressing various degrees of formality in relationships and thus is a language suitable to a world such as Jane Austen's, in which conversation takes the place of incidents and decorum in forms of address is so important. For instance, in the well-known effort of Lady Catherine to persuade Elizabeth to give up Darcy, Elizabeth's emphatic use of the most respectful of the pronouns, *domnia voastra*, in addressing herself to Lady Catherine is entirely effective in establishing the ironies of the dialogue. Generally, the Romanian translator makes good use of the pronoun of politeness, but sometimes she commits errors which are bound to cause misrepresentations of the original. Thus, because of Miss Bingley's unaccountable fluctuation between a formal and informal mode of address in her conversation with Darcy at Netherfield, a Romanian reader is likely to form a false impression of her as a woman unsure of her status in the world.

The divergence of the Romanian translation of *Pride and Prejudice* from the original text is ultimately determined by the lack of cultural equivalents for terms which define specific milieux. For instance, the Romanian language has no equivalents for such house divisions as 'breakfast room,' 'breakfast parlour' or 'dressing room.' For the first two phrases the translator has to employ the terms *salonas*, i.e., 'small lounge,' and *sufragerie mica*, i.e., 'small dining-room.' For 'dressing room,' on the other hand, the translator uses a more elaborate phrase made of the noun *budoar* for 'room' and the verb *sa se dezbrace* for 'dressing.' The word *budoar* has different connotations in Romanian from 'dressing room' in English. It designates a woman's private room which she would use not only for dressing but also, perhaps, for carrying on love affairs. Mrs Bennet would certainly have no need for such a room.

The lack of corresponding names of English rooms in Romanian is a minor matter; it does not affect the meaning of the novel directly. Of much greater consequence is the absence of full equivalence between Romanian and English words which relate to the rural world and social setting of *Pride and Prejudice*. The direct linguistic equivalents for such words as 'village,' 'landowner,' or 'estate' in Romanian are *sat, mosier,* and *mosie*. Culturally, however, these words would mean different things for a Romanian and an Englishman. An early-nineteenth-century Romanian village is hardly the place where the refined drawing-room conversations of *Pride and Prejudice* could take place. For a Romanian the village evokes a vast population of illiterate and exploited peasants or of peasant uprisings against the cruelty of rich landowners. Certainly the fact that no reference to peasants is made by any of the characters of *Pride and Prejudice* makes the village of the novel an improbable one for a Romanian. On the other hand, persons owning an estate as large as Pemberley become *mosieri,* that is, 'landowners' – and cannot be dissociated in the mind of a Romanian reader from practices of peasant exploitation. Also, a Romanian landowner is neither cultivated nor refined. His manners or language do not differ very much from those of the peasants. A *mosier* like Darcy has no correlative in the reality of life in a Romanian village.

How much, then, of the intention of the original novel is retained in translation? An educated Romanian reader may know that the English village has a socio-economic structure different from the Romanian village and he may be able to suppress the negative associations of such words as *mosier.* He will also understand quite well the eagerness of a mother to marry her daughters, the formality of polite relationships between members of the family or friends, or the desperate efforts of Lady Catherine to save Darcy from his misalliance with a person of inferior social rank. The Romanian society of the early nineteenth century was as inflexible about class distinctions and imposed equal pressures on a woman regarding marriage as the society of Jane Austen's time. Yet, partly because of inherent differences in the semantic and grammatical structure of the Romanian and English languages and partly because of mistakes made by the translator, the sustained mastery of Jane Austen's style is lost in translation. And if it is true indeed that the main triumph of *Pride and Prejudice* is, as critics describe it, a 'triumph of style,' then what a Romanian reader misses is the triumph.

RUSSIA

Considering the interest of Russian readers in English literature and the activity of the Soviet translation industry, it is remarkable that I. S. Maršak's translation of *Pride and Prejudice (Gordost' i predubeždenie* [Moscow: Nauka, 1967]) is the first Russian version of Jane Austen's famous novel. It is professionally done and effectively presented. Maršak is the son of the noted translator and poet, Samuil Jakovlevič Maršak, who helped with the early chapters; and neither father nor son can be faulted for his knowledge of English or his stylishness in Russian. The translation appeared in the distinguished series *Literaturnye pamjatniki (Literary Monuments),* along with a lengthy and knowledgeable critical essay by N. M. Demurova, and thirty pages of notes by Demurova and B. B. Tomasevškij. These notes are of exceptional value. Not only do they explain matters which must seem puzzling to the non-English reader and which the translation itself cannot make altogether clear (for example, the meanings of 'Mr,' 'Mrs,' and 'sir,' which have no exact equivalents in Russian); in addition, they supply a great deal of historical and social information (about the customs of the gentry, the English class system, whist, entails, and the like) which would be of considerable use to many readers of Jane Austen in the original.

What the Russian reader has before him is thus a translation of a high degree of literal accuracy, in which translator and editors have taken great care that no details, whether linguistic or social, remain murky. What he does not have is a reproduction of the style of Jane Austen's mind, the particular ironic flavor that accounts for so much of the effect of her novels. In part, the loss of the original's ironic tone is due to the breaking up of long sentences, virtually a necessity in a language whose words are so much longer than ours and whose capacity for the elegant is so much weaker. But the main cause seems to be a failure on the translator's part to perceive the tone rather than an inability to reproduce it. There is nothing in Russian vocabulary or syntax to prevent a perfectly literal translation of the novel's first sentence, for example; yet in Maršak's version, 'It is a truth universally acknowledged' becomes 'Everyone knows,' and instead of learning that the object of the knowledge 'must be in want of a wife,' we are told that he 'is obliged to try to find himself a wife.' There are no errors here, certainly, but the deliciously ironic aphorism has been transformed into a rather matter-of-fact statement, far less striking than in the English.

The dulling of edges is pervasive in this translation. Where the English Mr Bennet says to his wife, '*You* want to tell me, and I have no objection to hearing it,' his Russian counterpart avers woodenly, 'I am ready to hear you out, if you very much feel like telling me about it.' Mr Bennet's sarcastic 'Is that his design in settling here?' is toned down to 'Hmm, are those his plans?' Sometimes the translator manages to soften, blur, or dull the sharpness of the original by the most insignificant sort of alteration. When Lady Catherine, in her grandly dramatic interview with Elizabeth, declares that she knows the rumor about Elizabeth and Darcy must be a scandalous falsehood, Elizabeth retorts (with astonishment and disdain), 'If you believed it impossible to be true . . . I wonder you took the trouble of coming so far.' Maršak's only change is to preface Elizabeth's reply with a 'but'; but that 'but' significantly mitigates the iciness of Elizabeth's tone. It draws her into a closer relationship with Lady Catherine, making her statement part of the give and take of argument rather than the totally independent utterance of a young woman determined to remain totally independent of her opponent's influence.

Russian conversation would certainly call for such a 'but'; and it is characteristic of Maršak to Russianize Jane Austen's people through changes in their style of speech. To her husband's 'Is he married or single?' Mrs Bennet replies 'Oh! single, my dear, to be sure!' But the Russian Mrs Bennet speaks the language of Tolstoy: 'Single, my dear. That's the whole point, that he's single.' The greater emphasis, the repetition, the sense of a more immediate expression of a more vivid emotion – these belong to the Russian novel, not to the English. Similarly, Mrs Bennet's 'how can you be so tiresome?' becomes, in Maršak's Russian, 'today you are simply unbearable.' It is not only the brittle and ironic tone that is missing in this translation of *Pride and Prejudice*, it is the very decorum of English emotions.

SWEDEN

Stolthet och Fördom (translated by Gösta Olzon [Stockholm, 1968]) betrays signs of haste. It also illustrates all too abundantly the difficulties of translating Jane Austen into Swedish. While it is true that the force of Jane Austen's characters is so great as to leap over the barrier of language and thus delight the putative Stockholmer with something at least of the force of the original, the Swedish version is stiff and unnatural to a degree never intended by Jane Austen; and the translator's decision to follow English rules of agreement and punctuation makes for muddy Swedish. There are also distortions or mistakes of grave consequence.

Unfortunately the first chapter receives the worst treatment in the whole book. Mr and Mrs Bennet address each other 'kära du,' an expression that conveys more warmth and intimacy than the English 'my dear.' This is perhaps of minor importance and also a very difficult translation problem, but more serious is the fact that the translator fails to bring out clearly the contrast between these two characters. The delightful facetiousness of Mr Bennet is almost totally lost; he expresses himself clumsily and thereby gives the impression of being a less educated and witty person than in the original text. Mrs Bennet on the other hand is presented in a more favorable light than in the original. She is said to be 'en kvinna med medelgott förstånd, ringa bildning och ombytligt lynne' ('a woman of medium intelligence, little education, and changeable temperament'), which is a relatively positive statement and gives one the impression that although Mrs Bennet has little education she possèsses a fairly good intellect and has a lively temperament. This is a long way from Jane Austen's 'a woman of mean understanding, little information and uncertain temper'! It is also peculiar that in translating Mrs Bennet's statement that Lizzy is not 'half so good humoured as Lydia' Mr Olzon chooses the word 'snäll' for 'good humoured.' 'Snäll' means 'kind' and does not necessarily imply cheerfulness; thus the reader is misled about both sisters.

The tone in the Swedish version of the first letter from Mr Collins to Mr Bennet is pompous, as in the original, but to a lesser degree. For instance, instead of translating 'heal the breach' into a similar cliché, 'överbrygga klyftan' ('bridge the gap'), a more general rendering is given: 'förbättra förhållandet mellan oss' ('improve the relationship between ourselves'). Another difference is that in the Swedish version we read that Mr Collins considers himself happy to have been called to his valuable rectory by the Right Honourable Lady Catherine de Bourgh, widow of Sir Lewis de Bourgh, and nothing is mentioned about his being 'distinguished by the patronage' of Lady Catherine, nor anything about her 'bounty and beneficence'; the translator simply drops these items. Therefore there is really no need for Elizabeth to be so impressed by Mr Collins' 'extraordinary deference' to Lady Catherine; it does not come through in the letter.

Mr Collins asks Mr Bennet to 'forget' (glömma) rather than 'overlook' the fact that he is next in the entail, and he professes to 'feel sad' ('känna ledsnad') rather than to be 'concerned' about this, which makes him seem more hypocritical than perhaps Jane Austen intended. The translator skips the clause, 'which I can do without any inconvenience.' This passage is not unimportant: it reveals Mr Collins' narrow-minded selfishness in taking for granted that Lady Catherine's and his own convenience overrides that of his hosts. In the Swedish version he therefore seems less presumptuous – one is almost tempted to say he is a sensible man.

As the novel advances the translation gets better. By the time we reach the conversation between Lady Catherine and Elizabeth there is noticeable improvement. The language is more idiomatic, and the translator really manages to convey something of the rhetoric of the original. In order to achieve this he sometimes diverges from the English version, and does so to good advantage. The flaws result mainly from his translation being too slavishly bound at times to the original, or else from failing to bring out clearly the meaning of the original text, as in the passage 'You both did as much as you could in planning the marriage. Its completion depended on others,' which is translated 'Ni har båda gjort vad ni kunnat för att planera giftermälet. Men därmed är saken inte klar' ('You have both done what you could in order to plan the marriage. But the matter is not settled by that'). The Swedish version suggests that with some additional efforts Lady Catherine and her sister could perhaps have brought about the marriage, whereas the original clearly states that the mothers could not have complete control over the situation.

THREE ENGLISH VERSIONS

The three English versions of *Pride and Prejudice* to be considered are listed in order of publication:

1. *Pride and Prejudice* by Evelyn Attwood (Longman, 1946).

This version belongs to the Longman Simplified English Series and appears to have had considerable success. My copy (purchased at Blackwell's in 1973) lists fifteen new impressions issued since original publication, the latest in 1972. The book is printed in Hong Kong.

In a prefatory note the purpose of the Simplified English Series is declared to be 'to make enjoyable reading for people to whom English is a second or a foreign language.' Unusual words are avoided; difficult words are explained; long sentences are broken up. Four illustrations by C. E. Brock (from the Macmillan Illustrated Pocket Classics Edition) are included. There is a one-paragraph Introduction in which Jane Austen's birthdate and background are indicated and in which the editor asserts: 'Her world is a small one, but it is alive with truth and wit.' Immediately preceding chapter 1 is a list of persons in the story, together with brief identifying phrases ('Sir William Lucas, a prosperous merchant, knighted and retired,' 'Mr Bingley, a wealthy gentleman,' and so forth).

The level at which the series is pitched may be suggested by reference to the questions which appear on pages 152-60 following the last chapter. For chapter 1 these two questions are posed: '1. Explain the terms: to let; to take a house; to take possession; to settle in a place. 2. "The business of her life was to get her daughters married." Make a note of instances showing how Mrs Bennet carried out this aim.' The question at the back of the book about Mr Collins' letter is: 'What kind of man would you expect Mr Collins to be after reading his letter?' Of the confrontation between Lady Catherine and Elizabeth the questions are: '1. Explain: an air more than usually ungracious; to favour someone with one's company. 2. In what way was Lady Catherine "insolent and disagreeable"? 3. How would you describe Elizabeth's behaviour when Lady Catherine spoke so rudely to her?'

The annotations are sparse throughout, Evelyn Attwood having simplified the novel; but there is the following note to chapter 1: 'Nerves – a condition of mind in which a person is easily excited or upset.' There are three notes to the letter of Mr Collins. He writes, of course, from Hunsford, which Evelyn Attwood alters to Hunsford Parsonage: 'Parsonage (or vicarage – the house provided for the use of a priest (parson or vicar).' Jane Austen's 'Having received ordination at Easter' becomes 'Having lately taken holy orders,' and 'to take holy orders' is glossed as 'to become a priest.' Finally, Jane Austen's 'whose bounty and beneficence has preferred one to the valuable rectory of this parish' becomes 'whose generosity has granted me the valuable living in this district,' and 'living' is explained as follows: 'an appointment as a priest. These appointments were often in the hands of local landowners.'

About the three passages chosen for special comment in this essay, the following should be said in addition to the remarks made in connection with the Longman version as a whole.

The first two paragraphs of Jane Austen's chapter 1 are not attempted; Evelyn Attwood begins with Mrs Bennet's question to her husband, 'My dear Mr Bennet . . . ' The sense of distance between husband and wife is preserved in the replies of Mr Bennet which Jane Austen and Evelyn Attwood both represent in indirect discourse. The intention of Mrs Bennet to marry one of the daughters to Mr Bingley is faithfully rendered. The final paragraph is, however, a little less exploitive of ironic possibility than the original. Jane Austen has it: 'Mr Bennet was so odd a mixture of quick parts, sarcastic humour, reserve, and caprice'; but Evelyn Attwood: 'quick wits, sharp humour, reserve, and unexpected turns of mind' – a perhaps fair rendition of the whole collection of epithets, but one which makes the last item in the series anticlimactic because periphrastic. Mrs Bennet suffers a reduction. In Jane Austen the sentence 'She was a woman of mean understanding, little information, and uncertain temper' becomes 'She was a foolish woman.'

Figurative language, especially in its more ornate and fossilized forms, is Mr Collins' hallmark, and (as is true in foreign languages) specially difficult to render with the irony Jane Austen intended. Mr Collins does not express a wish 'to heal the breach' but 'to effect a reconciliation'; and there is no mention of 'the offered olive branch' (which even Mary finds 'not wholly new'). Mr Collins also conveys a considerably diminshed sense of self-importance: 'it shall be my earnest endeavour to demean myself with grateful respect towards her Ladyship, and be ever ready to perform those rites and ceremonies which are instituted by the Church of England' becomes, simply, 'I shall try to behave with grateful respect towards her Ladyship.' The multiple negations, so dear to the pompous heart, are also smoothed away: 'I cannot be otherwise than concerned at being the means of injuring your amiable daughters' becomes 'I am troubled at being the means of harming your fair daughters.'

The conversation between Lady Catherine and Elizabeth on the subject of the latter's possible engagement to Darcy is reduced from 5½ pages in the original to 2 in the Longman Simplified *Pride and Prejudice*; but much of the flavor of the longer version is, happily, preserved: there remains the sense of Lady Catherine's ill-considered impertinence outflanked by Elizabeth's resourceful wit and anger. But there are considerable losses too: when Elizabeth says of Darcy, 'Why may I not accept him?', Lady Catherine replies, 'Because honour, decorum, prudence, nay interest, forbid it.' All this, together with her ladyship's embroidery on the theme, is omitted from Evelyn Attwood's simplification. And, unfortunately, the ringing question 'Are the shades of Pemberley to be thus polluted?' is omitted altogether: how does one mix a metaphor in a simplified version?

2. *Pride and Prejudice*, abridgment and introduction by Anthea Bell (London, 1960).

This version belongs to Longman's Abridged Books series and has been reissued seven times since 1960. At the head of the list of the titles in this series (including *A Tale of Two Cities*, *The Moonstone*, and *Cry, the Beloved Country*) there is a note saying 'The limp edition of this series of abridged but unsimplified books includes comprehension and language exercises and a glossary.' The book is printed in Hong Kong.

The front matter includes a life of Jane Austen (1½ pages), a summary of the plot (1⅓ pages), and comments on the characters, of which the following appears under Fitzwilliam Darcy: 'In spite of his pride he is always just, and a good master to his tenants, and Elizabeth's reproach when he first proposes to her, that he has not behaved in a gentlemanly manner, leads him to become more civil.'

This being an unsimplified version, one expects (and finds) more complexity in the exercises at the end of the book than in Evelyn Attwood's version. Under chapter 1 there are 'things to find out' such as 'What social rules there were about "calling" on a newcomer to the district.' There is a category called 'comprehension,' under which are five questions, including 'What was so important to Mrs Bennet about the arrival of Mr Bingley?' There is a suggestion for writing a composition ('The Dangers of Being an Unmarried, Wealthy Young Man at the End of the Eighteenth Century'). There is a Section on Language, in which the student is asked to use certain phrases italicized here 'in sentences of your own' – for instance, 'He is to *take possession* before Michaelmas.'

In chapter I Jane Austen appears, as promised, in her own words; but in fewer words. These are omitted: 'that he came down on

Monday in a chaise and four to see the place, and was so much delighted with it that he agreed with Mr Morris immediately.' When Mrs Bennet declares to her husband, 'You must visit him as soon as he comes,' Mr Bennet replies, 'I see no occasion for that. You and the girls may go,' and so forth; but the Longman abridgment skips down to 'It is more than I engage for, I assure you,' thus omitting the teasing of Mrs Bennet by her husband ('As you are as handsome as any of them, Mr Bingley may like you the best of the party') and her revealingly vain rejoinder ('I certainly *have* had my share of beauty').

The letter from Mr Collins retains its original glory and is only slightly abridged.

The conversation between Lady Catherine and Elizabeth preserves much of its force, but something is lost as well. The fact that Lady Catherine's 'character has ever been celebrated for its sincerity and frankness' remains unsaid; correspondingly, Elizabeth's declaration that she does 'not pretend to possess equal frankness' is left out. The planning of the union 'while in their cradles' of Lady Catherine's daughter and Darcy is omitted, as is much of the detail about the aristocratic blood of her ladyship's family. And the climactic exchange, ending with 'Are the shades of Pemberley to be thus polluted?' is, considerably to the detriment of the scene, passed over, together with the final expressions of ultimate scorn.

3. *Pride and Prejudice,* retold by Joan Macintosh (Macmillan, 1962).

This version belongs to Macmillan's Stories to Remember, Senior Series, and has been reissued nine times since its original publication. The Senior Series list on the verso of the half-title includes one other work of Jane Austen (*Emma*), four Dickens novels, two by Wilkie Collins, and two by Tagore. The book is 'published by the Macmillan Company of India Ltd' and printed in Hong Kong. There is an introduction of 2 pages and 7 pages of explanatory notes at the end; ten Brock illustrations are included.

Joan Macintosh tells the reader in the introduction that Jane Austen's six novels are 'straightforward love stories, with happy endings, good plots, and a strong respect for domestic virtues.' She also says that the abridgment (which, for her, also involves simplification) cannot 'do justice to the original.'

The first chapter is abbreviated and simplified. 'Everyone knows that a single man with a large fortune needs a wife' lacks the aphoristic grandeur of the original, and 'needs' for 'must be in want of' collapses the ironies that Jane Austen achieved. The word 'fortune' is followed by a superscribed asterisk which takes the reader to the following note at the end of the book: '"Fortune" can mean "luck." But the owner of "a large fortune" is a man who has plenty of money.'

The phrase 'My dear Mr Bennet' is also explained as the usual form of address in Jane Austen's day; Joan Macintosh then goes on to say: 'Children called their parents "Sir" and "Madam" or "Papa" and "Mama." Nowdays husbands and wives call each other by their first name and children usually say "Mother" and "Father" or "Mummy" and "Daddy."' The remaining notes on the first chapter explain 'let,' 'carriage with four horses' as an index to wealth, and 'Lizzy' as a short form of 'Elizabeth.'

The Macintosh version of Mr Collins' letter is in a more subdued vein than Jane Austen's. For 'heal the breach' Mr Collins is now made to write 'end the quarrel'; and the olive branch is gone: 'I hope that you will be ready to excuse the fact that I am next in the entail of the Longbourn estate' replaces the more ornate original; and the pompous allusion to a curate at the end of the letter has disappeared entirely.

The exchange between Lady Catherine and Elizabeth is reduced by half, and there is inevitable loss of dramatic force in this celebrated conversation. While Lady Catherine's arrogance and stupidity are not wholly obscured, and while Elizabeth's capacity to resist and outwit her remain, the rendition is disappointingly tame. Lady Catherine's self-confessed reputation for candor is still communicated to Elizabeth, but in muted form. When Lady Catherine asks Elizabeth whether Mr Darcy has made an offer of marriage and Elizabeth has replied, 'Your Ladyship has declared it to be impossible,' Jane Austen then causes Lady Catherine to say, 'It ought to be so; it must be so, while he retains the use of his reason. But *your* arts and allurements may, in a moment of infatuation, have made him forget what he owes to himself and to all his family. You may have drawn him in.' This becomes: 'It ought to be. It must be, as long as he remains sane. But your arts may have made him forget what he owes to his family. You may have tricked him.' When Elizabeth asks why she may not accept Mr Darcy, her ladyship's reply ('Because honour, decorum, prudence, nay interest, forbid it') becomes drastically simplified: 'Because honour, decency and self-interest forbid it.' Nor do the shades of Pemberley make their appearance in the Stories to Remember series.

Of the three English versions of *Pride and Prejudice* discussed here it would be more tempting to wax superior and indignant if the example of Lady Catherine did not restrain such effusion. It was never to be expected that any simplification of Jane Austen would convey the force of the original; but the Longman abridgment has at least the virtue of retaining Jane Austen's own words. However, there may be a moral to be drawn: some authors are more difficult to translate than others; perhaps, therefore, some authors – Jane Austen among them – should stay at home. But would the loss not outweigh the gain?

A select bibliography

Compiled by John Halperin

[Editor's note: Despite the length of this bibliography, it is indeed
selective, especially with regard to the final category – uncollected
essays. I have listed throughout only what seem to be the most
important recent items. One further word of explanation is necessary.
The listing of uncollected essays in Section VI does not include many
of the most widely reprinted and well-known shorter pieces on Jane
Austen because such items are covered in Section V, which lists
collections of essays and the contents of each collection. In the
interests of economy, I have omitted full citation of the original
appearance of these reprinted pieces, which are readily available in
the collections themselves. Items listed in Section VI, then, have not
been reprinted in any discoverable available collection. Nineteenth-
century essays on Jane Austen also are not listed in Section VI.
Southam's *Critical Heritage* volume reprints the major criticism itself
through 1870; I have included a brief summary of its contents after
the listing in Section V.   J.H.]

I. TEXTS

The Novels of Jane Austen, ed. R.W. Chapman, 5 vols. (London:
    Oxford University Press, 1923; repr. 1926, 1933; rev. eds., 1943
    1946, 1948, 1954, 1959, 1965).
The Works of Jane Austen, ed. R.W. Chapman, Vol. VI: *Minor Works*
    (London: Oxford University Press, 1954; repr. 1958; rev. eds.,
    1963, 1965).

II. BIBLIOGRAPHICAL MATERIALS

Chapman, R. W., *Jane Austen: A Critical Bibliography* (Oxford, 1953; rev. ed., 1955).

Duffy, Joseph M., Jr, 'Jane Austen and the Nineteenth-Century Critics of Fiction 1812–1913' (University of Chicago dissertation, 1954, unpublished).

Hogan, C. B., 'Jane Austen and Her Early Public,' *Review of English Studies* (1950).

Keynes, Geoffrey, *Jane Austen: A Bibliography* (London, 1929).

Link, Frederick M., 'The Reputation of Jane Austen in the Twentieth Century' (Boston University dissertation, 1953, unpublished).

Page, Norman, 'A Short Guide to Jane Austen Studies,' *Critical Survey*, 3 (1968).

Pinion, F. B., *A Jane Austen Companion: A Critical Survey and Reference Book* (London, 1973).

Roth, Barry, and Weinsheimer, Joel (eds.), *An Annotated Bibliography of Jane Austen Studies, 1952–1972* (Charlottesville, Va., 1973).

Southam, B. C., 'General Tilney's Hot-Houses: Some Recent Jane Austen Studies and Texts,' *Ariel* (October 1971).

——, 'Introduction,' *Jane Austen: The Critical Heritage* (London and New York, 1968).

——, 'Jane Austen,' in *The English Novel: Select Bibliographical Guides*, ed. A. E. Dyson (Oxford, 1974).

Ward, William S., 'Three Hitherto Unnoted Contemporary Reviews of Jane Austen,' *Nineteenth-Century Fiction*, 26 (1972).

Watt, Ian, 'Introduction,' *Jane Austen: A Collection of Critical Essays* (Englewood Cliffs, N.J., 1963).

—— and Cady, Joseph, 'Jane Austen's Critics,' *Critical Quarterly* (1963).

III. BIOGRAPHIES AND LETTERS

Austen, Caroline, *My Aunt Jane Austen: A Memoir,* ed. R. W. Chapman (Alton, Hants., 1952).

Austen, Henry, 'Biographical Notice of the Author' (dated December 1817; published as preface to *Northanger Abbey* and *Persuasion,* London, 1818).

Austen-Leigh, J. E., *A Memoir of Jane Austen* (London, 1870).

Austen-Leigh, W. and R. A., *Jane Austen: Her Life and Letters* (London, 1913).

Chapman, R. W., *Jane Austen: Facts and Problems* (Oxford, 1948).

—— (ed.), *Jane Austen's Letters To Her Sister Cassandra and Others* (London and New York, 1932; 2nd ed., 1952).

—— (ed.), *Letters of Jane Austen 1796–1817* (London and New York, 1955).

Freeman, Jane, *Jane Austen in Bath* (Alton, Hants., 1969).

Grigson, Geoffrey, 'New Letters from Jane Austen's Home,' *Times Literary Supplement (19 August 1955).*

Hodge, Jane Aiken, *The Double Life of Jane Austen* (London, 1972).

Jenkins, Elizabeth, *Jane Austen* (London, 1938).

Laski, Marghanita, *Jane Austen and Her World* (New York, 1969).

Pilgrim, Constance, *Dear Jane: A Biographical Study of Jane Austen* (London, 1971).

Usborne, Margaret, 'Jane Austen – The Lefroys,' Spectator (29 February 1952).

Watson, Winifred, *Jane Austen in London* (Alton, Hants., 1960).

IV. CRITICAL STUDIES: BOOKS EXCLUSIVELY ON JANE AUSTEN

Apperson, G. L., *A Jane Austen Dictionary* (London, 1932; repr. New York, 1968).

Babb, Howard S., *Jane Austen's Novels: The Fabric of Dialogue* (Columbus, Ohio, 1962).

Bradbrook, Frank W., *Emma* (London and New York, 1961).

——, *Jane Austen and Her Predecessors* (Cambridge, England, 1966).

Brown, Lloyd W., *Bits of Ivory: Narrative Techniques in Jane Austen's Fiction* (Baton Rouge, La., 1973).

Burrows, J. F., *Jane Austen's Emma* (Sydney, 1968).

Craik, W. A., *Jane Austen in Her Time* (London, 1969).

——, *Jane Austen: The Six Novels* (London and New York, 1965).

Duckworth, Alistair M., *The Improvement of the Estate: A Study of Jane Austen's Novels* (Baltimore, 1971).

Firkins, O. W., *Jane Austen* (New York, 1965).

Fleishman, Avrom, *A Reading of Mansfield Park* (Minneapolis, 1967).

Gooneratne, Yasmine, *Jane Austen* (Cambridge, England, 1970).

Lascelles, Mary, *Jane Austen and Her Art* (Oxford and New York, 1939).

Liddell, Robert, *The Novels of Jane Austen* (London, 1963).

Litz, A. Walton, *Jane Austen: A Study of Her Artistic Development* (London and New York, 1965).

Mansell, Darrel, *The Novels of Jane Austen: An Interpretation* (London and New York, 1973).

Moler, Kenneth L., *Jane Austen's Art of Allusion* (Lincoln, Neb., 1968).

Mudrick, Marvin, *Jane Austen: Irony as Defense and Discovery* (Princeton, N.J., and London, 1952).

Nardin, Jane, *Those Elegant Decorums: The Concept of Propriety in Jane Austen's Novels* (Albany, 1973).

Select bibliography

Page, Norman, *The Language of Jane Austen* (Oxford, 1972).

Phillips, K. C., *Jane Austen's English* (London, 1970).

Sherry, Norman, *Jane Austen* (London, 1966).

Southam, B. C., *Jane Austen's Literary Manuscripts: A Study of the Novelist's Development through the Surviving Papers* (London and New York, 1964).

Tave, Stuart M., *Some Words of Jane Austen* (Chicago, 1973).

Ten Harmsel, Henrietta, *Jane Austen: A Study in Fictional Conventions* (The Hague, 1964).

Wiesenfarth, Joseph, *The Errand of Form: An Assay of Jane Austen's Art* (New York, 1967).

Wright, Andrew, *Jane Austen's Novels: A Study in Structure* (London and New York, 1953; rev. ed., 1964).

V. CRITICAL STUDIES: COLLECTIONS OF ESSAYS

Booth, Bradford A., (ed.), *Pride and Prejudice: Text, Backgrounds, Criticism* (New York, 1963). Includes critical pieces from the early twentieth century and also the following: Reuben A. Brower, 'Light and Bright and Sparkling: Irony and Fiction in *Pride and Prejudice*'; Andrew Wright, 'Elizabeth Bennet'; Dorothy Van Ghent, 'On *Pride and Prejudice*'; E. M. Halliday, 'Narrative Perspective in Pride and Prejudice.

Collected Reports of the Jane Austen Society, 1949–1965 (London, 1967). Includes guest speaker's annual address to the Jane Austen Society for the years 1956–65. Contents: 1956 – Sir Harold Nicolson, 'Jane Austen and Her Letters'; 1957 – Roger Fulford, 'Jane Austen's Dedication of *Emma* to the Prince Regent'; 1958– René Varin, 'The French Attitude towards Jane Austen's Works'; 1959 – E. G. Selwyn, 'Jane Austen's Clergymen'; 1960 – John Gore, 'First Impressions . . . and Last'; 1961 – Andrew Wright, 'Jane Austen from an American Viewpoint'; 1962 – Margaret Lane, 'Jane Austen's Use of the Domestic Interior'; 1963 – Elizabeth Jenkins, 'The Taste of Jane Austen's Day'; 1964 – David Cecil, 'Jane Austen's Lesser Works'; 1965 – L. P. Hartley, 'Jane Austen and the Abyss.'

Gray, Donald J. (ed.), *Pride and Prejudice: An Authoritative Text, Backgrounds, Reviews, and Essays in Criticism* (New York, 1966). Critical essays include the following: Donald J. Gray, 'Preface'; R. W. Chapman, 'Chronology of *Pride and Prejudice*'; Q. D. Leavis, '*Pride and Prejudice* and Jane Austen's Early Reading and Writing'; Richard Whately, 'Technique and Moral Effect in Jane Austen's Fiction'; G. H. Lewes, 'The Novels of Jane Austen'; Richard Simpson, 'Jane Austen as Ironist and Moralist'; A. C. Bradley, 'Jane Austen as Moralist and Humorist';

Reginald Farrer, 'Truth, Reality, and Good Sense in Jane Austen'; Mary Lascelles, 'The Narrative Art of *Pride and Prejudice*'; Samuel Kliger, 'Jane Austen's *Pride and Prejudice* in the Eighteenth-Century Mode'; Dorothy Van Ghent, 'On *Pride and Prejudice*'; Reuben A. Brower, 'Light and Bright and Sparkling: Irony and Fiction in *Pride and Prejudice*'; Marvin Mudrick, 'Irony as Discrimination in *Pride and Prejudice*'; Andrew Wright, 'Feeling and Complexity in *Pride and Prejudice*'; Howard S. Babb, 'Dialogue with Feeling: A Note on *Pride and Prejudice*'; E. M. Halliday, 'Narrative Perspective in *Pride and Prejudice*'; A. Walton Litz, 'The Marriage of Antitheses: Structure and Style in *Pride and Prejudice.*'

Heath, William (ed.), *Discussions of Jane Austen* (Boston, 1961). Contents: William Heath, 'Introduction'; Reginald Farrer, 'Jane Austen'; Virginia Woolf, 'Jane Austen'; H. W. Garrod, 'Jane Austen: A Depreciation'; D. W. Harding, 'Regulated Hatred: An Aspect of the Work of Jane Austen'; Walter Allen, 'Jane Austen'; C. S. Lewis, 'A Note on Jane Austen'; Frank O'Connor, 'Jane Austen: The Flight from Fancy'; Reuben A. Brower, 'Light and Bright and Sparkling: Irony and Fiction in *Pride and Prejudice*'; Reginald Farrer, 'On *Mansfield Park*'; Lionel Trilling, '*Mansfield Park*'; Kingsley Amis, 'What Became of Jane Austen? *Mansfield Park*'; Reginald Farrer, 'On *Emma*'; Arnold Kettle, '*Emma.*'

Lodge, David, (ed.), *Emma: A Casebook* (London, 1968). Contents: David Lodge, 'Introduction'; Arnold Kettle, '*Emma*'; Marvin Mudrick, 'Irony as Form: *Emma*'; Edgar F. Shannon, '*Emma*: Character and Construction'; Lionel Trilling, '*Emma* and the Legend of Jane Austen'; Mark Schorer, 'The Humiliation of Emma Woodhouse'; R. E. Hughes, 'The Education of Emma Woodhouse'; Wayne Booth, 'Control of Distance in Jane Austen's *Emma*'; Malcolm Bradbury, 'Jane Austen's *Emma*'; W. J. Harvey, 'The Plot of *Emma.*'

O'Neill, Judith, (ed.), *Critics on Jane Austen* (London, 1970). Contents: Judith O'Neill, 'Introduction'; Mary Lascelles, 'Jane Austen's Style'; D. W. Harding, 'Regulated Hatred: An Aspect of the Work of Jane Austen'; Leonard Woolf, 'The Economic Determinism of Jane Austen'; Reuben A. Brower, 'The Controlling Hand: Jane Austen and *Pride and Prejudice*'; Marvin Mudrick, '*Persuasion*: The Liberation of Feeling'; C. S. Lewis, 'Two Solitary Heroines'; Malcolm Bradbury, 'Jane Austen's *Emma*'; Thomas R. Edwards, Jr, 'The Difficult Beauty of *Mansfield Park*'; Laurence Lerner, '*Sense and Sensibility*: A Mixed-up Book.'

Parrish, Stephen M., (ed.), *Emma: An Authoritative Text, Backgrounds, Reviews, and Criticism* (New York, 1972). Critical essays include the following: Stephen M. Parrish, 'Preface'; Henry Austen, 'Biographical Notice'; extract from J. E. Austen-Leigh, *Memoir of Jane Austen*; Virginia Woolf, *'The Watsons'*; Walter Scott, review of *Emma*; G. H. Lewes, 'The Lady Novelists'; Richard Simpson, 'Jane Austen'; Henry James, 'The Lesson of Balzac'; A. C. Bradley, 'Jane Austen: A Lecture'; Reginald Farrer, 'Jane Austen, *ob.* July 18, 1817'; E. M. Forster, 'Jane Austen'; Mary Lascelles, 'The Narrator and His Reader'; Arnold Kettle, 'Jane Austen: *Emma*'; Wayne Booth, 'Control of Distance in Jane Austen's *Emma*'; Armour G. Craig, 'Jane Austen's *Emma*: The Truths and Disguises of Human Disclosure'; A. Walton Litz, 'The Limits of Freedom: *Emma*'; W. A. Craik, *'Emma'*; W. J. Harvey, 'The Plot of *Emma*.'

Rubinstein, E., (ed.), *Twentieth Century Interpretations of Pride and Prejudice: A Collection of Critical Essays* (Englewood Cliffs, N.J., 1969). Contents: E. Rubinstein, 'Introduction'; Dorothy Van Ghent, 'On *Pride and Prejudice*'; Reuben A. Brower, 'Light and Bright and Sparkling: Irony and Fiction in *Pride and Prejudice*'; Samuel Kliger, 'Jane Austen's *Pride and Prejudice* in the Eighteenth-Century Mode'; A. Walton Litz, 'Into the Nineteenth Century: *Pride and Prejudice*'; Mary Lascelles, 'Narrative Art in *Pride and Prejudice*'; E. M. Halliday, 'Narrative Perspective in *Pride and Prejudice*'; Mordecai Marcus, 'A Major Thematic Pattern in *Pride and Prejudice*'; Charles J. McCann, 'Setting and Character in *Pride and Prejudice*'; Andrew Wright, 'Heroines, Heroes, and Villains in *Pride and Prejudice*'; Douglas Bush, 'Mrs. Bennet and the Dark Gods: The Truth about Jane Austen.'

Southam, B. C., (ed.), *Critical Essays on Jane Austen* (London and New York, 1968). Contents: B. C. Southam, 'Introduction'; John Bayley, 'The "Irresponsibility" of Jane Austen'; Brigid Brophy, 'Jane Austen and the Stuarts'; Denis Donoghue, 'A View of *Mansfield Park*'; Robert Garis, 'Learning Experience and Change'; D. W. Harding, 'Character and Caricature in Jane Austen'; Gilbert Ryle, 'Jane Austen and the Moralists'; J. I. M. Stewart, 'Tradition and Miss Austen'; Tony Tanner, 'Jane Austen and "The Quiet Thing" – A Study of *Mansfield Park*'; Rachel Trickett, 'Jane Austen's Comedy and the Nineteenth Century'; Angus Wilson, 'The Neighbourhood of Tombuctoo: Conflicts in Jane Austen's Novels.'

Southam, B. C., (ed.), *Jane Austen: The Critical Heritage* (London and New York, 1968). Contents: B. C. Southam, 'Introduction'; includes essays, reviews, articles, extracts from books and letters, etc., during the period 1815–70. Among the major pieces reprinted in full or in part (see the 'Introduction' to the present volume for full discussion and citation) are Scott's review of

Emma, Henry Austen's 'Biographical Notice' of his sister, Whately's long essay, Lister's review, Macaulay's essay, several of G. H. Lewes's essays – including the full text of 'The Novels of Jane Austen,' Charlotte Bronte's letters to Lewes and W. S. Williams, Kirk's article, Pollock's article, Julia Kavanagh's essay, Dallas's review, full texts of the reviews of the Austen-Leigh *Memoir* by Mrs Oliphant and Richard Simpson and brief mention of attitudes toward Jane Austen expressed in one way or another by, among others, Miss Mitford, Henry Crabb Robinson, Southey, Coleridge, Wordsworth, Newman, Longfellow, Macready, and Fitzgerald.

Spector, R. D., (ed.), *Emma, with an Introduction, Notes, Biographical Sketch, and A Selection of Background Materials and Commentaries* (New York, 1969). Includes critical essays from the nineteenth and early twentieth centuries and also the following: R. D. Spector, 'Introduction: Creating A Masterpiece'; Q. D. Leavis, 'How *The Watsons* Became *Emma*'; B. C. Southam, 'Why *The Watsons* Did Not Become *Emma*'; Joseph M. Duffy, Jr, '*Emma:* The Awakening from Innocence'; Edgar F. Shannon, Jr, 'Rhythm in *Emma.*'

Watt, Ian, (ed.), *Jane Austen: A Collection of Critical Essays* (Englewood Cliffs, N.J., 1963). Contents: Ian Watt, 'Introduction'; Virginia Woolf, 'Jane Austen'; C. S. Lewis, 'A Note on Jane Austen'; Edmund Wilson, 'A Long Talk about Jane Austen'; Ian Watt, 'On *Sense and Sensibility*'; Alan D. McKillop, 'Critical Realism in *Northanger Abbey*'; Reuben A. Brower, 'Light and Bright and Sparkling: Irony and Fiction in *Pride and Prejudice*'; Marvin Mudrick, 'Irony as Discrimination: *Pride and Prejudice*'; Mark Schorer, 'The Humiliation of Emma Woodhouse'; Arnold Kettle '*Emma*'; Lionel Trilling, '*Mansfield Park*'; Kingsley Amis, 'What Became of Jane Austen? *Mansfield Park*': Andrew Wright, '*Persuasion*'; Donald Greene, 'Jane Austen and the Peerage'; D. W. Harding 'Regulated Hatred: An Aspect of the Work of Jane Austen.'

VI. CRITICAL STUDIES: UNCOLLECTED ESSAYS
(including essays in books on multiple subjects)

Auerbach, Nina, 'O Brave New World: Evolution and Revolution in *Persuasion,*' *English Literary History,* 39 (1972).

Banfield, Ann, 'The Moral Landscape of *Mansfield Park,*' *Nineteenth-Century Fiction,* 26 (1971).

Bradbrook, Frank W., 'Dr Johnson and Jane Austen,' *Notes and Queries,* 7 (1960).

——, 'Introduction' to *Pride and Prejudice* (New York, 1970).

Select bibliography

Bradbrook, M. C., 'A Note on Fanny Price,' *Essays in Criticism*, 5 (1955).

Bradbury, Malcolm, '*Persuasion* Again,' *EIC*, 18 (1968).

Branton, C. L., 'The Ordinations in Jane Austen's Novels,' *NCF*, 10 (1955).

Brissenden, R. F., 'La Philosophie dans le boudoir; or, A Young Lady's Entrance into the World,' in *Studies in Eighteenth-Century Culture II*, ed. Harold E. Pagliaro (Cleveland and London, 1972).

Brogan, Howard O., 'Science and Narrative Structure in Austen, Hardy, and Woolf,' *NCF*, 11 (1957).

Brophy, Brigid, 'Introduction' to *Pride and Prejudice* (London, 1967).

Brower, Reuben A., 'Introduction' to *Mansfield Park* (Boston, 1965).

Brown, Lloyd W., 'The Comic Conclusion in Jane Austen's Novels,' *Publications of the Modern Language Association*, 84 (1969).

Burchell, S. C., 'Jane Austen: The Theme of Isolation,' *NCF*, 10 (1955).

Burroway, Janet, 'The Irony of the Insufferable Prig: *Mansfield Park*,' *Critical Quarterly*, 9 (1967).

Carroll, David R., '*Mansfield Park, Daniel Deronda*, and Ordination,' *Modern Philology*, 62 (1965).

Cecil, David, 'Jane Austen,' in *Poets and Story-Tellers* (London, 1949).

——, 'A Note on Jane Austen's Scenery,' in *The Fine Art of Reading and Other Literary Studies* (Indianapolis, 1957).

——, '*Sense and Sensibility*,' in *The Fine Art of Reading and Other Literary Studies* (Indianapolis, 1957).

Chapman, R. W., 'Jane Austen's Titles,' *NCF*, 9 (1954).

——, 'A Reply to Mr Duffy on *Persuasion*,' *NCF*, 9 (1954).

Cohen, Louise D., 'Insight, the Essence of Jane Austen's Artistry,' *NCF*, 8 (1953).

Colby, R. A., '*Mansfield Park*: Fanny Price and the Christian Heroine,' in *Fiction with A Purpose* (Bloomington, Ind., 1967).

Cope, Zachary, 'Jane Austen's Last Illness,' *British Medical Journal* (18 July 1964).

Craik, W. A., 'Introduction' to *Persuasion* (London, 1969).

——, 'Introduction' to *Sense and Sensibility* (London, 1972).

Crane, R. S., '*Persuasion*,' in *The Idea of the Humanities and Other Essays Critical and Historical*, Vol. II (Chicago, 1967).

Daiches, David, 'Introduction' to *Persuasion* (New York, 1958).

——, 'Jane Austen, Karl Marx, and the Aristocratic Dance,' *American Scholar*, 17 (1948).

Dickens, Monica, 'Introduction' to *Mansfield Park* (London, 1972).

Donohue, Joseph W., Jr, 'Ordination and the Divided House at Mansfield Park,' *ELH*, 32 (1965).

Donovan, R. A., 'Mansfield Park and Jane Austen's Moral Universe,' in *The Shaping Vision: Imagination in the English Novel from Defoe to Dickens* (Ithaca, N.Y., 1966).

Dooley, D. J., 'Pride, Prejudice, and Vanity in Elizabeth Bennet,' *NCF*, 20 (1965).

Draffan, R. A., 'Mansfield Park: Jane Austen's Bleak House,' *EIC*, 19 (1969).

Drew, Philip, 'A Significant Incident in *Pride and Prejudice*,' *NCF*, 13 (1959).

Duckworth, Alistair M., 'Mansfield Park and Estate Improvements: Jane Austen's Grounds of Being,' *NCF*, 26 (1971).

Duffy, Joseph M., Jr, 'Moral Integrity and Moral Anarchy in *Mansfield Park*,' *ELH*, 23 (1956).

——, 'Structure and Idea in *Persuasion*,' *NCF*, 8 (1954).

Duncan-Jones, E. E., 'Jane Austen and Crabbe,' *Review of English Studies*, 5 (1954).

Edge, C. E., 'Mansfield Park and Ordination,' *NCF*, 16 (1961).

Ehrenpreis, A. H., 'Introduction' to *Northanger Abbey* (Baltimore, 1972).

——, 'Northanger Abbey: Jane Austen and Charlotte Smith,' *NCF*, 25 (1970).

Elsbree, Langdon, 'Jane Austen and the Dance of Fidelity and Complaisance,' *NCF*, 15 (1960).

Emden, C. S., 'The Composition of Northanger Abbey,' *RES*, 19 (1968).

Faverty, Frederic E., 'Introduction' to *Emma* (New York, 1961).

Fox, R. C., 'Elizabeth Bennet: Prejudice or Vanity?', *NCF*, 17 (1962).

Gallon, D. N., 'Comedy in Northanger Abbey,' *Modern Language Review*, 63 (1968).

Gillie, C., 'Sense and Sensibility: An Assessment,' *EIC*, 9 (1959).

Griffin, Cynthia, 'The Development of Realism in Jane Austen's Early Novels,' *ELH*, 30 (1963).

Gullans, C. B., 'Jane Austen's Mansfield Park and Dr. Johnson,' *NCF*, 27 (1972).

Halperin, John, 'Jane Austen,' in *The Language of Meditation: Four Studies in Nineteenth-Century Fiction* (Devon, 1973).

——, 'The Trouble with Mansfield Park,' *Studies in the Novel*, 6 (1974).

——, 'The Victorian Novel and Jane Austen,' in *Egoism and Self-Discovery in the Victorian Novel* (New York, 1974).

Harding, D. W., 'Introduction' to *Persuasion* (Baltimore, 1965).

Hellstrom, Ward, 'Francophobia in Emma,' *Studies in English Literature*, 5 (1965).

Hodge, Jane Aiken, 'Jane Austen and the Publishers,' *Cornhill*, 1071 (1972).

Hough, Graham, 'Afterword' to *Emma* (New York, 1964).

———, 'Narrative and Dialogue in Jane Austen,' *CritQ*, 12 (1970).

Karl, Frederick R., 'Jane Austen: The Necessity of Wit,' in *An Age of Fiction: The Nineteenth-Century British Novel* (New York, 1964).

Kaul, A. N., 'Jane Austen,' in *The Action of English Comedy* (New Haven, 1970).

Kearful, Frank J., 'Satire and the Form of the Novel: The Problem of Aesthetic Unity in *Northanger Abbey*,' *ELH*, 32 (1965).

Ker, W. P., 'Jane Austen,' in *On Modern Literature: Lectures and Addresses,* ed. Terence Spencer and James Sutherland (Oxford, 1955).

Kiely, Robert, '*Northanger Abbey:* Jane Austen, 1803,' in *The Romantic Novel in England* (Cambridge, Mass., 1972).

King, Noel J., 'Jane Austen in France,' *NCF*, 8 (1953).

Kirschbaum, Leo, 'The World of *Pride and Prejudice*,' in *Twelve Original Essays on Great English Novels,* ed. Charles Shapiro (Detroit, 1960).

Knoepflmacher, U. C., 'The Importance of Being Frank: Character and Letter-Writing in *Emma*,' *SEL*, 7 (1967).

Krieger, Murray, 'Postscript : The Naive Classic and the Merely Comic,' in *The Classic Vision: The Retreat from Extremity in Modern Literature* (Baltimore, 1971).

Kroeber, Karl, 'Jane Austen,' in *Styles in Fictional Structure: The Art of Jane Austen, Charlotte Brontë, George Eliot* (Princeton, N.J., 1971).

———, 'Perils of Quantification: The Exemplary Case of Jane Austen's *Emma*,' in *Statistics and Style,* ed. Lubomir Dolezel and R. W. Bailey (New York, 1969).

Kronenberger, Louis, 'Introduction' to *Emma* (New York, 1965).

———, 'Introduction' to *Sense and Sensibility* (New York, 1962).

———, 'Jane Austen: *Lady Susan* and *Pride and Prejudice*,' in *The Polished Surface: Essays in the Literature of Worldliness* (New York, 1969).

Lascelles, Mary, 'Introduction' to *Emma* (New York, 1964).

———, 'Introduction' to *Mansfield Park* (New York, 1963).

———, 'Introduction' to *Northanger Abbey* and *Persuasion* (New York, 1962).

———, 'Introduction' to *Pride and Prejudice* (New York, 1963).

———, 'Introduction' to *Sense and Sensibility,* (New York, 1962).

———, 'Jane Austen and Walter Scott: A Minor Point of Comparison,' in *Notions and Facts: Collected Criticism and Research* (Oxford, 1972).

Lawry, J. S., ' "Decided and Open": Structure in *Emma*,' *NCF*, 24 (1969).

Leavis, F. R., 'The Great Tradition,' in *The Great Tradition* (London, 1948).

Leavis, Q. D., 'Introduction' to *Mansfield Park* (London, 1957).

——, 'Introduction' to *Sense and Sensibility* (London, 1958).

——, 'Jane Austen,' in *A Selection from Scrutiny*, ed. F. R. Leavis (Cambridge, England, 1968).

Lerner, Laurence, 'Jane Austen,' in *The Truthtellers: Jane Austen, George Eliot, D. H. Lawrence* (London, 1967).

Levine, Jay, *'Lady Susan:* Jane Austen's Character of the Merry Widow,' *SEL*, 1 (1961).

Litz, A. Walton, 'The Chronology of *Mansfield Park*,' *N&Q*, 8 (1961).

——, 'Introduction' to *Pride and Prejudice* (New York, 1967).

——, *'The Loiterer:* A Reflection of Jane Austen's Early Environment,' *RES*, 12 (1961).

Lodge, David, 'Introduction' to *Emma* (New York, 1971).

——, 'A Question of Judgment: The Theatricals at Mansfield Park,' *NCF*, 17 (1963).

——, 'The Vocabulary of *Mansfield Park*,' in *Language of Fiction* (London and New York, 1966).

Loofbourow, John W., 'Introduction' to *Pride and Prejudice* (New York, 1969).

Mansell, Darrel, 'The Date of Jane Austen's Revision of *Northanger Abbey*,' *English Language Notes*, 7 (1969).

Mathison, J. K., *'Northanger Abbey* and Jane Austen's Conception of the Value of Fiction,' *ELH*, 24 (1957).

McKillop, Alan D., 'The Context of *Sense and Sensibility*,' *Rice Institute Pamphlets*, 44 (1958).

McMaster, Juliet, 'The Continuity of Jane Austen's Novels,' *SEL*, 10 (1970).

Minter, D. L., 'Aesthetic Vision and the World of *Emma*,' *NCF*, 21 (1966).

Moler, Kenneth L., *'Sense and Sensibility* and Its Sources,' *RES*, 17 (1966).

Moore, E. M., 'Emma and Miss Bates,' *SEL*, 9 (1969).

Mudrick, Marvin, 'Afterword' to *Mansfield Park* (New York, 1964).

——, 'Afterword' to *Persuasion* (New York, 1964).

Muir, Edwin, 'Jane Austen,' in *Essays on Literature and Society* (London and Cambridge, Mass., 1965).

Murrah, C., 'The Background of *Mansfield Park*,' in *From Jane Austen to Joseph Conrad*, ed. R. C. Rathburn and Martin Steinmann, Jr (Minneapolis, 1958).

Nash, Ralph, 'The Time Scheme for *Pride and Prejudice*,' *ELN*, 4 (1967).

Page, Norman, 'Categories of Speech in *Persuasion*,' *MLR*, 64 (1969).

Parks, Edd Winfield, 'Exegesis in Jane Austen's Novels,' *South Atlantic Quarterly*, 51 (1952).

——, 'A Human Failing in *Pride and Prejudice*?', *NCF*, 10 (1955).

Paulson, Ronald, 'Jane Austen: *Pride and Prejudice*,' in *Satire and the Novel in Eighteenth-Century England* (New Haven, 1967).

Pikoulis, John, 'Jane Austen: The Figure in the Carpet,' *NCF*, 27 (1972).

Poirer, Richard, 'Mark Twain, Jane Austen, and the Imagination of Society,' in *In Defense of Reading: A Reader's Approach to Literary Criticism*, ed. Reuben A. Brower and Richard Poirer (New York, 1962).

Priestley, J. B., 'Afterword' to *Pride and Prejudice*, in *Four English Novels* (New York, 1960).

——, 'Mr Collins,' in *The English Comic Characters* (London, 1963).

Pritchett, V. S., 'Introduction' to *Persuasion* (New York, 1966).

——, 'Introduction' to *Pride and Prejudice* (London, 1962).

Rosenfeld, Sybil, 'Jane Austen and Private Theatricals,' *Essays and Studies* 15 (1962).

Rubinstein, E., 'Jane Austen's Novels: The Metaphor of Rank,' in *Literary Monographs*, ed. Eric Rothstein and Richard N. Ringler (Madison, Wis., 1969).

Schorer, Mark, 'Fiction and the "Matrix of Analogy,"' *Kenyon Review*, 11 (1949).

——, 'Introduction' to *Pride and Prejudice* (Boston, 1956).

——, 'Pride Unprejudiced,' *Kenyon Review*, 18 (1956).

——, 'Technique as Discovery,' *Hudson Review*, 1 (1948).

Simon, Irene, 'Jane Austen and *The Art of the Novel*,' *E&S*, 43 (1962).

Southam, B. C., 'Interpolations to Jane Austen's *Volume the Third*,' *N&Q*, 9 (1962).

——, 'Jane Austen: A Broken Romance?', *N&Q*, 8 (1961).

——, 'Jane Austen's Juvenilia: The Question of Completeness,' *N&Q*, 11 (1964).

——, 'The Manuscript of Jane Austen's *Volume the First*,' *Library*, 5th Ser., 17 (1962).

——, 'Mrs Leavis and Miss Austen: The 'Critical Theory' Reconsidered,' *NCF*, 17 (1962).

——, '*Northanger Abbey*,' *TLS* (12 October 1962).

——, 'The Text of *Sanditon*,' *N&Q*, 8 (1961).

Steeves, Harrison R., 'And Jane Austen,' in *Before Jane Austen: The Shaping of the English Novel in the Eighteenth Century* (New York, 1965).

Stone, Donald D., 'Sense and Semantics in Jane Austen,' *NCF*, 25 (1970).

Suddaby, Elizabeth, 'Jane Austen and the Delphic Oracle,' *NCF*, 9 (1954).

Tanner, Tony, 'Introduction' to *Pride and Prejudice* (Baltimore, 1972).

——, 'Introduction' to *Sense and Sensibility* (Baltimore, 1969).

Ward, A. C., 'Introduction' to *Emma* (London, 1961).

——, 'Introduction' to *Mansfield Park* (London, 1964).

——, 'Introduction' to *Northanger Abbey* (London, 1960).

——, 'Introduction' to *Pride and Prejudice* (London, 1958).

——, 'Introduction' to *Sense and Sensibility* (London, 1953).

Watson, J. R., 'Mr Perry's Patients: A View of *Emma*,' *EIC*, 20 (1970).

Watt, Ian, 'Realism and the later tradition: a note,' in *The Rise of the Novel: Studies in Defoe, Richardson and Fielding* (Berkeley, 1957).

Weinsheimer, Joel, 'Chance and the Hierarchy of Marriage in *Pride and Prejudice*,' *ELH*, 39 (1972).

Welsh, Alexander, 'Introduction' to *Emma* (New York, 1963).

White, E. M., 'A Critical Theory of *Mansfield Park*,' *SEL*, 7 (1967).

——, '*Emma* and the Parodic Point of View,' *NCF*, 18 (1963).

Wiesenfarth, Joseph, '*Persuasion*: History and Myth,' *WC*, 2 (1971).

Wolfe, Thomas P., 'The Achievement of *Persuasion*,' *SEL*, 11 (1971).

Wright, Andrew, 'Introduction' to *Persuasion* (Boston, 1965).

——, 'A Reply to Mr Burchell on Jane Austen,' *NCF*, 11 (1956).

Zietlow, P. N., 'Luck and Fortuitous Circumstance in *Persuasion*: Two Interpretations,' *ELH*, 32 (1965).

Zimmerman, Everett, 'The Function of Parody in *Northanger Abbey*,' *Modern Language Quarterly*, 30 (1969).

——, 'Pride and Prejudice in *Pride and Prejudice*,' *NCF*, 23 (1968).

Contributors

R. F. H. BRISSENDEN holds degrees from the Universities of Sydney and Leeds and is currently Reader in English at the Australian National University, Canberra. He has been an editor of *Studies in the Eighteenth Century* and has published articles on eighteenth-century English literature, on Australian literature and on American literature. Mr Brissenden is also the author of a volume of poems. His most recent publication is *Virtue in Distress: Studies in the Novel of Sentiment from Richardson to Sade.*

REUBEN A. BROWER is Cabot Professor of English at Harvard University. His books include *The Fields of Light: An Experiment in Critical Reading, Alexander Pope: The Poetry of Allusion,* and *Hero and Saint: Shakespeare and the Graeco-Roman Heroic Tradition.* Mr Brower has edited *In Defense of Reading* and *On Translation,* and his latest publication is *Mirror on Mirror: Translation, Imitation, Parody.*

KATRIN RISTKOK BURLIN holds degrees from Northwestern University and Cornell University and currently is Lecturer in English and Dean of Freshmen at Bryn Mawr College. Her essay in this volume is part of a Princeton dissertation on Jane Austen's novels.

ALISTAIR M. DUCKWORTH is the author of *The Improvement of the Estate: A Study of Jane Austen's Novels.* Currently Associate Professor of English at the University of Florida, he has also taught at the University of Virginia, and was visiting professor in the Eleventh Summer Program in Modern Literature at the State University of New York at Buffalo in 1974.

331

Contributors

DONALD GREENE is Leo S. Bing Profesor of English at the University of Southern California. He has degrees from the Universities of Saskatchewan and London and Columbia University, and has taught at the Universities of Toronto, Wisconsin, New Mexico, California (Riverside) and Brandeis University. Mr. Greene has published extensively on eighteenth-century English literature, particularly Samuel Johnson.

BARBARA HARDY is Chairman of the Department of English at Birkbeck College, University of London, and present occupant of its Chair of Literature. She is the author of *The Novels of George Eliot, The Appropriate Form, The Moral Art of Dickens, The Exposure of Luxury: Radical Themes in Thackeray,* and the editor of *Middlemarch: Critical Approaches to the Novel* and *Critical Essays on George Eliot.* Mrs Hardy has just finished a new book, *The Narrative Imagination,* and is now working on a book on Jane Austen.

ROBERT B. HEILMAN is Professor of English at the University of Washington, where he was Chairman of the Department from 1948 to 1971. Two of his many books appeared in 1973 – *The Iceman, the Arsonist, and the Troubled Agent: Tragedy and Melodrama on the Modern Stage* and *The Ghost on the Ramparts and Other Essays in the Humanities.* Among Mr Heilman's other publications are *America in English Fiction 1760–1800, Tragedy and Melodrama: Versions of Experience,* two books on Shakespeare, and numerous essays on English and American fiction. In 1973 Kenyon College awarded him an L.H.D.

JANE AIKEN HODGE, daughter of poet Conrad Aiken, was educated at Oxford and Harvard. She is the author of ten historical novels set at the time of the Napoleonic wars, and two of modern suspense. In 1972 she published *Only A Novel: The Double Life of Jane Austen.* Mrs Hodge lives in Sussex and regularly reviews books for the *Weekly Post,* the *Sunday Telegraph* and *Books and Bookmen.*

KARL KROEBER, Professor and Chairman of the Department of English and Comparative Literature at Columbia University, has published extensively on the English Romantic poets and other nineteenth-century writers. His books include *Styles in Fictional Structure* and *Romantic Landscape Vision: Wordsworth and Constable.*

MARY LASCELLES was formerly Fellow and Vice-Principal and is now an Honorary Fellow of Somerville College, Oxford. Her books include *Jane Austen and Her Art, Shakespeare's 'Measure for Measure,' The Adversaries and Other Poems,* and *Notions and Facts: Collected Criticism and Research.* Miss Lascelles has edited Scott's and Jane Austen's novels in the Everyman series and Johnson's *A Journey to the Western Islands of Scotland* in the Yale edition of the works.

A. WALTON LITZ is professor and Chairman of the Department of English at Princeton University. He is the author of *Jane Austen: A Study of Her Artistic Development, The art of James Joyce* and *Introspective Voyager: The Poetic Development of Wallace Stevens.* Mr Litz has also edited *Modern American Fiction: Essays in Criticism;* a volume of essays on T. S. Eliot; a collection of *Major American Short Stories;* and, with Robert Scholes, Joyce's *Dubliners.*

KENNETH L MOLER is Professor of English at the University of Nebraska. He is the author of *Jane Austen's Art of Allusion* and has published essays on Jane Austen and other nineteenth-century authors in a number of literary journals.

MARVIN MUDRICK is the author of *Jane Austen: Irony as Defense and Discovery* and *On Culture and Literature,* and editor of the volume *Conrad: A Collection of Critical Essays.* His reviews and articles have appeared in the *Hudson Review* and many other literary journals. Mr Mudrick currently is Professor of English and Provost of the College of Creative Studies at the University of California, Santa Barbara.

STUART M. TAVE is William Rainey Harper Professor in the College and Professor of English and Chairman of the Department at the University of Chicago. He has published *The Amiable Humorist: A Study in the Comic Theory and Criticism of the Eighteenth and Early Nineteenth Centuries, New Essays by De Quincey, Some Words of Jane Austen,* and other studies in eighteenth- and nineteenth-century literature.

JOSEPH WIESENFARTH has published critical studies of Jane Austen and Henry James and numerous essays on English and American fiction. His most recently completed book is *George Eliot's Novels: Old Patterns and New Worlds.* Mr Wiesenfarth is Associate Professor of English at the University of Wisconsin, Madison.

ANDREW WRIGHT is Professor of English Literature at the University of California, San Diego. His books include *Jane Austen's*

Novels: A Study in Structure, Joyce Cary: A Preface to His Novels, Henry Fielding: Mask and Feast, and *Blake's Job: A Commentary.* In 1971 Mr Wright was named Fellow of the Royal Society of Literature.

EVERETT ZIMMERMAN is Associate Professor of English at the University of California, Santa Barbara. He is the author of *Defoe and the Novel* and has published articles on Jane Austen and Swift in several literary journals.

JOHN HALPERIN is Associate Professor and Director of Graduate Studies in the Department of English at the University of Southern California. His books include *The Language of Meditation: Four Studies in Nineteenth-Century Fiction, The Theory of the Novel: New Essays,* and *Egoism and Self-Discovery in the Victorian Novel.* Mr Halperin has published essays on Jane Austen and other novelists in several literary journals and has also edited a recent paperback edition of Henry James's *The Golden Bowl.* He is now completing a critical study of Trollope's parliamentary novels.